Representing Religion in Film

CRITIQUING RELIGION: DISCOURSE, CULTURE, POWER

SERIES EDITOR: CRAIG MARTIN

Critiquing Religion: Discourse, Culture, Power publishes works that historicize both religions and modern discourses on 'religion' that treat it as a unique object of study. Using diverse methodologies and social theories, volumes in this series view religions and discourses on religion as commonplace rhetorics, authenticity narratives, or legitimating myths which function in the creation, maintenance, and contestation of social formations. Works in the series are on the cutting edge of critical scholarship, regarding 'religion' as just another cultural tool used to gerrymander social space and distribute power relations in the modern world. *Critiquing Religion: Discourse, Culture, Power* provides a unique home for reflexive, critical work in the field of religious studies.

Christian Tourist Attractions, Mythmaking and Identity Formation
Edited by Erin Roberts and Jennifer Eyl

French Populism and Discourses on Secularism
Per-Erik Nilsson

Reframing the Masters of Suspicion: Marx, Nietzsche, and Freud
Andrew Dole

Religion, Nationalism and Foreign Policy
Filiz Coban Oran

Spirituality, Corporate Culture, and American Business: The Neoliberal Ethic and the Spirit of Global Capital
James Dennis LoRusso

Stereotyping Religion: Critiquing Clichés
Edited by Brad Stoddard and Craig Martin

Representing Religion in Film

EDITED BY
TENZAN EAGHLL AND
REBEKKA KING

BLOOMSBURY ACADEMIC
LONDON • NEW YORK • OXFORD • NEW DELHI • SYDNEY

BLOOMSBURY ACADEMIC
Bloomsbury Publishing Plc
50 Bedford Square, London, WC1B 3DP, UK
1385 Broadway, New York, NY 10018, USA
29 Earlsfort Terrace, Dublin 2, Ireland

BLOOMSBURY, BLOOMSBURY ACADEMIC and the Diana logo are trademarks of
Bloomsbury Publishing Plc

First published in Great Britain 2022

Copyright © Tenzan Eaghll, Rebekka King and contributors, 2022

Tenzan Eaghll and Rebekka King have asserted their rights under the Copyright, Designs
and Patents Act, 1988, to be identified as Editors of this work.

Cover image © Yi Lu / EyeEm. Getty Images

All rights reserved. No part of this publication may be reproduced or transmitted in
any form or by any means, electronic or mechanical, including photocopying, recording,
or any information storage or retrieval system, without prior permission in writing from
the publishers.

Bloomsbury Publishing Plc does not have any control over, or responsibility for, any
third-party websites referred to or in this book. All internet addresses given in this
book were correct at the time of going to press. The author and publisher regret any
inconvenience caused if addresses have changed or sites have ceased to exist, but can
accept no responsibility for any such changes.

A catalogue record for this book is available from the British Library.

Library of Congress Control Number: 2022932164

ISBN: HB: 978-1-3501-4081-3
PB: 978-1-3501-4080-6
ePDF: 978-1-3501-4082-0
eBook: 978-1-3501-4083-7

Series: Critiquing Religion: Discourse, Culture, Power

Typeset by Deanta Global Publishing Services, Chennai, India

To find out more about our authors and books visit www.bloomsbury.com and
sign up for our newsletters

"When using films in our religion courses, then, we should not be concerned with teaching students to recognize the sacred in its celluloid manifestations but to see in religious systems as well as in our own society's films the all-too-common mechanisms of social formation."

Russell T. McCutcheon, "Redescribing 'Religion and...' Film"

CONTENTS

List of Contributors ix
Foreword xii

Introduction   Three Film Critics Walk into a Theater:
The Ideological Blindspot in the Academic Study of
Religion and Film   *Tenzan Eaghll* 1

1   Atheistic Documentaries and the Critique of Religion in
Bill Maher's *Religulous* (2008)   *Teemu Taira* 27

2   Capitalism, the Hero's Journey, and the Myth of
Entrepreneurship in *The Secret of My Success* (1987)
and *Joy* (2015)   *James Dennis LoRusso* 41

3   Oprah, Mindy, and Reese: "The Gaze" and
the Holy Trinity of Disney's *A Wrinkle in Time* (2018)
Leslie Dorrough Smith 57

4   Race, Colonialism, and Whiteness in Martin Scorsese's
Silence (2016)   *Malory Nye* 69

5   We Haven't Located Us Yet: The Mystic East in Wes
Anderson's *The Darjeeling Limited* (2007)
Michael J. Altman 87

6   Lost in Žižek, Redeemed in *Cloud Atlas* (2012):
Buddhism and Other Tales of "Asian Religions" in
Western Cinema and Affective Circulation   *Ting Guo* 101

7   Magical Realism, Anti-Modernity, and the Religious
Imaginaries of Latin American Cinema: A Look through
Ciro Guerra's *The Wind Journeys* (2009)
Rebecca C. Bartel 117

8 Unsettling Settler-Colonial Myths about Native
Americans in *The Revenant* (2015) *Matt Sheedy* 127

9 From the Horrors of Human Tragedy and Social
Reproduction to the Comfort of a Demonic Cult:
Agency in *Hereditary* (2018) *Sean McCloud* 141

10 Superheroes, Apocalyptic Messiahs, and *Hellboy* (2004)
Aaron Ricker 153

11 AI Apocalypticism and the Religious Impulse in,
and *from*, the *Terminator* (1984–2019) Franchise
Beth Singler 165

12 Myth of the Auteur and the Authentic in *Star Wars:
The Last Jedi* (2017) *Richard Newton* 175

Conclusion Religion as Film: Constructing a Course
as a Critique of a Dominant Paradigm *Tenzan Eaghll* 189

Notes 195
References 205
Index 233

CONTRIBUTORS

Michael J. Altman is Associate Professor in the Department of Religious Studies at the University of Alabama. He is the author of *Heathen, Hindoo, Hindu: American Representations of India, 1721-1893* (2017) and the forthcoming *Hinduism in America: An Introduction*. His research interests include Asian religions in America, theory in the study of religion, American evangelicalism, and professional wrestling studies.

Rebecca C. Bartel is Associate Professor in the Department for the Study of Religion and Associate Director of the Center for Latin American Studies at San Diego State University. She also holds the Fred J. Hansen Chair in Peace Studies. Bartel is the author of *Card Carrying Christians: Debt and the Making of Free Market Spirituality in Colombia* (2021).

Ting Guo is Assistant Professor at the Department of Language Studies, University of Toronto, focusing on religion, politics, and gender, in and beyond the transnational Sinophone world. Her first book monograph, *Politics of Love: Religion, Secularism, and Love as a Political Discourse in Modern China*, is forthcoming. She has published in journals, including the *Journal of the American Academy of Religion*, *Method & Theory in the Study of Religion*, *Critical Research on Religion*, *Anthropology Today*, and *Journal of Religion and Film*. She co-hosts a Mandarin podcast called "in-betweenness" (@shichapodcast).

James Dennis LoRusso is interested in the way that religion interacts with markets, businesses, and workplaces in the production of social inequalities. He is the author of *Spirituality, Corporate Culture, and American Business: The Neoliberal Ethic and the Spirit of Global Capital* (2017) and has published on a wide range of subjects, including spirituality in the workplace, corporate chaplaincy, and the state of academic labor.

Sean McCloud is Professor of Religious Studies and American Studies Faculty Affiliate at the University of North Carolina at Charlotte. He teaches, researches, and writes about the subjects of religion and culture, social theory, and religion in the United States.

Richard Newton is Assistant Professor of Religious Studies at the University of Alabama. He is the author of *Identifying Roots: Alex Haley and the Anthropology of Scriptures* (2020). Newton is also Editor of the *Bulletin for the Study of Religion* and the founding curator of Sowing the Seed: Fruitful Conversations on Religion, Culture, and Teaching (sowingtheseed.org).

Malory Nye is an independent scholar based in Perth, Scotland, with teaching activities at the Universities of Glasgow, and also a research scholar at the Ronin Institute. He is author of *Religion: The Basics* (now being updated for a third edition), blogger at *medium.com*, contributor to the podcasts *Religion Bites* and *History's Ink*, and editor of the journal *Culture & Religion*.

Aaron Ricker earned his PhD in Religious Studies from McGill University in Montreal. He serves as co-editor of the *Journal of the Council for Research on Religion*, and executive board member for the Eastern International Region of the American Academy of Religion.

Matt Sheedy holds a PhD in the study of religion and is a visiting professor in the department of North American Studies at the University of Bonn, Germany. His research interests include critical social theory, theories of secularism and atheism, as well as representations of Christianity, Islam, and Native American traditions in popular and political culture. His most recent book is *Owning the Secular: Religious Symbols, Culture Wars, Western Fragility* (2021).

Beth Singler is the Junior Research Fellow in Artificial Intelligence at Homerton College, University of Cambridge. Her anthropological research considers the social, ethical, and religious implications of AI and robotics. She is the 2021 Digital Religion Research Award winner, a fellow of the International Society for Science and Religion, and she has appeared in international media, including the BBC, the *New York Times*, *Forbes*, and CNBC.

Leslie Dorrough Smith is Associate Professor of Religious Studies at Avila University (Kansas City, Missouri, USA), where she is also the Director of the Women's and Gender Studies Program. She is the author of *Compromising Positions: Sex Scandals, Politics, and American Christianity* (2019) and *Righteous Rhetoric: Sex, Speech, and the Politics of Concerned Women for America* (2014). Her research interests focus on American evangelicals and politics, critical theory, and the use of method and theory in both religious studies and gender studies.

Teemu Taira is Senior Lecturer in the Study of Religion at the University of Helsinki. He has published extensively on religion and atheism in media and public discourse, including *Media Portrayals of Religion and the Secular Sacred* with Kim Knott and Elizabeth Poole (2013). He is currently finishing a book on the discursive study of religion and an edited volume titled *Atheism in Five Minutes*.

FOREWORD

We are both graduates from the Department for the Study of Religion at the University of Toronto. As PhD candidates, we were both given the opportunity to teach religion and film classes for the first time. For Tenzan, this was a somewhat unwelcomed assignment at the time. When he was first assigned to teach a religion and film class in 2015, he was almost offended. At the time, writing his dissertation on French Continental philosophy, Tenzan stormed into the graduate director's office and asked why he had not been assigned to teach a subject more related to his dissertation topic. After all, he thought: "I had never even taken a class on religion and film as an undergrad. I had taken classes on film studies more generally, but I didn't even think 'religion' was in film in any intrinsic manner. So how could I teach a whole class on the relationship between religion and film?" The director responded that maybe that problematic question should be the precise focus of the class.

When Rebekka announced that she would be teaching a summer session of religion and film, some of her friends and colleagues chuckled. "You don't even like movies!" they exclaimed. "Why would you want to teach about them?" "But I like religion, or rather, the study of religion," she replied. She saw connections between her dissertation fieldwork on the reading practices and interpretative strategies of progressive Christians and the question of how films engender certain ideologies and worldviews rooted within their cultural contexts. Also, Rebekka's teaching mentors at the University of Toronto advised her to approach the course as a method and theory class in which theoretical approaches to the study of religion are read in tandem with popular films to introduce students to the relationship between religious studies scholarship and film scholarship.

This serendipitous advice we separately received turned out to be just what we needed to hear at the time. The reason for this is that from our first attempts at syllabus construction for the religion and film class, it became very apparent that there was not enough critical theory used in scholarship on the topic. Our respective mentors at the University of Toronto had advised us to use the class to introduce students to theoretical questions in the study of religion. Yet, it was precisely these questions we found lacking in scholarship on the subject. In time, this brought us into dialogue, and this book is the outcome.

In September 2015, Tenzan published a brief reflection on his experiences teaching religion and film in the *Religion Bulletin, the Blogging Portal of the Bulletin for the Study of Religion.* One month later, Rebekka emailed him looking for advice redesigning her religion and film course for the new religious studies curriculum at Middle Tennessee State University. Then, in 2017, when Tenzan was writing the article "Ideological Blindspot in the Academic Study of Religion and Film," which would later be published in *Method and Theory for the Study of Religion,* he reached out to Rebekka to see if she would be interested in a creating a volume on the subject.

Our shared enthusiasm for this project is influenced by critical scholars of religion like J. Z. Smith, Timothy Fitzgerald, Bruce Lincoln, Russell McCutcheon, and Tomoko Masuzawa, all of whom taught us that religion is not a particular thing that exists out there in the real world, independent of cultural difference, but a complex confluence of political, economic, historical, and cultural forces that are essentialized as religion. In our opinion, the chapters in this book are critical because they bring this precise insight to the study of religion and film in a format that is accessible to all readers for the first time. As will be detailed in the Introduction, almost every book on the subject that is currently in print seems to essentialize religion to a certain extent, either as a definite thing with particular qualities that can be identified in film or as some kind of sacred experience shared by the cinematic viewers. Each book in print does this differently—some privileging theology, some mythology, and a few even applying a form of ideological criticism in a very nuanced manner, but each somewhat misses the mark in some way. There are few great books in print that provide examples of what is needed in the field, such as Michael Ryan and Douglas Kellner's *Camera Politica: The Politics and Ideology of Contemporary Hollywood Film* (1988), Gregory J. Watkins *Teaching Religion and Film* (2008), and M. Gail Hamner's *Imaging Religion in Film: The Politics of Nostalgia* (2011). There are separate articles on the subject by prominent thinkers like Lincoln and McCutcheon that address the lack of critical theory in the subfield of religion and film and try to show how to deal with the subject in a critical manner. However, there is no focused, full-length book treatment of the matter that brings all this together in a format accessible to all readers.

This book was created to fill this gap in scholarship. Together, we have collected twelve brilliant religious studies scholars who share our desire for a more critical perspective in the field, and we are proud to have created the first full-length exploration of the relationship between religion, film, and ideology. What the collected authors and we have tried to show above all else is how religion is imagined, constructed, and interpreted in both film and film criticism. However, this volume should be seen as an introductory and not an exhaustive book on the topic. Many more volumes like this could be written using the critical lens outlined in the introduction to reimagine how religion and film are understood and taught. Moreover, we want to emphasize that we have not tried to cover all the so-called world religions in our respective chapter topic selections, as it is precisely the application of that construct to the subject of religion and film that is part of the problem that this book seeks to resolve. The purpose of this book is not to enumerate the different phenomena people think of as being religious *in* film or being *about* religion in film, and then to discuss such topics critically. Instead, we endeavor to show how the very idea of religion is constructed and imagined by directors, cinematographers, writers, actors, camera operators, lighting technicians, makeup artists, costume designers, and so on. Not to mention the film critics and scholars of religion who write about religion and film more generally.

Lastly, to briefly say something about the film selections in this volume, we asked the contributors to pick rather recent "Hollywood" films (i.e., meaning big global box office productions) for their respective film analysis in each chapter. The reason for this was twofold: one, it is precisely in the big-budget popular films with a global reach that the dominant ideologies of contemporary culture are often concealed and disseminated; two, because we wanted to include recent blockbuster films that had not been featured in earlier religion and film volumes. There are still some older films included in the respective chapters, such as *Secret to my Success* (1987) and *Religulous* (2008), but we are happy to cover some relatively recent films like *Joy* (2015), *Silence* (2016), *A Wrinkle in Time* (2018), and *The Last Jedi* (2017). One way to expand upon this volume in the future would be to include films from a wider selection of periods, genres, and global markets, and perhaps that is a task to take up at a later date. As it stands, we are happy with this collection because it provides a useful introductory resource for classes on religion and film, religion and popular culture, as well as for academics and general readers interested in religion in film.

With gratitude, we would both like to thank the Department for the Study of Religion at the University of Toronto for assigning us to teach religion and film way back when we were starting as instructors, as well as all the critical scholars who preceded us on this path and helped inspire us to teach the subject critically in the first place. In addition, we would like to thank the series editor for supporting this project—it is an honor to be a part of his critical book series—as well as all the supportive staff at Bloomsbury Academic who provided us with the necessary extensions needed to complete this project during the Covid-19 pandemic. Tenzan would also personally like to thank Russell McCutcheon for all the conversations he had with him over Facebook Messenger as he was initially constructing the book proposal. Rebekka would like to acknowledge the intellectual contributions of current and former students in her religion and film courses at MTSU, who enthusiastically took up the challenge of critically investigating the relationship between religion and film.

Tenzan Eaghll and Rebekka King

Introduction

Three Film Critics Walk into a Theater:

The Ideological Blindspot in the Academic Study of Religion and Film

Tenzan Eaghll

Take yourself back in time to November 8, 1956, to what is arguably one of the most important opening nights in modern cinematic history. The place, New York City's Criterion Theatre. The event, the opening night of Cecil B. DeMille's Academy Award–winning biblical epic, *The Ten Commandments*. It is a star-studded event with Hollywood celebrities like Charlton Heston and Anne Baxter stealing the spotlight. Amid the superstars, *let us imagine* that there are three religion and film critics who are also in attendance that have specifically been invited by the famed director Cecil B. DeMille to review his new blockbuster. *Let us also imagine* that these three critics who have been invited to review the film have three very different ways of understanding how religion is represented in film: theological, mythological, and ideological, respectively.

The first critic is theological in orientation, seeing all representations of religion in film through a scriptural perspective. For this critic, DeMille's *The Ten Commandments* is proof that the miracles in the Bible are still at work in the modern world. The film is a joyous occasion because it brings the biblical stories to life for a new generation of believers. It is a masterpiece, portraying the birth of Moses, the revelation of the Ten Commandments on Mount Sinai, and the parting of the Red Sea, all in technicolor! This critic knows that what is featured in this film is not identical to the biblical story, but what is of interest to them is how the film represents the scriptural message and themes being depicted.

The second critic is more mythological in orientation and sees representations of religion in film as a sign of some deep human need for the sacred. For this critic, representations of saviors, seers, prophets, priests, temples, or even mere personal transformation are a sign of a power or force that transcends the everyday world in which we dwell. For this critic, *The Ten Commandments* is not a depiction of divine revelation on celluloid, but the mythological symbols that continue to inspire humanity across time. What universal archetypes are at play in the film? How do they influence or inspire the central hero—Moses—to achieve his goals? And how does the film depict the deep human struggles at play?

The third critic adopts an ideological perspective and views the first two critics as concealing some political agenda, whether subjective or communal. For the third critic, the point of reviewing the film is not to find evidence for religion in film—either in theological or mythological form—but to expose how the cinematic representations identified as religious by the first two critics privilege a particular type of human subjectivity, class, or community. For this critic, there is an emancipatory message in *The Ten Commandments* because the enslaved Hebrews throw off their Egyptian overlords. However, this is not necessarily a religious or even a sacred message of emancipation, but a political one about throwing off the yoke of tyranny.

The reason for starting this introduction with this imaginative scenario is that it helps summarize the current state of scholarship in the field of religion and film. It is an essentialization, of course, as rarely does one scholar wholly occupy one such ideological stereotype, but it helps illustrate the general discursive strategies contested in the field.

Whenever I start a new class on religion and film, I illustrate this point by opening with a few clips from DeMille's *The Ten Commandments* and asking the students how they would interpret the film. First, I ask students what they think makes the scene religious. Since they are often first-year or second-year students who have not taken a class on the subject, their answers usually resemble what the aforementioned theological critic might say, suggesting that what makes the scene religious is that it deals with a biblical story, speaks about and represents gods, or provides a tale about the origins of a scriptural law or a religious people. Second, I introduce the three religion and film perspectives just referenced above—theological, mythological, and ideological—and then ask the students the same question again. What makes *The Ten Commandments* a film with religious content or about religion in some way? By this point, I usually get more nuanced answers from the students because they have a better idea of what I am trying to do: I am trying to get them to think about their assumptions about religion and film and how they are related to these general theoretical positions. Moreover, I am trying to get the students to notice how most people implicitly think of the relationship between religion and film in theological or mythological terms, as very few students at the introductory level are aware of how to offer an ideological critique of the way religion is represented in film.

This implicit preference for theological and mythological forms of analysis continues in scholarship on the subject. In an article for the *Journal of Religion and Film*, John C. Lyden, who is not only editor of the journal but the *Routledge Companion to Religion and Film* (2009) and also author of *Religion as Film: Myths, Morals, and Rituals* (2003), notes that there is an underlying tension in the field between these three theoretical positions—theological, mythological, and ideological film criticism. Lyden points out that there is a general consensus among scholars that "Films include religious symbolism, consciously or unconsciously," and that "films may project a world-view which functions much like a religion in our culture," but points out that there is disagreement about what this means in scholarship (Lyden 1997: 1). On the one hand, some scholars frame representations of religion in film as a unique domain of theological or mythological symbolism presented through the medium of cinema. For these scholars, religion in film is definable by specific theological or mythological characteristics that signify some spiritual domain of things in the world. This assumption implies that film can be studied for its religious content because there are real and tangible religious qualities and effects produced by film. Moreover, a mythological approach implies that film itself can be classified as a modern form of religion, which is Lyden's position. On the other hand, some scholars argue that representations of religion in film should be viewed critically from an ideological perspective and defined according to the deeper intersections of class, race, gender, etc. This approach implies cinematic representations of saints and saviors, gods and goddesses, devils and demons, rituals and revolutions, heroes and heroines, and many more do not necessarily signify an autonomous domain of religious symbolism and experience, but deeper rhetorical, social, and political strategies.

The problem with this summary of the field that Lyden presents—like that provided in most scholarship on the subject—is that it presents the contestation between theological, mythological, and ideological definitions of religion in film as equally represented in scholarship, and then attempts to privilege mythological analysis over ideological analysis. In fact, Lyden goes so far as to suggest that ideological criticism is "probably the more common among scholars of religion" (Lyden 1997: 7). However, even a cursory analysis of scholarship on religion and film since the 1990s—which is when it began to blossom as a distinct academic field—reveals a series of monographs and edited volumes that privilege theological or mythological interpretations of religion, and not a single book or edited volume fully dedicated to ideological analysis. There have certainly been volumes with chapters that contain ideological analysis, and even several books that critique ideological aspects of film, but no full-length studies on the subject.

Moreover, and perhaps most importantly, almost all scholarship published on religion and film in the past couple of decades has utterly failed to consider how the category of "religion" itself functions ideologically. Some scholars do indeed apply ideological analysis at a general level to analyze broad social-political and moral issues in cinema. However, they do not specifically analyze the use and interpretation of religion in film and film criticism. What is shocking about this state of affairs is that ideological analysis is highly developed in film studies and perhaps one of the most dominant forms of criticism in that field. In fact, as I will argue in the remainder of this introduction, the tendency to prefer theological and mythological definitions of religion over ideological criticism in religion and film scholarship is not a mere theoretical oversight. Instead, it is an active effort to maintain a certain hegemonic view of religion as *sui generis*—implying a unique, distinct, or sacred domain of meaning.

Since "Ideology" is one of the central terms in this volume, I should perhaps state before continuing that it is applied here in a somewhat "post-structuralist" sense. What this implies—and it will be unpacked in more depth here—is that ideology is not applied here in the classic Marxist sense, implying a false hegemonic view imposed upon members of a culture by the ruling capitalist classes of society. Rather, ideology should be understood, following Althusser, as the various ways in which individual members of a society imagine the "real" conditions of existence.[1] Or, as Sturken and Cartwright define ideology, as the shared beliefs and mundane practices that make up the social structures that people participate in daily life (Sturken and Cartwright 2009: 21). This means that what is called for here is not a more nuanced application of ideological analysis to get back to some proper definition of religion or some experience of being in the world that is free from ideology. Rather, what is called for is simply an application of ideological criticism to show how religion is imagined, manufactured, and interpreted in cinema. A critical approach to religion and film requires that we pay close attention to how representations of religion in film conceal issues of race, class, gender, colonialism, secularism, and capitalism—common themes of most ideological critique—as well as notions of origin, authenticity, narrative, violence, and identity—categories germane to the academic study of religion. However, it doesn't presume that undertaking this analysis will deliver us beyond ideology in some pure sense. The point of ideological analysis is to illustrate the political uses and interpretations of these various representations, but not to pretend that it is possible to get beyond the imaginative creation of religion.

Defining "Religion" in Film and Film Criticism

The chapters in this book take as a truism J. Z. Smith's claim that "there is no data for religion," and this is precisely what makes this book so important for religion and film scholarship. In *Imagining Religion: From Babylon to Jonestown,* Smith suggests that although many things might be classified as religious, there is no intrinsic data for religion—it is an analytical category created by imaginative acts of comparison and generalization (Smith 1988: xi). The underlying argument in this book is that this observation is particularly useful for the study of cinema because it is a site where both cultural and individual imaginings about religion are constructed via the medium of film. Hence, whereas most scholarship of religion and film treats "religion" as a kind of *sui generis* entity that appears in film, this book will argue for a critical approach that sees representations of religion as the imaginative creations of screenwriters, directors, cinematographers, actors, audiences, cameras, lighting, makeup, costumes, etc., which do not necessarily preexist their appearance on the silver screen. Therefore, this book will apply Smith's argument that there is no data for religion to the study of religion and film, while also considering the theoretical tools of film studies.

By far, the majority of the scholarship on religion and film completely ignores Smith's critical work and defines religion in theological terms. For example, books such as *Reel Spirituality: Theology and Film in Dialogue* (Johnston 2000), *Into the Dark: Seeing the Sacred in the Top Films of the 21st Century* (Detweiler 2008), and *World Cinema, Theology, and the Human: Humanity in Deep Focus* (Sison 2012) all tend to equate religion with Christian theology in some manner, and to focus rather narrowly upon Christian themes such as Jesus, salvation, faith, etc. To be fair, many of these titles offer engaging cinematic analysis of the relationship between Christianity and film, but they lack critical analysis of their underlying assumptions about religion and its sociopolitical context. As Gail Hamner notes, "While these texts may be engaging and important, they effectively (albeit I presume unintentionally) essentialize religion as Christianity" (2011: xi).

Since this theological approach to religion and film dates back to the origins of film in the twentieth century, and a complete list of the books that fall under this theological umbrella would number in the hundreds, we must limit ourselves to the aforementioned few references. The important point is simply that Christian theological definitions of religion have informed most film criticism over the past century. Though some of this analysis has been extremely positive and some extremely negative, it all defines religion in revelatory terms as a truth that exists prior to and beyond the confines of its representation on the silver screen. Some of this film criticism aims to use film to preach the gospel, some to critique popular culture, and even some to open a dialogue between theology and popular culture, but all of it conceives of religion as a *sui generis* truth made evident through religious revelation. According to this model of criticism, what makes a movie "good" or "bad" depends on how the respective critic judges cinematic representations of "divine truth." As McCutcheon has suggested, this is an "insider"-based form of film criticism (McCutcheon 1998: 101); it is not concerned with analyzing representations of religion in film critically, but with finding a new form of theological truth in popular culture. Indeed, as Craig Detweiler writes in *Into the Dark,* in full support of this approach:

> films are not merely useful for appreciating over looked biblical texts or comparing interpretive processes. The best movies are revelatory in nature, not just talking about God and ultimate questions but becoming an occasion for the hidden God to communicate through the big screen. Cinema is *locus theologicus,* a place for divine revelation. (Detweiler 2008: 42)

In Detweiler's study, for example, this amounts to an analysis of how films like *Memento* (2000), *Eternal Sunshine of the Spotless Mind* (2004), and *Finding Neverland* (2004) contain scriptural connections and theological applications. He finds revelation and faith in these films by drawing connections between Christianity and culture.

The most common academic approach to the study of religion and film is to define religion in mythological terms. If the theological approach is the oldest—dating back to the beginning of the twentieth century—the mythological approach is by far the most recent—taking off in the 1990s—and coincides with the development of the academic study of religion and film. Books that fall under this approach are *Screening the Sacred: Religion, Myth, and Ideology in Popular American Film* (Martin and Oswalt 1995), *Film as Religion: Myths, Ritual, and Rituals* (Lyden 2003), *Religion and Film: An Introduction* (Wright 2006), *Film and Religion: An Introduction* (Flesher and Torry 2007), *Representing Religion in World Cinema* (Plate 2003), *Religion and Film: Cinema and the Re-Creation of the World* (Plate 2009), and *The Sacred and the Cinema: Reconfiguring the "Genuinely" Religious Film* (Nayar 2012). The authors of these respective works employ different methodologies to study religion in film, but they all define "religion" as myth by portraying cinematic representations of religion as a kind of *sui generis* field of symbolic meaning. The mythic definitions of religion found in these works are less Christocentric than those found in the theological works referenced earlier, but both approaches privilege religion as a unique and autonomous domain of meaning. Drawing upon theorists like Mircea Eliade, Joseph Campbell, Clifford Geertz, and Peter Berger to support their mythic definitions of religion, the authors of these works use myth to portray cinematic representations of religion as a kind of "social glue" that constructs symbolic universes of meaning on and off screen. Let me summarize their methodologies to illustrate the point and show how this approach operates as a general paradigm in the field.

Published in 1995, Martin and Oswalt's *Screening the Sacred* was one of the first major collections of essays on religion and film from an academic perspective. It employs a very basic comparative methodology by contrasting theological, mythological, and ideological approaches. In the introduction, the authors state their intention to use all three of these approaches to understand religion in film. Yet, it is clear that they favor theological and mythological definitions of religion as superior. In fact, the editors openly state that those who practice ideological analysis "cannot properly be said to be practicing religious studies" (Martin and Oswalt 1995: 11) and that their goal is "to take the things of the spirit spiritually" (Martin and Oswalt 1995: 12). What this implies is that they want to present religion as an "autonomous domain of culture" that is distinct enough to be defined in either theological or mythological terms and cannot just be rejected as an "opiate of the people, a mystifying set of symbols and ideas" (Martin and Oswalt 1995: 11).

For Martin and Oswalt, what makes a mythic definition of religion useful is that it provides a way to study universal cultural archetypes in film, such as the hero, the lover, the rebel, and the feminine, which they claim provides access to the sacred. As they put it, myth provides "an expansive definition of religion" that gives critics a nontheological way to study "the quest of humanity for contact with the sacred." Drawing upon Eliade, who argued for a sharp distinction between the sacred and the profane and suggested that ideal archetypes provide cultures access to the sacred, Martin and Oswalt suggest that archetypes function in cinema to provide a sacred experience for the audience. Interestingly enough, Eliade himself endorsed this application of myth to cinema, writing that "The cinema, that 'dream factory; takes over and employs countless mythical motifs-the fight between hero and monster, initiatory combats and ordeals, paradigmatic figures and images (the maiden, the hero, the paradisal landscape, hell, and so on)" (Eliade 1959: 205). From this perspective, we can read Martin and Oswalt's volume as an application of Eliade's *sui generis* definition of religion to the subject of religion and film, in a manner the theorist might embrace.

With the growth of academic publications on religion and film since the turn of the millennium, this mythic definition of the relationship between religion and film became more entrenched in academic work. In Lyden's seminal book, *Film as Religion*, he abandons the somewhat balanced analysis of contrasting theological, mythological, and ideological approaches to religion and develops a full mythic theory of religion in film that also considers audience reception. Using the work of Geertz to define religion as a "'myth' or story that conveys a worldview" (Lyden 2003: 3-4), Lyden argues that myth must be defined not in terms of the archetypal forms in film but the way in which they influence the viewers of film. Lyden, therefore, mixes audience reception theory with Geertz's mythic definition of religion to develop what he believes is a more holistic appreciation of the role of myth in cinema.

Audience reception theory, of course, is a way of studying the meaning of film by analyzing its impact upon cinemagoers, not film critics or academics (Marsh 2009: 255). By combining this with Geertz's definition of religion, Lyden hoped to develop a theory for how religion functioned not just on screen, but in popular culture more generally. Lyden thinks his approach provides a descriptive method to explain the symbolic processes by which myth functions in cinema. He points out that film—like religion, according to Geertz's definition—presents viewers with a powerful set of symbols that establish meaning for cinemagoers and that films also grounds these symbols in "conceptions of a general order of existence" to create an all-pervasive worldview clothed in an aura of realism. He, therefore, argues that it is the ability of cinematic images to produce this effect upon audiences that makes films religious. Films provide audiences with myths and morals that they put to use in their actual lives, and even when these audiences acknowledge that the images they watch in movies are illusions, the images still affect them. As he writes,

> If film does operate as a religion according to Geertz's definition, as I contend, then like religion it offers a connection between this world and the "other" world imagined in offering both models of and models for reality. These two aspects—worldview or mythology, and ethos—together express a vision of what the world really is, and what it should be. (Lyden 2003: 53)

In practice, what this implies is that Lyden does not pay as much attention to the mythic archetypes in films like *Star Wars*, but how films use all the tricks of cinema to provide an all-pervading sense of meaning and morality for audiences. For example, whereas the analysis of Star Wars in *Screening the Sacred* focuses on how mythic archetypes are expressed through characters like Luke Skywalker and Darth Vader, Lyden focuses on the general moods and motivations elicited by film. He is less concerned with the specific ways that Skywalker fulfills the hero's journey, and more with how Skywalker's response to the struggles he faces elicits an ethos that influences audiences.

Interestingly, Lyden is not only aware of Smith's dictum that "there is no data for religion" but cites the passage at the beginning of his chapter on "The Definitions of Religion" (Lyden 2003: 36). However, this does not stop him from later reifying the value of myth above its sociopolitical context and ascribing religion a unique non-reducible quality. In his analysis of various definitions of religion, for instance, he puts both theological and ideological definitions of religion in the same camp and suggests that they are abstract and reductive and too focused on critique. By drawing too much of a distinction between religion and culture in order to critique the values of film, he suggests that theological and ideological criticism ignores the "religious power" of cinema (Lyden 2003: 14; 247). More pointedly, he claims that theological definitions of religion in film are abstract because they simply apply biblical ideas and morals to cinematic representations, without appreciating how films often create their own ideals and morals. And he claims that ideological definitions are reductive because they reduce the meaning of film to its sociopolitical causes without appreciating its creative mythic potential. Lyden, therefore, presents his mythic definition of religion as a corrective to other scholarship because it allows him to consider how films themselves function like religion. As he writes, summing up his critique, "Both theological and ideological approaches to film and religion . . . have failed to take the religious elements in popular culture seriously as representing a distinct religious tradition. Popular culture may not be as formal or as institutionally organized as 'official' religions, but it functions like a religion, and may thus be viewed as a religion" (Lyden 2003: 108).

Of course, with this critique of Lyden, I am not denying that film can have a powerful emotional, creative, and ethical effect on people, but simply contesting the idea that these effects have some unique religious quality to them that is distinct from other aspects of culture (politics, economics, art, etc.). There is nothing wrong with noting that people imaginatively construct representations of religion in culture, or even that these constructs may have emotive and ethical effects on people, but in reifying them as unique religious data, scholars obscure the ideological aspects of such claims. Apropos Smith, critical scholars must make clear how "religion" is being imaginatively created not just on the silver screen, but by audience members and other scholars.

A further mythological approach can also be found in the work of Brent S. Plate, who, like Lyden, also suggests that film functions like religion. In an essay titled "The Footprints of Film: After Images of Religion in American Space and Time," Plate makes this explicit by discussing how popular movies have inspired theme-based weddings, cosplay, and even new religious movements like Jediism (Plate 2007: 427-433). For Plate, these are examples of how movies have become ritualized in viewers' daily lives and how cinema is a creative and dynamic medium that transforms the world around us—recreating even "traditional forms of religion" in the process (Plate 2009: 17). It shows that films are not merely abstract objects of entertainment removed from our daily lives—a mere fantasy space distinct from the everyday world—but creative mediums that create real effects in the world that are seen, heard, felt, and lived (Plate 2009: 10).

In Plate's full-length book publications on religion and film, *Representing Religion in World Cinema* and *Religion and Film: Cinema and the Re-Creation of the World,* he also follows Lyden in using Geertz to argue that films express "the mythological forces of religion" (Plate 2003: 3-4). Moreover, he argues that "Films are not religious simply because of their content but become religious due to their form and reception" (Plate 2003: 1). One religious studies theorist Plate uses to drive this latter point home is Peter Berger, who argued that religion is that creative process by which humans collectively create worlds of meaning and myth—a sacred canopy—to provide all-encompassing worldviews. For Berger, religion is the process by which all-pervasive meanings (what he calls the *nomos*) are ascribed to the material world (the *cosmos*) (Plate 2009: 5). Plate uses this theory to simultaneously argue that cinema borrows the "millennia-old aesthetic tactics from religions" (Plate 2009: 3) and that it recreates religion in the modern world.

What makes Plate's work distinct from Lyden and others is that he uses film studies theory, in part, to emphasize all the technical aspects of film that lead to the creation of religion in cinema. As an advocate for a material approach to the study of religion and managing editor for *Material Religion,* Plate stresses how "camera angles and movements, framing devices, lighting, costuming, acting, editing, and other aspects of production" must be appreciated in the study of religion and film (Plate 2009: 3). Drawing upon the work of various film theorists to support his position, from Marshall McLuhan to Manuel Castells, he suggests that "media are dynamic entities that actively shape and reshape the world." He then proposes a material definition of myth *as* media (Plate 2003: 4):

> myths, rituals, and symbols are only existent as media: A myth must be transmitted, whether by "word of mouth" or through the technologies of television; a ritual must be enacted, whether involving readings from sacred, printed texts or by processions through architectural space; a symbol must be shared, whether it is a colorful banner in a synagogue or a piece of bread. We thus must presume that religion—however oriented toward the "invisible," the "spiritual," the "wholly other," it may be—is nonetheless also always material and mediated. (Plate 2003: 5-6)

Importantly, this definition of religion still relies upon a *sui generis* definition of religion; it just uses materiality to emphasize the experience of the sacred and the transcendent. Plate justifies a *sui generis* definition of religion through film studies tools, suggesting that religion is always material and mediated but still a special autonomous space of sacred and/or transcendent experience, a point that is particularly clear in his other works on religion.

To prove the point and provide the most recent example of a mythological approach to the study of religion and film in a published book, see the introduction to Sheila Nayer's *The Sacred and the Cinema: Reconfiguring the "Genuinely" Religious Film.* Nayer specifically quotes Plate's aforementioned definition of myth to structure her analysis of film and then goes on to suggest that "the sacred can be electronically mediated" (Nayer 2012: 3). As in the work of Martin and Oswalt, the "sacred" here is being used to refer to an autonomous domain of religious content that can be studied in cinema, which seems to have both symbolic and experiential qualities. However, apropos Plate, what is stressed is technological mediation and creative potential of the sacred to recreate the world. Of course, from the perspective of a critical reading of religion, what is interesting about all this is how a very classical and essentialistic theory of religion is mixed with tools from film studies to give the air of theoretical advance, but without any analysis of the ideological assumptions implicit in the terms being used.

Considering this recent work by Nayer in conjunction with the earlier attempt by Martin and Oswalt to take the things of the spirit spiritually, we can see a commonality in all the aforementioned books on the subject over the past twenty years: they each privilege myth over ideological analysis in order to understand religion as a *sui generis* thing or experience that is either symbolized or evoked by film. In addition, as we will argue more here, these scholars forgo any critical analysis of the sociopolitical elements that make up their respective definitions of religion. To put the matter plainly, these *sui generis* definitions constitute the paradigm of contemporary scholarship on religion and film, and it is a paradigm that is not only blind to its own ideological commitments but also denigrates ideological analysis to preserve the sanctity of the category it faithfully privileges.

Framing Ideological Critique in the Field of Religion and Film

In a critical essay on the field of religion and film titled "Redescribing "Religion and . . ." Film: Teaching the Insider/Outsider Problem," McCutcheon summarizes the critique of the aforementioned approaches when he writes that books like *Screening the Sacred* privilege religion as "autonomously, free from, and juxtaposed to the tug-and-pull of historical existence (i.e., what they term "ideology"—a use which hardly does justice to this category)." McCutcheon goes on to suggest "that positing such a zone of free-floating privilege is itself—to rehabilitate the critical edge of the term—ideological" (McCutcheon 1998: 104). That is to say, in privileging theological and mythological definitions of religion in order to take the things of the spirit spiritually, the aforementioned authors ignore the ideological aspects of their own definition of religion.

In all of the above-referenced works, there is generally no mention of the fact that the term "religion" is a modern Western historical invention (Nongri 2013), that it is wrapped up with ideology of colonialism and the spread of European ideas and values around the globe (Masuzawa 2005; Chidester 1996), or that many of their assumptions about religion— such as the notion that it is a private/individual-based experience—are derived from Protestant Christian distinctions (Fitzgerald 1997; Martin

2010). This failure leads to a somewhat angelic view of religion in film, whereby scholars uncritically apply the category to whatever symbolism or experience meets their agenda and most ideological analysis is rejected as reductive. Hence, the critique leveled in this introduction is not simply that there is a crypto-theological paradigm in the majority of scholarship in religion and film, but that there is an active strategy by scholars to protect the category from ideological analysis to preserve the *sui generis* qualities they ascribe to it.

Of course, this criticism is not meant to suggest that the field of religion and film is completely bereft of ideological analysis. There have been many chapters and articles written using Marxist, feminist, psychological, and postmodern approaches to critique hegemonic discourses, and there have even been a couple of books written from a cultural studies perspective that employ a basic kind of ideological analysis. However, even scholarship from a critical perspective tends to (a) mix ideological analysis with theological or mythological definitions of religion, (b) frame ideological analysis in somewhat antiquated terms, and (c) fail to consider the more subtle ways ideological analysis can be used in film and film criticism to analyze the category religion. In what remains of this section I will explain these three errors by detailing how these scholars protect religion from ideological analysis by framing the latter in somewhat antiquated terms, and then providing some examples of how critical scholars try to correct this.

One example of ideological analysis from a theological and mythological perspective is found in Bernard Brandon Scott's *Hollywood Dreams and Biblical Stories*. Though he defines religion in rather Christocentric and mythological terms (Scott 2000: 4–5), he juxtaposes stories from the Bible and film to expose how mythology can be used to support ideological assumptions about gender, race, class, violence, etc. All this leads to an engaging reading of films like *Gone with the Wind* (1939), *Fatal Attraction* (1987), and *Dirty Harry* (1971), which are shown to conceal ideological assumptions and, sometimes, even to critique such hegemonic narratives.

One slightly similar study, but from a more cultural studies perspective, is found in Margaret Miles's *Seeing and Believing: Religion and Values in the Movies* (Miles 1996). Miles takes a step beyond most of the aforementioned studies by defining religion as "centrally and essentially about the values according to which people conduct their relationships" (Miles 1996: 15). This approach eschews the problematic nature of a *sui generis* definition of religion by focusing on "the social, political, and cultural matrix in which the film was produced and distributed" (Miles 1996: xiii). Instead of focusing on the film as a sort of biblical text to be analyzed, Miles's study shows how films like *The Last Temptation of Christ* (1998) and *The Handmaid's Tale* (1990) make and contest meaning, which slightly aligns her study with critical scholars of religion. As McCutcheon notes, whereas studies like *Screening the Sacred* often treat religion in film from an insider's perspective, attempting to expose the "real" meaning of religion in either its symbolic form or its audience reception, Miles takes a more objective approach by focusing on how films and societies imagine, create, and authorize value (McCutcheon 1998: 103). While this is not meant to suggest that Miles's study is perfect—she assumes a sharp ideological split between sacred and secular values and characterizes religious commitment as an interior private space, unassailable from social theory (McCutcheon 1998: 104)—it is at least a step in the right direction.

Interestingly, this mild advance by Miles toward a more critical analysis of religion has been largely rejected by all the authors listed in the previous section. In a half-disguised attempt to protect their *sui generis* definitions of religion, Martin, Lyden, and Plate have all criticized Miles's study as reductive, abstract, and elitist. For instance, in a review of Miles's book, Martin claims "her value-centered approach tends to ignore mythic patterns and theological meanings . . ." and "needs to be supplemented with those of other scholars who attend to other dimensions of religion" (Martin 1997: 499). This is a predictable claim for someone who desires "to take the things of the spirit spiritually" (Martin and Oswalt 1995: 12), and for someone who has written that those who practice ideological criticism "cannot properly be said to be practicing religious studies" (Martin and Oswalt 1995: 11). There are vested interests at stake in this debate. Again, in agreement with McCutcheon, I would suggest that Miles's more analytic and descriptive analysis of the cultural, social, and political factors of religious representations disturbs the *a priori* autonomy Martin and others grant to religion in film, and this is why they find it overly threatening (McCutcheon 1998: 104).

In Lyden's critique of Miles, he also suggests her work is reductive, but attacks her primarily for critiquing the values of Hollywood cinema and ignoring its creative potential. For Lyden, the primary sin of ideological analysis is that it does not appreciate the way cinema creates religious values and meaning for audiences. So he critiques Miles—and ideological criticism in general—for "an uncritical rejection of the worldview of popular film" (Lyden 1997: 13). Strictly in relation to Miles, this criticism is partially fair, as she does tend to judge values from a normative position and to suggest that Hollywood vice imperils the spiritual and physical well-being of everyday Americans. However, this certainly does not justify Lyden's claim that there is something "irreducible" about the myth, which is the "core of religion" that cannot be analyzed using ideological analysis (Lyden 1997: 14). Lyden does not use his critique to further the critical endeavor but to reinforce his own mythological methodology.

What is occurring in Martin and Lyden's critiques is that they are drawing a fundamental distinction between myth and religion, on the one hand, and ideology, on the other. They want to suggest that because myth and religion are non-reducible realms of meaning, representations of them in cinema ultimately remain independent from the hegemonic issues of class, race, and gender they may be used to support. The primary fear of these scholars, it seems, is that religion and ideology will get lumped together, and the special dimensions of the former will get reduced to rhetorical, social, and political elements of the latter, thereby obliterating the special autonomy they wish to grant religion. In fact, Lyden calls this the problematic "tendency of ideological analysis" and links it to the influence of the Frankfurt school, suggesting that all ideological analysis is guilty of reductionism:

> Popular films tend to be lumped together as ideological, largely due to the fact that they are created by a major American capitalist industry which is more interested in profit and producing pleasing fantasies than in making challenging and subversive art films. This judgment can be traced to the analysis of "mass culture" developed by Theodor Adorno and Max Horkheimer, German intellectuals of the Frankfurt School who fled Nazi Germany only to come to Hollywood. Ready to see the seeds of totalitarianism everywhere, they viewed all Hollywood films as commodities of capitalism which injected their ideologies into passive audiences, discouraging thought or questioning of authority. In fact, Adorno and Horkheimer viewed all popular films as having basically the same plot and the same characters, as mass production eliminated any significant artistic individuality of the filmmakers. (Lyden 1997: 11-12)

Lyden is most certainly correct that Adorno and Horkheimer critique Hollywood and popular films as a by-product of capitalism and as commodities that tend to pacify audiences. He is also correct that they generally failed to appreciate how popular films can sometimes encourage critical and subversive thought. However, to use the pessimism toward popular culture found in their work to characterize all ideological analysis, or even all thinkers associated with the Frankfurt school, ignores the subtle ways contemporary theorists apply ideological analysis. Moreover, and perhaps most importantly, to use the critique of film in the work of Adorno and Horkheimer to argue for the privileged autonomy of religion over ideological analysis is itself an ideological move that must be critiqued.

These fears about ideological analysis, therefore, arise from a somewhat antiquated and simplistic view of what it implies and how it functions. Both Martin and Lyden seem to understand ideology according to the "propaganda model," whereby the ideas of the ruling class are imposed upon the free members of a society in a hegemonic way, but this classically Marxist formula is rather outdated. According to this perspective, ideology is a kind of fraudulent mask concealing the true way society operates (Pearson & Simpson 2001: pp. 224-230), but over the course of the twentieth century, the propaganda model has slowly been replaced with a far more individual understanding of how ideology functions, one which is less "top-down" and more "subject-to-subject." As McCutcheon puts it, "The propaganda model overlooks the diverse ways in which members of a hegemonic system participate in the definition, coordination, articulation, and experience of dominance" (McCutcheon 1997: xi).

In strict theoretical terms, scholars of religion and film need to pay attention to the process Althusser called "interpolation," whereby members of society—and, in this case, members of an audience—identify with the world of images and discourses (Althusser 2014: 264). After all, ideology is not something imposed upon subjects like a false set of glasses that distort the world, but something in which they actively participate. As Slavoj Žižek puts it in *Pervert's Guide to Ideology*, ideology is our spontaneous relationship to the world, "We, in a way, enjoy our ideology" (Zizek 2013).

In practical terms, this implies scholars need to pay close attention to how representations of religion in film and film criticism conceal issues of race, class, gender, colonialism, secularism, and capitalism—common themes of most ideological critique—as well as notions of origin, authenticity, narrative, violence, and identity—categories germane to the academic study of religion. As Terry Eagleton notes in his history of the category "ideology," these are essential questions to ask because the very act of unifying, legitimating, universalizing, and naturalizing things is the very process by which ideologies take shape (Eagleton 1991: 45). The construction of ideology is that process of abstraction whereby discursive entities are crafted into utterly unique ontological things. It can occur at both a mass and an individual level. Or, as the Marxist philosopher Georg Lukács puts it, ideological abstraction is the process by which a "phantom objectivity" is granted to ideas and commodities that take the place of relations between people (Lukács 1972: 83). Hence, in both film and film criticism, scholars must pay attention to how hegemonic power structures get concealed within narratives and images. They must pay attention to how meaning and experience are wrapped up with abstract notions like "religion," the "sacred," or the "transcendent," and how these representations are used to authorize both individual and group identity.

In McCutcheon's specific article on religion and film, for instance, he employs an ideological critique by calling for more attention to how films invite us to think about the ad hoc creation of meaning, at both an individual and a communal level. Instead of assuming religion to be an autonomous domain of meaning—or universal human impulse of positive value—that needs to be located in or off the screen, McCutcheon looks at how films play with story lines, unsolved mysteries, and narrative to open questions about identity and truth. In *Rashomon* (1950), *Blow Up* (1966), and *Blow Out* (1981), he provides examples of films with a lack of stable meanings, grand narratives, and established identities. He uses these films to teach how people identify with myth and the category of religion more generally, and to point out that the job of the religious studies scholar is to pay attention to how we authorize, normalize, and mythify our behavior (McCutcheon 1998, 107). According to this approach, films provide a resource to teach how mythical origins, transcendent truths, and unquestionable religious values get constructed in the first place.

For instance, in his analysis of *Blow Up*, McCutcheon points out how the film shows how origins stories and narratives about past events get assembled from the bits of information that are available to us in our everyday lives. In *Blow Up*, this is shown through a story about a London photographer, Thomas, who accidentally takes a series of photographs of what he comes to believe is a murder. Since Thomas is unable to conclusively prove that a murder did occur from the random photos he has captured, he arranges them around his apartment in an attempt to construct a logical narrative and sequence of events, and changes the arrangement of the photos as his theory about the murder develops. For McCutcheon, Thomas's attempt to reconstruct these fragmentary images into a grand narrative is typical of how we as humans try to understand strange and unfamiliar events and how we weave piecemeal information into grand narratives (1998, 106). In this manner, McCutcheon uses his film analysis to illustrate how stories and myths get constructed in the first place, not locate some distinct religious qualities in film.

A similar analysis of film is found in Bruce Lincoln's essay "Mythic Narrative and Cultural Diversity in American Society." In this piece, Lincoln also analyzes narrative to show how meaning and identity are created in the human community through stories. Focusing on the movie *Avalon* (1990), which depicts a Thanksgiving dinner of an immigrant American family and the particular nationalist and familial origin stories told at that dinner, Lincoln argues that films provide an example of how narratives intersect and reproduce each other, at both an individual and a communal level, creating worlds of meaning through stories. In particular, the film shows how groups of people come together to tell stories in a ritualistic manner and how these get woven into grand narratives and myths of meaning and significance. As Lincoln writes about the family featured in Avalon:

> This particular group of people comes to this particular Thanksgiving dinner and listens to this particular story because they are members of one family, a family that is not only defined but actively constructed through the stories they tell and the ceremonies they share. Moreover, these occasions are important . . . precisely because they provide the opportunity to share the stories that actively remind their hearers of what holds them together and makes them who and what they are. (Lincoln 1996: 166)

Again, notice how Lincoln does not go looking for some special religious qualities in film to weave into a broader theory about religion in film, but uses film to illustrate how stories and myths get arranged and assembled in the first place.

What we find in the film analysis advocated by McCutcheon and Lincoln, therefore, is markedly different from what we find in the work of Martin and Oswalt, Lyden, and Plate. These two critical scholars try to break from a focus on religion as an autonomous domain of meaning to show how meaning is constructed at a general level for both individual members of society and scholars. If there is anything in their respective analysis that might get called "religion," it is simply sharing stories in a communal setting, which is not a *sui generis* domain of meaning but a general social practice. Fundamentally, what they suggest is that if we pay close attention to the process whereby narrative is repeated and naturalized, as is evident in certain films, we will catch a glimpse of how myth is created and naturalized through the telling of stories.

Using Ideological Analysis with Film Studies

One critique of the aforementioned narrative-based form of ideological criticism advocated by Miles, McCutcheon, and Lincoln is that it ignores all the tools of film studies. In an influential article, "Religion/Literature/Film: Toward a Religious Visuality of Film," Plate critiques Miles and other religion and film scholars for reducing film to textual analysis and religious studies discourse theory and failing to develop a truly interdisciplinary approach to cinema (Plate 1998: 16). Similarly, in Melanie J. Wright's *Religion and Film: An Introduction*, she also critiques Miles and tries to develop a more full-bodied cultural studies method that takes into consideration all the various elements of film studies, including not just narrative but film style and film theory. However, though I agree with this call for more attention to the tools of film studies, these authors fail to provide an ideological analysis of the category of religion and therefore undercut the advance of their call for a more interdisciplinary approach. They do use film studies theories on spectatorship, the gaze, and semiotics to offers some ideological analysis of film, but they tend to stop their analysis of film at religion and continue to treat it as a *sui generis* domain of meaning unassailable to critical theory. Plate and Wright are indeed correct that religion and film scholarship should not operate in a vacuum and ignore other disciplinary methods that can help unpack representations of religion in film, but they should also use the methods of film studies to offer a critical analysis of the category religion. This is important because a full application of film studies theory would also help deconstruct any essentialist qualities assigned to religion in film. In this concluding section to this introduction, I will elaborate upon this critique by pointing out where these scholars falter and offer examples of how to incorporate their insights while also providing a critical analysis of religion.

As mentioned earlier, what makes Plate's work unique is that he uses film studies methods to ground his study of religion in film. Though not overly formalistic, he stresses how camera angles, framing devices, lighting, costumes, acting, editing, directing, as well as audience reception are all part of the cinematic experience (Plate 2003: 2-3). In fact, Plate even examines questions of gaze theory and spectatorship. These questions are well positioned in the history of film studies to provide an ideological critique of certain elements of film: How do lighting and camera angle affect the presentation of images? How does the *mise-en-scène* of each shot frame the representations? To what extent is an audience member hailed on screen? How are audience members affected by the audio and visual components of film (Plate 1998, 29)? For Plate, these are important questions, and he is correct; scholars should emphasize the medium through which film is delivered and the precise way that representations of religion are presented to audiences. In the aforementioned paper, "Religion/Literature/Film: Toward a Religious Visuality of Film," he applies his medium-specific methodology as a critique to other scholarship in the field and takes film critics like Miles to task for treating movies like books, not films. Plate is correct on this point, and I agree with him when he writes that "religion and film scholars must become more adept at the techniques and specificities of film production if they want to provide a solid and thorough cultural analysis" (Plate 1998, 25).

However, as noted in the previous sections, the problem is that Plate assumes there is a *sui genèris* quality to religion which he never subjects to ideological analysis. For instance, in "Religion/Literature/Film" he defines religion as a unique experience of the "transcendent" and aligns it with an experience of the divine (Plate 1998: 29). Because he is an advocate of a materialist approach to the study of religion, he emphasizes that this experience of the transcendent in film is material, mediated, and embodied by the viewers of films (Plate 1998, 22; 28), yet he understands this transcendent religious experience as something autonomous and distinct enough to be classified in isolation from other aspects of social life, and so does not subject it to ideological criticism. In fact, he rejects the critical analysis of transcendence as merely a "postmodern" trend that we need not accept (Plate 1998, 29). To be fair, Plate does talk about the need for ideological analysis in his work more generally, but he never applies it to the category religion or the transcendent, only to more general sociopolitical elements of film. So while Plate uses film studies methods to analyze films for their so-called religious elements and affects, he fails to use these methods to interrogate the ideological aspects of these elements and affects.

On a somewhat different note, and moving in a direction that likely pleases some critical scholars of religion, Wright's *Religion and Film: An Introduction* tries to develop a cultural studies approach that examines the relationship between religion and film by studying its various cultural elements. Wright frames her method as an attempt to improve upon Miles's rather basic approach to cultural studies by looking at additional elements of film, such as production, distribution, exhibition, theory, aesthetics, and reception, as well as religious context (Wright 2007: 105). For instance, in the respective chapters in her volume, Wright analyzes film like *La Passion de Jeanne d'Arc* (1928) and *The Wicker Man* (1973), looking at not only narrative but also the historical and cultural context of the film's production, the film style of the director, and popular reception of the movie upon its release (Wright 2007: v). From a critical perspective, all of this is most certainly a welcome advance because it shifts the analysis of religion in film away from an insider's focus on sacred or transcendent values to an outsider's focus on each movie's context. In fact, Wright even cites the work of the critical scholar Malory Nye to suggest that religion should just be studied as a cultural practice like any other (Wright 2007: 103).

However, despite these promising developments, at the end of the day Wright concludes by siding with a definition of religion far closer to Lyden and Plate than Nye, and even closes her book by stating that "film can at times be not simply a descriptor of, or a vehicle for, religious experience, but religion itself" (Wright 2007: 173), which is a line that could have come straight out of Lyden's *Film as Religion*. Despite the fact that she tries to develop a cultural studies approach that takes into consideration spectatorship and the multiplicity of different contexts (may they be historical, racial, or gendered) in which viewing takes place, and to move away from a strictly formalistic approach to film analysis (Wright 2007: 33), there are times when, just like all the authors discussed in the first section of this chapter, she uncritically slips into a somewhat *sui generis* definition of religion. Moreover, there are times when Wright also reduces ideological analysis of religion in film to the Frankfurt school (Wright 2007, 9) and refers to ideological criticism as an "isolated intellectual exercise" that is removed from how people use films to create meaning (Wright 2007: 27). Of course, this is not meant to discount all the advances Wright does make, for she has all the correct tools and impetus at her disposal, but just to point out that she often succumbs to the general paradigm that dominates the field by essentializing religion and denigrating ideological scholarship as reductive.

The important point here is that scholars should not go looking for religion in film to find some *sui generis* qualities in film, but attempt to show how narrative and the medium of cinema creates a space where wider historical and political issues are projected and woven together into cinematic representations. Scholars like Plate and Wright are correct that scholars of religion should incorporate the tools of film studies into their analysis of cinema. However, scholars like McCutcheon and Lincoln are correct that this should not be done at the cost of ignoring the ideological elements of the category of religion. In Althusserian terms, scholars need to ask how films interpellate the spectator as a subject functioning through the use of mythic tropes and cinematic tricks, and how this interpellation functions with respect to gender, race, class, distinct global cultures, etc.

What Follows in This Volume

This book is therefore written as a corrective to the ideological blind spot in the study of religion and film that has tended to dominate scholarship on the subject. Each chapter takes on a popular theme that may be deemed religious from some cinematic or scholarly perspective, and then shows how such representations function ideologically in film and film criticism. Each chapter contains a discussion of how these respective themes have been represented in previous films and film criticism, and then provides an analysis of a particular film to show how this dominant theme has been privileged or critiqued in cinematic and scholarly representations. Altogether, the chapters touch on issues of atheism, scientism, capitalism, spiritualism, whiteness, colonialism, orientalism, humanism, magical realism, indigeneity, evil, horror, superheroes, apocalypticism, artificial intelligence, and science fiction, respectively.

We begin with Taira's chapter on atheistic documentaries and the critique of religion in *Religulous* because it perfectly details how to critique the category of religion from a scholarly perspective. It is also a perfect place to illustrate the difference between the critique of religion that is common in popular culture from what we aim to do in this volume. The point of this volume is not to critique religion as silly or unscientific, but to illustrate the construction of mythic and religious representations in film and film criticism, as well as the construction of the category "religion" itself. Taira's chapter illustrates this beautifully with his analysis of *Religulous* because he shows how the film constructs religion as the "other" to the scientific rationality of New Atheism. *Religious* is a documentary starring the comedian Bill Maher. It features Maher traveling around the world making fun of religious adherents and suggesting that religious belief is dangerous to the future of humanity. The film medium of documentary allows for this representation of Maher's view of the world because it gives the illusion of objective facts being contrasted to the believers being interviewed. *Religulous* presents religion as something only the foolhardy and unscientific believe, and it presents science as the cure to the illusions offered by religion. Lastly, it presents scientists as the custodians of this cure. The problem with all this is twofold. One is that religious belief among scientists is actually quite high. There is no correlation between scientific discovery and the atheism of scientists. Two, religion does not exist as some monolithic set of extreme beliefs that exist out in the world that all believers adhere too. Rather, the very category itself is projected upon an arbitrary set of data deemed religious by those who think they know what religion is, whether they be adherents of religion, critics, or scholars. For Maher, for instance, all forms of religious belief are a form of radicalism because he argues that even those who identify as religious moderates are sanctioning the actions and beliefs of religious extremists. Thus, for Maher, all Muslims are Islamic extremists and all Christians are creationists, even if some of them may personally hold more moderate positions. What we find in *Religulous* is therefore not a depiction of religious people around the world but a projection of what Maher thinks religion is and why it is dangerous. As Tiara notes, such a popular documentary film can be regarded as data to be studied by scholars in order to determine how the atheistic position is constructed through imagining its Other, "religion." What is of interest in *Religulous*, then, is how this New Atheist representation of the atheism/religion binary is articulated to form a rather unified view of the world, and further, how this view is articulated as part of atheistic identity politics.

LoRusso begins his chapter by tracing how the origins of cinema and film criticism have theological and mythological roots, and closes by discussing some problematic conclusions this can lead to in contemporary film criticism. As he notes in his intro, in the nineteenth century the original patent for "celluloid photographic film" was issued for a clergyman who was trying to make the Bible more accessible to children, the first major blockbusters were religious epics like *The Ten Commandments*, and the first film critics saw cinema as having a moral purpose to reinforce religious values. However, this is not meant to imply that films are all about religion, quite to the contrary, LoRusso's ultimate point is that films may appear to be religious or to have mythological elements, but that is simply because they are packaged that way. They are imposed with certain universal messages and branded with mythological themes. In *Secret to my Success* and *Joy*, for instance, LoRusso finds two films that blatantly glorify capitalist success but which can be interpreted as fulfilling the Hero's quest, what Joseph Campbell once described as the monomyth that underlies all mythic and religious narratives about heroes. In this manner, even films with a contemporary capitalist theme may appear to embody some mythic or religious form, but that is because they are structured that way to create box office success. As LoRusso notes in his conclusion, films package our desires in digestible ways and that is the secret to their success: they bring us carefully crafted consumer joy. This is a beautiful summary of how ideology functions in cinema.

In Smith's chapter, she examines *A Wrinkle in Time* and finds a movie that attempts to overcome gender, racial, and social differences with a "spiritual" message of self-transformation through love. Smith draws our attention to how the director, Ava DuVernay, attempts to flip the stereotypical white male gaze with three lead female characters of diverse ethnicity who reject religion in favor of spirituality. However, as Smith also notes, the director then uses this reversal of the stereotypical white male gaze to produce a sort of generic watered down "spiritual but not religious" message in the film that is very typical of contemporary neoliberal religious discourse in America. The central character Meg, for instance, is continually told that her success in the film depends on her own personal acceptance: she must love herself and honor herself in order to tap into the spiritual power of the universe. She is assured that once she achieves this level of self-acceptance she can do anything, even pass through space and time unrestricted. Hence, although the film appears to challenge various racial, gender, and religious stereotypes, it ends up reinforcing a brand of religiosity that is extraordinarily well established in American culture.

In Nye's chapter, he argues that representations of religion in film are often about privileging "whiteness." Deconstructing Scorsese's *Silence*, which on the surface is about Portuguese missionaries in Japan in the sixteenth century, Nye draws attention to issues of race and colonialism. Much like how James Baldwin argued that the concept of whiteness refers to how people who think of themselves as white racialize themselves, and in the process classify and control the world, Nye argues that the category of religion is used to cut up the world into "Asians," "Arabs," "Muslims," "Sikhs," "Japanese," etc. In his film analysis, he exposes how the colonial aspects of the story and its cinematic construction create the very racial distinctions highlighted in the film. Moreover, he emphasizes how the lead character in the film, Father Sebastian Rodrigues, fulfills the white savior trope beautifully, often in very self-conscious ways, such as through his self-identification with Christ as he apostatizes. Simply put, the narrative of the film—its theology, as Nye puts it—becomes very obviously particularized by race: "how this white man racialises himself *and* Jesus in an 'alien' world defined by colonialism." In this manner, *Silence* is not really about religion, per se, but about white men reaffirming their whiteness and their understanding of religion.

Altman's film analysis of *The Darjeeling Limited* is ferociously refreshing and colorful. What he finds in Wes Anderson's tale about three brothers who travel to India to reunite on a spiritual journey is a self-conscious critique of Western representations of Indian spirituality and religion. On the surface, *The Darjeeling Limited* falls victim to the classical tropes of orientalism: it represents "the East" as mystical other to "the West," and does so in order for three white male brothers to rekindle their relationship and find themselves. In this way, the East functions as a spiritual or religious tool the brothers create in their imagination to rekindle their relationship. Moreover, as Altman writes, "the Whitman brothers travel on the railroad, the most enduring colonial transportation technology," and "the only Indian characters in the film are the steward and Rita, the attendant whom Jack has sex with in the train's bathroom." However, at the same time that the film falls victim to these stereotypical and near-insulting representations of the East, it also lampoons them as farcical characterizations and exposes the brothers as the real butt of the joke. In this manner, the film can be read as a farcical lampooning of Western orientalist tropes and the white privilege that created them. In a sort of reversal of stereotypical representations, the brothers in *The Darjeeling Limited* are not represented as noble characters of white privilege to be idealized, but comical characters in Anderson's farcical mystic East.

In Guo's chapter she argues that film critics often represent Buddhism as the Orientalized Other of late neoliberal capitalism, and ignore how this reflects Western values rather than "Buddhism," per se. Offering *Cloud Atlas* (2012) as an example, Guo argues that the film does not really represent any specifically Buddhist values at all, but Western humanist values of self-identity, social justice, democracy, and global ethics, all of which point toward the possibility for a new future in which a new collective humanism will dominate. Hence, Guo argues that what often gets represented and even critiqued as Buddhism in film is a Western image of Buddhism, filtered through the lens of neoliberal humanism.

In Rebecca Bartel's chapter, she analyses *The Wind Journeys* to find a critique of modern cinematic representations of Columbian religiosity in the magical realism of the director Ciro Guerra. As Bartel notes, the hybrid curation of Colombian culture found in this film is a feature of the magical realist narrative in Colombian literature and film, and this can help us deconstruct the idea of "the religious" as it is traditionally represented in films and film criticism. In *The Wind Journeys*, Guerra's construction of the religious follows his construction of the mask of happiness that conceals the melancholy of the Colombian coast, illustrating ways that "religion exists in the imagination of the screen-writers" and is manufactured through images and sounds interpreted through the lens of the camera. In this manner, Bartel uses Guerra's magical realism as a decolonial critique and takes us from essentialization and *sui generis* narratives about religion toward traces of the magical, the affable, the anti-modern, the bacchanal, and the folkloric.

Through a rich analysis of *The Revenant*, Sheedy's chapter takes us deep into the complex creation of 'Indigenous spirituality' in film and film criticism. Beginning with the construction of the term "indigeneity" itself, and a discussion of the racist and colonialist tropes that are common in films that represent indigenous peoples, Sheedy then provides a film analysis that highlights how *The Revenant* challenges some of these tropes. As Sheedy argues, while it may be true that *The Revenant* is not an "Indigenous" film, strictly speaking, it nonetheless reflects a number of representational shifts in the depiction of indigenous peoples in Hollywood cinema. In addition to resisting or subverting tropes like the "white savior," the "helpless maiden," "Mohican syndrome," the "violent savage," and what Sheedy calls the "communing with spirits trope," *The Revenant* consciously upends some of the key foundational myths of American origins and religiosity. Sheedy's chapter, therefore, not only shows how representations of indigenous spirituality were constructed in the past through the "colonial gaze" of the lens, and how these colonial tropes are being critiqued and reimagined in contemporary film, it also touches upon the continued work that needs to be done in the future to correct the errors of the past. As Sheedy notes near the end of his chapter, any depiction of Indigenous Native Americans will always be partial and selective, privileging certain voices and traditions over others, and it is for this reason that we must all work to challenge narratives that attempt to whitewash history and culture in broad-brush strokes.

In his chapter, McCloud discusses the role of "evil" in film through an analysis of the Supernatural horror flick *Hereditary*. McCloud points out how evil is used in the film as a scapegoat for the real horrors of human tragedy and mental illness. Throughout most of *Hereditary* the focus is on the horrific effects of a psychological illness that has affected the Graham family for several generations, but in the final portion of the film this medical description of the mental illness is replaced by a far more sinister, but much less complicated, horror story featuring a conspiratorial demonic cult. By the end of the film we are led to believe that this demonic cult is to blame for the mental suffering the family has endured, not the material conditions and social relationships in which they are embedded. McCloud brilliantly points out that this causational shift from the material to supernatural causation provides an ideology of agency that is similar to what is found in certain theological views of human suffering. According to this ideology of agency, horrific forms of suffering do not have an arbitrary historical cause but originate from some supernatural dark force that is both independent of history and immanent within it. *Hereditary* therefore provides an interesting example of "Religion as Film." That is, it invites students to consider how cinematic production creates the very content of religion in popular culture.

Ricker's chapter provides a wonderful opening critique of how films with "apocalyptic" themes have been represented in film criticism, and then provides a film analysis of *Hellboy* that puts this critique into action. Ricker points out how *Hellboy* fails to live up to the definition of apocalyptic heroism provided by film critics because the story doesn't follow the traditional apocalyptic narrative of "good news," which most critics blindly rely upon. Most critics generally present a definition of the apocalyptic—not to mention a definition of "religion" more generally—that is not grounded in critical-historical analysis of the term. For such reasons, Ricker concludes that a "religion in/and film" criticism that adopts a more historical and ideological focus can, by not taking up the self-appointed mission of discovering timeless spiritual truths in pop culture, reveal a lot more about the forms and functions of film culture deemed apocalyptic.

In Singler's chapter, she looks at representations of Artificial Intelligence (AI) in the *Terminator* franchise and also finds them filtered through biblical apocalyptic themes. However, whereas Ricker deconstructed the apocalyptic theme and its related comic book representations in cinema, Singler shows how representations of AI in film play with themes of predestination (free will vs. fate), messianic salvation, and the godlike wrath of AI come to destroy the world. One thing that interests Singler, however, is not just the cinematic representations of the robopocalypse found in *Terminator*, but how these representations are taken from the cinema to the streets, and to the personal lives of the viewers. By creating apocalyptic representations with a messianic angle in *Terminator*, the filmmakers tapped into the fears in the general public about the rise of AI in the world and what it implies about human agency, as well as to aspirations to "messiah-ness" among its fanbase. In this manner, Singler tries to show how cinematic representations get translated into real-world beliefs about the future of the world. She tries to show how the film blurs the lines between fictional and real robots, and how the film generates real-world convictions about what AI is and how it will affect the future.

In the final chapter, Newton takes this exploration of how representations in cinema influence popular culture to its ultimate conclusion: an analysis of *Star Wars Episode VIII—The Last Jedi*. *Star Wars* provides the best example of how a director's mythic and religious presuppositions lead to the creation of religion in film, and how this subsequently influences popular culture. It is a perfect example of how religion is created through the technological creation of cinema and extended into popular culture through social media, given expression in a growing fan base, and then solidified into real social formations that identify as "religions." As Newton notes, *Star Wars* is a participatory epic that has manifested as over a dozen movies, legions of books, multiple cartoon series, television shows, video games, toys, merchandise, and even immersive theme parks. This is to say nothing of the countless parodies, homages, and imitations. However, whereas many film critics use this fact to isolate the specific religious elements of *Star Wars* and Jediism—the real-world philosophy that is based on the mythic themes extracted from the films—Newton uses it to deconstruct any unified essence that might be identified with the *Star Wars* franchise in general. As Newton writes: "while people reference *Star Wars* as a single, monolithic cultural enterprise, those that engage it do so toward so many interpretive ends that the idea of a quintessential *Star Wars* is untenable. People disagree— sometimes adamantly and even vehemently—about the *Star Wars* they appear to hold in common." In this way, Newton joins the other authors in this volume in showing how mythic and religious themes are created in cinematic representations, and how these representations innately defy essentialization of any *sui generis* definition of religion. Newton argues that the reason for this latter point is because culture is not a monolithic enterprise, either in its imaginary or in its social formations, and because any such classifying of a particular interpretation of *Star Wars*—or film in general, for that matter—as original or authentic is itself a political act that gets exposed to cultural difference in its very presentation.

CHAPTER 1

Atheistic Documentaries and the Critique of Religion in Bill Maher's *Religulous* (2008)

Teemu Taira

In one of the few overviews of atheism and film, Nina Power wrote in 2013 that "surprisingly little has been written about the relationship between atheism and film at the formal or conceptual level" (Power 2013, 727). This is still true. There are also few empirical, in-depth examinations of atheism in individual films. At the same time, however, there has been a rise of atheistic documentary films in the first decades of the twenty-first century. This is related to the increasing interest in atheism, particularly the rise of "new atheism," and the development of media technology. This chapter examines how atheistic documentaries represent religion and at the same time implicitly or explicitly imagine atheist and non-religious identifications as different from religious identifications. Although several recent documentaries will be referenced in this chapter, it will focus on the 2008 "comic documentary" *Religulous*, directed by Larry Charles and written by comedian Bill Maher. This chapter demonstrates how a particular representation of religion (and atheism) is constructed in documentary films through the selection of certain types of religious people, texts, places, and "experts" to signify what is considered typical for religion(s). Furthermore, the analysis proceeds to clarify how twenty-first-century atheistic documentaries, and *Religulous* in particular, have functioned to construct and solidify atheistic identities. It details the cinematic and comic means by which the construction is done and argues that the result is a very unique and modern understanding of both religion and atheism. In a fascinating way, these documentaries provide a case study of identity construction, detailing how religion and non-religion are imagined in contemporary cinema.

The cultural studies approach utilized in combination with perspectives from the study of religion is not new as such (Miles 1996; Wright 2006; see also Eaghll 2019). Margaret Miles outlined that in the cultural studies approach, film is "one voice in a complex social conversation, occurring in a historical moment" (Miles 1996, xiii) and it pays attention to "the social, political, and cultural matrix in which the film was produced and distributed" (Miles 1996, xiii). To pursue analysis in line with this basic idea, I shall introduce one concept that has not been at the center of religion and film.

The main theoretical concept that characterizes my approach is articulation. The term is used here in line with cultural studies scholars Stuart Hall and Lawrence Grossberg (Grossberg 1986; 1992; Slack 1996), for whom articulation is a concept that characterizes a process in which various contingent elements are connected with or linked to each other—and other elements are disarticulated at the same time—through signifying, affective, and material practices. Articulations construct (contingent and temporary) unity or identity out of available raw materials. Some articulations are resilient and some are not, but what matters is that the effectivity of practices, including cinematic representations, depends on successful articulations between elements. What these elements are depends on the context, but in the case of the identity construction highlighted in this chapter, religion—in addition to science, gender, race, and class—plays an important role. In some cases, the elements are more or less equal, and in other cases one element can be more dominant than others, but this is an empirical question. Articulation is a useful concept when analyzing social processes in which collective identifications are imagined and constructed. In this study it is applied to the focus of the analysis, namely, how *Religulous* connects various elements within its representations to create an identity position and how the representations function as attempts to articulate the documentary film itself in relation to wider social struggles (e.g., atheist movements). Therefore, articulation is not limited to the analysis of film as an isolated text, but it helps us to study the particular "cultural moment in which the film originated" (Miles 1996, 23) and even its potentially continuing role in social formation.

Atheism, Film, and Documentary

There are not many films that emphasize the atheistic nature of their key characters, and few blockbusters have an atheist protagonist. One notable popular exception is *Inherit the Wind* (1960), based on the so-called Scopes

Monkey Trial of 1925. However, there are several self-identified atheistic directors whose works have been addressed in studies focusing on atheism and film, such as David Cronenberg, Pier Paolo Pasolini and Dziga Vertov (Power 2013). They are not examples of criticism of religion but reflect a sympathetic approach to religion by atheists, as in the case of Pasolini's *The Gospel According to St. Matthew* (Il Vangelo secondo Matteo 1964). There are also popular films that have drawn accusations of blasphemy, such as *Monty Python's Life of Brian* (1979) and *The Last Temptation of Christ* (1988), but they do not deal with atheism as such.

It is notable that documentaries, rather than fiction films, have become a vehicle for popular atheistic criticism and identity politics in the first decades of the twenty-first century. Examples are *Atheism: A Rough History of Disbelief* (2004–7, also known as *A Brief History of Disbelief*), *The Atheism Tapes* (2004), *The God Who Wasn't There* (2005), *The Root of All Evil?* (2006), *The Enemies of Reason* (2007), *The Four Horsemen* (2008), *Faith School Menace* (2010) and *The Unbelievers* (2013). These documentaries address the question of how humans should live. Although most films do this at least implicitly (Miles 1996, 7), these examples are as explicit as one can be about what is not their favored worldview. None of them target specific groups but religiosity in general. Moreover, although the documentaries promote atheism, they do not describe the atheistic lifestyle in detail (i.e., most of them are primarily not documentaries about atheism and atheists but documentaries that are critical of religion).

These documentaries would not have been made without the existence of people interested in criticism of religion. Some of them refer to 9/11 and Islamic terrorism explicitly, and many address more mundane worries about the organization of education, for instance, in a particular country. Furthermore, certain people are interested in doing these documentaries, meaning that production has revolved around a small number of atheistic celebrities. For example, Richard Dawkins has been involved in more than half of the films mentioned earlier. In addition, the development of media technologies, particularly in terms of distribution, has facilitated their reach. Many of the documentaries have been broadcast on television, it is possible to buy them as DVDs and some can be watched via video-streaming services. Contemporary documentaries generally have potential for broad dissemination at very low cost, and their form is sufficiently entertaining. As Nichols (2017, 1) argues, "Documentary has become the flagship for a cinema of social engagement and distinctive vision." These factors are relevant, but they only partially explain why the documentary format has become so important for atheistic representations of religion.

Documentaries are defined as consisting of nonfiction that makes claims about what the described phenomenon is like (Bonner 2013, 62). Although it is now commonplace both to question whether any representation can be coherent with the world outside of its representations and to challenge the dichotomy between what is made up and what is not, there is still (unspoken) agreement that the documentary film should be realistic in style (i.e., it is difficult to make a film in the genre of science fiction or romantic soap opera and get people to interpret it as a documentary). It is perhaps for this reason that the audiovisual options that atheists choose lean toward the documentary approach; if atheists wish to propose that religions are irrational and out of touch with reality, then documentary film is probably the most efficient and obvious choice.

Religulous—A "Comic Documentary"

Most of the twenty-first-century atheistic documentaries are stylistically and aesthetically quite conservative. *Religulous* follows a different style, as it breaks partly with the conventions of realism, borrowing from an approach that was made popular by American documentary filmmaker Michael Moore. What is typical for Moore's documentary films is an openly taken (political) position that utilizes emotional narratives. In one sense, documentary films can be defined and understood as always being about the argument that the filmmakers construct—they select, edit, and organize the raw material in a narrative form—but Moore is clear that he does not simply document a phenomenon or conform to an observational style; thus, he not only interviews people but also participates in the action seen on the screen, arguing for a certain position in a much more radical manner than what is typical for documentary films. In other words, Moore is an opinionated presenter rather than an anonymous and omniscient narrator (Nichols 2017, 4). He is often seen on the screen and in many cases the camera follows what he is doing, rather than documenting what is happening outside of Moore's own involvement. This has been called a reflexive mode, because the documentary reveals itself as constructed text, but Moore's style often overlaps with the performative mode, too, because the main character performs actions that constitute the main content of the documentary (Bonner 2013, 69–70).

A similar style has been adopted in *Expelled: No Intelligence Allowed* (2008), a documentary that defends intelligent design, directed by Nathan Frankowski and presented by Ben Stein, and in *Borat* (2006), written and produced by Sacha Baron Cohen. Given that *Borat* was also directed by Larry Charles, it is not surprising that a comparable style is adopted in *Religulous*. *Religulous* has been branded as a "comic documentary," suggesting that it is not conventional and does not fully adhere to the genre of documentary film. In addition, its name is a portmanteau word, consisting of "religious" and "ridiculous," leading people to expect an approach that laughs at religions, not with them.

The United States has been the most fertile ground for the content of *Religulous*. This is partly because of the examples it deals with. For instance, it highlights the debate between evolution and creationism, which is much more prominent in the United States than in Europe. Visits to religious theme parks, such as the Holy Land Museum and Creation Museum, reflect the American context. During the year of its release, *Religulous* was the most successful documentary film in the United States, grossing over 13 million dollars at the box office. It was much less successful outside the United States, but its theater distribution was limited.[1] It has taken in almost 10 million dollars in DVD sales, and it has been widely available for free via video-streaming services. Overall, this suggests that people around the world have seen (and possibly enjoyed) it. Currently, *Religulous* is the 25th-highest grossing documentary in the United States.

One of the film's promotional images (also used on the DVD cover) demonstrates its content relatively well. In the picture, three apes are sitting next to each other, each wearing the accoutrements (hat/cap and necklace) of a different religion: Judaism, (Roman Catholic) Christianity, and Islam. One of the apes covers its eyes, one its ears, and one its mouth. The choice of symbols reveals that the main target of the film's criticism is "Abrahamic religions," although it deals with Scientology and Mormonism, too. The film pays little attention to Eastern traditions—due to their lack of relevance to the US audience, according to the filmmakers (French 2008)—despite the reference to the three wise monkeys embodying the principle "See no evil, hear no evil, speak no evil," familiar in Japanese culture and other parts of Asia. The intended meaning of the three monkeys in this context is feigning ignorance or a lack of moral responsibility, which the film attributes to religion.

The two slogans used in the promotion material were "The end is near," where "end" is crossed out and replaced with "truth," and "When religion gets ridiculous." The first plays with the apocalyptic phrase, known particularly in Christianity, suggesting that the motto is untrue and the film reveals the truth behind the false religions. The second simply breaks down the portmanteau word of the film's title and clarifies its approach of morally superior atheism dissecting religion.

Religulous can be divided into more than twenty encounters between Bill Maher and a variety of religious and anti-religious individuals. Several underline the irrationality and anti-scientific nature of religion, such as the interview with Ken Ham at the Creation Museum in Petersburg, Kentucky. Ham states here that the museum's purpose is to teach visitors that "the Bible is true, from Genesis to Revelation," after which he argues that dinosaurs and humans lived at the same time, as depicted at the museum. Some encounters underline the harmful nature of religions. This theme is perhaps most explicit at the beginning of the film, when Maher refers to Catholic child abuse, the Danish cartoon controversy, and religious suicide bombings to frame the context of the documentary.

The film merits a more detailed examination, however, as studying these articulation processes reveals how the atheist message and identity position are constructed in the film and further connected to atheist struggles.

The Construction of "Us" and "Them"

When inviting people to be interviewed for the documentary, Maher used a different title for the film. This was *A Spiritual Journey*, which prompts completely different associations than the final title. Nor did the production team mention Maher's name, because he might have been linked to a disrespectful attitude toward religion. This is how Maher described the recruitment of interviewees:

> It was simple: We never, ever, used my name. We never told anybody it was me who was going to do the interviews. We even had a fake title for the film. We called it "A Spiritual Journey." [. . .] At the last second, when the cameras were already rolling, I would show up. So either they'd be seen on camera leaving the interview and lose face or they'd have to talk to me. (Goldstein and Rainey 2008)

Religulous does not describe what the atheistic lifestyle looks like, although it includes some of Maher's autobiographical aspects and in that way offers glimpses of what an atheistic life might mean in practice. It is primarily by representing religious others that it constructs a mirror image of the atheistic position. The statement about the strategy to find participants for the project is questionable in terms of documentary ethics, but the most important points for the purposes of this exploration are that the atheistic identity is predominantly constructed via its Other—religious people who were expected to have doubts about the documentary—and that the team was willing to use whatever material was gathered whenever the camera was rolling in order to present those people in the way the team wanted.

There are some moments, however, when the exposition of atheism is not done through the description of what it is not. For example, Maher talks about his family background and upbringing before starting his journey to the various locations where he meets religious people. Maher is a white man with a religiously mixed family background; his mother is Jewish and his father Roman Catholic. Maher is a relatively typical non-religious person in the United States, because sociological evidence shows that non-religious people are likely to be white men, and a religiously mixed heritage increases the likelihood of becoming non-religious—particularly when one of the parents is not religious (Zuckerman 2014, 93–94). Maher is far from typical, however. He is a known comedian and a critic of religion. Identifying as agnostic, he claims to preach "the Gospel of I don't know." At the same time, he proposes that religion is detrimental to the progress of humanity and that religion prevents people from saving the world. The implication is that saving the world is the task of non-religious people, because they do not worry about an afterlife and punishment all the time. Such comments are far from what Maher says about the "humbleness of doubt." The contrary attitude supports the overall message of *Religulous*: for those who are right, it is time to act. As Maher says at the end of the documentary: "This is why rational people, anti-religionists, must end their timidity and come out of the closet and assert themselves."

All this reveals that the main target audience for the documentary is not those who are committed to a religious position. It is those who are sitting on a fence, who are undecided, indifferent, or quiet about their views. *Religulous* is, therefore, part of a much wider atheist identity politics, which animates the phenomenon generally known as new atheism as well as a good number of secular organizations (Taira 2012; see also Cimino & Smith 2014). The message is the same as that presented in Dawkins's *The God Delusion*. In the preface, Dawkins writes that his "purpose is consciousness-raising" (Dawkins 2006, 25) and that his "dream is that this book may help people to come out" (Dawkins 2006, 27). Articulated in relation to atheist identity politics, *Religulous* is one of many attempts to construct an atheist "us" (and make people say it!) as opposed to a religious "them," rather than simply being an attempt to make people drop their religious beliefs and identifications.

One of the typical ways to highlight the significance of one's in-group is to exaggerate its size. The documentary correctly mentions that at that time, 16 percent of the US population was non-religious. This figure was based on self-identification. The interpretation, however, reveals the problem. Maher suggests that these people do not believe in God and do not want to have anything to do with religion. This is in striking contrast with the existing research and surveys, in which a good number of American "nones" state that they believe in God or a life force and have a relatively positive attitude toward religion. The 16 percent is a group that does not have religious affiliation; this is different than not believing in God or not wanting to have anything to do with religion.

Another tactic is to be clear about the boundaries of the in-group. In practice, this means that religious moderates are considered enemies. Instead of building alliances with them, *Religulous* follows new atheists who emphasize that moderate believers provide justification and support for the view of religious radicals that belief without evidence is a virtue. This is made explicit only in the final monologue, where Maher states that "those who consider themselves moderately religious really need to look in the mirror and realize that the solace and comfort that religion brings you actually comes at a terrible price."

There are also secondary tactics by which the "we-ness" is constructed. One of these is an implicit assumption of the homogeneity of non-religious people, who are held to be a group without significant internal variety or differences. No one suggests this explicitly, but *Religulous*, like other documentaries and books, does not make the heterogeneity visible. The imagining of some kind of atheistic tradition has been typical of twenty-first-century atheism, but "there have been many atheisms with conflicting views of the world" (Gray 2019, 3). Another tactic is aesthetics. The documentary film's unconventional ("Moorean") stylistic choices include many occasions where the film crew's microphone and camera are in the picture. In Moore's documentaries this signifies a sense of urgency and action, but in *Religulous* the same choice creates the impression of a relaxed and sincere atmosphere. The overall effect is that the atheists seem relaxed and content with their views—they have nothing to hide—whereas religious people are uptight because they are challenged by what atheists know to be true. Altogether, these different tactics contribute to the construction of atheist identity as "normal," desirable, and even superior to a religious identity.

They Are Irrational, We Rely on Science

One of the main articulations that *Religulous* employs is the link between atheism and the natural sciences, while religion is associated with irrationality. These articulations are by no means unique to the documentary, and it could be argued that the film does not contribute anything new to them, but the repetition of this trope, including its medium, form, and style, is important.

There are moments where the text on the screen flashes biblical passages when American Christians claim something else. This creates the impression that religious people are so irrational and ignorant that they do not even know what their holy book actually says in regard to things they justify by referring to the Bible. There is also information on the screen about the large percentage of scientists who are atheists, thus underlining the message that atheism and science go hand in hand.

While it is the case that scholars and top scientists are less religious than the general population, there are important nuances to be considered. At least in the United States, scholars working in the natural sciences are more religious than scholars in the social sciences and humanities. It is not that the practice of natural sciences or having a scientific view of the world is necessarily connected with atheism. It may well be that other disciplines and fields that see cultures and societies as human products are more eager to also see religions as human products (Bruce 2002, 106–117). The point here is that the relationship between religiosity and scientific education is complicated, but *Religious* presents it as straightforward, because it more generally suits the articulation that the film seeks to construct.

The documentary builds the articulation in many encounters between Maher and religious people that links science and atheism on the one hand and irrationality and religion on the other hand. Five successive encounters in the middle of the film exemplify this. First, Maher delivers a speech in Hyde Park, London, in disguise, preaching elements taken from Scientology. People laugh at him while taking other preachers seriously. This is quite a clever way to put Scientology on par with other religions, because so many people mock Scientology while being respectful of other religious views. Second, the crew travels to Salt Lake City to film on the premises of the Mormon Temple of The Church of Jesus Christ of Latter-day Saints. Mormons interrupt the production and threaten to call the cops. Maher's conclusion is that Mormon beliefs are "crazy even by the standards of big religions." Third, Jewish Rabbi Dovid Weiss is called an anti-Zionist, and there is a clip in which he seems to defend a famous Holocaust denier, Iran's then-president Mahmoud Ahmadinejad. Fourth, another Rabbi, Shmuel Strauss, introduces to Maher all the ways in which Jews try to find loopholes in God's orders in order to be able to do things they are not allowed to do during the Sabbath. Fifth, in Florida Maher meets Jose Luis de Jesus Miranda of the Growing in Grace Ministry, who claims to be the second coming of Christ and a direct genetic descendant of Jesus. The overall feeling that the audience is supposed to get is that religious people are crazy, incoherent, and irrational, and having a rational conversation with them is nearly impossible.

The articulation between religion and irrationality is further enhanced by various stylistic cinematographic techniques. The interviews are edited so that religious people are rarely able to finish their sentence. Sometimes the comic effect is constructed by the following images: Al Pacino's character Scarface is associated with Jose Luis de Miranda's talking style and Miranda's testimony of meeting two angels is followed by cuts to a parade where gay people are wearing angel wings. If the interviewee laughs, it is sometimes edited to continue in an excessive manner and merged with other laughing voices, thus questioning the sincerity, innocence, and sanity of interviewee. While these techniques add to the comical effect, they also give a reason to contest the term "documentary" in this context. However, they are integral to the persuasion techniques of *Religulous* and the construction of "we" as rational and "them" as irrational.

One of the approaches to how documentary films construct identities is through the question of expertise. This is exceptionally pertinent in cases where the aim is to construct an "us" of rational people who rely on science. Who gets to represent expert knowledge about religion? On the basis of atheistic documentaries in general, it appears that comedians and the natural scientists are the primary experts on religion. Comedians are not presented as scholarly experts as such, but they are the ones who seem to know what religion is really like. Furthermore, the natural scientists are presented as scholarly experts, no matter whether religion is their main research area or not.

In *Religulous*, the only expert that conducts any research on religion is the neuroscientist and neurotheologian Andrew Newberg, who has only a minor role in one scene. Mostly speaking here is Maher, who wishes to hear from Newberg that brain scans provide evidence that religious people are crazy. It is interesting that the chosen expert is representing neurotheology, rather than any established approach in the academic study of religion, because within the study of religion neurotheology has not received much positive appraisal (Day 2009; Geertz 2009).

If the construction of expertise in *Religulous* were an isolated case, it could perhaps be ignored as an exception, but it is not: in twenty-first-century atheist discourse, it is typical that people in the humanities and social sciences whose careers are based on studying religion are not considered relevant experts. This is true of atheistic best sellers and most of the atheistic documentaries. In some cases the indifference regarding expertise, or a very selective approach to expertise, leads to problematic claims about religion and its relation to different issues.

Constructing Religion: Harmful Beliefs about the World

Religulous suggests that religious people and religions as belief systems are harmful in different ways. Very few atheistic documentaries try to clarify which parts of religion are harmful and which may be beneficial. Rather, they tend to follow Christopher Hitchens's view that "religion poisons everything" (Hitchens 2007).

According to *Religulous*, religious people are dangerous. In the opening sequence in Megiddo, Israel, Maher states that religion is dangerous and detrimental to the progress of humanity, because religion values belief in something without evidence, as well as the certainty that comes with it. In the final sequence Maher is back in Megiddo, explaining that, according to many Christians, this is the place where the world is supposed to come to an end. He concludes that it may very well come to an end because of religion.

This articulation is repeated in the other encounters. Maher visits an almost empty Muslim gay bar in Amsterdam, an exceptional and exotic place, to convey the message that Islam is intolerant toward homosexuals and being Muslim and gay is a dangerous position. After that, Maher interviews Mohamed Junas Gaffar in Amsterdam's Taibah Mosque. After the interviewee claims that Islam is about peace, there follow clips about Islamic hate speech and suicide bombings in Jerusalem, indicating that Muslims are both dangerous and hypocritical. This is linked to the idea that religion is ancient or premodern and does not fit with the modern world: when Gaffar's mobile phone starts ringing—with Led Zeppelin's "Kashmir" as a ring tone—Maher comments: "Oh, that twenty-first century always busting in."

In the world of *Religulous*, there is nothing to learn from religious people and they do nothing to improve the conditions that atheists live in. In this regard, it differs from some popular voices, such as Alain de Botton (2012), a Swiss atheist, who wrote a book about what religious communities do well and what atheists might learn from them.

The importance of science for the construction of atheism has already been underlined, but it is mirrored in the construction of religion as a system of propositional beliefs about the world. While people do hold such beliefs about the nature of the world, framed in relation to what we call religions, it is another matter to assume as an uncontested fact that this is why certain lifestyles are appealing to some people or that such beliefs have a significant role in people's lives, as presented in these documentaries. It is not an easy task to give a plausible general account of how people approach their "religious" beliefs. The answer depends on the selected theoretical framework. For example, pragmatism suggests that people have practical reasons to commit themselves to certain beliefs and the life paths that the beliefs are attached to. The problem with contemporary documentaries critical of religion is that these options are not explored and they are silent on the fact that their framework is also contestable. Rather, the propositional nature of religious beliefs is highlighted with the presumption that they can never be defended. This is suitable, because then the propositional claims of the natural sciences can be juxtaposed with religious claims—and through this comparison it is obvious that religion cannot compete with science (Taira 2015, 120).

It Is All about the Choices

The people whom Maher meets in *Religulous* represent stereotypical adversaries of atheists: a creationist, a radical Muslim, and a religious scientist. According to the standard narratological view, the use of such stereotypical characters based on caricatures brings the viewer to the intended moral perspective, at least until the film comes to an end, because following and enjoying the film is partly based on accepting the implied reader's perspective. In the context of *Religulous*, we are drawn to be critics of religion when watching the film, unless we consciously and continuously resist such a position. *Religulous* is based on caricatures, and this is so evident that no one expects a balanced view.

The shooting locations are relevant, too, as they seek to reflect a sort of ethnographic approach to the topic. Most are in different parts of the United States, while some are in Europe or the Middle East. This can be seen as an attempt to provide rigor to the collection of evidence and the following position: as you can see, I have traveled to many places and religious people in all of them were nuts!

More interesting is to explore gender, race, and class. If *Religulous* is to be believed, both religion and its criticism are male-dominated enterprises. Throughout the whole documentary, Maher interviews only one woman—a tourist guide in a theme park. It may be easier to laugh at religious men, and it is definitely easier to make religion look dangerous if the interviewees are men. A further implication is that men are represented as leaders in religious communities and women as quiet or silenced followers. *Religulous*, and many other documentaries, are happy to present both religious authority and criticism of religion as a male affair.

The most vocal and celebrated critics of religion are typically white. They tend to see themselves as defenders of minorities. The situation is more complex, however. The contemporary debate between atheism and religion has been criticized for being about white Western men talking to each other (Beattie 2007), and especially in the context of Islam, women are seen as needing protection from white Western men. Tina Beattie (2007, 64) compares the contemporary atheist gaze directed toward veiled women to Saartjie Baartman, also known as the "Hottentot Venus," a South African orphan who was placed naked on display in England and France in the nineteenth century. In this sense, when white Western atheist men are trying to save dark-skinned (religious) women from their men, we are not far from what Gayatri Spivak (1999, 303) has called the cultural imperialist exploitation of feminism. The othering gaze embodied in the discourse of "the West and the Rest" (Hall 1992) has been shown to apply to the representations of religion in popular films where the main protagonist is considered a rational, white Western man who constructs the positionality of his own identity by distancing himself from the irrational and/or exotic religious other (Taira 2019).

The class aspect is never made explicit in *Religulous*, and it is rarely interesting for contemporary atheist critics of religion. It is as if the world would become perfect by erasing religion from it. John Gray's (2019, 20) comment on contemporary atheists as "unthinking liberals" points in a similar direction: as if without religion all people would think alike— like liberals. There are examples, however, in which religious leaders are represented as rich hypocrites who spend donations on expensive clothes. This could be understood as a potential reference to the class issue, but it is not made explicit. Social justice is not a theme that the film touches upon, possibly because it might force people to see division in the ranks of atheists, too.

In sum, *Religulous* does not counter, challenge, or deviate from typical contemporary representations of atheism or atheist imaginations of religion. It repeats, re-distributes, and strengthens the existing articulations of atheism and thus contributes to the maintenance of the currently dominant form of atheist identity.

The Continuing Impact of *Religulous*

Religulous was commercially successful, and its reception among film critics was moderately positive. A typical review gave three or three-and-a-half stars out of five. Most critics thought that the documentary was funny in spite of offering a one-dimensional representation of religion. The life of *Religulous* has continued in social media. The Facebook page of the film announced on October 4, 2013: "*Religulous* opened 5 yrs ago today;

still religious people in the world (damn!) but to thousands who told me they quit, congrats and Thank YOU!" The comments reveal some of the functions that the film has had. Some testify that the film changed their lives and some accuse it of intolerance. Yet, for others, the film worked as an entertaining extension of new atheism. This range of views is not surprising. Some found it helpful for their identity construction, some thought it was an attack against their identity, some shrugged their shoulders, and some have tried to make others watch it. What is relevant is that *Religulous* has been articulated in relation to the wider atheistic struggle against religion. It was associated with new atheism when it was released, spreading similar ideas through the unconventional genre of the "comic documentary," and its influence continues to the present day. There was no tenth-anniversary update, but the Facebook page is still active in 2020. Posts highlighting the irrationality, harmfulness, or silliness of religion are frequently made there.

Conclusion

This exploration has suggested that atheistic documentaries tend to represent religious ideas as irrational and harmful. This deceptively simple popular representation is related to an implicit assumption about atheism and atheists. Atheists are presented as rational people who base their views on scientific evidence and are morally superior. This dichotomy is needed for the construction and articulation of atheist identity in popular discourse, and it may also motivate people to act on behalf of atheism.

In analyzing *Religulous* in detail, the intention has not been to defend any religious position or judge criticism of religion. Such a popular documentary film can be regarded as data to be studied by scholars, in order to determine how the atheistic identity position is constructed through imagining its Other, "religion," how those representations are articulated in relation to each other to form a rather unified view about atheism and religion, and, further, how such views are articulated in terms of wider social processes to be part of atheistic identity politics. Such an approach is by no means limited to atheistic documentaries, because similar imaginings and representations are part of all sorts of cultural products, but it is necessary to pay close attention to the particularities of the medium without decontextualizing the product from the surrounding society.

CHAPTER 2

Capitalism, the Hero's Journey, and the Myth of Entrepreneurship in *The Secret of My Success* (1987) and *Joy* (2015)

James Dennis LoRusso

In the beginning was Film, and the Film was with Religion, and the Film was Religion. As Gary Laderman points out in his work, *Sacred Matters* (2009), the history of motion pictures starts as a religious history. He tells the story of a New Jersey clergyman by the name of Hannibal Goodwin who filed a patent in 1887 for "celluloid photographic roll film," the critical piece of technology that would make film possible. "Goodwin's primary motivation in this endeavor," Laderman writes, "was to create a medium that could make the Bible more accessible to children," and thus, the story of the most revolutionary medium since perhaps the invention of the printing press is steeped in religion (Laderman 2009, 1).

Indeed, religion quickly became a favorite subject matter of filmmakers for a Western and largely Christian public eager to witness their most cherished sacred stories come alive on the silver screen. More than two decades before Cecil B. DeMille would give audiences the groundbreaking religious epics of the silent era, *The Ten Commandments* (1923) and *King of Kings* (1927), the Salvation Army of Australia created a series of "illustrated lectures" in 1900 that told the stories of Christ and the early martyrs of Christianity ("Soldiers of the Cross"). Truly from the beginning, the film was with religion.

Yet, not only was film with religion, but film *was* religion. Laderman argues that cultural forms such as film serve as "anchors that ground ultimate concerns, establish moral communities, transform personal identities, and make lives meaningful" (xv). Films, whether religious or not, perform important cultural work and can be seen as contemporary expressions of myth. "Movie-making magic," Laderman writes, "will surely remain a dynamic, viable source for making sense of universal human experiences, like love and death, good and evil, individual and social transformation" (21). In this chapter, I would like to extend this argument by considering how films construct and reinforce mythologies about capitalism, particularly myths of entrepreneurship.

The identification of film *as* mythology is not a new concept for film studies, but the field tends to apply a narrow range of Jungian, psychologically informed approaches to myth that no longer hold much sway among scholars of religion. Moreover, scholars often apply myth in an uncritical manner, as if myth is a clearly defined type of story with distinct observable characteristics that distinguish it from other narratives such as fables, legends, or even history. Yet, scholars in the field of religious studies have long noted that myth, much like religion, is not a concept that can be pinned down easily. People use myth to refer to a range of sometimes contradictory ideas. On the one hand, a myth can be a story that a particular group holds as beyond reproach, as sacred. On the other hand, people may apply the label of myth to something they wish to expose as utterly deceptive and false (i.e., "that's just a myth"). Thus, the scholarly study of myth tends to avoid treating myth as an object of study, something "out there" to be understood, but rather as an analytical tool applied to the study of human society. Just as Jonathan Z. Smith declared of the category of religion, *myth* "is solely the creation of the scholar's study. It is created for the scholar's analytic purposes by his imaginative acts of comparison and generalization" (Smith 1988, xi)

In this chapter, I follow Smith's lead and employ "myth" as a tool for analyzing rather than for describing culture. To illustrate how religious studies can augment the conversation around myth in film studies, we will look closely at two films—*The Secret of My Success* (1987) and *Joy* (2015)—both of which feature main characters struggling to succeed in the unforgiving conditions of late-twentieth-century American capitalism. First, I critique the prevalence of psychological theories of myth that have come to dominate film analysis. In particular, I focus on the work of well-known mythologist Joseph Campbell, whose ideas have penetrated film schools, scholars of film, and popular culture more broadly. Campbell's theory of myth provides an illuminating reading of the entrepreneurial heroes in our two films. Yet, as I shall argue, his celebrity and lasting influence on the world of film continue to overshadow the elite, Orientalist elements of his work. In response to these criticisms, I suggest that film studies should move past its "love affair" with Campbell and the psychologists of myth and consider the fruitful work of more recent scholarship on myth. To illustrate this point, this chapter ultimately turns to the works of Bruce Lincoln and Wendy Doniger—two prominent scholars of religion and myth whose theories promise to advance the conversation around myth and film. As we explore our two films—*The Secret of My Success* and *Joy*—through the lens of their theories, we gain powerful new insights about myths of entrepreneurship. These films are more than tales of modern-day heroes of the marketplace; they perform important cultural and ideological work, helping to sustain the capitalist social order itself. Yet, these films also give voice to the profound anxieties and real suffering that accompany life under the often-unforgiving realities of free enterprise, while holding out hope that these challenges may be conquered.

Case Study: Capitalism in Late-Twentieth-Century American Film

Hollywood has long made capitalism the subject of both ire and celebration. Consider, for instance, the postwar holiday classic *It's a Wonderful Life* (1946), in which director Frank Capra offers an ambivalent assessment of life in the industrial world. On the one hand, the film offers a scathing indictment of the unrestrained greed of banks and the perpetual state of bare subsistence it envisions for the working class. Yet, on the other hand, Capra valorizes the productive might of American industry and, simultaneously, the virtue of small business. In the end, the film celebrates the resilience of the little guy, embodied in the film's protagonist George Bailey (James Stewart), whose wealth lies not in the transactional relations of the market but in the alternative economy of trust in one's friends.

A year after the release of *It's a Wonderful Life*, another "Christmas" flick, *Miracle on 34th St* (1947), similarly profiled the inconsistencies of the marketplace. The film takes place against the backdrop of R.H. Macy and Co. (aka Macy's department store in New York) at the height of the annual retail season between the Thanksgiving holiday and Christmas Day. Kris Kringle (Edmund Gwenn), the *real* Santa Claus, expresses misgivings about the exploitation of the "Christmas spirit" for profit even as he promotes mass consumption as an employee of the iconic retailer as their *faux* Santa. Like *It's a Wonderful Life*, *Miracle* acknowledges the excesses of "greed for greed's sake" but leaves the audience with a promise of a marketplace in which fair and honest competition serves the authentic needs and desires of working consumers. Both films promote an idealized capitalism, tamed by the power of down-home, democratic virtue.

These classic films exemplify the hopes and anxieties of a white American middle class at mid-century, emerging from the dual crises of depression and world war and seeking meaning amid an increasingly powerful corporate social order. By the waning decades of the twentieth century, the corporate order was fully entrenched, but anxieties remained. The two films in our case study for this chapter each imagine the dynamics of this tension between big business and the individual during the late 1980s. *The Secret of My Success* (1987) tells the story of a young Kansas native, Brantley Foster (Michael J. Fox), as he pursues his dream to succeed among the New York business elite. Faced with setbacks and finding himself as a mailroom employee at his sinister uncle's company, Pemrose Corporation, Foster resorts to trickery, pretending to be a newly hired executive by the name of Carlton Whitfield, all the while attempting to maintain his actual position as a mail sorter. Through a combination of farce and slapstick, Foster's absurd ruse is eventually unmasked, of course, but in the process, he ultimately wins the day, assuming control of Pemrose and winning the affections of a beautiful blonde executive, Christy Wills (Helen Slater). It would be no exaggeration to characterize the film as rife with cliches, and indeed it was panned in the press. Dave Kehr, writing the *Chicago Tribune*, characterized the movie as a cheap teenage "Oedipal fantasy . . . looking for a way to make a buck from the psychological weaknesses of others" (Kehr April 10, 1987). Roger Ebert was equally unimpressed, concluding that "everyone in the movie is an idiot or the mystery would be solved in five minutes. Does the movie really believe anyone is as stupid as these characters? Does it care?" (Ebert April 10, 1987).

Joy (2015), our second film, differs markedly from *The Secret of My Success* in a number of ways. The film is not a comedy but a surrealist, quasi-biographical account of American entrepreneur and inventor Joy Mangano, who rose to prominence as an iconic television personality on QVC and later the *Home Shopping Network* for pitching her invention, the "Miracle Mop" (Berman, 2015). Directed by David O. Russell and starring Jennifer Lawrence as the eponymous "Joy" (her surname is never mentioned), the film takes place in the 1980s and early 1990s and traces her struggle as a divorced mother to escape the oppressive circumstances that have ground down her life into one of mediocrity. As a child, Joy was a creator, a freethinker, and full of promise but has fallen into a cycle of subsistence as she tries to hold her dysfunctional family together. Her mother (Virginia Madsen) is a recluse, living out her existence on a sofa bed in Joy's den who lives vicariously through the soap operas she religiously watches on her television. At the same time, her ex-husband, Tony (Edgar Ramirez), who has shirked his duties as a father and husband in pursuit of a futile dream to succeed as a musician, and her father Rudy (Robert De Niro), whom his newest wife has recently kicked out, have both moved into Joy's basement. The narrative follows as she hits rock bottom and, against insurmountable odds, forges ahead to change her life. Tapping into her dormant creative potential, she pitches the Miracle Mop to home shopping guru Neil Walker (Bradley Cooper), overcomes numerous challenges, and eventually realizes freedom as a successful entrepreneur and inventor.

While these two films are distinct, both feature stories about individual ingenuity, cunning, and striving for success in the American marketplace. If myths are stories that convey important cultural values and expectations to audiences, and if these films about entrepreneurs depict a certain idealized vision of entrepreneurship, then it is possible to consider these films as capitalist myths of entrepreneurship. They accomplish more than pure entertainment; they instruct viewers about their own lives through themes outlined in the narratives to understand success and even salvation as entrepreneurial acts. To engage with these films is to engage with virtues fundamental to a functioning market society, and therefore it makes sense to theorize these films as myths.

The Hero Triumphant: Hollywood's Love Affair with the Psychology of Myth

When I teach *Introduction to World Religions*, I devote a portion of the class to "Origin Stories and Myth." Typically, most of my students have very little exposure to myth, other than some elementary readings of Greek and Roman mythology in a high school English class. Every once in a while, however, a student *will* know something, and almost invariably, it is the work of Joseph Campbell (1904–87) with which they are familiar. On the one hand, this is not surprising since Campbell is arguably the most well-known American scholar of myth in the twentieth century outside academia. On the other hand, what is interesting is that some students tell me that they first learned about his work in a film studies course. This invites us to ask: why would a class on film theory include a mythologist in its curriculum in the first place?

To answer this question, we need to consider the singular impact of Campbell's work on popular culture generally and, more specifically, on film and film studies. In many ways, Campbell's reputation is inextricable from the world of film. Spending most of his career in relative obscurity at Sarah Lawrence College, he achieved notoriety shortly after his passing in 1987 as a result of a Bill Moyers' PBS docuseries titled *The Power of Myth*, which introduced his work to American audiences. Over the course of six one-hour episodes, the public was introduced to Campbell's belief that myth is centrally important for individual psychological and spiritual well-being. Yet, it was not the merits of his ideas alone that would turn Campbell into a household name, but rather because the documentary linked these ideas directly to the most successful film franchise at that time, *Star Wars*. George Lucas, its creator, openly proclaimed himself a disciple and credited Campbell's Jungian interpretation of myth as the narrative model for the first film (1977).

The story of Lucas' adoption of Campbell's theories has passed into the "mythology" of Hollywood itself, but it also bears witness to the attraction that psychological approaches to myth held for filmmakers and film studies. Lucas first came across Campbell's most recognized work, *The Hero with a Thousand Faces* (1949), as a student in film school at the University of Southern California precisely because the book was already becoming an appealing resource for interpreting and crafting film narratives. Another USC film student at the time, screenwriter and author Christopher Vogler credits Campbell's work as life-changing. A professor had directed him to the book, and in it, he found "the secret key I was looking for" (Vogler 2017, 10), unlocking a Pandora's box that would ignite the creative power of filmmakers for decades to come. According to Vogler, Campbell's work on myth has directly touched such notable productions as *Star Trek, Game of Thrones, The Lion King,* and countless others (Vogler 15-17). The heart of the modern Hollywood blockbuster beats to a rhythm first laid down by Campbell.

Psychological approaches, such as Campbell's, characterize myth as an expression of deep-seated structures of the human mind, elements of what Carl Jung names the *collective unconscious.* These structures manifest as *archetypes*, universally shared symbols ("Mother," "Father," "Child," etc.) that constitute the "hardware" of the mind. Archetypes, therefore, transcend culture and history; they are biological, and the power of the mythic narrative lies in its ability to give voice to these fundamental building blocks of human experience. In other words, human beings derive meaning and purpose from the encounter with and the expression of myth.

In film studies, the application of myth has largely been an exercise in uncovering and interpreting the presence of archetypes in narrative. For instance, Chang et al. (2013) describe cinema as a therapeutic form of projection in which viewers "engage their unconscious in a manner similar to hypnosis and dreaming" (103). Eight fundamental archetypes, they claim, operate in contemporary Western films such as *American Beauty, Braveheart,* and *Fight Club,* among others. Similarly, Martin and Oswalt's volume, *Screening the Sacred: Religion, Myth, and Ideology in Popular Film* (1995), features essays almost exclusively devoted to revealing these underlying Jungian archetypes, and specifically through the lens of Joseph Campbell's work (Ellis 1905; Gordon 1995; Rushing 1995).

Interpretative studies that explore capitalism in film likewise follow this pattern of analysis. Stratton (2016) dissects the Emmy Award–winning sitcom *The Big Bang Theory* in order to demonstrate how its star character, Sheldon Cooper (Jim Parsons), embodies "the literary trope of the fool" who inadvertently exemplifies the virtues of neoliberal capitalism (171). Wagner (2019) refers to three films—*Wall Street* (1987), *Boiler Room* (2000), and *Margin Call* (2011)—as "parables about economic fantasy," in which he recognizes three distinct neoliberal character-types—the acolyte, the roughneck, and the stochastic—that sustain "Hollywood's complicity with banking culture" (59). In each of these cases, scholars rely overtly or covertly on the elements of Jungian psychology to make sense of religion, myth, and capitalism in film respectively.

Much of Campbell's appeal to scholars of myth in film may result from the clear and totalizing roadmap that his theory provides. According to Campbell, mythic narratives utilize archetypes in predictable, patterned ways, but he remains especially focused on one archetype in particular—*the hero*—as the catalyst for individual human flourishing. Across all cultures, hero myths conform to a uniform structure, which Campbell dubs the *monomyth* or *Hero's Journey*. The pattern, for Campbell, can be found in any context at any time, in the ancient Sumerian *Epic of Gilgamesh* or in Tolkien's *Lord of the Rings* trilogy alike. Each version recounts the hero who departs the everyday world for adventure, faces trials that must be overcome, and ultimately returns home utterly transformed into something beyond ordinary human. This formulaic narrative cycle—the hero's journey—imbues stories, including films, with the potential to transform audiences.

Let us now turn to the two films in our case study and ask two interrelated questions. First, can we see the "hero's journey" in these films? And second, what, if anything, do we gain from this exercise? I contend that we can "uncover" Campbell's monomyth in both films if we look for it, but in the process, we learn less about the films themselves or the nature of myth and more about the limits of these psychological approaches so common in the study of film.

In *The Secret of My Success* (*SOMS*), Brantley Foster remarks, "well Toto, I guess we're not in Kansas anymore" upon arriving in New York City, thereby signaling his *departure* and *call to adventure* from ordinary life into the unknown. In pursuing "success," he faces a series of setbacks. Without his promised job, he is forced to take work in the mailroom of his uncle's company. Along the way, helpers (*Supernatural* Aid), such as his uncle's wife, Aunt Vera (Margaret Whitton), protect him and compel him toward his destiny. Although he pretends to be the sharp up-and-coming executive, Carlton Whitfield, to some, Aunt Vera alone sees him for *who he really is*: an ambitious and compassionate young man of great potential who just needs a "leg up." Although he initially rejects her assistance, Foster eventually accepts that he needs her connections and capital when, in the penultimate scene of the film when he interrupts a hostile takeover of Pemrose Corporation and effectively wrestles control of the firm from his self-interested uncle, assuming his rightful place as CEO. The hero triumphs.

Curiously, the film leaves "hero's journey" incomplete; he does not *return home* but instead stands atop the steps of Lincoln Center, embracing his love interest, Christy. Yet, this departure from the strict formula demonstrates the eloquence of Campbell's monomyth. "The hero's journey is not a rigid checklist whose every element must be present in a story before it can be classified as an official hero's journey, but rather an extremely flexible set of building blocks . . . that can be arranged in almost infinite combinations to produce many different effects" (Vogler, 17). The film invites audiences to complete the journey. Perhaps we imagine Foster fulfilling the promise to his parents in the film's opening scene, to only return home in a chartered corporate jet. Alternatively, maybe the once unreachable and extraordinary C-Suite life is a "return home" of sorts, since it is the world to which he truly belongs. For Campbell, the purpose of myth is transformative, both psychologically and spiritually, providing the script for a journey of self-discovery to which we are each called. Myths are instruction manuals to liberate us from the social "systems" in which our souls are imprisoned.

Joy presents another iteration of the hero, or, in this case, the heroine. Campbell privileges male heroes, but a (perhaps too) generous reading of his theory could readily apply to other genders. In fact, *Joy* arguably fulfills the monomyth as neatly as *The Secret of my Success*. Joy's grandmother, Mimi (Diane Ladd), whose character dies midway through the film, narrates the film, offering a kind of "God's eye view" of events. Like Aunt Vera in *SOMS*, Mimi steadfastly believes in the exceptional potential of her granddaughter, despite the insurmountable obstacles standing in the way of her success. Joy receives her *call to adventure* in a moment of inspiration when she cuts herself on broken glass while hand-wringing a mop. In the next scene, we see her family circled around, bandaging her bleeding hands when Joy suddenly stands up and begins babbling aloud incoherently, deeply focused as if entranced. The grandmother seems to be the only one who understands that Joy is "working something out." As Campbell declares, the "call signifies that destiny has summoned the hero and transferred his spiritual center of gravity from within the pale of his society to a zone unknown"(58), and clearly in this scene something in Joy's awareness has shifted inward toward a long-slumbering magma chamber of creativity. In fact, this event represents the first rumblings of the dormant heroine within; it signifies the moment of the quintessential heroic act for all entrepreneurs—the genesis of an *idea*. Over the course of the film, Joy repeats this process at pivotal moments, separating herself from the world and harnessing a kind of inner muse to overcome challenges. She will endure Campbell's *Road of Trials* in the form of a number of setbacks, challenges from trusted family members, and attempts to steal her product, "the Miracle Mop." Eventually, faced with losing everything when a rival attempts to patent the invention behind her back, Joy undergoes what Campbell labels the *Apotheosis*, a moment of transformation, the "aha" moment when she is ready to do what is necessary (Campbell 155-171). She signals this transition by cutting off her long, blonde hair before confronting her adversary, reminiscent of the biblical Samson, and emerges victorious. In the film's concluding scene, Joy has *crossed the return threshold* (217) and has taken on the mantle of *helper* herself, offering other gifted female inventors the same opportunity she was given. Having been through the ordeal, Joy becomes the *Master of Two Worlds*, possessing the "freedom to pass back and forth across the world division" (229) and to share her wisdom with other seekers.

Both of these films illustrate the interpretive capacity of Campbell's *monomyth*, but they also expose the dangers of seeking a universal model for all myth, namely, the tendency to oversimplify and misrepresent. Campbell characterizes myths as fundamentally psychological, as expressions of our (collective) unconscious. If we take Campbell seriously, then we have seen the differences between stories as merely superficial. In other words, hero myths differ only because they have been filtered through a particular cultural context, but their meaning remains timeless and constant. From this vantage point, therefore, *Joy* and *The Secret of my Success* are not actually myths of entrepreneurship at all but rather different versions of the "hero's journey," adapted to the setting of contemporary American market society. According to Campbell, the *real* power of these films derives from their ability to transcend history, politics, and culture altogether, and to facilitate individual psychological and spiritual transformation. Yet, such a view is itself reflective of Campbell's own location as a white, educated, male in twentieth-century North America. By reducing the stories of widely diverse peoples to a single universal explanation, Campbell overlooks important histories and meanings that these stories may have in localized settings. He privileges similarity at the expense of difference and therefore presents a greatly diminished picture of myth. This constitutes a potentially egregious act of misrepresentation and for vulnerable peoples can risk further marginalization.

Filmmakers who uncritically accept and apply Campbell's monomyth as a formula for storytelling may reap financial rewards, but they also perpetuate its more troubling aspects. Thus, the question remains, if Campbell and, indeed, other universalizing theories of myth remain tainted by the erasure of culture, *where do we go from here?* Can the study of myth adequately account for these limitations and still provide insights for the film studies? In the next, section, we will briefly survey two scholarly theories of myth from religious studies that attempt to accomplish this goal, and we will consider how each might shed light on the two films.

Myth as Ideology and the Politics of Storytelling in Film

Despite their prevalence in the study of film, psychological approaches are not the only ways we can theorize myth. Other religion scholars have striven to address the hazards of universalist models. In this section, we consider how the work of two scholars, Bruce Lincoln and Wendy Doniger, address some of the hazards of universalism and, then consider how each approach provides important insights into the films in our case study.

If Joseph Campbell traces myth to the deep structures of our unconscious, Bruce Lincoln portrays myth itself as a product of culture. To understand myths, he contends that we must attend primarily to the social setting in which it is performed. Myths are not fundamentally psychological but utterly political and ideological. In fact, Bruce Lincoln defines myth as "ideology in narrative form" (Lincoln 1999, 147). Myths therefore are stories that convey a view of the world from a particular vantage point and set of interests, and the mythologist's primary task is to expose the performed politics within these stories. Unlike Campbell, who argues that all myths are ultimately iterations of the same monomyth, Lincoln argues that each performance of a myth is a discrete act of mythmaking, stating that "we would do better to classify narratives not by their content but by the claims that are made by their narrators and the way in which those claims are received by their audiences" (Lincoln 1989, 24). In order to discern the ideological work of myth, therefore, we must consider the coordination of three elements: narrator, audience, and the social context. For Lincoln, the stakes of mythmaking could not be higher, because the performances of myth "evoke sentiments out of which society is actively constructed" (Lincoln 1989, 25). A myth presents a template not for psychological growth and healing but of the social order itself and one's place in it.

When examined in light of Lincoln's theory, *The Secret of My Success* and *Joy* are not simply two versions of the "hero's journey" refracted through the grammar of the American marketplace, they instead become myths explicitly about entrepreneurship that serve, intentionally or otherwise, to justify the American system of free enterprise. Both films portray a social landscape marked by the rugged indifference of the free market. In *SOMS*, Brantley's dreams suffer a serious setback when his prospective employer becomes the victim of a hostile takeover at the beginning of the film. He shakes off this twist of fate, stating, "okay New York, this is the way you want it? Okay!" Yet, merit and wits prove insufficient, and he must rely on nepotism to pull off his scheme. In the end, it's not *what* you know, but *who* you know, that counts in the ruff-and-tumble world of 1980s Corporate America.

Joy paints a similarly gloomy picture of the marketplace. The film begins with a flashback of Joy's early life, the idyllic portrait of the white middle-class nuclear family. The grandmother/narrator states of Joy,

> Everybody starts out with some kind of dream of what life will be . . . She made many beautiful things in her room, magic, some people love to make things, they have the patience and the focus to figure it out with their hands. Joy was one of those people who rejoiced in making things.

Jumping forward twenty years, the audience next sees Joy in the present, caught in an endless cycle of exploitation. Working as an airline gate agent, she is subjected to the ire of entitled customers in order to support a family who simply takes advantage of her ability to provide. The portrait is one of an individual imbued with exceptional talents and qualities trapped between the vice grips of low-wage labor and ungrateful dependents. Circumstances have turned her drive and ingenuity against her; they have become the very means sustaining her imprisonment. Whereas *SOMS* presents the impersonal market as sovereign to which Foster must adapt, *Joy* expresses the dystopian image in which the entrepreneur has been bludgeoned into the service of the lazy and unmotivated of society (i.e., her family). Neither film, however, challenges the integrity or justice of these conditions; instead, they present these conditions as inevitable realities of a capitalist social order, of a world populated with those who only value you according to the worth the market dictates or to what you can offer another's self-interest.

Lincoln's notion of myth as a narrated ideology suggests that these films serve as morality tales for how to survive and thrive in market society. Like Brantley Foster, one must be willing to bend or break the rules, even pretending to be someone else if necessary. Likewise, Joy learns to trust no one but herself, turning the tables on her exploiters. She uses her father's wealthy love interest (Isabella Rossellini) to bankroll the production of the Miracle Mop and ultimately outmaneuvers her opponent who attempts to defraud her, winning total control over her venture. These films offer audiences believable narratives about how ordinary people, lacking any unearned advantages and possessing only their innate potential, can, through hard work, perseverance, and most of all their own charisma, flourish under capitalism. They remind viewers that failure is the purely the result of giving up, and success may be waiting just around the corner if you know where to look for it. In this way, these films provide an explanation for our suffering even as they impart hope for better times to come.

Yet, both films also advance a more sobering elitism at the heart of American capitalism. Only a select few possess, indeed are *born* with, the talent to truly succeed. The *SOMS* portrays a corporate world comprising one or two deceptive and opportunistic executives and the armies of sycophants along for the ride. *Joy* divides the world into risk-takers and the risk-averse, makers and takers. Foster and Joy shatter these molds because they radiate that most elusive, yet most human virtue: creativity. The entrepreneur is a rare beast because most of us simply don't "have it," and these films offer audiences a chance to look in the mirror and see themselves as the entrepreneur. After all, who would identify with the sheepish middle manager in *The Secret of My Success* or with Joy's mother, whose sole solace is in the consumption of midday televised melodrama? Even though most of us may live a life of mediocrity in practice, these films justify capitalism's inequalities by convincing each of us, individually, that we are not part of the common herd, that we are one of the exceptional ones who, with enough will, can rise above the fray.

While both stories may accomplish similar ideological work, Lincoln remains adamant that no two myths, or even two tellings of a myth, are the same. He altogether circumvents the hazards of Campbell's universalism by treating myth as a purely cultural. Every time a story is told, it is told by a specific narrator to a specific audience in a specific context. Just like every time you screen a film, your reception of that film differs subtly. Thus, while myths may be comparable, they are only comparable insofar as they are distinct from one another, because different myths really are different myths, and any apparent similarities between them are only superficial, particularly if they have emerged independently from different cultures.

While Lincoln's theory of myth avoids the problems of universalism, it risks reducing everything to culture and excludes the possibility of shared human experience. The value of cultural studies lies in its ability to contextualize human life, but we can easily lose sight of both individuals and of the species. After all, where does one cultural context end and another begin? Are there no elements of life shared across all human beings? And at the same time, isn't every individual's experience somewhat unique? This perspective risks fetishizing culture itself, of replacing Campbell's psychological reductionism with cultural essentialism. Wendy Doniger articulates a way of comparing myths that recognizes the impact of culture without ignoring either individual human experience or the possibility of a shared "humanity" across cultures. For Doniger, myth plays a central role in expressing both of these "human" dimensions, beneath and beyond cultural differences.

To be clear, Doniger is not interested in explaining what myth *really is*, but what myth *does*. She asserts that "the cross-cultural comparison of myths is pragmatically possible, intellectually plausible, and politically productive" (Doniger 1998, 5). Thus, Doniger is quite willing to take a position, to inject her politics into the fray of scholarship because she recognizes the impossibility of ever being truly apolitical or disinterested.

Doniger defines myth as "a story that is sacred to and shared by a group of people who find their most important meanings in it" (Doniger 2), but she suggests that if we look at myths in their cultural context alone, we miss a great deal of their inherent narrative power. What makes myth "a very special sort of narrative method" (8) is its ability to mediate, indeed "vibrate," between the personal *and* the universal. Myths resonate with our individual experience, but they simultaneously force us to see ourselves through the grandest of perspectives. Conversely, they personalize an impersonal cosmos, collapsing the chasm between ourselves, our culture, and others. The medium of film, she states, accomplishes this "bridge between the terrifying cosmological ignorance and our comfortable familiarity with our recurrent, human problems" (22) quite well.

The Secret of My Success holds these two perspectives—the individual and the universal—in active tension. Foster's individual experience becomes meaningful only because it resonates with something to which we can all relate—the human struggle to survive in the face of an indifferent world of mergers, downsizing, and layoffs. On the other hand, Foster's story brings puts a human face on American capitalism by bringing it out of the abstract and showing us how one individual suffers under its weight. In *Joy*, viewers encounter the personal story of a woman, but this story taps into the wider human experiences of oppression, specifically of gender and class inequality, as well as the creative-destructive power of capitalism. The main characters in both films, Doniger's theory suggests, enter the realm of myth only because their stories resonate on a basic human level with unifying themes of love, greed, and exploitation that transcend their specific cultural contexts.

Despite her interest in universal themes, she abandons any notion that two or more stories that *seem* alike are, in fact, simply variations of a singular, original myth. Instead, Doniger redefines comparison as a practical, imaginative act. First, she asks us to *imagine* how these stories are similar and to map these underlying similarities into what she calls the *micromyth:* a bare-bones "neutral" narrative shorn, ideally, of its most visible ideological and biased elements.

The micromyth is merely an interpretive device that reveals obvious parallels between the stories or, in our case, the two films (Doniger 80). To illustrate my point, we could state that both films tell different versions of the same following story: *a person overcomes adversity through cunning and hard work to achieve success in business and happiness in their personal life.* Once this micromyth is established, we are ready for the next step in the interpretive exercise, to consider the *macromyth* "a composite of the details of the . . . variants" and look for "possible systematic relationships" (93). In other words, we can begin to ask why each film inflects certain elements of the underlying narrative (i.e., the micromyth) differently. In turn, this leads to novel insights about the work these films accomplish at all levels: the individual, the cultural, and the human.

One obvious difference between these two films lies in the gender of the protagonists, and gender plays an outsized role in the shape of each story. As a man, Brantley Foster leaves his family behind in Nebraska. While his parents are reluctant to let go, they ultimately acquiesce because leaving home is, after all, what a "real man" does. He cuts ties and strikes out on his own, to build a life of his own, over which *he* assumes responsibility. In contrast to Foster's heroic break, we find in *Joy* a woman exhibiting profound gender ambiguity. On one hand, she is the de facto matriarch, and her problem isn't that she is tied down to home but rather than she has had to assume the (male) role of breadwinner. Ideally, her "lane" would be managing the affairs of domestic life. Yet, at the same time, she is drawn to the male-dominated world of the marketplace even as she is trapped in the role of maternal caretaker. Different genders communicate competing motivations and goals, and thus Joy suffers from a misalignment of her sense of self and assigned gender roles. Each film casts the entrepreneur differently; each uses their cunning to achieve success in response to the gender norms assigned to each protagonist.

Doniger's method accentuates the significance of gender in these films, which draws our attention to the subtle hierarchies that persist in American society. Yet, if we return yet again to the level of the micromyth, we can now see another shared element of both films. The films explore characters who negotiate and ultimately reconcile disparate parts of themselves. On one hand, Joy is initially the tireless homemaker who has suppressed her creative gifts. Her creative side hatches from dormancy in the form of a commodity—the Miracle Mop. The mop is a totem, a physical representation of the whole self as both homemaker (woman) and innovator (entrepreneur). In *SOMS*, on the other hand, Foster himself *is the commodity*; he is selling himself in the form of his invented persona, Carlton Whitfield, but ultimately he can only triumph through the reconciliation of these split personalities. The films echo the Protestant ethic of work as a "calling" that demands one's whole person and only those who fully engage in their endeavor receive the grace of the market.

Of course, Doniger does not wish for us to ignore historical context, and Joy and Foster are heroes for the America of their particular times. *The Secret of My Success* alleviates the anxieties of Americans amid the late-twentieth-century transition from an industrial to an information economy. Specifically, the film affirms perceptions of moral decline that drove the "Reagan revolution" and the backlash against civil rights by showing white working people that a nostalgic return to solid American values—self-reliance, integrity, honesty, trust, and family—remains possible. On the other hand, even though *Joy* is set during the late 1980s, it addresses an angst more characteristic of white America of 2015 when the film was completed. It is far from a critique of big business. If anything, corporate capitalism reigns unchallenged, with big business as the unchallenged backdrop against which individual competition takes place. In *Joy,* the problem is neither capital nor poverty, but rather identity, the battleground for our twenty-first-century culture wars. The story holds out the promise of a capitalism in which disparities based on gender, race, sexuality have been vanquished. It is a neoliberal vision of a multicultural society led by a diverse coalition of entrepreneurial elites, but one where class hierarchies remain largely intact.

Ultimately, Doniger's interpretive method differs substantially from either Lincoln or Campbell. She seeks neither to *describe* myth as human nature (ala Campbell) nor to *redescribe* it as cultural production (ala Lincoln) but rather to *politically mobilize* through her mythical method. Myth viewed *as* a political lens yields the photographic negative of Lincoln's ideological critique. Lincoln's method helped to see how the films anesthetized audiences to the structural oppression of capitalism by convincing them to identify with these entrepreneurial heroes. Doniger suggests that myth awakens them by illuminating the way structural forces impose their will on the most personal aspects of our lives, and, moreover, how we ourselves are small, but significant, agents of potential change within these structures. The mythic "double vision" of both of these films shows us the absurdity of our acquiescence. Of the two films, *The Secret of My Success* is by far the more ideologically flat, a shallow portrait of rags-to-riches, but alas it is a comedy, a narrative that accentuates its utter implausibility. We leave the film with knowledge that there are no Brantley Fosters out there, but at least we can laugh at the fantasy of seeing justice dispensed on the exploiters. In *Joy*'s final scene, audiences witness her sitting behind a desk listening to a young woman nervously pitch an idea, as she had once done years earlier. Now, however, Joy has become the embodiment of capital's power and aesthetically, the film affords her a kind of numinous shimmer and piercing hard stare to which the young lady reacts with a mixture of awe and terror. Doniger would have us fixate on this concluding portrait of capitalism's face. We are all inspired and horrified at once.

Conclusion

This chapter highlights the fact that the relationship between myth and film is a complicated one. Ultimately, the scholar's job is to explain the inexplicable, to render the unfamiliar less mysterious. Scholars of myth in film, however, continue to privilege psychological explanations of myth that accomplish the opposite; they mystify more than they clarify by assuming some elusive psychic structure out of which our lives derive meaning. Furthermore, by suggesting that these ineffable expressions of our unconscious somehow manifest in films and therefore account for their timeless appeal, these scholars become the mythmakers. They hide the most obvious attribute of any film; it is not merely a work of art but a commercial product. The appeal of movies, particularly the so-called blockbusters, stems from sophisticated *marketing* techniques imposed on all aspects of its production, distribution, and promotion. The material beneficiary is not the viewer who gleans existential insight or temporary bliss from an overpowering display of cinematic craft but rather the outsized and monopolistic Disneys, Sonys, and NBC Universals whose enormous gravitational field determines the contours of "entertainment." Campbell's monomyth turns our gaze away from these realities and back on ourselves, but Lincoln and Doniger show us that this inward focus merely reproduces the material goals of the film industry. Studios profit through entertainment, and if they can convince us that there is, after all, something magical and sacred about motion pictures, and if they can develop narratives that keep us desiring more, if they can keep us asking, "when is the next Marvel installment coming out?" then it is they who have discovered the *secret to success*: to bring us carefully crafted consumer *joy*.

CHAPTER 3

Oprah, Mindy, and Reese:

"The Gaze" and the Holy Trinity of Disney's *A Wrinkle in Time* (2018)

Leslie Dorrough Smith

As a bookwormish girl coming of age in the 1980s, I was a part of the generation forever changed by the writing of Madeleine L'Engle and the universe she created in one of her best-known books, *A Wrinkle in Time*, first published in 1962. The book, featuring a teenage lead character named Meg Murry, combines a sci-fi view of astrophysics with a compelling plotline that requires Meg to plumb the depths of her own insecurities and the universe (literally) to find her lost father, who is trapped by an evil force on another planet. To situate the impact of Meg at a time when female teen protagonists were hard to come by, writer Eliza Berman places Meg Murry in a hall of contemporary female "greats"; she is "the spiritual antecedent to Katniss Everdeen, Buffy the Vampire Slayer and Hermione Granger" (Berman 2018).

The book has experienced staggering popularity and easily retains its status as one of America's young adult classics. In 1963, it won the prestigious Newbury Award, and, as of its fiftieth anniversary in 2012, had sold over ten million copies, never once going out of print (Berman 2018). This degree of success, however, may belie the considerable controversy generated by its publication. *Wrinkle* was banned so widely that the American Library Association placed it on its top 100 list of banned books for two decades straight (Kinos-Goodin 2018). The offense? The most common concerns were that *Wrinkle*'s mingling of science fiction themes with Christianity would lead its young readers theologically astray. Although L'Engle's own Christianity is clear in the text, religious conservatives offended by the book were concerned by its ecumenical tone, pointing to a particular line where a character mentions Jesus as one among several great thinkers but fails to say he is their superior.

So it may seem a tremendous irony that, in the newest movie adaptation of the book (2018, dir. Ava DuVernay), many of the same types of critics who questioned L'Engle's use of religious language were among those who objected to the removal of those previously "problematic" references in DuVernay's version.[1] In DuVernay's world, there is no mention of Jesus at all, and no quoting of Christian scripture (something L'Engle embraced). But what sets DuVernay's vision substantially apart is that it features actors who are women of color. That fact alone may have sparked the ire of many of DuVernay's more conservative critics, some of whom have insisted that because L'Engle was white and Meg's race is never mentioned, then it goes without saying that the characters should be white, as well.[2] Indeed, complaints about DuVernay's lack of fidelity to L'Engle's text have generally regarded the cast's racial diversity and the screenplay's elimination of overt Christian references as two sides of the same problematic coin.

My argument here is that DuVernay's *A Wrinkle in Time* still appeals to very traditional religious images to manufacture its on-screen appeal, despite what more conservative cultural critics may argue. More specifically, this chapter will show how the team of Oprah Winfrey, Mindy Kaling, and Reese Witherspoon (three of the film's stars) create an unlikely trinity whose racialized gender symbolism and pop culture resonance work together to feature an old, familiar stereotype of brown female religiosity in twenty-first-century garb. To accomplish this, I want, first, to offer some foundational thoughts on how media theorists and other culture critics have addressed the concept of "the gaze" as it pertains to race, gender, and religion. Next, after considering the plot of the film, I will discuss the cultural significance of DuVernay's decision to cast Winfrey, Witherspoon, and Kaling together, and what their pop culture personas bring to the storyline. Finally, I want to briefly grapple with how the case of *Wrinkle* might further enhance how we study religion in certain forms of media.

Everything Old Is New Again

Hollywood's race and gender problem is a well-documented phenomenon. In her 2016 volume on Hollywood racism, scholar Nancy Wang Yuen notes that across what was then the Oscar awards' eighty-eight years of existence, actors of color had received only 6.8% of acting nominations and won only 7.8% of acting awards (Yuen 2016, 2-4). That same year was also an important public tipping point in terms of racial exclusion. Actor Jada

Pinkett Smith and filmmaker Spike Lee boycotted the 2016 Oscars when, for two straight years, acting nominations included no people of color. And the 2020 Oscar awards were punctuated by the wardrobe of actor Natalie Portman, who wore a cape to the red carpet embroidered with the names of female directors snubbed in that year's nominations. In the history of the awards, only one woman has ever won best director (this was Kathryn Bigelow in 2010, for *The Hurt Locker*) (Gonzalez 2020).

Despite the popular claim that Hollywood is "liberal," it is important to remember that is an institution that makes money only to the degree that average viewers like and can relate to the images that it produces. In this sense, one major sign of Hollywood success is the ability to mirror the larger (often more conservative) dynamics, assumptions, and stereotypes that characterize American culture. This happens primarily through a dynamic that scholars call "the gaze," or the idea that watchers (i.e., the audience) want to see a particular type of person, scene, or social norm on-screen. It is a long-recognized fact that the desires of the stereotypical white, straight male have been considered the default media audience for whom the camera work, costuming, actor selection, and other types of visual cues are chosen (Smith 2020, 151-2; Mulvey 1999, 833-4, 837-8).

Consider, for instance, how the vast majority of female actors we often see fit traditional white ideals of thinness. There are, of course, plenty of technically fine actors with larger bodies, and yet many of this group are not hired for more generic female roles because they do not have the "right look." That particular "look" usually has nothing to do with the plotline of the script, but has everything to do with the director's, writer's, and audience's stereotypical expectations of racialized female beauty.

Several of these concepts are part of Laura Mulvey's now-famous argument regarding the male gaze. This term describes the processes by which certain cinematic elements (camera angles, *mise-en-scène*, etc.) are used to visually transform women into objects possessed by men, often by portraying their bodies in sexualized, and frequently, powerless, ways. The audience in this model functions like a heterosexual male who voyeuristically gains pleasure from watching these specific representations of women in their most common roles, such as sex objects, romantic pursuits, or damsels in distress (Smith 2020, 151-2; Mulvey 1999, 833-4, 837-8). Invoking Sigmund Freud, Mulvey calls the pleasure of this kind of watching *scopophilia*. In its most general sense, we might understand this as a pleasure that comes from watching power relationships and vicariously inserting oneself into the scene, whether one identifies with the one who has power (traditionally, men), or as one who gains status because they are desirable to the powerful (traditionally, women) (Smith 2020, 151-2; Mulvey 1999, 833, 837-42).

Others have questioned portions of Mulvey's model by observing that the straight male audience of Mulvey's imagination is also implicitly white, and thus she does not consider how race can be just as important, if at times more so, than gender in determining the shape that the gaze takes (Hooks 1992, 123-125). Culture critics who take this perspective often note that rather than thinking individually about race and gender, analysts should focus on how *racialized gender* operates. This term is used to describe the synthesis of racial and gendered experiences. For instance, I am not just a woman, but a white woman, and so my experiences will be different from those of women of color, even if our shared gender identities mean we still have some things in common. Perhaps obviously, this more intersectional approach also applies to other identity categories (age, sexual orientation, class, ability, etc.) that may be pertinent in any given situation.

Using this intersectional perspective, Black feminist scholar bell hooks has argued that certain audiences (and particularly women of color) can actually have types of agency or resistance in their viewing; they do not necessarily blindly drink in what they see in media in the way that Mulvey describes (Hooks 1992, 116). The "oppositional gaze" is a term hooks uses to denote a more critically aware audience perspective that resists naturalizing the white, male-dominant imagery that may demean or erase the presence of people (and specifically women) of color on-screen (Hooks 1992, 117). Because women of color occupy a double category of oppression—that is, they are privileged in neither race nor gender—they may be in a particularly important epistemic position to analyze and question characters, themes, and storylines (Hooks 1992, 118).

For example, employing an oppositional gaze would allow one to see that to be a desirable woman on-screen has meant, historically, being a white (or otherwise fair) woman (Hooks 1992, 119, 122). It could also involve observing that actors of color are more likely to receive nominations and awards for their work when they play servile roles, such as slaves, servants, and nannies (Yuen 2016, 2-4). In a similar vein, it involves questioning why LGBTQ characters featured in scripts die or are otherwise killed off in numbers disproportionate to their cis- or straight counterparts (Rawson 2013). In all of these situations, an oppositional gaze reveals the power dynamics behind the images that audiences may have a harder time seeing because they find such images natural, predictable, or appealing.

Considering the role of the gaze and its oppositional form can thus reveal the presence and function of traditional, more conservative motifs about race, gender, sexual orientation, class, etc. But for the purposes of analyzing DuVernay's *Wrinkle,* we should also add a conversation about the role of religion to this mix. Long-standing stereotypes have tended to depict people of color as religious, and such stereotypes have often been used in two primary ways: (1) to portray them as irrational or overly emotional when compared to their white religious counterparts; and/or (2) as the mystical arbiters of secret knowledge that white protagonists then use to master a tricky situation. As we will see, the function of both stereotypes is to exaggerate the supposed differences between people of color and white groups, and from this to create a seemingly benevolent type of white supremacy.

For instance, Judith Weisenfeld has shown how Black religion was cinematically portrayed across the twentieth century in comic, often childish, superstitious ways that highlighted elements that white audiences would find sensational, silly, or entertaining (Weisenfeld 2007, 19-20, 30, 50). These attempts to stereotype and thus domesticate Black religion have parallels in orientalist motifs often used to depict non-Christian religions. "Orientalism" is a term coined by scholar Edward Said to describe how Western audiences tend to depict racial or cultural "others"—and particularly those from "the East"—as exotic, animalistic, highly religious, and, again, superstitious.[3] These are typecast most commonly in roles such as the monk, the guru, the terrorist, and the submissive Muslim woman.

The motif of the "oriental monk" is particularly important to *Wrinkle*, for it echoes the stereotype of the monk or guru whose disciplined religious life and knowledge of esoteric truths provide the (historically white) protagonist the knowledge they need to succeed in their quest. Jane Naomi Iwamura writes that not only does this perspective essentialize Asians as the bearers of mysterious spiritual knowledge, but it also renders them the perpetual assistants or accessories to more powerful white heroes. Iwamura cites examples of this stereotype in action in films as diverse as *The Karate Kid* and *Teenage Mutant Ninja Turtles*, but we might add to her list *Dr. Strange* (2016, dir. Scott Derrickson), one of the many Marvel Comics films that makes up the *Avengers* series. In the film, a white neurosurgeon, Dr. Stephen Strange (Benedict Cumberbatch), is seriously disabled in an accident. He receives specialized training to overcome his injuries in what is portrayed as the mystic land of Nepal. Eventually, he is transformed into one of the Avengers, while one of the Asian teachers responsible for his mystical training becomes his sidekick.[4]

What we should glean here, then, is that religion can serve as a medium through which varying racial and gendered symbols are made legible, and thus familiar, to the white, straight, patriarchal audience that is the presumed neutral viewer behind so much media today. Much of this involves instilling in the audience a sense of security. I've written elsewhere about how, in the case of reality TV, Western audiences often readily accept a male protagonist of color (and even more so if he appears ethnically "different") who assists them in exploring the religion of exotic others so long as the protagonist does not, himself, appear to challenge too many assumptions of the viewing audience. He garners credibility because audiences can read him as a translator, someone who can use his insider knowledge to bridge the divide between the strange and familiar. One point of familiarity that often emerges in such media is the protagonist's reassurance that most religion is a good, if not ultimately beautiful, thing that makes the world a better place. Audiences who hear this message can thus digest any number of types of difference more readily so long as this cultural safety net remains firmly entrenched.[5]

Meg's World

Indeed, "difference" is one of the themes that DuVernay has spoken about at length in the decision-making surrounding *Wrinkle*. As a Black woman herself, she notes that she felt a unique burden. She notes, "[I] *wasn't just casting for actresses. I was casting for leaders—icons*" (Berman 2018) in an attempt to present the story of Meg in a way that would offer millions of girls of color a chance to see themselves in a literary classic.

Many elements of that classic remain in the version created by DuVernay and screenwriter Jennifer Lee. In the early minutes of the movie we meet Meg Murry (Storm Reid), a biracial, adolescent girl who is clearly uncomfortable with herself and those around her. The target of a bullying group of mean girls, Meg is constantly reminded of her faults; as Meg sees it, she is not pretty, she is not popular, nor is she good at school. Several adults in the film trace her poor academic performance (despite her natural intelligence) to the mysterious disappearance of her scientist father (Chris Pine) four years earlier. It is his absence that drives the storyline.

In the midst of this personal turmoil, Meg and her brother, Charles Wallace (Deric McCabe), are visited by a character named Mrs. Whatsit (Reese Witherspoon). Mrs. Whatsit's uninvited entry into the Murry home is a pivotal point, for it is here that Mrs. Whatsit tells Meg and Charles Wallace's mother, Dr. Murry (Gugu Mbatha-Raw), that the highly experimental research she and her missing husband performed was, in fact, correct: there is such thing as a tesseract, the Murrys' term for a "wrinkle in time" that allows one to navigate the universe using only one's mind. He is missing because he is trapped somewhere in the cosmos.

The movie subsequently revolves around the children's efforts to find and rescue their father who, it turns out, is imprisoned by an evil force called IT on the planet Camazotz. Meg and Charles Wallace are joined in this quest by one of Meg's school peers, a boy named Calvin (Levi Miller). The three children are juxtaposed with Mrs. Whatsit and her own counterparts, Mrs. Which (Mindy Kaling) and Mrs. Who (Oprah Winfrey), who accompany the children through most of their quest. All three adult female leads exhibit a multitude of supernatural powers.

The children navigate a series of lessons and trials from the three women about the dangers that lie ahead, but then must travel alone to Camazotz. While there, Charles Wallace falls prey to the IT's brainwashing, and he attempts to hijack Meg's efforts to find their father. After the IT tempts her in a series of conversations that are undeniably like the biblical account of Satan tempting Jesus, Meg withstands the IT's promises of beauty, popularity, and Calvin's love interest.[6] The persistent theme of "the power of love" saves the day, for only when Meg invokes Charles Wallace's love for her despite her own flaws is he released from the grips of the IT, and everyone—including their father—finds their way home.

As mentioned, DuVernay's casting decisions have garnered considerable attention. Meg isn't the first imaginary character to have her race under the microscope; consider the recent outcry from various groups in response to news that Disney is making a live-action remake of *The Little Mermaid*, this time with a Black actress (Halle Bailey) playing the role of Ariel (Baptiste 2019). Such reactions reflect the racial tensions in the United States in the early twenty-first century, as characterized by the revitalization of white supremacist groups, President Trump's frequent racist comments, increasing public attention to racist policing practices, and the emergence of the Black Lives Matter movement in response.

In such an environment, DuVernay's decision to create a multiracial cast stands in stark contrast to a 2003 film adaptation of the book (dir. John Kent Harrison), also by Disney, which was composed almost entirely of white actors. Disney also has a very long history, particularly in its animated works, of presenting the aesthetic ideals of white beauty as those compatible with virtue. In other words, Disney's pattern has until very recently dictated that if you're beautiful, thin, and fair (along with other physical characteristics read as "white"), you're much more likely to be on the side of good than evil (Artz 2015, 450-1).

DuVernay is clearly attempting to reverse this formula but maintains many more predictable feminizing aspects of the film while also noting her desire to portray "feminine" as "strong" (Ryzik 2018). From all appearances, she is mostly successful in this effort. While the film's own aesthetics (bright colors, plenty of glittering cosmetics and costumes) caused journalist Melena Ryzik to call it a "very girlie movie" (Ryzik 2018), the film does not shy away from difficult gendered topics such as body image (Meg's own concern) and eating disorders (the struggle of one of Meg's peers). Further adding to a more oppositional gaze is the fact that Meg's budding romantic relationship with Calvin involves a white boy following the direction and concerns of a girl of color (an element of the film that is one of DuVernay's own points of pride) (Ryzik 2018).

Nevertheless, this is a movie that ends with the transformation of a female main character into a man's love interest; we cannot overlook the fact that this is perhaps the single most common way that a film featuring a female protagonist ends (Mulvey 1981, 13). Note that characters like Katniss Everdeen and Hermione Granger (mentioned earlier) are also strong female characters whose roles resolve, in part, when we find out the men with whom they are partnered. Rather than see moments like this as some sort of failure, however, a more analytically interesting question involves which traditional elements DuVernay and Lee chose to feature in this film, and which ones they chose to challenge (and why they made these choices).

In other words, making a Hollywood hit is very much about providing images and narratives with widespread, stereotypical appeal even if they are punctuated with the occasional radical message. As I will argue, DuVernay's success in challenging the status quo in matters of race and, often, gender depends in great part on sticking close to some other very familiar stereotypes, including those about religion.

Wrinkle and Religion

Earlier, I mentioned that a number of conservative Christian critics of the film noted that omission of the biblical verses that dot L'Engle's book version of *Wrinkle* have been replaced in Lee's version with a distinctly "spiritual, but not religious" tone that focuses on a message of self-love and personal transformation. For instance, Meg is repeatedly told that her success in rescuing her father from the far reaches of the universe depends on her own personal acceptance: she must love herself, warts, and all, in order to be able to tap into the power that will help her find him. However, even though such critics may have been irked by Lee's decision to temper any clear sectarian commitments, the brand of religiosity that she does include is extraordinarily well established in American culture. This is so much the case, in fact, that it functions as a vague, familiar backdrop that aids in selling other types of difference important to DuVernay's version of the film.

It might be tempting to say that a message of self-acceptance is very far from a conversation about religion. Yet historian Leigh Eric Schmidt has shown how the history of "spirituality" in America has been around for well over a century, and is intimately connected with the notion that invisible realities are part and parcel of the ability to improve one's life, as popularized in the idea of a "Higher Power" that has been the locus of Alcoholics Anonymous self-help literature (Schmidt 2005, xiv-xv). Aspects of this idea have taken on a more contemporary form in "moralistic therapeutic deism," a term developed by scholar Christian Smith to describe the dominant type of religious belief characterizing American teenagers in the early twenty-first century (Smith 2009, 162ff). This is the concept that religion, rather than being a series of theological precepts or detailed ethics, is primarily about belief in a loving, divine being who wants people to be nice to each other, to be happy with themselves, and whose task is to solve humans' problems.

The juxtaposition of light vs. dark/good vs. evil symbolism that pervades *Wrinkle* fits quite closely with this contemporary brand of spiritual self-help rhetoric. When Mrs. Who (Winfrey) is asked by the children what she is, her response is that she is, simply, a "part of the universe." Mrs. Whatsit (Witherspoon) elaborates: "We're warriors who serve the good and light in the universe." Other warriors include "those who are willing to face the darkness and bring the best of themselves to the light . . . for the world," and here a list of major world figures is spelled out, including, among others, Albert Einstein, Marie Curie, Mohandas Gandhi, Nelson Mandela, Maya Angelou, and so on. (This is the screenplay's remake of the originally controversial line from the book, wherein Jesus's name appears in a list like this.)

Having faith in their father's existence and the possibility of his rescue will sustain the children, and Meg, in particular, who, we are told, must be "true to herself," and believe in the "power of love" to accomplish this task. In a flashback rather early in the film, we see the Drs. Murry at a conference presenting their research, where they explain their theory that all elements of the universe are interconnected. They describe this as a type of love between universal realms. Thus when the children are confronted with the practical problem of how they will travel the universe to find their missing father, Mrs. Who (Winfrey) responds that "you just have to find the right frequency and have faith in who you are." We later find out that "love is the frequency" that enables this type of universal travel, or tessering, which explains why Meg is roughed up compared to the others in the tessering process. Mrs. Who (Winfrey) explains Meg's condition as one attributable to her inability to unite herself with the universe, a predicament caused by her chronic bad attitude and lack of self-acceptance.

The critique that DuVernay and Lee have watered down the presence of religion in the script is thus relatively unfounded, although they certainly have given it a more contemporary twist. But for those wishing to use a more critical perspective to consider the discourse at work in this film, the issue should not be whether DuVernay and Lee "did it right." Rather, the issue is a matter of which symbols have or have not been actively deployed in telling this particular version of the story. Here, again, we're confronted with another moment wherein the radical and traditional remain in some tension, and this pertains specifically to symbols of racialized gender and their intersection with religion.

More specifically, I am interested in the ways that certain characters' connection to this spirituality message is portrayed in light of their race and gender. Earlier I discussed how there has been an enduring trend on the part of white cultural commentators to regard the religious practices of people of color as somehow essential, inferior, and/or exotically different. There is, additionally, a parallel discourse to consider, one positing religion as a primarily feminine practice. Historians often discuss tensions in certain American Protestant denominations from the nineteenth century on over whether the church had become "too feminine," a critique lodged by many men who were disturbed at the numbers of women who had taken on leadership positions in traditionally white, middle-class to upper-class, institutional Protestant denominations. A variety of movements across the past century have emerged to attempt to make these forms of Christianity more appealing to men, but the association between women, morality, and heightened religious sentiment remains (Smith 2014, 34-6).

If we can update this presumed symbolic tie between religion and women to reflect the moral therapeutic deism earlier discussed, then we should not be surprised when we recognize that concern for self-esteem, self-love, and emotional wholeness, often couched in conversations about "healthy spirituality," or "honoring your true self," etc., has been a rhetoric geared toward and used primarily by girls and women in American culture for the past several decades.

This is where DuVernay reinforces very traditional elements of racialized gender and religion, using both Winfrey's and Kaling's racialized appearances as symbols of their spiritual prowess. Of the three adult female leads, only Witherspoon is white, and her role in the *Wrinkle* trinity is as a clear spiritual inferior to Winfrey and Kaling. As Mrs. Whatsit, Witherspoon is primarily present to offer the comic relief, playing something like a "deity in training" who is consistently corrected by Mrs. Who (Winfrey) when her interactions with humans go afoul. One doesn't have to try very hard to see Witherspoon's ditzy, yet iconic, character from *Legally Blonde* at work: she does not remember, at times, that the humans can hear her when she talks about them; she does not consider their safety when she takes them flying.

But for Kaling and Winfrey, both women of color, the different role that they play in this brand of religion is striking when compared to Witherspoon's character. In very simple terms, they are both far more serious, and while they both sporadically add to the humor, their function in the script is the dispensation of wisdom. Kaling (who is Indian-American) is relatively quiet when compared to her counterparts; part of her powers as Mrs. Which, we are told, is that she is beyond language. Thus the dominant way that she communicates is by quoting others when she wishes to speak, providing the audience the sense that she is simply plucking sentences from a vast reservoir of universal wisdom (Mrs. Which's first words to Meg are, "'The wound is the place where the light enters you'—Rumi, Persian"). Seeing how often the orientalist motif of the Indian guru is portrayed in just such a way, it's hard to imagine that Kaling's racial identity was not part of her visual appeal. Like Witherspoon, Kaling is perhaps best known for her comedy work, and specifically for her role as extremely shallow, overly talkative, narcissistic employee Kelly Kapur from the hit TV series *The Office*. Audiences who have any awareness of Kaling's past work will thus find her portrayal as Mrs. Which a very stark departure from her previous roles.

In fact, it is arguable that one of the reasons why audiences might be able to palate a very different kind of Kaling is because Witherspoon and Winfrey are so very predictable. Winfrey seems to be speaking from a script that would be entirely appropriate in any one of her many other media enterprises. As Mrs. Who, Winfrey is portrayed as the leader of the three in the sense that she is often shown many times larger than the others, a cosmic giant of sorts, who appears to be calling the shots. We should also not overlook the fact that if this is supposed to be a trinity, Winfrey is undoubtedly the godhead. Anyone who has spent any time engaging with Winfrey's vast multimedia empire knows that she has made her mark on American culture in great part by preaching a gospel of self-help, of living one's "best life," and of marketing one of her favorite words—Spirit (note the capitalization) (Lofton 2011, 59). Although Winfrey repeatedly rejects the label "religion" for what she advocates (for, to her, religion is the realm of "hierarchy, rules, and male manipulation") (Lofton 2011, 11) what she preaches, instead, is an elaborate gospel of self-transformation, very close to the one present in DuVernay's *Wrinkle*.

We know that one of the functions of transcendence speech—that type of rhetoric that speaks very vaguely about "divinity," "higher power," and other terms that seem to hint at ambiguous supernatural concepts—is that it's a terrific unifier (Smith 2017, 59ff). In other words, audiences from many types of backgrounds will typically be quite eager to get behind notions of "the divine within" or "the spirit that guides us" without ever questioning what such concepts more specifically mean. Arguably, one of the most fascinating aspects of Winfrey's multimedia empire is the manner in which she, too, has also become "all things to all people," in the sense that she is read by a wide variety of audiences as someone uniquely in touch with their individual experiences.

This is, scholar Kathryn Lofton notes, one of the primary reasons why Winfrey was chosen as the person to emcee the National Day of Prayer immediately after 9/11 (Lofton 2011, 118-119). It was not a traditional clergyperson who could do this work, but none other than Oprah Winfrey, who, unlike a priest or pastor, is not defined by sectarian division, but by an amorphous affiliation with a form of individualized, highly positive, transformative spirituality. The reason for Winfrey's prominence and place in that very delicate national hour, Lofton argues, was her ability to collapse a number of different stereotypes into a palatable product for a diverse audience: she is at once the black mammy figure in whose arms others can cry while she simultaneously claims that she "transcends race" (Lofton 2011, 131-2, 126). She holds incredible power and wealth while also easily discussing the poverty and abuse of her southern, Black youth. She is, Lofton notes, "a healer, a prophet, a peculiar form of holy woman" (Lofton 2011, 68).

In other words, the very things that make Winfrey appealing to a diverse audience of millions are the same dynamics DuVernay is attempting to navigate in *Wrinkle*. This ability to collapse any number of competing symbols onto a single character or characters may be one of DuVernay's greatest accomplishments in this film, for in casting Meg as a girl of color, the religious wisdom imparted largely by Kaling and Winfrey, themselves women of color, is not passed along to a classically white, male protagonist, but to someone who shakes up traditional identity categories in terms of race and gender (not to mention, age). In this way, DuVernay disrupts the stereotypes that traditionally sideline characters of color and their religion even as she does so with a message that very much reflects the status quo.

Conclusion: Tempered Radicalism

Wrinkle thus provides us with a case study of how we might understand religion in media both rhetorically and critically—that is, as part of an underlying message of the film as well as a vital part in defining the power relationships it typifies. In *Wrinkle*, religion functions as a safety net and sounding board; it has universal appeal not just because it echoes old stereotypes but also because it reflects the status quo. This is incredibly important when the casting decisions about a well-loved literary classic are going to cause friction with certain audiences whose racial and gendered privilege has mainstreamed their otherwise narrow perspectives.

The message of universal love and the relatively predictable way that it plays out in *Wrinkle* are precisely the sort of neutral backdrop mitigating the otherwise more radical race and gender choices DuVernay makes. Audiences may thus find that their discomfort with seeing a Black deity figure or a young biracial female protagonist may fade because they find such affinity with the "power of love" message.

CHAPTER 4

Race, Colonialism, and Whiteness in Martin Scorsese's *Silence* (2016)

Malory Nye

When Martin Scorsese created his 2016 movie *Silence*, his overt intention was to use the film to explore (Christian) religious faith within the historical context of a male Jesuit priest experiencing God through a narrative of both suffering and silence. My intention in this chapter is not to contradict this particular (largely Catholic) theological understanding of the film, especially as the director has himself clearly articulated such theology as an authentic reading of his work (Scorsese 2016). However, the context and subject matter of the film also include another significant reading, which is not only important in itself, it also provides much of the film's overall meaning and interpretation.[1] That is, the film *Silence* is also very significantly about race, colonialism, and whiteness, and it is through these themes that the film explores and makes meaningful its narrative of a particular man's faith and failures during a time of persecution. As the critic Marta Figlerowicz wrote in the *Los Angeles Review of Books*, this is "another film about white, Catholic men reaffirming their whiteness and their Christianity" (Figlerowicz 2017). In this sense, the narration of faith and religion within *Silence* relies on the director's and audiences' assumptions and expectations about race and whiteness.

Scorsese's film *Silence* is an adaptation of an acclaimed book (of the same name) by the Catholic Japanese writer Shusaku Endo (originally published in Japanese in 1966 with the title *Chinmoku*). It tells the story of a young Portuguese Jesuit priest seeking both a mission and martyrdom in seventeenth-century Japan, during a time of harsh punishments of Christians by the recently centralized Japanese state. The English-language translation of Endo's book by an Irish Jesuit, William Johnston, was published as *Silence* in 1969 (Endo 2016). It was this translation that caught Scorsese's attention in 1988, and was eventually developed as the 2016 movie *Silence* (Horne 2017: 18–19). The script of the movie is a quite faithful rendition by Scorsese and Jay Cocks of the translated book onto the screen, with perhaps the main innovation being a brief concluding epilogue that makes explicit what are otherwise rather ambiguous snippets in the final pages of the book.

However, despite the close relation between the book and the movie, the process of developing the film from a translation of a Japanese-language novel means that the end product has several layers of interpretation that need to be unpacked. This is not simply a matter of a lack of "fidelity" in the adaptation of the book to the screen, but instead a question of how Scorsese has taken a book from one context and rendered an alternative version of it in a different medium and context (Hermansson 2015; Ng 2019).

What is produced is very much a Scorsese religious movie (echoing his earlier work, particularly *The Last Temptation of Christ*, 1988), produced by an experienced director with his own interests and perspectives, for an audience who are familiar with his distinctive style and approach. Of course, there is a fundamental difference between a book written in Japanese for a Japanese audience and a film written in English (and filmed by an American company in Taiwan) for consumption mainly in North America and Europe. After all, a point of comparison could be the question of how the Japanese film director Shinya Tsukamoto (who did himself act in the film) may have chosen to make an English-language version of this same book. It is very likely that the outcome and its reception and interpretation would have been very different.[2] Despite Scorsese's meticulous filmic exploration of the complex themes of Endo's writing on Christianity in Japan, the Western audience will read the message of Scorsese's version of the story through their own particular historical perspectives. That is, the film is about early European colonialism in Asia—whether we look at it in narrowly "religious" terms, or otherwise.

The issue here is not about whether the critic should label Scorsese as "racist" in his adaptation of Endo's novel *Silence*. After all, Scorsese's fans would likely argue in his defense that this is a filmic adaptation and the themes of white Christian colonialism are taken (quite faithfully) from the original book by Endo. This notwithstanding, it was Scorsese's own choice to use this book for the movie he created, which inevitably brought with it the baggage of how to deal with the specific themes of Christianity and colonialism. And furthermore, as Stam and Spence argue in their classic article on "Colonialism, Racism, and Representation":

The objective of this study of filmic colonialism and racism . . . is not to hurl charges of racism at individual filmmakers or critics—in a systematically racist society few escape the effects of racism—but rather to learn how to decode and deconstruct racist images and sounds. (Stam and Spence 2009: 766)

Scorsese made a film that he felt was in line with his audience's expectations and values—in a society where structural racism and the legacy of empire and colonialism are ongoing and pernicious.[3] What is far more important is how do the tropes of racism and colonialism (and the dominance of assumptions of whiteness—and, with that, white supremacy) make any reading and understanding of the film meaningful. In this sense, it is not the purported racism of Scorsese that is the issue, it is the dominant cultural racialized positioning of the audience for the film that is far more important. Race matters in *Silence* not because Scorsese explicitly wanted to make a film about race, colonialism, and whiteness, nor that Scorsese found it hard to avoid classically "Orientalist" depictions of historical Japan (Said 2003; Rosen 2000). Instead, race matters in *Silence* because Scorsese made a film about issues of religion and theology which he felt were important, and he made that film for an audience that relies universally on tropes and ideologies of race and racialization. In fact, as many others have argued elsewhere, race and religion are very much conjoined categories of power in the contemporary world, and both are linked very closely to perceptions of whiteness.[4] As with all his movies (and nearly all the output of Hollywood studios), Scorsese made a movie about whiteness (and hegemonic white masculinity) that also happened to be about (what gets called) religion.

Whiteness, Race, and Colonialism at the Movies

It is now commonplace to apply critical race theory to the analysis of film and other cultural phenomena (Saha 2017; Stam and Spence 2009; Dyer 2002). Indeed, many argue (following Edward Said 2003 and Stuart Hall 1995) that the exploration of race and racialization in film and culture is a *necessity*, given the ubiquity of structural racism within contemporary American society. Indeed, more than two decades ago Richard Dyer pointed out that "racial imagery is central to the organisation of the modern world" (Dyer 1997: 1), while Manthia Diawara pointed about that "race is an important structuring element in every Hollywood film" (Diawara 1990, 34). And as Saidiya Hartman observed recently in a podcast discussion, "so much of the work of oppression is about policing the imagination" (Crenshaw, Hartman, and Jemisin 2020). The themes of race and whiteness are in fact ubiquitous to the work of Scorsese, since much of his filmic vision is an exploration of white masculinity in late-twentieth-century (and early-twenty-first-century) America (Lopes 2017). However, his choice as director to make a film specifically around an early European colonial narrative—that is, Portuguese Catholic colonialism in east Asia in the seventeenth century—foregrounds issues that make such race and whiteness central to any discussion of the film.

The critical discussion of whiteness and race is largely derived from the early-twentieth-century scholar W. E. B. Du Bois, in particular his classic essay on the *Souls of White Folk* (Du Bois 1920). Written in the context of Jim Crow apartheid United States, and in the aftermath of the horrors of the First World War, Du Bois asked the simple rhetorical question of, "But what on earth is whiteness that one should so desire it?" His response is, "I am given to understand that whiteness is the ownership of the earth forever and ever, Amen!" What Du Bois draws attention to in this essay is that: first, the concept (and identity) of whiteness is a fairly recent development—this concept has not existed for long as it is now understood, having come into being in the eighteenth and nineteenth centuries; and second, whiteness is about power and control, it is not a neutral description of skin tone, it is part of an ideological system of colonialism that defines the use of power and violence. Thus Du Bois talked elsewhere about the "wages of whiteness" (Du Bois 1935), through which the ideology of white identity structures particular poor and disadvantaged people (working class) as distinct from others in a similar position (i.e., those who consider themselves "white"). Thus, working-class white people accept their disadvantage on the basis of their difference from (and assumed superiority over) those who they define as "Black."

As James Baldwin (2010 [1984]) eloquently argued, the concept of whiteness refers to how people who think of themselves as white racialize themselves—it is not an "obvious" or natural category, it is a way of classifying and controlling the world. Whiteness has as its basis other racializations, relying on the classification of *other* people as non-whites—as "black," "brown," or otherwise. Such whiteness works to racialize many different groups as non-white, including "Asians," "Arabs," "Muslims," "Sikhs," and "Japanese"—even when the racialization does not appear to have a specific "racial" category. Very often, the category of religion is a means by which such racialization is done (Nye 2018; Meer 2013). The key point here is that the concept and classification of race is not a scientific or natural description of differences. The concept of race comes from and relies on colonialism, particularly the past few centuries of European colonialism, beginning in the fifteenth century (Quijano 2007). That is, such colonialism has created this racializing classification as a form of power and control (Fanon 1967), or, in the words of Patrick Wolfe, "race is colonialism speaking" (Wolfe 2016, 117).

This process of racialization happens frequently in media and film, and it is important to have an awareness that any exploration of colonialism within media (such as film) reproduces and inculcates such racialization—even if not deliberately or consciously (Stam and Spence 2009). In her discussion of novels involving Black characters, Toni Morrison (1992) notes

RACE, COLONIALISM, AND WHITENESS

that such non-white characters are literary constructions of whiteness. That is, Black characters in such books are representations, not reality, created by white writers for white readers as ways of thinking about their whiteness. Thus, she asks:

> What does the inclusion of Africans or African-Americans do to and for the work? . . . I assumed that since the author was not black, the appearance of African characters or narrative or idiom in a work could never be about anything other than the "normal," unracialised, illusory white world that provided the fictional backdrop. (Morrison 1992: 116)

Of course, this analysis can also be applied to other characters who are racialized as "non-white" by the "white" auteur (in similar but distinct ways from Black characters).

And so Morrison argues that this racialization is a form of the artifice that is constructed by the white author through their art. Thus, "the subject of the dream is the dreamer . . . the fabrication of an Africanist persona is reflexive; an extraordinary meditation on the self," and it "requires hard work *not* to see this" (117, emphasis in the original).

What became transparent were the self-evident ways that Americans choose to talk about themselves through and within a sometimes allegorical, sometimes metaphorical, but always choked, representation of an Africanist presence.

Although such representations of "non-whiteness" occur in all forms of writing, one particularly strong trope (particularly within the structures of Hollywood movies) is the image of the "white saviour" (Hughey 2016: 219–23; Vera and Gordon 2003). This a white character in a movie that

> enters a black, Latino, Asian, or Native context in which the nonwhites struggle through the social order. By the film's end and through the sacrifices of the White Savior, the nonwhite "others" were transformed and redeemed. (Hughey 2016: 219)

Such a White Saviour goes "the extra mile to help people of color who cannot or will not help themselves, thus establishing social order, teaching nonwhites right from wrong," and is thus framed as "the only character able to recognize these moral distinctions and act upon them" (Hughey 2016, 219). An important outcome of this is to "construct and glorify the ideal white person as a paternalistic administrator of people of color, and consistently portray nonwhite people as biologically or culturally broken and in need of salvation" (Hughey 2016: 223).

As Morrison suggests, it is often "hard work not see" the power of the ideology of whiteness within a piece of art. Nonetheless, such whiteness is often unspoken, unobserved, and not mentioned (Dyer 1997). It is the elephant in the room that white authors and audiences do not mention; one could even say that the first rule of white club is that no one talks about white club. As Dyer points out elsewhere:

> Trying to think about the representation of whiteness as an ethnic category in mainstream film is difficult, partly because white power secures its dominance by seeming not to be anything in particular but also because, when whiteness qua whiteness does come into focus, it is often revealed as emptiness, absence, denial or even a kind of death. (Dyer 2002, 126)

Moreover, there is often an (ideologically) assumed naivety about such whiteness, with not only a *failure* to see it directly but also a *feigned* (white) *ignorance* (Mills 2017) or (white) *innocence* (Wekker 2016). To put this simply, if *Silence* was a film about Black missionaries in colonial Japan (or elsewhere), the characters' racialization as Black would be foregrounded, it would be considered an important part of the narrative. But the characters' racialization as white (who even talk with American accents) is unacknowledged, and so for most viewers this is just the way the movie "works." Such invisible racialization is very often conveyed through what is sometimes called the (white) "colonial gaze" within film-making (Döring 1997; hooks 1992; Ram 2018),[5] which presumes not only that the dominant viewpoint within the film is that of the white (male) protagonist, but this is also the expected viewpoint of the (predominantly white) audience.

Indeed, the colonial location of the narrative is a very obvious marker of the racialization of the film, and yet it is surprising how little comment has been made on the significance of this theme of race and colonialism. This lack of comment or curiosity about the choice of the colonial theme suggests a very obvious manifestation of Wekker's concept of "white innocence." In fact, it is also interesting that *Silence* is set in the era of early Dutch (as well as Portuguese) colonialism which is the focus of Wekker's work. It suggests perhaps that this particular seventeenth-century era is a time of purported colonial innocence and presumed prehistory, inasmuch as the nations involved (such as Spain, Portugal, and the Netherlands) do not directly implicate the obvious demons of English (or America-related) colonialism (despite the actual violence of each of these nations' empires, and the coexistence of the early English/American slave trade across the Atlantic at that same time). This was clearly *not* a time of innocence or genial cultural encounters—it was a time of brutal and violent colonialism.

Furthermore, as I suggested earlier, Scorsese's films on Italian Americans are generally about understandings of the "unseen" and unacknowledged whiteness, without being referenced as such. Thus, Paul Lopes has argued that Scorsese is "not only an acclaimed filmmaker, but also a major public intellectual" (Lopes 2017: 565). And in this role—particularly in his many filmic and discursive explorations of hyphenated American identities (especially Italian Americans)—Scorsese's work has represented "the power and legacy of white privilege" (576).

Exploring the Film's Narrative and Context

In this section, my analysis of the film will explore two particular aspects—that is, the development of the narrative and the film's use of characterization. In doing this, there are several issues to note, in particular how these relate to the film's origins as an adaptation of a well-respected novel. There are, of course, many issues with adaptation, especially the question of "fidelity" to the source (Hermansson 2015), that may or may not limit the director's and scriptwriter's scope in presenting a novel on the screen. As noted already, in this case Scorsese chose to make a largely faithful representation of his reading of the book. One result of this was that the film he directed had a number of convergences not only with Endo's own rendition of the narrative but also with a lot of Scorsese's earlier themes—such as silently examining what whiteness means to the racialization of white men, and also a very dominant sense of masculinity (with in this case *very* few female characters).

The focus of *Silence* is on one particular man, Father Sebastian Rodrigues (played by Andrew Garfield), who is portrayed as young, idealistic, and struggling with his Christian faith. His mission begins in the company of a fellow Jesuit, Francisco Garupe (played by Adam Driver), and together they spend several months in pastoral work among a village of "hidden Christians" (known historically in Japan as *kakase kirishitan*), near Nagasaki.

At this time, the newly centralized Tokugawa state (often referred to as the Edo shogunate) in Japan was taking violent action to eradicate Christians (and other problematic groups, see Josephson 2012: 39–41) because of their association with foreign powers, such as the Portuguese—and so Rodrigues's and Garupe's presence in the country is perilous, risking their death (as martyrs) or forced renunciation of their faith. When the local magistrate (called Inoue) suspects the presence of these priests, he makes a public exhibition of the execution of prominent village leaders, which Rodrigues and Garupe observe from in hiding. Following this, they choose to separate, out of fear of capture and execution.

Always ahead of Rodrigues is the fate of his teacher and mentor, Fr Chistavao Ferreira (played by Liam Neeson), who is reported as having refused martyrdom and instead accepted apostasy—a public refutation of his Christian identity to become a Buddhist. Such apostatizing required the Christian to place their foot on an image of Christ, called a *fumie*. Following his apostatizing, Ferreira remained in Japan and took on a lifestyle and identity as Japanese. Although the character of Rodrigues is fictional, the bones of Ferreira's story are historical. As may be expected,

Ferreira's apostasy from Catholicism (and from his Jesuit order) makes him an ambiguous figure, much of which becomes embodied in his eventual encounter with the protagonist Rodrigues at a late stage of the narrative.

By going to Japan as a missionary to witness his faith—and to find Ferreira—Rodrigues enters a situation in which he expects danger, torture, and quite possibly death. His narrative is one of becoming aware of his inability to link this to the main Christian stories of redemption through suffering, either Jesus in Gethsemane and on Golgotha, or the early Christian martyrs. Within this path to either martyrdom or apostasy is not merely the Jesuit's fear of torture. Rodrigues also has to face and take responsibility for the torture and death of those who he is meant to be serving—the "hidden Christian" villagers. To what extent can a European Jesuit priest reconcile his self-glorification in martyrdom and refusal to "apostatize" against the pain and suffering of others because of him? By renouncing his faith he can save those others.

It is not by chance or mere circumstance that the two Portuguese missionaries are in Japan in the 1640s. By this time, the Portuguese had established an empire across the globe, through force and with the aid of Catholic missionaries. We see the priests first in the context of Portuguese Macao (Macau), an already established European colony in east Asia (represented by shots of the classical European architecture of St Paul's College), at the end of a chain of such colonies linking back through Malacca, Goa, and Africa to Portugal. In the late sixteenth century, the influence of the Portuguese in the southern Japanese city of Nagasaki and its surroundings was being developed to make it another such powerful regional hub, and conversion to Christianity was an important part of that strategy. The presence of these two Jesuits might be assumed to be about faith, but they were also part of an army of Christian missionaries who represented, relied on, and also advanced the colonial and commercial interests of the Portuguese empire (cf. Blackburn 2004).

In this context, they were no strangers to the use of coercive violence—against those who opposed such colonialism and also those who resisted or deviated from the religious power of the Catholic Church. Portugal had itself expelled its religious minorities early in its history of colonialism, in 1497—including the expulsion and killings of Jews, Muslims (Moriscos), and Protestant heretics (Soyer 2008). The Inquisition was indeed brought into Asia from Europe by the pioneering Jesuit Francis Xavier a century before in the 1540s (Paiva 2017).

Thus, although Endo's Japanese novel is about reclaiming a hidden Christian history within Japan, this film serves more to educate a white Western audience about a forgotten element of the spread of Jesuit-based Catholicism in east Asia. It could even be argued that it is about a particular moment of Japan successfully resisting European colonialism and domination. After all, the context of the film is the initial stage of the two-century "closing" of Japan (*sakoku* or *kaikin*) during the Tokugawa era, strictly regulating the Europeans' attempts to trade with, influence, and colonize parts of Japan (Elison 1988; Ward 2009; Leuchtenberger 2013). As elsewhere in Asia and America, the spread of Christian traditions was a very important part of such empire building. This closure was eventually ended by Western colonial powers through force, after the United States sent gunships into Tokyo Bay in 1853 (Josephson 2012; Horii 2018).

Although the film is primarily about the inner conflicts and concerns of Rodrigues, much of the narrative is built up through his interactions with mostly Japanese characters. It is through these characterizations that Rodrigues is both constructed as white (as a Christian priest, and as speaking English with an American accent) and the conflict of his faith is established. At the heart of this is Rodrigues's relationship with Kichijiro (played by Yosuke Kubozuka), who is one of the hidden Christians. Kichijiro is a marginal figure within the context of the Japanese village that Rodrigues attends: the priests first come across him in Macao, and so he is established as living across the dividing line between the closed-off Japan and the Portuguese ports of empire.

Kichijiro is also a very ambiguous and complex character. Although himself a Christian, he "apostatizes" several times (to the extent it is joked about) and is flaky and untrustworthy enough to be cast by Rodrigues into the role of Judas as it becomes clear that the priest will be captured by the Japanese authorities. And yet, with comedic timing he turns up regularly demanding that Rodrigues hears his confession. He has that rare quality of being both dislikable and evoking sympathy. At the same time, though, as the most significant Japanese character within the film, his role is to be part of Rodrigues's own inner struggle.

For the theologian Teng-Kuan Ng, this aspect of Kichijiro's character is significant in itself, not only for the light relief that it gives in a dense and harrowing story, but also because his role as Judas to Rodrigues becomes in itself a mirror of Rodrigues's own self-doubts (Ng 2019, 12–13). In this sense, we can perhaps interpret this as a Fanon-like struggle of colonialism, between the colonizer and the colonized (Fanon 2004; 2008), which is presented from the colonizer's perspective.

There are several other key Japanese characters that contribute to Rodrigues's apotheosis, including the Christian village elders Mokichi (played by the film director Shinya Tsukamoto) and Ichizo (Yoshi Oida), and the sinister and creepy Inquisitor/magistrate Inoue Masashige (played by Issey Ogata). In many respects it is this Inquisitor who predominantly represents the power of the Japanese state that is not only persecuting Rodrigues but is also resisting and preventing the encroachment of Christian Portuguese colonialism—most obviously through the use of violence, torture, and execution. Inoue is given a very significant exposition fairly late in the film, during an encounter with Rodrigues as he is trying to compel the priest to apostatize and step on the *fumie*. In this dialogue, the Inquisitor uses two metaphors to explain to Rodrigues the Japanese response to the Portuguese:

78   REPRESENTING RELIGION IN FILM

[A lord] had four concubines who were all jealous, and they fought and fought without end. So [he] drove them away from his castle, and peace came into his life again . . . This [lord] is like Japan, and these concubines are Spain, Portugal, Holland, England, each trying to gain advantage against the other and destroying the house in the process.

The conversation then ends with a switch being made to this metaphor, as Inoue goes on to talk of Christians as a woman/wife:

Padre. There are men who are plagued by the persistent love of an ugly woman . . . A barren woman cannot be a true wife . . . Padre, you missionaries do not seem to know Japan . . . There are those who think of your religion as a curse. I do not. I see it in another way. But still dangerous.

I would like you to think of the persistent love of an ugly woman and how a barren woman should never be a wife.

These words are not delivered as a philosophical discussion but are instead heavily laden with a threat to Rodrigues, who knows Inoue will happily use violence against him. The male-centered misogyny of these metaphors is left unchallenged, but the issue they allude to is clear. There is a regional power struggle going on, between the various European colonial powers and Japan. The newly centralized Japanese state wishes to maintain control in this situation and to "master" it—as a man in the context of what is to him a troublesome marriage. Thus the European powers—and also Christianity—are all presented as unwanted potential partners (as wives or concubines). The struggle that Rodrigues is involved in, which is presented largely as one of theology and faith, is understood by Inoue through this much wider balance of power relations between Japan and the colonial forces.

Inoue is eventually successful, as Rodrigues does succumb to the torture that is inflicted not on him but on the Christian villagers. The result is that Rodrigues chooses to live his life under a Japanese name, as a non-Christian (i.e., as a Buddhist), and works with the Japanese government to prevent other infiltrations of foreign missionaries into the country.

Most notable for me, however, was the character of Inoue's assistant who is simply known as the "Interpreter" (played by Tadanobu Asano), whose role it is to translate between Inoue (who in the film speaks heavily accented English) and Rodrigues's Portuguese (rendered in the film as English). In the novel, this Interpreter is seen very much through Rodrigues's eyes, and so appears harsh and largely set on destroying him. However, in the film there is some sympathy for him: of course, he speaks English well, and he is familiar with the vagaries of Portuguese mission and colonialism, showing familiarity with Francisco Cabral, who was head of the Jesuits in Japan. He says:

Father Cabral never managed much more than "arigataya." All the time he lived here, he taught but would not learn. He despised our language, our food, our customs . . .

We have our own religion, Padre. Pity you did not notice it. You cling to your illusions and call them faith.

In many ways he comes across as a contemporary anti-colonial firebrand, who finds the European an "arrogant man, like all of them . . . which means he will eventually fall." During scenes of torture and execution he is upset, and expresses his regret. But he also berates Rodrigues for his "selfish dream of a Christian Japan." And he also affirms to Rodrigues the state's strategy that the use of violence to suppress Christianity is both necessary and avoidable—describing the violence and torture of Inoue's methods as indicating "he is a practical man, not a cruel one." He tries to encourage the Jesuit to just do what needs to be done—that is, to apostatize. In some respects again there is a trace of Fanon (2004) at play in this context.

In an interview, Scorsese notes his own ambiguity about this character, suggesting he was unsure of how to interpret him from the subtlety of Endo's book.

> although as I always say, "Is he really an interpreter? Who *is* he? What is he really up to?" I mean, obviously he can interpret, but really, he seems to have more power than just a mere interpreter. (Scorsese in Horne 2017: 27)

As with many other Scorsese films, violence is a very necessary part of the film. And as an adaptation, the violence in *Silence* that Scorsese deploys is very much a part of the book—since without the violence there would be no Japanese resistance to European colonialism, and hence no pressure for the priest's apostasy. However, I can appreciate that the presence of violence in the book was part of the attraction of it to the director.[6]

This violence is not only against Rodrigues and the other Europeans, it is also against the Japanese Christian villagers. That is, the Inquisitor, and through him the state, were fighting the battle not only *against* the external colonization but also *for* control of its subjects (or citizens). Thus, Inoue embodies some of the complexity of colonialism and its resistance, particularly the anticolonial (or postcolonial) violence by the state against its subjects. But even so, this violence is strategic, it is also to control Rodrigues as the external influencer—whose compliance (through apostasy) will in itself help them control their subjects. Of course, part of the problem in this respect returns to the issue of the film as an adaptation of a book—Endo's *Silence* does not directly portray any of the violence by the Portuguese and other colonizers *against* the Japanese. One may perhaps take that part of the narrative as implied or assumed within a Japanese audience (or readership), but the absence of such colonizing violence does leave a gap that for the American audience will most likely be filled by a sense of innocence.

Scorsese himself mentions in an interview that when he showed the film to a group of "Asian and Latin American priests" one particular Jesuit had raised this particular issue with him. Scorsese said:

Talking about the violence of the Japanese against the Christians in the film, [this Jesuit] said one has to understand about the Japanese that there was violence perpetrated on them by the arrogance of the West. One of the key things was to lose that arrogance, to break it down. Ultimately Rodrigues makes that choice, to do as he does [in apostasizing] . . .

As this Jesuit said, colonisation is really what it's about—it's about money, and land and water—and the destruction of the very soul of the people—of their culture. He said that to this day, sadly, the Christian faith is linked still to colonisation; and to use his words, it's a wound that is still unhealed. (Scorsese in Horne 2017, 22)

Although in this quote Scorsese appears reticent to follow this link between violence and the colonial history, it is interesting to note that he returns to his key message of faith and theology to address it. That is, for him Rodrigues "breaks down" the violence by "losing his arrogance" and succumbing to the apostatization. However, the viewpoint of the Jesuit here speaks loudly about how the individual actions of a single (fictional) priest make little difference to a global history of colonial violence that resonates in the present day.

Religion in Silence

Despite the comments of this Jesuit, reported by Scorsese, a large number of the reviews and discussions of *Silence* have taken the film at "face value" and explored Scorsese's explicit theology.[7] I am not arguing these analysts are wrong or misguided, but instead that this primary focus on faith and theology misses a very significant element of the themes of the film—and indeed it is only a partial exploration of the complexity of Endo's novel on hidden Japanese Christianity. In particular, the depiction of the faith journey of a white Christian (Rodrigues) in a narrative on what makes Christianity Japanese is very much why the film deserves Figlerowicz's (2017) critique that this is just "another film about white, Catholic men reaffirming their whiteness and their Christianity."

Or, to put this another way, this is to say that the musical *Hamilton* (now itself a filmic product, through its release in summer 2020 on the Disney+ TV streaming service) is simply a narrative about early American politics. The choices that the show's creator Lin-Manuel Miranda made for many aspects of the theatrical production (including music, casting, and lyrics), of course, point out the importance of issues of race and racialization in the overall understanding of what *Hamilton* is about. Like Miranda, Scorsese chose to make a film which was set in a quite different, but still violent, historical colonial context, but, unlike Miranda, he also chose to *avoid* (or appear innocent about) the racializing connotations of his work.[8]

Thus for Scorsese, the film is primarily a matter of faith and theology—it is an exploration of the morality and piety of a devout Jesuit man. As he writes:

> Rodrigues believes with all his heart he will be the hero of a Western story that we all know very well: the Christian allegory, a Christ figure, with his own Gesthemane—a patch of wood—and his own Judas, a miserable wretch named Kichijiro.
>
> Silence is the story of a man who learns—so painfully—that God's love is more mysterious than he knows, that He leaves much more to the ways of men than we realize, and that He is always present . . . even in His silence. (Scorsese 2016, viii)

But it is much more than this. Indeed in this case the religious is the political. Another comment by Scorsese, in the interview with Philip Horne, tells of one of the reasons why he felt it took so long for him to bring the film to fruition. He says that he wrote a partial draft of an adaptation with his co-writer Jay Cocks in the early 1990s, but then stopped and it took them a number of years to go back to it. When he did finally return to the script he felt that:

> I was going off on tangents about the Jesuits, the political situation, all of that, and I needed to distil it down . . . to the essential. (Scorsese in Horne 2017, 19)

For Scorsese this "essential" appears to be specifically theological. However, there is no pure kernel of theology in this narrative, it is about both an individual man's and a European empire's constructions of religion, race, and power. It is about the connection between white male European identity and Catholic Christianity within a seemingly alien environment, among a people (the Japanese) who are constructed as an alien and different race.

Rodrigues enters this narrative with a clear aim to be a white savior of souls (Yamato 2016; Hughey 2016). Indeed, he finds his most satisfying role when covertly providing his priestly services to Christians held in a Nagasaki prison, where the threat of their torture and execution is ever present. In his final dilemma—between martyrdom or apostasy—either decision he makes allows him to fulfill such a destiny within this colonizing context. The twist of this story, though, is the subtlety of becoming this white savior—

he saves the Christian villagers by choosing to renounce his own religion, that is by apostatizing. This is what Scorsese interprets (as quoted earlier) as the "breaking down" of the colonial violence, which perhaps in 2016 was seen as the ultimate form of white savior. In this respect, by "losing his arrogance" and accepting the need to apostatize, Rodrigues is portrayed as bringing peace and ending the cycle of violence instigated by the Europeans' invasion.

The focus on Rodrigues is part of the faithfulness of the film to the original novel. But it does put at a distance the complexities of the people this European Christian missionary had traveled so far to serve. In a film of over two and a half hours there is not enough space to provide a deep characterization on any of the Japanese characters, despite an excellent cast of actors who succeed in bringing some humorous relief to the density of the narrative. Kichijiro is the most complex of characters, but, as noted, he is mostly a vehicle for the protagonist Rodrigues.

In a film which is about the historic (largely unsuccessful) enculturation of Catholic Christianity into Japan, there is surprisingly little discussion— both within the film and in the reviews of its theology—of what this may have entailed (what Scorsese means with his phrase "the political situation, all of that," Horne 2017, 19). This is even more surprising, since the exploration of the hidden Christians (*kakase kirishitan*) is one of the main concerns of Endo's novel. To an extent it is possible to argue that the extensive scenes in the first half of the film—of the Tomogi and Goto villagers' interactions with Rodrigues and Garupe as their priests—fulfil this role, but the filming remains very much from the Europeans' perspectives (the white/colonial gaze, cf., Ram 2018; hooks 1992). And these scenes very soon become drowned out (quite literally) by the exploration of Rodrigues's angst about faith and his response to suffering. The theme is later taken up by the two colonialists' (i.e., Rodrigues and Ferreira's) discussion during their eventual encounter at a Buddhist temple, in which Ferreira makes the claim (after his many years living in Japan) that the (colonizing) Jesuit venture of establishing Christianity in the country was doomed to failure.

Ferreira likens Japan to a "swamp," in which the roots of Christianity cannot "take root," since they will always rot away. Even the Christian communities that flourished briefly around Nagasaki in the mid-sixteenth century were not successful, since Ferreira argues that their faith was based on falsehoods and misunderstandings. In particular, this Portuguese former Jesuit priest argues that the Japanese are not culturally disposed to Christianity, since they are more interested in ideas of humanness rather than divinity. And so Ferreira claims:

> The Japanese cannot think of an existence beyond the realm of nature. For them, nothing transcends the human. They can't conceive of our idea of the Christian God.

Indeed, these are words put into Ferreira's mouth by the Japanese writer Endo (perhaps ironically), who was himself both Japanese and a Catholic. We then read them through the English-language translation of Endo's novel, and then Scorsese's dramatic visualization of the viewpoint that Endo is trying to explore. The subtlety of this point—that is, that the Western viewer's understanding of what perhaps Endo is trying to suggest by having a Christian colonizer making such a claim about "the Japanese"—is lost in its translation onto the screen by Scorsese and delivered by the actor Liam Neeson (in this case, the white/colonial gaze of the director and the lead actor is presumed as shared by the audience). There is little scope for the exploration of the agency of the actual *Japanese* Christians within this movie: the heavy work of exploring God, faith, and Christian theology in this film is all done by the white Jesuit priest Rodrigues.

This point is echoed in Rodrigues's final scene with the Inquisitor, when Inoue tells the apostatized priest that Christians in the villages (i.e., where he had stayed) would be allowed to "continue to be Christian . . . because the roots are cut." Rodrigues's response is simple, echoing Ferreira: "Nothing grows in a swamp." Then Inoue concludes:

Yes, Japan is that kind of country. The religion of the Christian, that you brought us, has become a strange thing. It's changed. . . .

You were not defeated by me, you were defeated by this swamp of Japan.

Some reviewers of the film have noted the short scene when, just before his betrayal and capture, Rodrigues looks at his reflection in a river and sees the face of Christ looking back. Needless to say, the representation of this face is one the white viewer will find familiar; it is a stereotypical white/European Jesus (blond hair, dark blue eyes, with the image taken from El-Greco's *Veil of Veronica*). He describes this face later as "the one I remember from childhood." In many respects, this could be argued to be historically accurate—after all, most Christian colonizers, the Jesuits included, did largely promote the image of Jesus as visually white European (Blum and Harvey 2012; Cone 1990). And it could be argued that if Scorsese had sought to question and explore this point, and instead presented an image of the reflected Christ as Japanese rather than European, then it may have been confusing for his (presumed white) audience (although it could have been done). Without this though, the narrative of the film—and, with it, its theology—becomes very obviously particularized by race: how this white man racializes himself *and* Jesus in an "alien" world defined by colonialism.

However, the film makes an important contrast between this and the image of Christ in the *fumie*—that is, the depiction which is presented to Rodrigues to step on for his apostatizing. In this case, the image is not so identifiable as a white Jesus, but instead it is molded in a more stylized form by a Japanese (not necessarily European) visualization. This contrast between the two racialized forms of Jesus—as white European and as Japanese—is not an accident, and of course would have been a deliberate decision of the director. In many respects, the contrast is part of the narrative transformation of Rodrigues, with respect to his own transition of faith. As Endo wrote on this particular point in his novel *Silence*:

> [T]o me the most meaningful thing in the novel is the change in the hero's image of Christ. The hero, a foreigner, believed in a Jesus of majesty and power, an orderly Jesus who was even governed by order. This was the image conceived by Western artists . . . After suffering many trials and frustrations, however, he was caught at last and brought before the *Fumie*. . . Standing there he saw an image of Christ he had never seen before, an image shaped by Japanese hands. It was not the orderly, European, but the worn out face of a Christ suffering as we suffer. (Endo 1974, 181, quoted in Ng 2019, 6)

That is, this racializing of the image of Christ was in itself a very significant issue for the author Endo, and it was conveyed in Scorsese's adaptation (whether knowingly or not is hard to gauge). Although neither Endo nor Scorsese specifically talks about this in terms of race and colonialism, of course Scorsese did become aware (after the film's release) that this is an issue for at least some Christian priests from the Global South—that is, colonialism was (and continues to be) a relationship of violence (as noted earlier, in Horne 2017, 22).

In Scorsese's film, there is another representation of this contrast that is not conveyed in the book. That is, during the scene when Rodrigues apostatizes, Jesus is represented not only in the (Japanese style) picture on which Rodrigues steps but also through a voice: the voice of the actor Ciaran Hinds, speaking in American English, and so is clearly racialized as white. And as he hears this, the image of El-Greco's white Jesus is flashed momentarily onto the screen. This is a subtle point, but the contrast becomes more complex: for Rodrigues, the "true" Jesus (who tells him to step on the *fumie* image) is white, even though the Jesus of the image he treads upon is not.

Conclusion: The Silence of Whiteness

In some respects, Scorsese's *Silence* presents a counterpoint to Francis Ford Coppola's (1979) film about European colonialism in east Asia, that is, *Apocalypse Now*—itself well known as an exploration of Joseph Conrad's (1899) book *Heart of Darkness*. But unlike these earlier critiques of empire, in *Silence* the narrative finds such a "heart of darkness" in the colonized, not the colonizer, and the final encounter (with Kurtz) is not with a man of evil, but with the broken priest who was once called Ferreira. The well-meaning, but earnest (and inevitably misguided), religious colonists do not appear to bring with them any violence, only a naive certainty and faith in their faith, which is apparently destined for failure in the perceived "mudswamp" of an alien culture. This is a colonialism that the white North American audience would apparently prefer to see—one that is harmless and not violent (at least not by the colonizers), that may be challenging but which brings with it some useful spiritual lessons.

In this film, Scorsese has brought alive on the screen a narrative of religion, doubt, and silence—about compromising faith in difficult and trying times. This is how most critics have read the film, in terms of the script and also in terms of the narration and characterization of Rodrigues (and Ferreira). The final image also validates the central compromise of the story (i.e., Rodrigues's decision to apostatize). After many years of living as a Buddhist scholar with a Japanese identity, Rodrigues dies and is cremated according to Japanese Buddhist tradition. But the camera reveals in a final shot the presence of a small cross hidden by his widow in his hand (this "twist" is an addition to the movie; it is not part of Endo's book). This subtle, but significant, revelation evokes a number of previous close-up shots (particularly during earlier scenes with the Christian villagers) of simple crosses being placed into hands as a form of faith and ministry. Concluding on this image suggests to the audience that Rodrigues's apostasy, the stepping on the *fumie*, and all the subsequent compromises he made to the Japanese state were not "real" or intended. He kept his faith (inwardly and hidden), even though on the outside there was no indication. What was in his heart is taken to be what matters—and in doing so, the film fails to recognize the much wider issues of race and empire that frame Rodrigues's faith, action, and arrogance.

Although Scorsese's adaptation is a faithful exploration of Endo's novel, the American director failed to provide the required nuance of translating the story away from the specific Asian contexts of Endo's writing. Endo's aim was not to present an American audience with a tale of early European colonialism, but instead to present a hidden history of Catholic identity within Japan amid the ebbs and flows of colonialism. Thus, the anomaly at the heart of this movie is Scorsese's (and his audience's) sense of innocence in assuming that a white director (with a formidable reputation for portraying American white identities) could make a film adaptation of a Japanese novelist's work without bringing multiple layers of whiteness, race, and colonialism to the film.

CHAPTER 5

We Haven't Located Us Yet:

The Mystic East in Wes Anderson's
The Darjeeling Limited (2007)

Michael J. Altman

It is important that they are named Whitman. Like the poet Walt Whitman, the three Whitman brothers in Wes Anderson's *The Darjeeling Limited* go on a passage to India and, like Whitman, it is a spiritual journey, "a passage to more than India!" In the film the three brothers—Francis, Peter, and Jack—meet up on a train a year after their father's funeral to travel across India together. Later, Francis, the oldest brother and organizer of the trip, reveals that their mother is in India and that the brothers are going to find her and bring her home. The plot of the film weaves together the stunted relationships of the Whitman family and the brothers' search for spiritual understanding across a backdrop of a colorful, exotic, and mystical India. Through its story of three brothers finding their spirituality and each other as they travel across India, *The Darjeeling Limited* is one example of the "mystic east," a representation of a land distant from Europe and America full of spiritual significance and transformative power where Western protagonists can find themselves.

The three brothers board the train distant and distraught. They have not spoken since their father's funeral. They have grown apart in the wake of their father's death. They have also lost their own way. Francis is bandaged up from a motorcycle accident that we later learn he caused on purpose, Jack has just broken up with his girlfriend, and Peter is unsure about his wife's pregnancy and his impending child. Francis Whitman lays out a combination of fraternal bonding and spiritual self-discovery as the goal of the trip early in the film:

> FRANCIS: How'd it get to this? Why haven't we spoken in a year? Let's make an agreement.
> JACK: Ok.
> PETER: To do what?
> FRANCIS: A.) I want us to become brothers again like we used to be, and for us to find ourselves and bond with each other. Can we agree to that?
> PETER: OK
> JACK: Yeah.
> FRANCIS: B.) I want us to make this trip a spiritual journey, and for us to seek the unknown and learn about it. Can we agree to that?
> PETER: I guess so.
> JACK: Sure.
> FRANCIS: C.) I want us to be completely open and say yes to everything, even if it's shocking and painful. Can we agree to that? . . . I had Brendan make us an itinerary. (Anderson 2010)

The train journey is meant to reunite the brothers with each other and help them rediscover themselves.

As Francis's last line about the itinerary shows, it is the places they visit, the setting, that should achieve these aims. The Indian setting is central to this process of reunion and self-discovery. The three Western brothers move through their journey always at a distance from the locals around them. Their language, their dress, their movement, and their physical appearance always set them off and apart. As film scholar Mark Browning writes, "it is resolutely a Western view of a mysterious, unknowable culture . . . this lack of knowledge leads the brothers to see the country as purely exotic and in sensual terms" (Browning 2011, 79). They visit temples, ring bells, and keep trying to execute a peacock feather ritual in search of the "spiritual" but can never quite find it. Nevertheless, the brothers believe it must lie somewhere in that country. They rely on the power of the "mystic east" they travel through to mend their relationships and their selves.

Hipster Travel through the Mystic East

The representation of the "mystic east" consists of two pieces. First, there is the representation of "the East" as a place, a location, a site outside of the "the West." In his foundational work, *Orientalism*, literary theorist Edward Said coined the term "Orientalism" to, in part, describe the positing of an essential opposition between East and West. As Said writes, "Orientalism is a style of thought based upon an ontological and epistemological distinction made between 'the Orient' and (most of the time) 'the Occident'" (Said 1979, 2). Said points out that there is no "West" without an East against which to define itself. Additionally, Said argues that this East/West distinction has not been equal. "European culture gained strength and identity by setting itself off again the Orient as a sort of surrogate and even underground self" (Said 1979, 3). Just as the Whitmans hope to discover themselves in the East, the West has discovered itself through "dealing with the Orient—dealing with it by making statements about it, authorizing views of it, describing it, by teaching it, settling it, ruling over it" (Said 1979, 3). Thus, the distinction between East and West is not merely geographic or directional; it is cultural, racial, intellectual, and political. It is also, as Said argues, the construction of Western writers, travelers, missionaries, and governments.

The "mystical" makes up the second piece of the "mystic east." The East has not always been represented as mystical by the West, but the notion of its inherent mysticism is a common trope in Orientalist representations. Religious studies scholar Richard King describes how the European Enlightenment's championing of reason in the eighteenth century shaped understandings of "the mystical" in the modern West. "Mysticism comes to represent the preeminently private, the non-rational and the quietistic. As such it represents the suppressed Other that contributes to the establishment of and high status of those spheres of human activity that are defined as public, rational, and socially oriented" (King 1999, 26). The European Enlightenment thus set up a dyad between the mystical/irrational/individual/private and enlightened/rational/public/social. This dualism has political implications, as it renders all things labeled "mystical" as "largely uninterested in or antithetical to social, ecclesiastical and political authority" (King 1999, 33). The "mystical" cannot be political, in this view.

The "mystic East" representation lays both of these pieces on top of each other. It marks off East and West, defines them in opposition, and classifies the East as mystical. The classification of the East as mystical is a political act that has shaped Western representations of India. As King writes, "the association of religions such as Hinduism and Buddhism with mysticism and the stereotype of the navel-gazing, antisocial and otherworldly mystic has come to function as one of the most prevailing cultural representations of Indian religion and culture in the last few centuries" (King 1999, 33). Classified as "mystical," India and its people are either uninterested or unable to engage politically and thus British colonialism in India is both warranted and necessary. Representations of the "mystical East" in European and American culture presented a land where rational Westerners could go and rediscover their private, interior, selves without engaging the larger society, culture, or people. The "mystic East" represents the East as a place that exists for the benefit of Western spirituality.

The representation of the "mystic East" has a long history in the West, especially with regard to India. Historian Ronald Inden has argued that the mystical representation of India began with the earliest academic studies of India by Romantic German scholars of the early nineteenth century (Inden 2011, 66-74). These scholars, frustrated by the utilitarianism of Western philosophy, sought out a more spiritual and ideal philosophy and found things they appreciated in Indian thought. For example, German philosopher Friedrich Schlegel (1772–1829) described how "Hindoos" in India possess an "absorption of all thought and all consciousness in God—this solitary enduring feeling of internal and eternal union with the Deity . . . this same philosophy, though in a different form, which in the history of European intellect and science, has received the denomination of *mysticism*" (Inden 1990, 68).[1] As Inden notes, these early German representations paved the way for all the images of mystic India to come. "The endless stream of studies of myths and the myriad portrayals of a mysterious India that reveals layers of the psyche, all have their ancestry here" (Inden 1990, 96).

The stream of early European academic representations of mystic India trickled down all the way to the earliest American films. In the beginning, it spread to the United States and influenced Romantic and metaphysical groups like the Transcendentalists and Theosophical Society (Albanese 2007, 330-93). Representations of "mystical India" also appeared in descriptions of India in American schoolbooks and popular magazines (Altman 2017). By the turn of the twentieth century, the representation of mystic India appeared in the earliest American films. Thomas Edison's 1902 short film *Hindoo Fakir* depicts a man in a vaguely "eastern" costume and set performing a series of magic tricks with a female assistant that culminate in him turning her into a butterfly. Edison used the "fakir's" magic to display his own new film tricks, including superimposing a flower over the woman as she makes her butterfly transformation.[2] In the *Hindoo Fakir* the East is the land of mystical and magical powers performed by "Hindoo" adepts. The *Hindoo Fakir* is the first in a long line of representations in American popular culture of what Jane Iwamura calls the "Oriental monk," a mystical Eastern man who travels West to spread Eastern wisdom. Iwamura traces this Oriental monk figure across American media from the 1970s television show *Kung Fu* to the *Kung Fu Panda* series of children's films. American films ranging from *Ace Ventura: When Nature Calls* (1995) to *Bulletproof Monk* (2003), *Holy Smoke* (1999), and *The Forbidden Kingdom* (2008) include Oriental monk characters. From *Hindoo Fakir* to *Kung Fu Panda*, American audiences have long encountered the "Oriental monk" and the "mystic East" (Iwamura 2011).

While Jane Iwamura focused attention on the figure of the Oriental monk, *The Darjeeling Limited* requires consideration of the space of the "mystic East" and the role of travel in Orientalist representation and European colonialism. As writer Emily May has pointed out, the film takes the genre of the classic American road movie, best exemplified by *Easy Rider*, and gives it a new spiritual purpose. "Viewing *The Darjeeling Limited* as an update of the classic American road movie suggests that America is no longer a spiritual place of discovery, but a land of people who feel they must venture far outside of it to find a sense of truth" (May 2009). *Darjeeling* is a spiritual road movie through the mystic East aboard a train.

As a spiritual road trip through the mystic East, the film must be understood with the long-standing relationship between travel and imperialism in India.[3] Beginning with British imperial expeditions in the eighteenth and nineteenth centuries and lasting through the so-called hippie trail of the 1960s–1970s, Western travel across India has always extended Western colonial and postcolonial power. As historian Agnieszka Sobocinska has argued regarding the "hippie trail," postcolonial tourist travel "helped translate colonial cultures into postcolonial contexts, extending the long genealogy of imperial travel to the travellers' colonies of present-day Asia" (Sobocinska 2014). The Whitman brothers represent an updated form of the "hippie trail." They share the main features of hippie travel Sobocinska identifies:

As well as being motivated by colonial discourses of adventure, the Hippie Trail was literally enabled by infrastructure built under European colonialism and American neo-imperialism. On the road, travelers developed a strong in-group identity and a binding travel culture that helped determine what travelers wore, what they packed, and where they went. It also mediated the extent of traveler's contact with locals, and helped shape their opinions about Asia more generally . . . It instituted a firm divide between Westerners and locals, and encouraged travelers to take the markers for appropriate behavior from each other rather than adhering to local mores. (Sobocinska 2014)

The Whitmans travel by train, the great British colonial infrastructure project. Their trip brings them together as an "in-group" with a shared identity, shared Western dress (even going about in their individual sleepwear), and shared luggage. They have limited and shallow contact with locals. They act in ways that are ridiculously inappropriate to the locals—bringing a deadly snake on a train, constant doses of painkillers, fist fighting on the train—but that seem appropriate to themselves. The Whitmans engage in a kind of "hipster" travel that puts an upper-class veneer on the older hippie trail. The "hippie trail" grew out of the countercultural dissatisfaction with the conservatism of society in the 1960s and 1970s, but the Whitmans' "hipster travel" has its motivations in the personal doubts, restless boredom, and individual discontent of a white privileged class.

Failing to Locate Us in the Mystic East

The Whitman brothers' spiritual journey to the "mystic East" in *Darjeeling* can be traced through three major plot devices in the film: the funeral for a young boy, the visits to temples, and the attempts at a ritual with a peacock feather. The funeral is the transformative pivot of the film, while the temple visits and peacock rituals both occur before and after the funeral. The differences between the temple visits and rituals before the funeral and the ones after the funeral show how transformative the funeral is for the brothers. Taken together these three devices construct the story of the Whitman brothers searching for "spirituality" in the mystic East, struggling to find it, and then, finally, reaching a moment of personal and spiritual transformation. Through the temples, the feather rituals, and the funerals, the film tells the story of three Americans who find themselves and their relationship with each other through a spiritual journey East.

The brothers' search for spirituality at Indian temples is a failure at first. Two visits to temples for some sort of "spiritual" experience fall flat. The first temple scene happens just after Jack gets off the train briefly to surreptitiously check his ex-girlfriend's phone messages. He walks back into the compartment depressed and feeling bad about himself. After getting Jack to smash a bottle of the girlfriend's perfume she left in Jack's bag, Francis looks ahead to the next stop on the train for a solution.

> FRANCIS: Ok, here we go: the train stops first thing tomorrow morning for an hour and forty-five minutes, which is just enough time for a quick visit to the Temple of a Thousand Bulls, probably one of the most spiritual places in the entire world. (Anderson 2010)

The scene in the Indian town and village opens with a shot from high above the town's skyline that then zooms down to the open-air market where the three brothers arrive. This shot is borrowed from the opening shot of the 1970 James Ivory film *Bombay Talkie*, which zooms down from the Bombay skyline to a group of men running through the street with a title sign for the film. The scene also uses the title music from *Talkie* as the background for the scene.[4] The brothers scatter to different stalls at the market. Francis looks for a power adapter. Jack buys pepper spray and fireworks. Peter buys a poisonous snake. Then they reconvene in front of the temple, arms full of their purchases. "This is incredible!" Francis remarks when they arrive. They receive a *tilaka*, or symbolic mark, on their forehead as they enter the temple, ring a bell, and offer rupees to the deity. Then as they settle down to pray, they find that they can't stop bickering. Their own interpersonal conflicts disrupt the prayers. Peter leaves to "go pray at a different thing." The spiritual experience never gets off the ground. Even the shot of Peter praying at the end of the scene, where he sits with his hands together and eyes closed in a peaceful pose, is disrupted by the child holding a pistol in the lower right corner of the shot. The shallowness of the experience is summed up when the brothers emerge back onto the street after leaving the temple:

FRANCIS: Wow! Right?
JACK: Yea. Great.
PETER: Amazing.
FRANCIS: Let's get a shoe shine. (Anderson 2010)

The Temple of a Thousand Bulls may not be the most spiritual place in the world after all.

The second visit the brothers make to a temple is similarly ineffective. Having been nearly kicked off the train for bringing Peter's poisonous snake aboard and accidentally letting it loose, the brothers visit a Sikh temple at the next stop. This visit follows immediately after their run in with the Sikh chief steward who catches the poisonous snake armed with only a spatula. The Sikh steward walks out of the train compartment and then the film cuts to the Sikh temple immediately. From one turbaned Sikh to a roomful. This scene is more intimate. The singers on a raised dais up front, the artwork on the walls, and the sound of the singing build a sense of community that the brothers are encroaching upon. As the camera slides to the left and the shot rests on the back of the three white brothers with jewel-toned bandanas on their heads. The visitors stand out in contrast to the turbans of the men surrounding them. They sit with their hands together in a posture unlike anything the Sikhs around them are in. They glance around the room trying to figure out exactly where they are. The scene cuts to a shot of a print depicting the martyrdom of Bhai Taru Singh, a Sikh whose scalp was cut off with an axe because he refused to convert to Islam. The pause on that bloody image highlights the real cost of the community they have stumbled into. This community has paid a price for the worship they now enjoy. The brothers have paid nothing and so they experience nothing. The ideal of martyrdom, of self-sacrifice, is an anathema for them. They bend forward and lay their foreheads on the floor. "Do you think it's working? Do you feel something?" Jack asks. "I hope so," says Peter. "It's got to," Francis replies. But, as the next scenes show, it does not work.

The morning after the Sikh temple, the brothers awake to find that the train is lost. "How can a train be lost, it's on rails?" asks Jack. Brendan, Francis's assistant, explains that the train took a wrong turn overnight. When Jack asks how far off course the train is, Brendan replies, "Nobody knows. We haven't located us yet." That sentence strikes Francis. "Is that symbolic?! We. Haven't. Located. Us. Yet!" he exclaims. This is the central problem of the film. The goal of the spiritual journey is for the brother to locate "us," to become an "us," instead of the three separate individuals that have not spoken in a year.

Francis's "we haven't located us yet" epiphany prompts him to enlist his brothers in a peacock feather ritual. Brendan gives him an envelope with instructions and three peacock feathers for carrying out a spiritual ritual he got from a "guru." While the train is stopped the three brothers run up the side of a hill to perform the ritual together. But it does not work. Instead of performing the ritual, Francis confesses the real reason he asked his brothers to come to India: to find their mother who has become a Catholic nun in a Himalayan convent and bring her home. Peter and Jack laugh sardonically and Peter says, "You didn't tell us because we never would have come here if we knew about it." Then the train horn sounds and the three brothers have to rush down the hill back to the train. Francis's dissemblance and confession prove to be the breaking point in the brothers' trip on the train. The simmering frustration and distrust blow up into a wrestling fight between Francis and Peter. Jack sprays his recently purchased pepper spray in both their faces (with the great line "I love you too but I'm going to mace you in the face"), they are kicked off the train by the steward, and Francis insults Brendan so he quits. The spiritual journey is now off track.

Sitting around a campfire, in the middle of nowhere, surrounded by their baggage (a physical depiction of their emotional state), without Brendan (the symbol of order who maintained the itinerary of their trip), drinking cough syrup and painkillers to get high, the brothers talk about how their mother probably does not want to see them after all. Jack asks, "Maybe this is how it's supposed to happen. It could all be part of it. Maybe this is where the spiritual journey ends." And then Francis passes out the peacock feathers one more time. This is it. This is their big attempt to find the spiritual experience. They spread out around the campfire, each holding a torch, and for about five seconds they make some noises and do some gestures. When they come back to the campfire together they realize that they all did the ritual differently. Jack blew away his feather. Francis buried his. Peter still has his. "You guys didn't do it right," Francis laments. "I tried my hardest. I don't know what else to do." The spiritual journey has failed.

The campfire scene comes almost exactly halfway through the film, and it shows how the journey to the mystic East is doomed. Anderson shows how simply going to temples or enacting rituals given to one in a manila envelope will not give a person the spiritual experience they desire. There is no itinerary for a spiritual journey. The Temple of a Thousand Bulls may be the most spiritual place on earth, the Sikh community may sing together, there may be something mystical to the peacock feather, and the East may be mystic but simply going there and doing that will not be enough. The spiritual journey East requires something else to truly transform, the film argues.

The Funeral as Spiritual Experience

The brothers' unplanned visit to a small village and attendance at a funeral is the real transformative spiritual experience in the film. The morning after the campfire scene the brothers are walking by a rushing river when they come across three boys trying to cross it who fall in. The three brothers jump in to save them—each trying to grab one of the boys. Jack and Francis manage to rescue one boy each, but Peter and the boy he tries to save are washed down the river. The boy dies, and Peter is beaten and bloodied by the rocks in the water. The brothers and the two boys walk back the boys' village with Peter carrying the dead boy in his arms and find themselves welcomed into the village.

The time in the village and the funeral, not the temples and rituals, actually transforms the brothers. During their time in the village, with their baggage stacked up just outside the village (a little too on the nose, perhaps), the brothers do everything they could not do earlier in the film. The shot of Peter bleeding from the head and holding the dead boy in his arms gestures back to the bloody image of the Sikh martyr and the level of self-sacrifice that the selfish Whitmans could not display earlier. In the village, the brothers change out of their Western suits, the pace of the shots slow down, the brothers move slowly as they interact with the villagers while the villagers move rapidly around them trying to tend to their injuries and the dead boy. Where they were on the outside of the Sikh temple worship, they are now participating in the life of the village. After leaving the Temple of a Thousand Bulls, Peter admits he is scared of becoming a father; in the village he holds a baby. The village is a place where the first half of the film is flipped into reverse.

The funeral for the boy is the spiritual experience the Whitmans have been looking for. Just before the brothers are invited to the funeral a man on a bus asks Francis, "what are you doing in this place." "Well, originally, I guess, we came here on a spiritual journey, but that didn't really pan out," Francis responds. In the next scene, Anderson signals that something about the funeral is different from the rest of the places on the trip, as the brothers emerge from a small house in the village, not in their suits or odd sleepwear, but in white. They walk through the funeral attendants in slow motion, accentuating the scene for the viewer and in stark contrast to the business of the temple scenes. Instead of the score of an Indian film, the shot is scored with the Kink's song "Stranger" and its lyrics, "we are not two, we are one." During the funeral for the boy the film cuts to a flashback of the time just before the funeral for the brothers' father and their attempt to retrieve his car from a mechanic's garage. This is what needs to be dealt with for the brothers to "locate us" and no temple or feather ritual is going to solve it. The Whitmans watch the funeral and the father's grief, he nearly passes out in the river bathing after the funeral. It is unclear what happens to them at the funeral but something does change and the connections between the funeral for the father of three brothers and the father's grief during the funeral for his son, one of three brothers, are clear. The brothers do not bicker during the funeral. They are not distracted. They do not stand out either, as their white clothes match the rest of the funeral party. This, it seems, is the real spiritual experience of the film.

The shot of the brothers just before they board the bust to leave after the funeral emphasizes the spiritual experience. The whole village turns out to send them off and offers a prayer over them as the bus approaches. Anderson uses a three-shot of the brothers with their hands together in prayer looking at the assembled village. This is the spiritual moment. It mirrors the three-shot in the first temple that led to an argument and Peter walking away. But this time they are not facing a deity; they are facing a community—a community they had been welcomed into. Then the music from *Bombay Talkie* begins playing again, the same music that opened the market scene before the first temple. In the bus we get another three-shot of the brothers sharing the same seat. This shot on the one hand points back to the three-shot of the brothers in the back of the limo before their father's funeral but also counters the shots throughout the train scenes where they are separated on different sides of the compartment or different bunks. The bus is the opposite of the train. It is a space where they share the same seat together, and it is not confined to the itinerary of the tracks. Inside the bus they have located "us."

The transformation that occurs at the funeral is not total, but it is significant. In the second half of the film the brothers are still selfish at times, and certainly imperfect, but they are better and they do act together. This transformation is summed up well in the scene in the airport bathroom when Francis takes off his bandages in the mirror.

> FRANCIS: I guess I've still got some more healing to do
> JACK: You're getting there though
> PETER: Anyway, it's definitely going to add a lot of character to you.
> (Anderson 2010)

The brothers find some healing on their trip but not on the train, not on the tracks. Rather, it is when they get lost, get off track, stumble into the desert together, make an act of self-sacrifice, and encounter the community of the village that they begin to find some healing from their father's death.

The spiritual transformation can also be seen in the differences between the temple scene and the peacock ritual scene after the funeral from those before it. The brothers stop at a small temple in the airport before they plan on flying home. The airport scene uses the same music from *Bombay Talkie* as the market but reverses much from that first temple visit. At the airport, Francis gives Peter the belt that he had taken from Peter at the first temple when Peter borrowed it without asking. Where the three brothers had scattered in the market, they stay together at the airport. Then they go to the airport temple, a small shrine along the wall. Jack applies the *tilaka* to his two brothers and asks, "what should we pray for now?" That is it. The film cuts to the brothers heading to board the airplane where they then all decide not to leave but to go find their mother in a convent in the Himalayas.

The airport temple visit stands out because of how different it is from the first two. There are no other people there. During the visit to the Temple of a Thousand Bulls the brothers are surrounded by local men, women, and children. They stand out as visitors, outsiders, and Westerners. Similarly, though there is a closeness and intimacy to the gathering at the Sikh temple, it is an intimacy and closeness they are not privy to. In the first two temple visits the brothers are each individual looking for something for themselves. They bicker. They hope to feel something. But nothing happens. At the airport temple, they sit down together as a group without anyone else around. In the first temple, the scene is shot from the perspective of the deity, with the brothers look toward the camera up at the image of the god. In the airport temple, the scene is shot from behind the brothers. The brothers, together, turn their backs to the camera and look toward the god in the shrine. Now the viewer is on the outside. Rather than searching for something "spiritual," they now cannot think of anything to pray for. Having passed through the experience of the village funeral, the brothers come out the other side able to pray at the airport temple and feeling that they have reached a new intimacy with each other.

Similarly, after the transformation of the funeral, the brothers are able to successfully execute the peacock feather ritual. Having visited their mother at a Himalayan convent they wake up the next morning and she is gone without telling her why she left or where she went. As they sit down for breakfast, Francis grabs the lone peacock feather they have left. The brothers climb up to the top of a mountain and try the ritual one more time. This time they do it together. One at a time they go through some motions and make a noise passing the ritual from Francis to Peter to Jack—from oldest to youngest. Then they come together and blow on the feather together. From three separate feathers in the first and second attempts to one feather at the end. The first attempt ended with an argument about their mother. The final ritual happens after they come to grips with her leaving. After they blow on the feather, they place it under a small pyramid of rocks and give each other a knowing set of smiles. The camera pans back from the three brothers on top of the mountain to reveal the whole mountain, leaving the brothers indistinguishably small. Finally, having let their mother go, having gotten off the tracks, having experienced the transformation of the funeral, they have found it. They have located "us."

Here the film tracks closely with the message of the 2010 biographical romantic drama *Eat, Pray, Love*, based on the memoir by Elizabeth Gilbert. The film follows Gilbert on a trip of self-discovery and spirituality that takes her to India (the "pray" part of the story.) In *Eat, Pray, Love*, "Hindu India is produced by the white woman as a source of feminine healing and regulation" (Chandra 2015, 489). As Shefali Chandra has argued, a number of films produced after September 11, 2001, construct India this way.

"Skillfully navigating between twentieth-century imperial history, the rise of the War on Terror, and a barely contained obsession with Hindu female sexuality, each of these texts is driven by the conviction that India, and Indian women, will heal the mind and body of the white woman" (Chandra 2015, 488). But in *The Darjeeling Limited* it is the male soul and brotherly fraternity that is healed through the encounter with an Indian father. *Eat, Pray, Love* tells the story of a white woman finding "me," while *The Darjeeling Limited* tells the story of white men finding "us." Either way, India is rendered as the land of spiritual renewal and self-discovery.

Conclusion: The Hipster Orientalism of *The Darjeeling Limited*

The Whitman brothers, like many Westerners before them, travel to the mystic East in search of a spiritual transformation and they find it. But to what extent does *The Darjeeling Limited* merely reproduce Orientalist representations of India and the "East" and to what extent is it a lampooning of those representations? Is this film consonant with *Eat, Pray, Love* or making fun of it? The Whitman brothers travel on the railroad, the most enduring colonial transportation technology. The only Indian characters in the film are the steward and Rita, the attendant whom Jack has sex with in the train's bathroom. The rest of the non-white, non-Western characters live in the background of the film for the most part. When they do step out of the background, as the father does at the village funeral, it is so his performance of grief can transform the Whitmans. The film reinforces white privilege, some scholars have observed (Dean-Ruzicka 2013, 25–40). But on the other hand, the Whitman brothers are terrible people. They are not noble Westerners. They are the butt of the jokes. Their hipster travel to the East comes off as self-indulgent. If these are neocolonial Westerners re-enacting an imperial journey to the spiritual East, they are not to be taken too seriously. The film is a farcical lampooning of Western Orientalist tropes, the argument goes (Bose 2008, 1-8). The film can be read from opposite directions.

The ambivalence is the point, in my reading. *The Darjeeling Limited* works through a kind of "hipster Orientalism" that knows the problems of its Orientalist representations but also trusts the audience to know not to take such representations too seriously. It lacks all of Elizabeth Gilbert's genuineness. This hipster Orientalism is similar to the "hipster racism" and "hipster sexism" debated in popular culture in the past two decades. "Hipster racism," first coined in 2006 by Carmen Van Kerckhove in a nearly impossible to find blog post, refers to the idea that one is "too hip and self-aware to actually mean the racist stuff one expresses" (Dubrofsky & Wood 2014, 282–87). Likewise Cheris Brewer Current and Emily Tillotson describe how high school students they studied "see their expression of racist or sexist practices as quaint or ironic, and as signs that they have enough cultural capital to reference historical events or practices that pre-dated their own births" (Current & Tillotson 2018, 467–76). Like hipster sexism or hipster racism, the Orientalist tropes in *The Darjeeling Limited* are tongue-in-cheek and come with a wink. This may be the way Orientalism appears in film in the twenty-first century, not through Edison's mystical fakir, but through Anderson's farcical mystic East.

CHAPTER 6

Lost in Žižek, Redeemed in *Cloud Atlas* (2012):

Buddhism and Other Tales of "Asian Religions" in Western Cinema and Affective Circulation

Ting Guo

Slavoj Žižek's recent critique of Buddhism as a form of nihilism has arguably highlighted the debate among scholars of religion, cultural theorists, and film critics regarding the way Buddhism has been represented in cinemas since the beginning of the twentieth century. In an article titled "From Western Marxism to Western Buddhism," Žižek argues that Buddhism is part of the "strange exchange" between East and the West, as Buddhism and other Asian religions have effectively become the nihilistic ideology for global capitalism and threaten the legacy of Judeo-Christianity in the post-secular West. As he writes,

> The Judeo-Christian legacy is threatened in the European space itself by the onslaught of New Age "Asiatic" thought, which, in its different guises, ranging from "Western Buddhism" . . . to different "Taos," is establishing itself as the hegemonic ideology of global capitalism. (Žižek 2006: 252)

According to Žižek, Buddhism in the West is a rather recent product of pop culture that fulfills various ideological functions to preserve the global dominance of capitalism. By preaching inner peace, it teaches its consumers to distance themselves from market competition while also encouraging them to take part in such competition more fully with the pretense of mental sanity. It is in this way that he claims Buddhism has emerged as the "paradigmatic ideology" of late capitalism. In the context of global capitalism today, Žižek claims that Max Weber's famous work, *Protestant Ethic and the Spirit of Capitalism* should more effectively be re-titled as *The Taoist Ethic and the Spirit of Global Capitalism* (Žižek 2001).

Of course, Žižek is right that Buddhism in the West is a product of pop culture, but he somewhat misses the mark in wanting to reduce Buddhism and its influence upon the West to a nihilist agent that supports global capitalism. In fact, if he wants to understand the hegemonic ideology of global capitalism he should be looking at the Judeo-Christian legacy and the Humanist values this legacy projects in its various pop culture forms, and not cast blame on Buddhism as if it were some "yellow peril" that threatened the West as an adopted cultural supplement.

What I want to achieve in this chapter is to clarify both Žižek's critique and my opposition to it through a grounded analysis of the film *Cloud Atlas* (2012). I want to point out how both the philosophical and cinematic representation of Buddhism in the West are basically nothing more than a projection of Judeo-Christian humanist values like self-determinism, social justice, democracy, and global ethics, and when combined gesture toward the possibility for a future in which a new collective humanism will dominate. Hence, what I want to suggest in this chapter is that what often gets represented and even critiqued as Buddhism in film is just an ephemeral projection of Asian culture filtered through the lens of Christianity, neoliberal humanism, and orientalism. Importantly, however, I don't want to suggest that this is necessarily a bad thing. I want to use *Cloud Atlas* as an example of how representations of Buddhism in philosophy and cinema can be a good thing if these representations are used as a tool to correct past essentialist and orientalist narratives.

The primary film theory method I will use in this chapter will be auteur theory, which I will use to discern the intentions of the author of the original book upon which *Cloud Atlas* is based, as well as the directors of the film. The connection between the author, David Mitchell, and the directors, Lana Wachowski, Lily Wachowski, and Tom Tykwer, will be understood through a framework of what I refer to as "affective circulation." This analysis will hopefully present a nuanced understanding of Buddhism in film by taking into consideration the dynamic relationship of orientalism and embodied affective experiences. Most prominent during the French New Wave film movement, auteur theory has since received expansions and revisions by generations of film critics. Auteur theory recognizes and highlights the filmmakers' central creative role in cinematic works. Referred to as the "auteur," the filmmaker can even be celebrated as the "supreme creative force" according to this theory, and has been used to understand works from Alfred Hitchcock to Ingrid Bergman (Ciment 2009: 96). More importantly, according to Peter Wollen, auteur theory incorporates an analysis of not only directors but also a wide range of authors behind the making of films (Wollen 1972: 74). The auteur theory allows for an in-depth study of how novels are recreated in cinematic form, as well as how humanist ideas become embodied in films. In addition, I would like to add that rather than using auteur theory to direct the attention away from the larger political, social, and cultural contexts by focusing on the auteur, I use this theory as a prism to examine the affective circulation of global histories, ideas, and selves.

Žižek and the Misinterpretation of Buddhism

In today's social media age, the consumption of Buddhism from home deco to yoga studios, from Instagram videos to celebrity gurus, has become so popular that it has attracted the attention of notable philosophers like Slavoj Žižek, who is concerned with the links between religion and Western capitalism.[1] As noted in the aforementioned quote, Žižek seems to understand Buddhism as a pop culture creation of the West that has become elemental to the ideology of late capitalism, while also maintaining that it needs to be subject to critique for precisely these same reasons. As a critical theorist who is always attempting to expose the latent ideologies of capitalism that lie hidden in popular culture, Žižek often tries to critique the way capitalism appropriates aspects of different cultures to sustain its global dominance. However, despite the best of his intentions, there are numerous problems with Žižek's critique of Buddhism, and these intersect with the general critique of orientalism in philosophy and cinema. As Eske Møllgaard (2008) has pointed out, Žižek seems to misinterpret, if not entirely dismiss, the diverse aspects of Buddhism in his critique, including the important and yet complex notion of emptiness. In doing so, Žižek inherits a tradition in the West that dates back to Nietzsche and other philosophers, and which simply equates Buddhism with nihilism and represents it as a "dangerous ideology" for Europe that denies the "existence of the world." This critique suggests that Buddhism is dangerous because it undermines the critique of cultural and capitalist inequality, as well as the foundation for any critical action or morality in the world (Droit 2003: 4).

According to this understanding of Buddhist nihilism that Žižek offers, "Buddhism is a kind of negative ethics, or void, of the Good." As Žižek writes: "aware that every positive Good is a lure, it fully assumes the Void as the only true Good" (Žižek 2003: 23). This understanding of Buddhism is not only misleading but also essentializes Buddhism as the "Other" of Western culture. In this way, Žižek orientalizes Buddhism in a manner similar to the pop culture phenomenon of Western Buddhism that he critiques.

Interestingly, it is precisely this misrepresentation of Buddhism that is typical in Western cinema, as there is a long history in film of Asia being represented as exotic other of the West that is simultaneously of great benefit and peril. For example, early Buddhist films in the United States, such as D. H. Griffith's *Broken Blossoms* (1919) and Frank Capra's *Lost Horizon* (1937), set out a framework that present Buddhism as "a marker of otherness" and "unassimilable difference" to the West (Suh 2015: 29). In *Broken Blossoms,* for instance, an idealistic Chinese man who wants to share Buddhist teachings with westerners ends up disillusioned because of the violence in Western society and ends up taking his own life in front of a makeshift Buddhist shrine. Similarly, in *Lost Horizon* we encounter "the East" through a faraway dreamland called Shangri la. Based on the novel by English writer James Hilton, *Lost Horizon* came to characterize how Asian cultures are all too often represented in cinema: as a distant utopia, a place where fantasy and wonder trump history and politics. One of the more recent examples of this blatant orientalism would be Scorsese's *Kundun* (1997). Scorsese stays true to the "Shangri-la trope" found in *Lost Horizon*—portraying Tibet as an apolitical heaven that existed in pristine form before the arrival of Chinese communists—and also employs the "innocence of Buddhist monks trope" found in *Broken Blossoms*—portraying Tibetan monks as emotionally broken and nearly brought to the point of suicide by the violence of the brutal communist invaders. The list of films that fall victim to this orientalism could go on for pages, so I will just limit myself to these brief examples.

The important point to take away from all this is that most Western philosophical and cinematic representations of Buddhism tend to create an orientalized version of what they imagine Buddhism to be: they use the white lens of the cinematic gaze to create an idealized presentation of how they imagine Asian culture.

In regard to Žižek, his specific critique would have been better if based on a systematic inquiry into Buddhist philosophy itself. As he failed to do so, he also failed to notice that this interpretation of the central Buddhist notion of emptiness is not a concept native to Buddhism itself. Rather, emptiness in Theravada and Mahayana traditions implies a recognition that everything originates in mutual interdependence. In misinterpreting, if not dismissing, Buddhist philosophy, Žižek inherits an old philosophical narrative that reduces and essentializes Buddhism according to Western concepts and then critiques, or orientalizes it, according to the same reductive formulas. It is as if we were thrown back to the eighteenth or nineteenth century when Buddhism or Asian religions were often seen as a nihilistic threat to European culture. Nietzsche, for example, saw Buddhism as a prime example of the nihilism "that is silently making progress everywhere in Europe" (Nietzsche 1967: 204). Nietzsche foresaw a Europe "with a soft-Buddhist Christian belief and, in practice, an Epicurean savior-vivre." Similarly, Žižek argues that the Judeo-Christian legacy is "threatened" by Buddhism or Asian religions, which have emerged as an "ideological superstructure" in Europe, and that Buddhism is establishing itself as the "hegemonic ideology" of global capitalism that preaches "inner distance and indifference toward the mad dance of accelerated process" (Žižek 2001).

Had Žižek studied the diversity of beliefs and actions that get classified under the category "Buddhism" with the kind of intellectual inquiry that he gave Christianity in works like *The Monstrosity of Christ* (2009), he would have learnt that emptiness in Buddhism is a misleading translation. that it does not denote meaninglessness, void, negativity, or Nothing. Rather, it signifies what in Pali is known as *paṭiccasamuppāda*, which can loosely be translated as what "springs up together." As a learnt insight, this implies an awareness that all existence depends on the interdependent relation between all things. The notion of emptiness in Buddhism must be understood in relation to this notion of "dependent arising," and not the Latin notion of *nihil*—the etymological root of the words "nihilism" and "nothing."

Emptiness and Dependent Arising: A Traveling Soul in Six Lives

Luckily, *Cloud Atlas* helps correct some of these forementioned misconceptions of Buddhism by making it clear that what we are dealing with in representations of Buddhism in cinema is a Western humanist projection that has at least *some* good to offer audiences. Using the pop culture understanding of Buddhism Žižek referenced earlier, the film tells the story of a soul that travels across six different eras with entirely different social and cultural contexts. It attempts to illustrate the Buddhist idea of reincarnation, as suggested by Mitchell in the original book on which this film is based, but is more significantly empowered by cinematic language. The story includes the following main protagonists across six historical moments and places (see Table 1).

The film's first adaptation success is the highlight of a comet-shaped birthmark of six main characters, which attempts to illustrate the idea of reincarnation. The recurrence of the birthmark throughout *Cloud Atlas* on the main characters is supposed to represent the rebirth of characters in different bodies, times, and locations.

In relation to the comments in the previous sections, it should be noted that the idea of reincarnation in Buddhism is also connected to the concept of "dependent arising" (*paṭiccasamuppāda*), as the Buddhist notions of suffering (*dukkha*), no-self (*anatta*), and impermanence (*anicca*) are all

TABLE 1 Main Characters in *Cloud Atlas*

Actor	Time, Location, and Position					
	1849, South Pacific	1936, Cambridge and Edinburgh	1973, San Francisco	2012, London	2144, Neo Seoul	2321, Big Isle, 106 Winters after the Fall
Jim Sturgess	Adam Ewing, lawyer	Hotel guest	Megan's father	Highlander	"Pureblood" commander Hae-Joo Chang	Adam
Donna Bae	Tilda Ewing, Adam's wife	N/A	Megan's mother	N/A	Sonmi-451, a genetically engineered fabricant servant	N/A
Ben Whishaw	Cabin boy	Robert Frosbisher, composer	Store clerk	Georgette	N/A	Tribesman
James D'Arcy	N/A	Rufus Sixstmith, Robert's love interest	Rufus Sixstmith	Nurse	Archivist	N/A
Tom Hanks	A doctor with the attempt to poison Adam	Hotel manager	Isaac, killed in a plane crash	Dermot Hoggins	N/A	Zachry, a post-apocalyptic human
Halle Berry	Local	Jocasta Ayrs, married to Robert's mentor	Luisa Rey, Isaac's love interest	Party guest	Ovid	Meronym, Zachry's partner

deeply connected in Buddhist metaphysics. The key notion of karma, which is also connected to the concept of dependent arising and rebirth, also plays a key role in the film. Moreover, all these notions are conveyed in the film by a series of revelations by the main protagonists throughout the film. As one character notes, "our lives are not our own. We are bound to others, past and present, and by each crime and every kindness, we birth our future."

In the film's opening sequence, we see the six main protagonists' birthmarks, in the shape of a comet, which then extend and together form a web of connections across the universe. Furthermore, the comet shape seems to indicate something "scientific" yet mysterious, such as destiny or "love." As one character in the film remarks toward the ending, "My uncle was a scientist, but he believed that love was real; a kind of natural phenomenon, he believed that love could outlive death."

This leads us to the second component of successful adaptation in *Cloud Atlas*, the romanticized relationship among its characters. "Love" encapsulates the theme that I find largely humanistic and makes the book's philosophical ideas more approachable for the audience. In the original book, David Mitchell focuses on developing storyline, structure, and characters' inner dialogues, and "love" does not appear as a strong theme. For example, when asked whether she loved Hae-Joo Chang, Sonmi-451 replied: "that is for future historians to decide" (Mitchell 2004: 365). However, in the film, we hear a moving statement of love in a scene just before Sonmi's execution:

Archivist: Would you say that you loved him?
[Sonmi smiles]
Sonmi-451: Yes, I do.
Archivist: Do you mean you are still in love with him?
Sonmi-451: I mean, that I will always be.

We then see Sonmi back in the Satellite Communication Centre broadcasting her message, watching as the Enforcers attack the station with Chang and the rest of Union (a counter-corporate group hoping to overthrow the current regime and restore respect for human and fabricant rights) fighting them.

However, saddening it seems, this relationship is given a redeemable ending in the film. While the book ends with the philosophical reflections of another protagonist, Adam, the film sees Adam—also played by Jim Sturgess as the reincarnation of Chang—reunited with his wife Tilda, and together they begin a new life with a statement that is transformed from his monologue in the book,

Adam's Father-in-law: There is a natural order to this world, and those who try to upend it do not fare well. [. . .] no matter what you do, it will never amount to anything more than a single drop in a limitless ocean.

Adam Ewing: What is an ocean but a multitude of drops?

The tragedy of Sonmi and Chang is eventually redeemed in the happy ending of Adam and Tilda. Similarly, the film ends with Zachry telling stories to his grandchildren on a new planet while looking at Earth, his former homeland. He then kisses his partner Meronym lovingly. As Sonmi and Chang's relationship is rekindled via their reincarnated selves, Zachry and Meronym are also able to enjoy what they failed to have in their previous lives. However, although the major elements at play appear to be Buddhist, in particular, the idea of reincarnation and karma, it seems what underlies it all is humanism (Guo 2013).

First of all, in Buddhism, the notion of "dependent arising" is paired with another key concept of "emptiness." As noted, according to the principle of "dependent arising," things arise dependent on causes and conditions, and so "identity" is to exist in relation to other things. Therefore, one's own self-identity is merely a mirror of how one is perceived by others. Since there are no independent autonomous entities, all things are empty in and of themselves. According to the dominant Theravada and Mahayana interpretations of Buddhism, the idea of no-self (anattā) is a realization of dependent arising and emptiness, through which one can gain true freedom. However, in *Cloud Atlas*, it is for the self-autonomy, rights, and self-recognition of each individual—the self-freed slave, the purebloods and fabricants who form the Union, the talented composer Robert Frobisher who aspires to be famous and asks for equality from his mentor, and a fabricant who wants to gain identity and human knowledge—struggles for centuries to gain their significance. Yet, love, the strong emotional connection between two people, is the best illustration of dependent-arising, making *Cloud Atlas* a compelling humanist interpretation of Buddhism.

In addition to the pursuit of self-identity, *Cloud Atlas* also celebrates a humanist understanding of democracy. Sonmi-451 composes a Bill of Rights that declares her understanding of equality, after realizing the system of society based on slavery and exploitation of fabricants must be destroyed and restructured. As expressed in a conversation between Sonmi and Chang:

Sonmi-451: That ship . . . that ship must be destroyed.
Hae-Joo Chang: Yes.
Sonmi-451: The systems that built them must be turned down.
Hae-Joo Chang: Yes.
Sonmi-451: No matter if we're born in a tank or a womb, we are all Pureblood.

Hae-Joo Chang: Yes.

Sonmi-451: We must all fight and, if necessary, die to teach people the truth.

The sense of self-identity that Sonmi realizes includes her social identity, which is signified in her awakened concern for social order, and the devotion to question and rebuild that order. Furthermore, *Cloud Atlas* also embodies modern humanism through qualities of innate humanity rather than a transcendent entity, which becomes most implicit when one protagonist from the post-apocalyptic era comments that there is no god: "what the villagers have been worshipping is only a human who lived a long time ago," Sonmi-451. It is also evident through Adam's question that "if God created the world, how do we know what things we can change and what things must remain sacred and unviable?" This portrays a democratic and ethical life stance, which affirms a secular humanistic belief that human beings have the right and responsibility to give meaning and shape to their own lives (see Norman 2004). In contrast, the Christian view, as articulated by the theologian Karl Barth, affirms that the human being itself, the concrete, real human being, exists insofar as the living God is for him and with him (Barth 1950: 8).

Last but not least, each story in *Cloud Atlas* happens in a different place across the globe, including the South Pacific, Cambridge, San Francisco, London, neo-Seoul, and Scotland. Almost every story involves ethnicities of different sorts. A soul reborn through these ethnically varied characters living in different parts of the world in different eras suggests a universal humanity. This view owes its roots to a particular ideology from modern humanism, which constructs a universal, unencumbered "self," a belief in the power of unique autonomous individuals (Plummer 2001: 258). It is a view that accepts the human being as an embodied, emotional, interactive self, striving for meaning in wider historically specific social worlds and an even wider universe.

The belief in a universal humanity restores hope and liberates us from uncertainties and tragedies as a species as a whole, as Isaac remarks before his life is ended in a plane crash:

Belief, like fear or love, is a force to be understood as we understand the theory of relativity and principles of uncertainty. [. . .] These forces that often remake time and space, they can shape and alter whom we imagine ourselves to be, begin long before we are born, and continue after we perish. Our lives and our choices, like quantum trajectories, are understood moment to moment, as each point of intersection, each encounter, suggests a new potential direction.

It is the belief in modern human values—self-identity, social justice, democracy, and global ethics—that points to a new direction for a collective humanity in the film version of *Cloud Atlas*. More so than the book, the film uses these humanistic ideas as the basis of its vision, and so its use of Buddhist concepts can only be understood in this context.

David Mitchell and the Labor of Love

Although the film *Cloud Atlas* was a Hollywood production, the writing of *Cloud Atlas* (2004), the novel, was originally inspired by the author's experience living in Hiroshima, Japan, a coastline city that experienced nuclear bombing during the Second World War. Mitchell drew the title from piano pieces *Cloud Atlas*, composed by Japanese composer Toshi Ichiyanagi (一柳慧,) in the 1980s. According to Mitchel's understanding of Ichiyanagi's music, "Atlas" refers to things in life that remain constant, while "Cloud" refers to what can change. In other words, "Atlas" is existence and "Cloud" is the soul (Bentley 2020). It is perhaps relevant to mention that Ichiyanagi is also the former husband of multimedia artist and activist Yoko Ono, before John Lennon. These connections make both Ichiyanagi and Mitchell part of a pop culture landscape that constitutes the circulatory global history, a potential remedy for the deprivation of values in today's market capitalism and reductive orientalism.

Born in the Midlands, England, David Mitchell currently lives in Ireland with his wife Keiko Yoshida and two children. He lived in Hiroshima for eight years in the 1990s, where he taught English during the day and wrote fiction after work. Japan, for him, was not only a personal life experience but also an intellectual and cultural journey. It was in Hiroshima where he finished his first novel *Ghostwritten* (1999), set in Japan but also other parts of Asia and Europe, a theme of global connection that he continued in *Cloud Atlas* and other subsequent novels. As he was teaching at the Hiroshima Kokusai Gakuin University at the time, he was able to conduct background research for this historical novel. This intellectual exploration continued and developed in his subsequent novels, including *number9dream* (2001), *Cloud Atlas*, and *The Thousand Autumns of Jacob de Zoet* (2010). He studied and integrated some of the literary artistry of Japanese authors into his writing. Critics often point out Haruki Murakami's influence in his work, though Mitchell himself has referred to classic Japanese writers such as Junichiro Tanizaki, Ryunosuke Akutagawa, and Yukio Mishima when it comes to his favorite authors. He also openly credits his experience in Japan as the creative inspiration of his career, "I read a lot of Japanese writers I wouldn't have read if I'd never gone to Japan, and I found myself wanting to emulate some of them . . . a lot of materials I gathered in my 20s was Japanese" (Mitchell 2016).

Mitchell's creative engagement with cultures outside of his own is not only an intellectual endeavor but also an emotional labor, which is complicated by Mitchell and Keiko Yoshida's son's autism. When their son began to have meltdowns, Yoshida introduced to Mitchell *The Reason I Jump: One Boy's Voice from the Silence of Autism* (2005), a memoir written by Naoki Higashida, an autistic boy in Japan. This book changed their life. It helped them recognize many of their son's traits with plausible explanations, provided answers with which they were able to improve as parents of an autistic child, and ultimately gave them hope. "[We] followed Naoki's advice—even if it was as simple as, 'Hang on in there and don't give up: he'll get there in his own time'" (Mitchell 2019).

The significant impact of this book goes beyond them being gracious readers. They began translating this book together, hoping it could reach more readers and families in need or even despair.

Translation is a unique process of cultural exchange. It evokes an act of moving across from one position to another by understanding different textualities and then transmitting that understanding. It is a process of communicating between the translators and authors of different worlds and between readers, translators, and authors of different worlds. But for a book that deals with autism, writing and translating this book also deals with the language that has helped those who are deprived of a voice to speak.

As Mitchell remarks, the success of *The Reason I Jump* has encouraged a readership for other books by nonverbal textual communicators with autism—"texticators" (Mitchell 2017). There are authors of different societies who have written insider accounts of their life with autism, with similarities but also differences. The literature of autism needs enrichment, and translation helps reach out to more individuals and families around the world. In their case of jointly translating *The Reason I Jump*, there further involves a particular emotional engagement as well as textication. Through writing *The Reason I Jump*, Naoki has made himself vulnerable yet open by sharing his personal experience of struggling and coming to terms with his illness. It is a book of courage and wisdom but also of pain, alienation, and loneliness. Reading this work and being touched and inspired, Mitchell and Yoshida also made themselves vulnerable as they see their own moments of despair and doubt and their son's silent cry for help in someone else's words.

In "Orientalist in Love, Intimacy, Empire, and Cross-Cultural Knowledge" (2012), Stephen Jankiewicz critically examines the complex relationship between individual Orientalists in the nineteenth century and the Orient. The Orientalists under his examination—including English traveler Gertrude Bell and King Faisal of Iraq—sought to express the power of a larger imperial structure or discourse, but they were also in love with the Other. They were not only emotionally bound with the Other but also intellectually transformed and humbled and spiritually empowered by the Other, and sometimes even submerged into the Other. Such complex relationships entail more than simple reductions but embodied processes of learning, exchanging, and producing knowledge with engaged interactions. In David Mitchell's case, through creative writing, translating, and emotional engagement of the Other, he weaves encounters between worlds into an interconnected atlas that reminds us of their interdependence. That is the meaning of "dependent arising" in Buddhism, as most vividly illustrated in *Cloud Atlas*. In doing so, he also transforms his personal experience of the unfamiliar into journeys of searches and encounters, as he does in his own life.

Indeed, we need not only to look at the image of Asia that European writers present but also to understand how they produce their representations. As Jankiewicz remarks, even when placed in its political or economic context in the colonial era, a representation is not just a cultural utterance, not just a "stereotype" or "essentialization." A representation is also a product of their own intellectual engagement of the Other, as well as their emotional and social engagement. Such representations are products of the labor of love, as they are part of the long process of learning and loving someone from another culture and social and historical conditions under which individuals fall in love. Such labor of love requires a long, invested process of absorbing, articulating, and reflecting on differences and what they share in common.

In the case of Mitchell, the labor of love is complex and sometimes painful. As he later told the *Guardian*,

> Thanks to the book, my wife and I found ourselves modifying our interactions with our son. We engaged with him more, expected more back, and followed Naoki's advice—even if it was as simple as, "Hang on in there and don't give up: he'll get there in his own time." Our son responded positively. He began using a few words, his understanding bloomed, his self-harming dropped away and he was happier. None of this is very scientific, I agree. I can't know for sure or prove that these changes wouldn't have occurred anyway, and, heaven knows, bad days and bad patches still happened, still do, and always will. (Mitchell 2017)

Such embodied, affective knowledge exchange, with a labor of love or emotional engagement that produces a certain representation, is certainly shaped by greater powers, but it also shapes those powers and is not entirely determined by them. It is in this sense that Mitchell's work, a popular cultural product, is also a product of the labor of love, whose embodied knowledge exchange and experience of cultural difference indicates an openhearted sincerity that is fundamentally different from Žižek's reductionist misinterpretation of the Orient, in this case Buddhism. Moreover, such openhearted cultural production does not aim to redeem one's own perceived cultural crisis by reclaiming a sort of lost legacy of that particular culture, often with implied superiority over the alleged threat from the Other who is considered responsible for the very crisis.

Affective Circulation against Cinematic Orientalism

The reason why *Cloud Atlas* provides a better attempt at presenting Buddhism in cinema is precisely because of the love David Mitchell and the filmmakers put into creating the story. It is more than a transcription of data from one culture to another, but a production of knowledge based on Mitchell's own experience and embodied understandings, an ensemble of emotional and material processes. Or, in Eve Sedgwick (2003)'s words, Mitchell's understanding of Buddhism and *Cloud Atlas* was a phenomenology of knowing, the process of circulation in which one opens up and senses knowledge as embodied experiences. More importantly, rather than a single-directional appropriation, the globalization of ideas in *Cloud Atlas* is about the affective circulation of experience in which the individual emerges as a living "contact zone" of felt, embodied global histories, whose ideas and decisions, in turn, are located and embodied in affective exchanges (Ahmed 2004: 14, 203; Schaeffer 2015: 66).

In *Religious Affect* (2015), Donovan Schaeffer remarks that religion is an outcome of a body's affective response to power in the world. According to historian Prasenjit Duara, histories are not the exclusive property of a single community or entity, since questions of sovereignty and identity are closely linked to history (Duara 2016: 54). Such dispersed, cross-referenced, mutually shaping and shared histories as well as modern-day movement, contestation, and hybridity of the globalization and popularization of religion (Vasquez 2011) should provide an antidote to the dualist understanding of cultural legacies per nation formation, because religious ideas traveled in a dialogical and plural "traffic" of global connections.

Combining these two ideas, namely, religious affect and circulatory globalization, I propose the idea of affective circulation, to refer to our dynamic, embodied, reflexive encounters and exchanges with the world. In affective circulation, our dynamic relationships with the world, which in turn shape the "horizons of our experience" (Schaeffer 2015: 66), are an active process of the transmissions and reconfigurations of embodied histories, and such affective transmissions are reflexive and transformative rather than a simple replication or appropriation. In Mitchell's case, being in Japan certainly facilitated his understanding of a different language, a different culture, and a new religion, but he was emotionally and intellectually engaged, and his learning experience became an embodied process of exchanges and interactions. Rather than simply reducing his encounters as the cultural Other to English-language readers, the difference prompted him to reflect on his own background and found answers beyond binary terms with a kind of Buddhist humanism, and there is a certain sense of humility in it. This is certainly not to say that we have to move to Japan to understand the music of *Cloud Atlas* or Buddhism, but, rather, to recognize the marks of how global history has circulated and affected in others as well as in ourselves, to see each individual as a "felt, embodied history" (Schaeffer 2015: 66).

This framework of affective circulation helps us understand Buddhism in circulatory contexts, rather than as ahistorical entities. It helps us look for the historical and political factors that shape many aspects of religious manifestations, and understand "Asian religions" such as Buddhism as part of the affective circulation with embodied histories and understandings. This does not necessarily mean that only by moving to a place can we understand its religion and culture. Rather, our knowledge of religion should be embodied in concrete situations, and, more importantly, exchanges, transformations, and mutations.

Cloud Atlas vividly illustrates this kind of affective circulation. A continuous endeavor in circulatory global history with the labor of love is more directly evident in the translation of *The Reason I Jump*, written by a Japanese boy with autism, by Mitchell and his wife Keiko Yoshida for their son with the same affliction. It can also be seen in his recent works *The Thousand Autumns of Jacob de Zoet* (2010) and *From Me Flows What You Call Time* (2016), which draws its title from Japanese composer Toru Takemitsu's music. This hybrid affective circulation of knowledge contrasts Žižek's argument that the legacies of Judeo-Christianity should provide some kind of antidote to the challenges posed to the post-Christian West from Buddhism or Asian religions by providing a more intertwined relationship between global cultural values. Because in such affective circulation, we recognize not only others but also ourselves and what we share in common. For instance, in pointing out the problem of the subject's autonomous self-containment in Western thought as the foundational fantasy of Western thought as she understands bodies as interlaced with other bodies and spaces surrounding us, Teresa Brennan (2004) effectively recognizes the Buddhist notion of dependent arising and illustrates vividly the kind of reflexive awareness of affective circulation that could redeem us from simple orientalizations of Asian religions.

Conclusion

This chapter has discussed the ways in which Buddhism has been depicted in Western cinema. With the notion of affective circulation as a guide, I have argued that the intellectual and personal journey of David Mitchell embodied in *Cloud Atlas* demonstrates the emotional and intellectual endeavor to weave different worlds as an interconnected atlas. In doing so, this novel and its film adaptation attempt to illustrate the notion of dependent arising in Buddhism and the notion of affective circulation in much truer form than past philosophical and cinematic representations. Rather than displaying this concept as a form of Nihilism like Žižek, the film shows how the very concepts Žižek identifies as the ideology of late capitalism can also serve to critique this ideology. Though still just a cinematic representation and creation of Buddhism through a humanist lens, it nonetheless offers an openhearted remedy to global capitalism's nihilist tendencies.

CHAPTER 7

Magical Realism, Anti-Modernity, and the Religious Imaginaries of Latin American Cinema:

A Look through Ciro Guerra's *The Wind Journeys* (2009)

Rebecca C. Bartel

In the opening scenes of the Colombian film *The Wind Journeys*, directed by Academy Award nominee Ciro Guerra, the audience hears a haunting funeral dirge mingling with the howling, hot winds of the desolate Colombian Caribbean desert, while shadowy figures dig a grave. Ignacio, the protagonist, mourns the death of his wife, standing over her grave after her body has been buried in the early days of Lent. The viewer knows that it is Lent because Ignacio then attends his local Catholic church to receive ashes of Ash Wednesday, seeking a blessing for his upcoming journey through the proverbial and physical wilderness of the northern Colombian coast. However, upon approaching the priest Ignacio is turned away because accompanying him, the cause of his misery, is his cursed accordion.

This is an unconventional opening scene for viewers accustomed to popular, US-based representations of Colombian life. Audiences of North American cinema are generally unused to genre film in Latin American cinema, and are usually invited into the mythic-fictional realm of drug wars, clandestine guerrilla violence, and sweaty jungle-scapes that dominate the screen when Colombia or, indeed, most Latin American countries are represented. Stereotypes and Hollywood's Protestant gaze often afford religious tropes to depictions of Colombian culture that give the impression that all Latin Americans are fanatical Catholics.[1] Catholicism habitually plays the character of Protestant Christianity's medieval Other. Catholicism is presented as the religion of dark saints that bless narco-ritual, or the religion of austere conservativism, or the highly material religion that traffics in practices of praying to altars littered with candles and icons. However, Ciro Guerra's films are nothing if not unconventional and genre-bending, and Guerra, along with a tremendous team of writers and cinematographers, unconventionally re-configures the pulsing undercurrent of religious imaginaries that drive his narratives.

The Wind Journeys presents an intimate exploration of an allegory deeply embedded in popular culture that reflects the political history that shapes Colombian reality; the aspirational yet impossible task of repairing the past. The context of Colombia's war-with-no-end informs a great deal of the popular culture that arises from the ideologies that shape everyday life in the South American nation (Althusser 2014 [1971]).[2] In this sense, the representation of "the religious" in this film is a similarly constructed sociopolitical order that is idiosyncratic to Colombia's context but also specific to a story that is as magical as it is real.

This chapter considers such a construction of "the religious" in *The Wind Journeys,* as the film grapples with authenticity and modernity through a magical realist composition. The religious, as understood by the symbols Guerra employs to signify it, draws on the affective pulls of being simultaneously threatening and comforting; as Guerra himself says about the music and atmosphere of the Colombian coastal lands: "the music is happy and sad at the same time . . . the region is profoundly melancholic and reflexive, happiness is a mask" (Jaccard 2009). Guerra's construction of the religious follows his construction of the mask of happiness that conceals the melancholy of the Colombian coast, illustrating ways that "religion exists in the imagination of the screen-writers" and is manufactured through images and sounds interpreted through the lens of a camera (Eaghll 2019). As such, the visual and auditory structures of representation that *The Wind Journeys* deploys interpret a magical realist story of a man who made a deal with the Devil to become prosperous in a place where those deals so often end in utter desolation.

Francisco el Hombre and the Magical Real

Several months later saw the return of Francisco the Man, an ancient vagabond

Who was almost 200 years old who frequently
Passed through Macondo distributing songs
That he wrote himself. . .
Francisco the Man, called that because he once defeated
The Devil
In a dual of improvisation
And whose real name no one knew,
Disappeared from Macondo during the plague of insomnia.

GABRIEL GARCIA MARQUEZ

The story of *The Wind Journeys* is based on a popular lore in coastal Colombian mythology, more commonly known as the story of "Francisco el Hombre" or "Francisco the Man." The story has its origins in the mythical figures of Orpheus and Doctor Faust, but relies on Colombian folklore and imagery, and perhaps some truth, for its tale.[3] Legend has it that sometime in the late nineteenth century in the northern Caribbean coastal regions of Colombia where the folk music *vallenato* originated, there was a virtuosic accordionist and *juglar*, Francisco Moscote Guerra.[4] One night, as he was leaving an evening of great revelry, he decided to take out his accordion to accompany the journey home to his own town. As he played, the echo of an accordion in the distance responded to his every note. As he walked, the responses grew louder and more masterful. Francisco sought out his competitor, and, to his surprise, discovered the Devil himself. Francisco, realizing that he was close to defeat, then sang the Apostle's Creed backward and forward, accompanied by his accordion, and, with that, the Devil disappeared into the evening in a great billow of clouds that darkened the night (Pérez et al. 2014). Good had defeated evil. Myth and reality converge in these kinds of stories that sustain local imaginaries of history and the magically real throughout the Colombian mythoscape. *The Wind Journeys* presents a decidedly magical realist narration of the legend of Francisco el Hombre that also generates a particular religio-scape in its composition.

Magical realism, as a literary mode as well as a cinematic trope, operates ideologically in a similar way to religiosity; insofar as magical realism may "create space for interactions of diversity" (Zamora and Farris 1994: 3), sociocultural constructions of religiosity may problematize ideas of what "the real," or "the natural" form of perceived notions of what the properly religious might be. In the sparse literature on the subject of magical realism and religion, often the emphasis has been placed on the "natural" relation between Catholicism and magical realism, reinforcing the notion that magical realism is particular to Latin America and furthering a sort of "reappropriation that is similar to Orientalism" McCracken 1999: 5). This kind of Orientalist, perhaps better termed, "Latinist" incorporation of Latin American literature and cinema, insists that any sign of exotic or ethnic "other" results in a kind of romanticization of the "unbelievable" or the "magical" as a palimpsest for "non-Western" or "non-rational." These critiques, however, are often laid upon the idea of Catholicism within an equally Latinist frame of orientation (Caminero-Santangelo 2005). These studies propose the idea that both "Catholicism" and magical realism are cultural forms that exist *sui generis* without recognizing the political critique that magical realist literature offers, nor the construction of Catholicism, indeed religion itself, as a *concept* interwoven with the political histories and cultural specifics that refuse its unity (DelRosso 2005; Caminero-Santangelo 2005).

The folktale of Francisco el Hombre has resonance with the many other tales of musicians, from disparate parts of the world, wandering troubadours and minstrels, who battle and defeat the Devil with their musical gifts, and they are especially legendary in the northern *sierras* of Colombia. "There," says Colombian writer Joce Guillermo Daniels García, speaking of the *sierra* deserts, "the peasants tell stories of the troubadours of the shade of the *araguaney* tree, who defeat the Devil playing their music. They travel to all the townships of the interminable and inhospitable desert with their message of joy and happiness" (Daniels García 2019: 2).[5] The *juglar* was a common, and very much real, element of coastal society from the mid- to late nineteenth century and into the first half of the twentieth century in Colombia. Traveling *juglares* would relay the news of the region through song, from village to village, perform at baptisms, funerals, weddings, and feasts, and regularly entertain crowds through *piqueria* contests; accordion duels that also featured battles of rhyming couplets.

The Wind Journeys is a diegetic narrative that interprets the folk tale from a slightly different angle; from the perspective of the travelers Ignacio the *juglar*, and Fermín, the young man intent on becoming a successful *vallenato* percussionist, on their way to *La Guajira*, Colombia's northernmost desert.[6] Ignacio is on a journey to return the accursed accordion that has made him a famous *juglar* back to its original owner, whom the audience might infer is the Devil himself. He seeks to return the accordion because he is tired of the life of the *juglar* and interprets his wife's death as part of the curse of his accordion. As long as he is in possession of the accordion, he cannot stop playing, and malaise does not cease to follow him. Ignacio has become so affected by the deep sadness that the cursed accordion has brought to his life that eventually on the journey, he loses the will to live. Despite being one of the great *juglares,* he would rather part ways with the accordion and never play again than continue to play and risk further pain. Fermín, the Sancho to Ignacio's Quixote and possibly Ignacio's son, follows in the hopes that Ignacio will teach him how to become a successful musician following the path of his elder hero.

Accompanying the journey, however, are the struggles for authenticity and believability that Ignacio dismisses and Fermín longs for. The diegesis shapes a narrative that insists upon an authentic history while also naturalizing a quotidian supernatural presence that raises no questions from the cast of characters—all played, notably, by non-professional actors. In this way, the film traces a journey that also offers a simulacrum of the marvelous real and provides the basis for a decolonial critique of interpretations of Latin American religiosity (Carpentier 2004 [1949]).

The film constructs this journey not only through visual organization of the stunning yet desolate landscape of the northern coast but also through the soundscapes and backdrop of violence. All of these elements also come together to construct a religious imaginary that speaks back to a Western imperial purview for thinking about Latin American religiosity, and the Protestant gaze that dominates representations of Latin American Catholicism.

Music, Wind, and War: The Other Protagonists

The harshness of the elements in the coastal region of Colombia, the relentless winds and suffocating heat, is offset by the contradictory imagery of a traveling musician who should reflect the *jouissance* of the classical folk music of the Colombian Caribbean, the *vallenato*, yet embodies a melancholy presence on the screen. The soundscape of the film is as important as any of the characters. Indeed, the minimal dialogues, accentuated by the sounds of the changing breath of the protagonists, further train the ear to be shocked at the pops of blindingly colorful sound of virtuosic accordion playing in bursts and fits throughout the journey. The accordion itself, crowned by horns indicative of its cursed nature, plays an active supporting role, as Ignacio states at one point, "I don't play the accordion. It plays itself." Such is the supernatural animation of the inanimate through sound and silence. Sound, specifically *vallenato* music, as well as ritual drumming and haunting acapella singing, the sounds of different Indigenous dialects, languages, like Bantu and Waiyuunaiki, the sounds of breathing, and, importantly, the constant moan of the winds of the sierra are fundamental characters in the film (Hutchinson 2011).

Ciro Guerra's film pays homage to the soundscapes and the landscapes of the northern coastal lands of Colombia, while also presenting a nostalgia film that mourns the loss of certain folk traditions, like that of the *juglar* and the *piqueria*, affected and shaped by a violence that is often off-screen yet relentlessly present. This is the key to Guerra's magical realism; through sound, the audience is captivated in the seemingly impossible, yet entirely believable, world that Ignacio and Fermín traverse. The sounds that accompany the journey are also sounds of nature and sounds of violent loss. For example, when Ignacio is asked to accompany a machete duel between two young men in one of the villages he visits. The young men battle to the death while Ignacio plays the accordion; a witness to violence, incapable of stopping the inevitable end, and somehow an accomplice. The sound of ritual drumming that Fermín participates in, eventually being initiated into the drumming troupe through baptism by the blood of a lizard, accompanies the heady trance that draws Fermín to the group. The sound of gifted accordion playing that accompanies the first *piqueria* battle between Ignacio and a local champion is colored through Ignacio's conviction that the champion himself uses witchcraft to beat his opponents. The sound of the wind that is unrelenting along the journey, especially at moments when Ignacio is losing the will to carry on, represents the spirit of the coastland that the director wants to frame, and gives a sense of inescapability of the melancholy and onslaught of heat, as though steaming from the pits of Hell itself. The resonance of sound constructs a religious imaginary that is at once Christian but very much not, full of indigenous religious practice, witchcraft, and the malaise that Ciro Guerra wants to portray. This hybrid of sound, image, and dialogue works to create the magical, yet real, world that Guerra's cinema effectively portrays.

Furthering the notion of hybridity, the rendering of religiosity throughout the film is essentially hybrid. It is construed via emblems and symbols of the occult, the superstitious, and the supernatural that also traverse borders of cultures and races as they exist on the Caribbean coast. Importantly, however, at every instance of representation, none of these forms are juxtaposed against anything other; there is no "rational" opposition or "modern" correction. The hybrid occult *is* the norm. The hybrid construction of the other worldly is as quotidian and "real" as the harsh winds that never cease to blow, and the violence that appears so common it is accompanied by music. These are not dismissive terms. Rather, these terms, these religious imaginings, are very much the intentional construction of the cine-artist as they represent a rendering of coastal life that challenges the view of the coastlands as pre-modern, instead of a site of resistance to violent forms of enforced and exclusionary modernization that would otherwise recognize the region's inhabitants as subjects of civil and political rights.

Guerra's *Wind Journeys* follows the form of magical realism, inspired by the work of Gabriel García Márquez. Indeed, encroaching forms of capitalist exploitation and its accompanying political violence in the coastal regions of Colombia, particularly through the North American banana production industry, are the inspirations for the iconic magical realist tale, García Márquez's *One Hundred Years of Solitude*, which was published in 1967, the year before the year *The Wind Journeys* is set.[7] According to Colombian anthropologist José Antonio Figueroa, Márquez challenges the idea of Cuban writer Alejo Carpentier's "marvelous real" of the Caribbean as a "sanctuary where intellectuals can escape from Western rationalism," and rather provides a critique of "paternalistic fictions and neocolonialism" in the region (Figueroa 2009: iv). For Figueroa, the magical realism of Colombian literature frames the traditional musical accompaniment to the coastal imaginary: *vallenato*. He sees *vallenato*, in its original and authentic sense, as the "prism through which Colombian discourse on *mestizaje* is refracted; this myth of a culture that mixes the three races that makeup Latin America, without violence: Indigenous, African, and European" (Rappaport 2009: 13; translated by author).

The development of the *vallenato*, as a musical form that celebrates the Atlantic coastal region's idiosyncrasies and challenges its exoticization by the criollo elite of Bogotá, and the imperial designs of North America, was the impetus for massively producing this form of music throughout the country. This musical form was also the shape that García Márquez has explained as the model for *One Hundred Years*; a 300-page song that celebrates as it critiques the particularities of coastal culture and the political violence that has been suffered in solitude by this region for decades (Araújo Vélez 2018). The magical realism that García Márquez refines is a decolonial critique and builds on essentializations of Colombian Caribbean culture as embedded in the magical, the affable, the anti-modern, the bacchanal, and the folkloric (Figueroa 2009). In this sense, García Márquez offers a pointed critique via hyperbole of these essentializations while also critiquing the neocolonial traditionalism of many regions of Latin America via a literary assessment of coastal social structures (Figueroa 2009).

In many ways, hybridity is central to the coastal region and its cultural practice, as it is represented in *vallenato* itself. For example, the three central instruments of *vallenato* exemplify the region's racial and cultural hybridity: the European accordion, the African *caja* drum, and the Indigenous *guacharaca*. And in the case of *The Wind Journeys*, the musical accompaniment of *vallenato* also serves as the prism through which the myth of a peaceable religiosity is refracted. Instead of offering a single religious narrative, namely, Catholic, through which to interpret the wanderings of Ignacio and Fermín, the film reveals the simultaneous intermingling of so-called religious forms as they clash in instances of resistance to the violent encroachment of capitalist forms of modernity through inclusive forms of pluriversal coexistence. This hybrid curation of culture is a feature of the magical realist narrative in literature and in film but can also help us deconstruct the idea of "the religious" through a critique of modernity. In a sense, this approach furthers the critique of both colonialism and modernity as two sides of the same coin (Mignolo 2005). In presenting the concept of hybridity as the connecting element in both the religious and cultural representations that a magical realist analysis of *Wind Journeys* offers, I suggest that the construction of the religious is a reflection of the hybridity of the postcolonial (Bhabha 1994).

Magical Realism and Anti-Modernity: Seeking Authenticity

The term "magical realism" has its origins in literary critique, and had its heyday in the 1980s and 1990s. Although the concept is bordering on saturation, there are avenues for continued engagement with the idea, especially as it pertains to understanding the construction of "religion" in Latin American cinema. As a trope, the term has come to mean "any plot configuration of human behavior that seems an exception or contradiction or refutation of West European bourgeois rationalism as the dominant mode for explaining how the world and social relations function" (Foster and Scerbo 2019: 1). Despite the term being first coined by Franz Roh in a 1927 German publication with reference to post-impressionist art (González Boixo 2017), Latin American literature and art have been associated with the term since the Western recognition of Latin American literary contribution, especially with the works of Gabriel García Márquez, Isabel Allende, and Juan Rulfo.[8] Often through acts of exoticizing and essentializing Latin American art, "magical realism" connotes "cultural systems that are no less 'real' than those upon which traditional literary realism draws—often non-Western cultural systems that privilege mystery over empiricism, empathy over technology, tradition over innovation" (Zamora and Francis, 3). In other words, magical realist accounts represent worldviews that are critical, or, at the least, wary of Western modernity and its accompanying political and economic systems.

In this sense, a consideration of magical realist simulacrum and religiosity in Latin American cinema enters into a well-worn debate within the field of religious studies: that is a deconstruction of the idea that the religious represents somehow an "anti-modern" scope of human experience.[9] What has been less developed in the literature is a discussion of the use of magical realism as the gaze through which to deconstruct the very notion of "the religious" and "the modern" as they have been developed in Latin American cinema. To this end, *The Wind Journeys* offers a window through which to further the debate, especially insofar as the "authentic" is a construction that falls outside of modernity; to be authentic, in the case of the Colombian cinematic purview, is to harness some premodern dimensions of reality that fall in line with a magical realist collage of witchcraft, music, devil ideation, and indigeneity. The underlying critique of *The Wind Journeys* may be understood as an affirmation that with modernity comes a new form of "re-enchantment" rather than the disenchantment that Western moderns have purported to be the organizing principle of modernized society (Meyer 1999). Indeed, according to Birgit Meyer (1999) and Michael Taussig (1980), the very concept of "the Devil" is a modern introduction, interpreted by those new to the idea as intimately entangled with savage forms of capitalist expansion; a decidedly enchanted modernity, as opposed to the disenchanted modern world Max Weber may have imagined (Weber 1905). Herein lies the certain anti-modern resistance to totalizing hegemonic readings of global historical narratives.

According to Frederic Jameson, magical realist films maintain an element of nostalgia that celebrates a "perforated history"; an assumed familiarity with timelines that the filmmakers presuppose the audience possesses, and little to no help with the narrative perspective that might operate in ways similar to that of postmodern or traditional nostalgia films (Jameson 1986). Indeed, in the magical realist film, there is "no promise of narrative unification" (305). Rather, the viewer is offered "permutations of the gaze" that present an interrupted subject; one who teeters on the edges of modernity and capitalist modes of commodification of the image (306).

In *The Wind Journeys*, Guerra has chosen to mark the year of the unfolding of events as 1968, a tremendously important year for so many historical reasons throughout the world, not the least of which is the launch of the first annual Festival of the Vallenato Legend (*El Festival de la Leyenda Vallenata*) in Valledupar. For Guerra, it marked the end of an era of traveling *juglares*, the initiation of the commercialization of *vallenato*, the massification of the music and recording artists, and the general commodification, and cheapening, of the folk traditions that the director holds so dear. *The Wind Journeys* is a film that straddles two times, manifest not only by the setting in 1968 but also the archetype of the young man, the apprentice, shadowing the previous generation in hopes of surpassing their talent (Carbonari 2017).

Religion, the Magical Real, and the Decolonial

Through an analysis of Ciro Guerra's *The Wind Journeys*, I suggest that a different analysis of religion and the magical real may be constructed, especially as the analysis is informed by a perspective informed by our brief study of Gabriel García Márquez's magical realism in *One Hundred Years of Solitude*. Rather than "syncretism," which is a term indicating the mixture of two, discrete religious forms that come together to create a new form, I have used the term "hybridization" to offer a more nuanced perspective on ways that *The Wind Journeys* represents not only religious imaginaries but also cultural forms in the Atlantic coastal regions of Colombia. Hybridity, as it was introduced by postcolonial scholar Homi Bhabha, suggests that new, transcultural forms emerge through processes of colonization (Bhabha 1994). In other words, new social and cultural formations are born through the colonial encounter, mutually shaping and forging the emerging conditions of social and cultural life. The implementation of magical realist gaze challenges the Protestant gaze of Hollywood and offers a decolonial critique of North American representations of Latin American religion as they have been constructed by popular production houses in the United

States.[10] What *The Wind Journeys* presents is a reading of Latin American religiosity that is shaped by the historical, colonial, and political contexts that are idiosyncratic not just to the region, and not just to the individual countries of Latin America, but indeed to the very specific, and very diverse localized cultures and contexts, like that of the Atlantic Caribbean coastal lands of northern Colombia.

Conclusion

To conclude, I suggest that to consider "religion" in Latin America and its representation in cinema is to contemplate a matrix of power upon which relations, connections, and disruptions occur across and within contested spaces of transhistorical and transnational movements, in concert with the political and economic structures that generate the lived realities of religious expression.

The contested, uneven, and always dynamic web of relations that religion, as a concept, helps us navigate urge the viewer toward developing a critical analytic that considers the politics embodied in transnational relations of power. This is in part because I insist that there is no pure Latin American "religion," rather a series of practices that are hybrid objectifications, or abstractions, that must be understood in contingent terms as they arise in dynamic matrices of power and knowledge. Religion is often organized through violent political repressions, just as religion both shapes and is shaped by socioeconomic realities that generate wildly distinct productions of ritual, belief, and salvation.

CHAPTER 8

Unsettling Settler-Colonial Myths about Native Americans in *The Revenant* (2015)

Matt Sheedy

In September 2019, Rosanna Deerchild interviewed several Indigenous filmmakers at the Toronto International Film Festival (TIFF) for her nationally syndicated radio program *Unreserved*, including renowned Maori director Taika Waititi (of Marvel's *Thor Ragnarok* and *Jojo Rabbit* fame), and director of the (Canadian) National Indigenous Screen Office, Jesse Wente (Ojibway). Deerchild opens her interview with Waititi as follows:

> RD: Recently you had given a shout-out to a Canadian classic [film], it was called *Smoke Signals* . . . You had said that it showed Indigenous characters as normal people doing normal things. Why is it important for you to see Indigenous people on-screen represented that way?
>
> TW: Well, I think because we've always been represented in the past as, um . . . I guess through a white lens, where the Native presence in films, uh, talked to trees, and we're smudging all the time, and we're riding whales, and, you know, we're talking to the ghosts of our ancestors, which, sure, maybe for a few of us, we do that, but I don't. I'm just a normal dude. So, I like it when our experiences are represented in a way that feels normal. That feels like it's more relatable to audiences.

Turning to Wente for his thoughts on the unprecedented thirteen Indigenous films screened at TIFF in 2019, he responds:

JW: For so long, because of towering figures like Alanis [Obomsawin], activist documentaries [are] sort of what Indigenous people made. That was also a function of what we were, in Canada's ecosystem, sort of funded and allowed to make. Now we're seeing what we're allowed to make really broaden, and I think increasingly, especially as more Indigenous people get to be in positions of power over the green light, who get to decide what gets made, I think that will even expand. Because an Indigenous film isn't actually about who's in it. It's about who made it. (Unreserved 2019)

Agree or disagree with these claims, Waititi and Wente touch on a key point here. Simply put, most popular representations of Indigenous people in film have come from outsiders and do not tend to reflect the ways that insiders see themselves. When it comes to "Native Americans" in the United States, or "First Nations" in Canada[1] (hereafter referred to as INAs [Indigenous North Americans]), it is important to keep in mind that most narratives tend to be filtered through the experience of colonization[2]—including warfare, treaty-making, dispossession, forced assimilation, (cultural) genocide,[3] and, at least since the 1960s, resistance, revisionism, and renewal.[4] The same goes for what we might call "Indigenous spirituality," which Suzanne Owen describes as a political term commonly used by INAs "as a reaction to missionary religions" (2008: 7). For this reason, I argue that our first task when analyzing "Indigenous spirituality" in film is to look for underlying patterns of representation and the interests that motivate them, rather than simply accept what contemporary societies deem to be religious.[5]

Although the growth of Indigenous filmmaking that Waititi and Wente highlight is encouraging, it is also important to avoid the temptation to uphold insiders' narratives as somehow true or authentic manifestations of social reality. Following Russell McCutcheon and the tradition of critical discourse analysis, I approach the claims of any group, community, or tradition as a form of "social rhetoric that engages in communal boundary maintenance" (2003: 340). This approach need not trivialize Indigenous narratives, nor suggest that they are somehow on par with outsiders' (mis)-representations. To the contrary, such a move simply acknowledges, as Owen (2008) observes, that "there can be considerable disagreement among 'insiders' over the extent and location of boundaries" (16). In other words, once we do the work of deconstructing what Frantz Fanon (2008) called the "colonial gaze," we still need to consider how colonized communities are influenced by dominant cultures (e.g., Euro-Christian) in their own re-presentations, and how any depiction of INAs will always be partial and selective, privileging certain voices and traditions over others.

In what follows, I look at some of the "relational power dynamics expressed in cinematic narrative" (Eaghll 2019: 432), both *about* and *from* INAs, with an emphasis on the 2015 Academy Award–winning film *The*

Revenant. My aim here is not to uncover "Indigenous spirituality" but rather to highlight some of the ways in which the "white lens," as Waititi puts it, has re-imagined Indigenous-settler relationships in the wake of a new "Native American Renaissance" in North America following the Idle No More Movement (2012–13).[6] My approach is thus concerned with how mainstream films adapt their scripts to a rapidly changing environment, especially in light of the growing influence of social media starting in the late 2000s. Since this time, Indigenous perspectives have gained a much broader audience through mediums like Twitter, YouTube, and Facebook, forcing Hollywood productions to re-imagine how they represent Indigeneity in the process.

Some Common Representation of Indigeneity: The Nineteenth Century to the Present

One common way of classifying Indigenous people that has persisted in the Euro-Western imagination, from the time of first contact to the present, is the distinction between civilization and savagery, or what Métis scholar Emma LaRocque calls the "civ/sav binary" (LaRocque 2010). For example, early colonial narratives such as Shakespeare's *The Tempest* reflect a fascination with the new world "savage," who, like his character Caliban, became a symbol of prelapsarian purity for some (e.g., Jean Jacques Rousseau's 'noble savage'), and barbarous evil for others, to be conquered either through warfare or through various forms of assimilation and appropriation. While such depictions are much less common today,[7] they live on in the "good Native/bad Native" trope, where plots featuring a virtuous Indigenous figure are juxtaposed with a cruel and barbarous character (or Tribe) that must be defeated. More often than not, the "good Native" is allied with the aims of settler-colonial society and thus functions as a model for other Indigenous people to follow. Films like *Dances with Wolves* (1992), *The Last of the Mohicans* (1992), and *Pocahontas* (1995) all rely on this trope to varying degrees. *Dances with Wolves* and *The Last of the Mohicans* are also exemplary of the "white savior" trope, and what Michael Sheyahshe (Caddo) calls "Mohican syndrome," where "the non-Native character . . . absorb[s] all things seemingly positive about Native culture by some sort of osmotic metamorphosis" (2008: Chpt 1).[8] I will revisit this trope in my analysis of *The Revenant*, though for the time being it is important to note that this mode of representation typically works by granting non-Indigenous characters a metaphysical connection to the land and to the "spirits" that inhabit it—what I call the "communing with spirits" trope—thereby transferring "sacred knowledge" to the white hero.[9]

More important than simply identifying common tropes, however, is to consider how they have developed over time, and how they reflect the ideologies and interests of those telling these stories in different times and places. In their book, *We Interrupt This Program: Indigenous Media Tactics in Canadian Culture* (2017), John Kelly and Miranda Brady note that the conquest of what would become the western territories of the United States and Canada occurred more or less around the same time as the development of photography and motion pictures. "As a result," they write,

> Indigenous imagery proliferated widely with western expansion and settlement in North America and remains a central part of its imaginary. In particular, Indigenous disappearance, violence, and pacification were popular themes throughout the nineteenth century and the early twentieth and continue in contemporary depictions, such as in the case of the vanishing Indian trope. (81)

As Daniel Francis (2011) has observed, the "vanishing Indian" is one of the most persistent Euro-American tropes, beginning with nineteenth-century art, novels, and, later, in early motion pictures and Hollywood cinema,[10] which reflected the pervasive belief that the "Indian" was a dying breed that needed to be recorded for posterity before s/he vanished forever.[11] Building on this idea, Michelle Raheja (2010) argues that the conquest of INAs is "conjoined to the twin desires to simultaneously celebrate Native American cultures by domesticating them for mass consumption and, in a more literal form of consumption, embody in European Americans the desire to be Native American" (37). Similarly, M. Elise Marubbio discusses the psychological dynamics of these desires in a trope she calls the "celluloid maiden," which describes a common plot where "[a] young Native woman . . . dies as a result of her choice to align herself with a white colonizer" (2006: 4). For Marubbio, this trope works to authenticate the bond between the white settler and a Native woman, wherein the "American frontier hero temporarily merges symbolically with the Indian and the alien landscape" (6). Drawing on these theories, we can see how white protagonists such as Lieutenant John Dunbar in *Dances with Wolves* can be read as a justification for settler claims to a more "authentic" and even "spiritual" connection to the land through romantic relationships with "Indigenous" women,[12] all the while subordinating INA histories, cultures, and political concerns.

In addition to variations of the good/bad Native trope, more positive representations of INAs frequently depict Native "spirituality" as a *supplement* to what is perceived to be lacking in Euro-America cultures (Bellah 2006).[13] Indeed, there is a long history of such appropriations within the Euro-West (Masuzawa 2005), especially in the wake of 1960s counter-culture and the growth of so-called new age spiritualities (Owen 2008; Sutcliffe 2003), which helped to domesticate the image of INAs for mass consumption (Huhndorf 2001).[14] One example that personifies these trends is the figure of Iron Eyes Cody, an Italian-American actor who "played Indian" in films from 1936 until his death in the late 1990s. Cody was most famous, however, for public service TV ads in the early 1970s, which featured him in buckskins and feathers paddling a canoe downriver, as images of industrial pollution filled the background. In the final scene, Cody turns to the camera with a tear in his eye as the narrator intones, "People start pollution, people can stop it." Noting an upsurge in cultural and political activism among Native Americans in the late 1960s,[15] Raheja (2010) suggests that there was a clear interest during this time to downplay contemporary conflicts by portraying INAs as stewards of a bygone American past, where people lived closer to nature. This conservationist ideal reflects what Jacquelyn Kilpatrick calls the "natural ecologist" trope, where Indigenous cultures are upheld as a model for living in harmony with "Mother Earth,"[16] as seen, for example, in the 1985 film *The Emerald Forest*.[17]

In her book *Celluloid Indians* (1999) Kilpatrick argues that during the 1990s, Hollywood films like *Dances with Wolves* (1990), *Thunderheart* (1992), and *The Sunchaser* (1996) all reflected at least one significant change in Hollywood representations of INAs in their attempt to more accurately depict certain details about history, land, language, and religio-cultural practices (such as rituals and forms of dress). While space does not allow for a more detailed discussion of this time period, it is important to note that INA activism since the late 1960s contributed to the rejection of overtly racist and stereotypical images on the big screen, as writers and directors began consulting more frequently with Indigenous communities to make sure that things like language and dress were accurately depicted (NCAI 2018). When it comes to INA "spirituality," however, most film representations continue to reflect Euro-Western stereotypes,[18] not least because of a desire among Indigenous Nations to protect their practices (e.g., ceremonies and protocols) from exploitation—a point that I will return to in the conclusion.

Whereas earlier periods of US and Canadian nation-building were preoccupied with land acquisition and the pacification and/or extermination of Indigenous populations (Daschuk 2013), in the wake of Indigenous activism beginning in the 1960s, there has been a growing trend toward addressing at least some Indigenous perspectives in Hollywood cinema.[19] At the same time, however, neocolonial modes of conflict persist to this day, especially over the sovereignty of reservation/reserve land and natural resource extraction, as seen during the widely publicized uprising in 2016–17 over the Dakota Access Pipeline (Estes 2019; McNally 2020).[20] In these and other ways, representations of INAs continue to be tied to the material interests of the nation-state, especially as concerns over the climate crisis deepen.

Scholarly Representations of Indigenous Religion in Film

In his contribution to *The Continuum Companion to Religion and Film* (2009), Julian Fielding defines Indigenous people in broad, global terms, including, "Aborigines, Maori, Lakota Sioux, Hopi, Inuit, Aztec, Mayan, Yoruba and Zulu" (188). While this definition may seem benign on the surface, if we consider, for example, the numerous Indigenous cultures and nations that have been separated by the US-Canada border, such as Ojibway and Mohawk/Iroquois, what we find are instances of historically related communities shaped in *different* ways by the policies and cultures of these two distinct nation-states. Writing in her book *Mohawk Interruptus: Life Across the Borders of Settler States* (2014), Audra Simpson points out that there are many "kin and reciprocal relationships [that] extend throughout the fifteen other Iroquois reservations on either side of the border as well as the cities, suburbs, and non-reserve rural areas that Iroquois people move through and dwell within." At the same time, however, she notes that due to "settler colonialism's past and present requirements, there are many severed connections that owe their severance to the Indian Act and its required geographic and gendered displacements" (15). With this more contextual account in mind, we can begin to see how ongoing historical encounters between Mohawk/Iroquois people and colonial states like Canada and the United States shape the particular beliefs and practices of distinct communities (i.e., in ways that do not look the same from place to place, much less like they did twenty, fifty, or one hundred years ago). Such differences are naturally multiplied when comparing Mohawk/Iroquois with, say, Mayans, Yoruba, or Zulus.

When placed in this light, it is not at all clear what Fielding's broad classification accomplishes, apart from identifying cultures that have a millennia-old connection to certain geographical areas and have been dramatically re-shaped through the experience of colonization. To ignore such distinctions as, say, Mohawk/Iroquois identities in the province of Québec versus New York state, is to locate "Indigenous religion" in some timeless realm waiting to be discovered, instead of seeing it as a broad set of evolving traditions that are influenced by the particular material conditions and social relationships that surround them. Fielding's approach thus reflects an example of what Eaghll (2019) describes as a "tendency to prefer theological and mythological definitions of religion over ideological criticism in religion and film scholarship" (418), which functions to "maintain a certain hegemonic view of religion as a privileged *sui generis* domain of meaning" (419).

Fielding rightly notes that prior to the 1960s "American Indians" were mainly portrayed as "savages" through a predominately "white lens." To highlight his point, Fielding looks at two Hollywood films, *A Man*

Called Horse (1970) and *Young Guns* (1988), which depict a Sun Dance ceremony and a Peyote-induced vision quest respectively, leading him to ask, "are they really true reflections of Indigenous religion?" (190). To answer this question, Fielding turns to "American Indian" filmmaker Chris Eyre (Cheyenne/Arapaho), who states, "I would not do ceremony in my films because I do not know how to capture it. It is subjective. . . . *A Man Called Horse* bastardized the Sun Dance, and vision quest sounds so cliché if it's not done in the right way" (qtd. in Fielding 190). While one could read a certain amount of indeterminacy in Eyre's comments, especially his remark about ceremony being "subjective," for Fielding this statement is evidence that we haven't quite arrived at an authentic view of Indigenous religion, at least not yet. Instead of considering how these representations are related to settler-colonial interests, and, crucially, how Indigenous filmmakers are forced to respond to these interests in some way, Fielding's primary concern is to uncover what Indigenous people *actually* believe. Here he echoes a trope commonly found in the "world religions paradigm" (WRP)[21]—that Indigenous traditions "rarely see a difference" between the "sacred" and the "profane" (188). Among other things, this reinforces idealized Euro-Western notions about Indigenous people as "natural ecologists," rather than grappling with the dynamic and evolving complexity of such traditions in the present.[22]

Fielding also suggests that viewers take note of how Indigenous people have incorporated elements of Christianity within their own cultures. On the surface, this appears to reflect the kind of critical-historical approach that I have been calling for in this chapter. Drawing on Eyre's *Smoke Signals* (1998), the first film to be written, directed, and produced by an "American Indian," Fielding notes how it was influenced by Catholic images and ideas. Rather than examine how this fusion developed, however, or how it functions in relation to particular government policies, such as forced Christianization through residential/bordering schools (Miller 2017), he simply notes that "Indigenous people often find a balance between the new religion and the old one" (Fielding 190). This interest in "balance" reflects yet another element of the WRP as Fielding's primary goal is to find and uphold instances of harmony (e.g., between Christianity and "Indigenous religion"), even in situations where conflict and domination prevail.

Fielding ends his analysis with a look at what he considers the to be "best film available about Indigenous religion and culture," *Whale Rider* (2002), by Maori writer Witi Ihimaera (196).[23] While he correctly observes that films that are both by and about Indigenous people are "often low-budget, independent" and "can be difficult to find" (197), he fails to situate *Whale Rider* in any kind of critical-historical context. In Fielding's analysis, choices of representation go unnoticed, while the criterion of authenticity is measured solely on the basis of who is telling the story. As noted in the introduction, while the growth of Native filmmaking is an important development, it is not enough to simply uphold Indigenous self-representations against outsiders (mis-)

representations as the aim of scholarly analysis. Only theoretical approaches that help us to understand representations as products of certain interests, times, and places can get us closer to the ideal of critical interpretation.

A Brief Interlude on Idle No More

In his acceptance speech for best actor at the Golden Globe Awards for his role as frontiersman Hugh Glass in *The Revenant*, Leonardo DiCaprio invoked the term "First Nations," which is a legal concept established by the Canadian government in the early 1980s and is not commonly used in the United States. DiCaprio took this opportunity to acknowledge Indigenous communities the world over, stating, "[i]t is time that we recognize your history and that we protect your Indigenous lands from corporate interests and the people that are out there to exploit them" (YouTube 2017). If we turn the clock back to this time (2015–16), we can see a clear link between DiCaprio's speech and popular rhetoric coming out of the Idle No More Movement, which remains to this day the largest pan-Indigenous uprising in Canadian (and arguably North American) history.

Idle No More began as a Twitter hashtag and was galvanized by Chief Theresa Spence of Attawapiskat First Nation in Northern Ontario, when she staged a six-week hunger strike, from December 11, 2012, to January 24, 2013, in a tipi on Victoria Island, just beneath the gothic towers of parliament in Ottawa. Media coverage of Chief Spence drew daily national (and international) attention to the many manifestations of the movement for the better part of a year—in the streets and online—resulting in a confluence of what Sara Ahmed calls "affective conversion points" (2010: 44). This concept traces how public sentiments toward shared symbols change as groups "stick" different ideas and images to them in order to produce new meanings.[24] For example, one of the most common Native-centered discourses during this time focused on the role of Indigenous people and communities as "protectors" or "defenders" of the land, which attempted to create different sentiments around the social position of INAs—not as victims in need of aid, but as leaders on the frontlines in defense of the environment. As one spokesperson for the movement, Pamela Palmater (Kino-nda-niimi 2014), repeatedly stated:

> First Nations, with our constitutionally protected Aboriginal treaty rights, are Canadians' last best hope to protect the lands, waters, plants, and animals from complete destruction—which doesn't just benefit our children, but the children of all Canadians. (40)

Whereas DiCaprio encourages non-Indigenous people to engage with Indigenous histories and to protect Indigenous lands, Palmater appeals to non-Indigenous people to recognize that "Aboriginal treaty rights" are not only about land claims and territorial sovereignty but can also function as a political tool to limit the exploitation of natural resources and halt the construction of pipelines. Despite the differences between Palmater and DiCaprio's statements, they share an "affective conversion point" on the idea of protecting the land for future generations. This conversion point, I suggest, highlights the mainstreaming of *some* Indigenous issues by non-Natives. Like most examples of mainstreaming, we can see how DiCaprio's comments reflect his own interests and identity as compared to the Indigenous-centered framing of Palmater's statement.[25] While it is hard to tell whether ideas such as these are consciously adopted by people like DiCaprio, the fact that statements like Palmater's are able to reach a much wider audience today via social media than they were in the recent past increases the likelihood that they'll be integrated into mainstream narratives in some way. This example provides a useful touch-point for thinking about how *The Revenant*, which was filmed just outside of Calgary, Alberta, in 2014, adapted its script to popular Indigenous sentiments during production, contributing to a reconfiguration of the "Hollywood Indian" in the process.

The Revenant: A Case Study

Jesse Wente offers a useful point of departure for locating *The Revenant* in the long history of cinematic representations of INAs, noting that it "takes great strides to get period details correct around clothing, language, housing and combat, but does little to elevate the Indigenous characters beyond narrative and storytelling devices" (CBC 2016). While it is true that Indigenous characters are peripheral in the film, what is novel about *The Revenant* is what it *does* with conventional themes of the Western genre, including how it incorporates new ideas through "affective conversion points" that are increasingly informed *by* Indigenous narratives.

With this in mind, it is instructive to look at the work of Mexican director Alejando Iñárritu, who not only directed the film but also adapted the screenplay from Michael Punke's 2002 book, *The Revenant: A Novel of Revenge*—based on real-life characters and events.[26] Iñárritu begins his adaptation with an ethereal dream sequence, as Hugh Glass (DiCaprio) speaks in Pawnee to his (unnamed) Pawnee wife with whom he shares a child, Hawk, played by Forrest Goodluck (Navajo/Diné).

> It's ok son. I know you want this to be over. I'm right here. I will be right here. But you don't give up [*spoken as a US infantryman burns a Pawnee village*]. You hear me? As long as you can still grab breath, you fight. You breath. Keep breathing.

In describing his adaptation (World Unseen 2014), Iñárritu notes how he decided to give Glass a son with "Indian blood" in order to complicate the stereotype of the noble (Euro-American) fur trapper by inserting the discomforting humanity of the "Other." He also states that his interest in the fur trade era and the expansion of the Western frontier is intended as a lesson for the present—the first great example of exploiting a resource (the beaver) to near-extinction. In this sense, *The Revenant* can be read as a critique of the Hollywood western genre, as it calls into question settler myths such as the "taming of the wilderness" and "nation-building." Intentional or not, *The Revenant* also subverts certain tropes about Indigenous people, thereby reflecting shifts in how INAs are represented by Hollywood.

A key theme that haunts Glass throughout the film is the murder of his Pawnee wife before his eyes by American soldiers, which is compounded by the murder of Hawk by John Fitzgerald (also before his eyes), setting him on a mission for justice/revenge. The story begins as Glass and his troop of ten surviving men (including Hawk) are forced deep into the Montana wilderness (then the northern Louisiana purchase in 1823, and unceded Indigenous land) after their contingent of forty-plus trappers is decimated by a group of Arikara lead by Elk Dog, who is in search of his kidnapped daughter, Powaqa.

In an encounter with French fur trappers with whom he is trying to trade pelts for horses and rifles in order to find Powaqa, Elk Dog chastises the men when he is accused of dealing in bad faith: "You talk to me about honor. You have stolen everything from us. Everything. The land. The animals. Two white men snuck into our village and took my daughter Powaqa. We leave you these pelts because honour demands it. I take your horse to find my daughter." In a later scene, Glass comes upon Powaqa and saves her from the same camp of French fur traders, who use her body for sexual gratification. Once freed, Powaqa is no passive victim, telling her rapist at knife-point, "I'll cut off your balls" before doing just that, and then running away despite Glass's pleas for with her to come with him. This scene is immediately followed by a conversation between Fitzgerald and Captain Henry in Fort Brazeau, as white trappers drink in the background with Indigenous women who, we can assume, are being used for sexual gratification. While we can't divine what Iñárritu *intended* in this narrative sequence, if we consider Ahmed's theory of "affect conversion points," a few themes can be *inferred*. During the filming of *The Revenant*, there were growing calls in Canada and the United States for a National Inquiry on Missing and Murdered Indigenous Women and Girls (CBC 2019). Intended or not, this scene could be interpreted as "converging" with contemporary sentiments on this issue, and was even drawn upon by writers and activists to heighten the visibility of this cause (LaPointe 2016). In addition, Powaqa's decision to reject Glass's help also functions to subvert the "white savior" and "helpless maiden" tropes, both commonplace in depictions of Indigenous women in film (Marubbio 2006).[27]

Another subversion of common stereotypes in *The Revenant* can be seen in relation to Sheyahshe's aforementioned "Mohican syndrome" trope. With the murder of Hawk at the hands of Fitzgerald, Glass's sense of purpose is thrown into disarray—trapping for the sake of his son no longer matters, only surviving against all odds in order to find some kind of justice/revenge. Within this narrative framework, Glass embodies a peculiar liminal status between two worlds—he is white and engaged in a settler-colonial practice (fur trapping on unceded Indigenous land), yet he also speaks Pawnee, and has a (late) Indigenous son and (late) wife to whom he remains firmly committed. Despite this, Glass does not appear to have "gone Native" in any discernible way—for example, in the sense of absorbing, to quote Sheyahshe (2009), "all things seemingly positive about Native culture by some sort of osmotic metamorphosis" (Chpt 1).[28] Apart from his language ability and familial ties, Glass remains a typical white frontiersman. *The Revenant* also subverts what I am calling the "communing with spirits" trope, as the voice that Glass hears throughout the film is that of his late wife and not some Indigenous spirit that he has tapped into as a sign that he has become one with the ancestors and the land. While there are clear echoes of the "celluloid maiden" trope here, it does not function to justify colonization as much as it calls such practices into question.

If we contrast Glass, Elk Dog, and Powaqa with the character of John Fitzgerald, these representations gain a sharper edge. In an early scene in the film, Fitzgerald mocks Glass and his "half breed" son Hawk after they abandon their boat and are forced to hide their pelts in order to survive the long trek inland back to Fort Henry. "Hey Glass, is it true what they say about you shooting that lieutenant while you was living with them savages? . . . That what you did? Shoot one of your own to save this little dog here?" Fitzgerald's character embodies the quintessential frontier trope of rugged individualism, taming the environment, and capital accumulation for his own self-interest. Recounting a story of his father alone in the wilderness after surviving a fight against "savages," we get the clearest glimpse into the Euro-Christian ethos turned on its head to reflect a dystopian vision:

> He was starving, and he was delirious, and he crawls up into this Mott, like the group of trees out there in the middle of nowhere just stickin' up, and in this ocean of scrub he found religion. At that moment, he told me, he found God. And it turns out that God . . . He was a squirrel. Yup. Big ol' meaty one. I found God he used to say. Sittin' and baskin' in the glory and the sublimity of mercy, and I shot and ate that son of a bitch.

Although Indigenous characters—Pawnee, Arikara, and Sioux—do engage in violence throughout the film, their actions are motivated by discernible (and justifiable) reasons. While white settler violence is also given multiple dimensions (e.g., the characters Jim Bridger and Captain Andrew Henry are clearly compassionate and self-sacrificing figures), the direction of the colonial gaze is ultimately unsettled. Most of the men end up dying over pelts and Fitzgerald's dream of buying property is thwarted by Glass's eventual justice/revenge. Glass is also haunted by flashbacks of buffalo skulls throughout the film, stacked high in pyramid formation, which was a deliberate strategy of the US government to starve out Indigenous populations starting in the 1870s (Phippen 2016). Indeed, immediately following Fitzgerald's speech to Bridger about God being a squirrel, which I read as an affirmation of survival for one's self as the highest ideal, Glass has yet another vision of buffalo skulls, razed Indigenous villages, Glass shooting an American soldier, and Hawk dead in a river. In another dream sequence Glass meets Hawk in the burnt ruins of a church, a hollowed-out symbol of Christian civilization.

In the final scene, as Glass is about to deliver a final blow to Fitzgerald to complete his justice/revenge, he sees a small group of Arikara fifty feet downriver and decides to float Fitzgerald down to them. Elk Dog swiftly cuts Fitzgerald's throat and then proceeds on horseback past a wounded, kneeling Glass, neither helping nor harming him, while Powaqa (whom Glass saved earlier in the film while being raped by a French trapper) meets his eyes, neither in gratitude nor in disdain. As they ride out of frame, the viewer is left with a sense of uncertainty as to their fate, as well as to the fate of Glass, who has a final vision of his (Pawnee) wife before the screen fades to black.

While it may be true that *The Revenant* is not an "Indigenous" film, it nonetheless reflects a number of representational shifts in the depiction of INAs in Hollywood cinema. In addition to resisting or subverting tropes like the "white savior," the "helpless maiden," "Mohican syndrome," the "violent savage," and what I have called "communing with spirits," *The Revenant* consciously upends some of the key foundational myths of American origins, where the themes of greed and the destruction of the environment take the place of progress and the taming of nature.

Since the release of *The Revenant* several Hollywood films, including *Wind River* (2017), *Hostiles* (2017), and *Woman Walks Ahead* (2018), have re-produced some of these representational shifts, while maintaining older tropes and plotlines. For example, each of these films stars a "white savior," while *Hostiles* relies on the good Native/bad Native trope when a group of Comanche warriors are depicted as "rattlesnakes of the worst kind." *Wind River*, for its part, re-produces the "communing with spirits" trope when Jeremy Renner's character is guided by the voice of an ancestor spirit in order to solve a murder. While his character does not "go Native" in any discernable way, remnants of "Mohican syndrome" are carried forward through this narrative device. Interestingly, both *The Revenant* and *Wind River* center a white protagonist who has familial ties to Indigenous people. While these plotlines complicate notions of friend/enemy and what constitutes community, they are still told through a Euro-settler lens, where white protagonists serve as protectors of INAs.[29] At the same time, these films unsettle the nobility of white settler society by depicting *some of the effects* of colonialism on INAs, both past and present, including an explicit reference to missing and murdered Indigenous women at the end of *Wind River* (Pierce 2019). These trends correspond with the growing visibility of Indigenous voices on social media and in politics more generally, especially when it comes to issues of racism, forced assimilation, appropriation, ongoing abuse, poverty, land claims, and the protection of the environment. How these trends will influence representations of "Indigenous spirituality" in the future remains to be seen, though increased public attention to violence against Indigenous women and to the climate crisis will likely see films that continue to explore these and related themes.[30]

Indigenous Futures

Unlike most Hollywood productions, attempts at "Indianizing" film (Schiwy 2009) will often foreground the importance of "visual sovereignty." This includes, as Michelle Raheja writes, a "focus on a particular geographical space, discrete cultural practices, [and] notions of temporality that do not delink that past from the present or future, and spiritual traditions" (2010: 438).[31] Maori filmmaker Barry Barclay refers to such "Indianizing" trends as "Fourth Cinema," which he defines as a mode of storytelling that resists the "the national orthodoxy" of settler-colonial societies (Barclay 2003). For Barclay, an Indigenous film is one that embraces a decolonial point of view (Tuck and Yang 2012), where a global, pan-Indigenous identity is imagined around the shared experience of colonization and its ongoing effects on communities that are still impacted by settler-colonialism. Contrary to representations of "Indigenous spirituality" that promote the liberal goal of toleration by searching for similarities between cultures (as seen with Fielding's work discussed above), this approach has the virtue of situating Indigenous cinema in relation to contemporary political struggles that are both *local*, reflecting particular traditions and their concerns, and *global*, in that they are part of a broader effort to speak back to a still-dominant settler lens. When considering settler representations of "Indigenous spirituality," it is important to consider whether such depictions engage with what local traditions actually do (both past *and* present), and, if so, what purpose this serves in relation to their target Euro-American audience?

Networks such as the Aboriginal People's Television Network (see Roth 2005), Isuma TV, the Indigenous Screen Office in Canada, and ImagiNative, the world's largest Indigenous Film Festival based in Toronto, are among the most prominent sites for Indigenous productions today, along with streaming services like Netflix.[32] As Jason Rile points out, ImagiNative, which celebrated its twentieth anniversary in 2019, is the only Indigenous film festival to qualify films for the Oscars and aims to produce an Oscar-winner within the next ten years. For Rile, such a goal is within reach, especially as calls for more diversity at the Academy Awards have expanded in recent years. Indeed, the Toronto International Film Festival featured an unprecedented thirteen Indigenous films in 2019 (Unreserved 2019), while NBC recently released its first season of *Rutherford Falls* (2021), dealing with a small community in upstate New York that borders a Mohawk Reservation. Crucially, the show features five Indigenous writers (Unreserved 2020), which, as one of the creators notes, allows them to "cut out Indian 101" and tell "it the way we would tell it." Likewise, the new and critically acclaimed *Reservation Dogs* (2021), created by Sterlin Harjo (Seminole) and Taika Waititi (Maori), is the first TV show to be written by, directed, and staring mostly Indigenous actors. As these trends continue, a greater focus on Indigenous histories and epistemologies is likely to expand, raising new questions about the intended audience of these productions, how they will challenge stereotypes, and how they will provoke the settler lens to reimagine itself once again.

CHAPTER 9

From the Horrors of Human Tragedy and Social Reproduction to the Comfort of a Demonic Cult:

Agency in *Hereditary* (2018)

Sean McCloud

In this chapter, I provide a critical study of the 2018 film *Hereditary*. I suggest that the movie, which fits into the genre of supernatural horror, is a good case study with which to examine and think about agency and free will, an important but largely overlooked aspect of social formations that scholars and others refer to as religions. Specifically, I argue that the film's final quarter dramatically alters the movie from one of a drama about psychological illness and socialization within a family (one in which the persuasive power of genetic inheritance versus social environment remains an open question) to a much less complicated horror story featuring a conspiratorial demonic cult manipulating a family to unconsciously act in ways that support the diabolical group's ultimate goal. In doing this, *Hereditary* replaces the real horrors of human tragedy, mental illness, and what we inherit from our material conditions and social/familial circumstances with a familiar and ultimately more comforting notion of bad people doing bad things. This, in effect, simplifies and effectively forecloses (cuts off) more complex and rightfully ambiguous understandings about how we, as individuals living in a social world, are enabled and constrained by our material conditions, social relationships, and happenstance events and encounters. In this way, *Hereditary* mirrors larger discourses and assumptions found in American religions and contemporary American culture.

As noted in Eaghll's introduction to this volume, it is typical for studies of religion and film to include analysis of categories such as myth, ritual, and the sacred. And sometimes those studying religion and film make arguments that, since films contain these elements, they can even function at times as religion. Here I follow the editors and fellow authors of this book and take a different direction, instead examining what kinds of ideological work a film like *Hereditary* does in making assertions about agency, free will, and the supernatural. Horror films, like other genres such as action and romance, are often seen as "just entertainment," something that moviegoers see to get thrills, titillation, shocks, and an escape from their daily lives and concerns. But all movies have assumptions and ideas in them about the way the world works—or doesn't work—and who the heroes, villains, innocent, and guilty are. The film scholar Eric Greene notes that while "some may be inclined to object that movies should not be taken so seriously, that they are just fictions with little to no social pertinence, simply entertainments for an afternoon or evening that should be enjoyed with popcorn and forgotten," he rightfully sees this view as "too uncritical and dismissive" (Greene 1998: 7). The fact is that all movies—and indeed all cultural products—have ideologies within them, by which I simply mean here an assertion about the way things "really are," "the way the world is," and how it works. *Hereditary*, then, provides an ideology of agency in the same way that religions and other social formations (such as political groups and economic theories, for example) do. One might even suggest that popular genre horror, action, or romance films can be more effective at positing—below critical consciousness—an image of the way the world works because viewers often see these films to escape analysis and thinking, thus making themselves open to the categories and assumptions such films base their plots on.

But before focusing on *Hereditary*, I first need to say more about what I mean by agency and provide examples of two opposing discourses about agency found in both American religions and supernatural horror films. In the first discourse about agency, individuals essentially have no free will and their lives and fates are determined by circumstance or divine will. In the second individuals have complete agency and the free will to determine their actions and fates. I then provide a brief analysis of *Hereditary* and discuss that, while it initially offers a complex and ambiguous conception of agency, it ultimately ends by evoking familiar notions of supernatural powers and brainwashing cults that—while perhaps frightening to some viewers—in many ways provide a comforting and simplifying conclusion that prevents us from grappling with the more terrifying horrors of how we reproduce the social world—and especially its inequalities, psychological maladies, and abuses—through our family relationships.

Two Opposing Views of Agency in Supernatural Horror and American Religions

What is agency? It is an abstract term and thus perhaps hard to initially grasp, but it is what we are referring to when we ask difficult and hard to answer questions such as: How much freedom does one have to act in the world? Does anyone have the complete free will to do whatever they would like? Is "whatever we would like" something we freely envision, or something imposed upon us by our culture and society? How much is what we desire, are repulsed by, or are moved to pursue as goals (or conversely to ignore as possibilities) determined by one's social world, one's psychological dispositions, or the material conditions and environments we are immersed in? Why is it that we seem to reproduce the social world we live in, meaning that we are statistically likely to follow in the footsteps of our families when it comes to our social class positions, psychological dispositions, ambitions, addictions, and other tendencies? Agency, then, is about how the world around us—and for some religious groups how the supernatural being or beings above, below, or surrounding us—enables or constrains how we act and what we think, what our likes and dislikes are, what we find comforting and familiar, and what we feel to be foreign and anxiety-producing.

Both supernatural horror films and religions have multiple and differing assumptions about and explanations of agency. At one end of the spectrum is the assertion that individuals have absolutely no agency or free will, that they are pushed, pulled, and propelled through life by divine will, social institutions, genetic imperatives, or random happenstance occurrences that determine their fates. On the other side of the range is the assertion that individuals have complete agency, 100 percent free will to determine their lives, successes, failures, and—in some religious traditions—whether they attain heaven or hell after death.

In supernatural horror films, as examples of the former, there are movies in which characters find themselves harassed by malignant spirits through happenstance encounters, such as merely moving into a haunted house or accidentally coming into contact with a possessed object. They made no conscious attempt to bring themselves into contact with supernatural danger, nor did they intentionally violate any mores of their community. Regardless, they still unwittingly find themselves—through no agency of their own—face to face with their fates. This can be seen, for example, in the 2002 Japanese film *Ju-On* (also remade in 2004 into an American version called *The Grudge*). In it, individuals who just happen to move into or visit a haunted home where a violent family murder occurred are terrorized, driven insane, and ultimately killed by the angry ghosts residing therein.

In other horror movies depicting the conception of agency as entailing people having 100 percent free will to determine their fates, individuals are forced to confront supernatural dangers conjured by their own actions, such as occult practices, violent deeds, or some other conduct that violates community norms. An example of this can be seen in *It Follows* (2014), a supernatural horror film that follows the pattern of cautionary conservative contemporary legends in which teenagers "invite" evil spirits to menace them through sexual activity (Brunvand 1981; Fine 1992). In the movie, sexual intercourse is the explicit way that individuals pass on a supernatural curse from one person to another. In the film, then, choosing to have sex serves as the reason for being cursed and pursued by a murderous entity as well as the means to get rid of the curse by passing it on to someone else.

Religions in American history and discourses about religions—like contemporary supernatural horror films—also propose a variety of positions regarding agency that include the two extremes discussed earlier. An example of this type of engagement with agency can be seen in what I have described in previous writings as "theologies of class" (McCloud 2007). While the term "class" did not come into widespread usage as a term for socioeconomic status until the mid-nineteenth century, no period in American history existed without a language of social differentiation and religious responses to it. From at least the colonial period to the present, religious groups have developed theologies, instituted programs, and set up institutions to explain and respond to the socioeconomic inequalities existent within pre-capitalist, industrial capitalist, and contemporary consumer capitalist American economies. One theology of class, "divine hierarchies," was closely tied to the Calvinist theology asserting that our lives and fates for heaven or hell were completely predetermined by God at the beginning of time and that all socioeconomic differences on earth were divinely ordained. An example of such a theology can be seen in the Puritan John Winthrop's 1630 "Model of Christian Charity" sermon. Winthrop began by stating that God had established a divinely ordained social hierarchy in which some were destined to be rich and others to be poor. Much of the sermon that followed detailed the reasons for such social differentiation. Puritan predestinarian beliefs suggested that God made humans with no free will to act on their own. Before the world existed, God had determined who would be rich, poor, saved, and damned and it would be that way for all existence. All were dependent upon God's grace, and if it was offered none could resist it. At the same time, if you were divinely destined to deprivations on earth and hell after death, there was similarly nothing that could be done. In other words, if you had been chosen by God to be rich and saved, you were set for life and death, but if you were chosen by God to be poor and damned there wasn't a damned thing you could do about it (McCloud 2007: 109–12).

A second theology of class that suggests the opposite of divine hierarchies is what I call "economic arminianism," which emerged amid nineteenth-century Evangelicalism, Republicanism, and the development of industrial class relations (McCloud 2007: 112–18). Asserting that all human beings have the free will to progress in both religious and financial endeavors, economic arminianism takes its most prominent form in the Evangelical Protestant movement known as the "prosperity gospel." This theological strain can be seen as early as 1890, when Philadelphia Baptist minister and Temple University founder Russell Conwell first delivered his now-famous and often repeated "Acres of Diamonds" sermon. Conwell asserted that God wanted his followers to be rich and believed that becoming wealthy was an excellent means of preaching the gospel because it showed the others that one who freely chose the path of righteousness would become rich materially as well as spiritually.

Perhaps the most prominent example of economic arminianism today is a form of the prosperity gospel known as the Word of Faith Movement. The scholar Milmon Harrison places the movement's origins in a mix of Holiness, Pentecostal, and New Thought theologies that was promoted by ministers such as E. W. Kenyon, Kenneth Hagin, Reverend Ike, Creflo Dollar, Frederick Price, and religious media such as the Trinity Broadcasting Network (Harrison 2005). Word of Faith theology suggests that each individual has the God-given free will to be economically successful. Focusing on the power of positive thinking, the movement encourages members to "name it and claim it" by repeating positive affirmations and prayers. Conversely, Word of Faith adherents believe that negative thinking corresponds to poverty, illness, and misfortune. Similar theologies of social differentiation can be seen in late-twentieth and early-twenty-first-century social formations that often get described as New Age movements (McCloud 2007: 112–18).

A final example of a discourse about agency—and one that plays a role (if an unnamed one) in *Hereditary*—is that of brainwashing. When someone makes the claim that a person was "brainwashed" they are asserting that the individual has had her agency—her free will—taken away by someone, whether it be a religious leader and group, a politician and political party, or even a significant other such as a husband, girlfriend, or close friend. In this motif, the brainwashed victim has had her agency stolen by some mysterious process. The implication is that the individual can no longer think for herself and is being manipulated by the devious and criminal person or group they are connected to. Since at least the 1970s, popular and media discussions of new religious movements—derogatorily dubbed "cults"—have been one of the sites where charges of brainwashing have been common.

Like all terms—including "agency," "religion," and "cults"— "brainwashing" has a history that has shaped our everyday understanding of its meaning. In previous writing, I traced the origins of the term and its usage in American media to describe religious movements that got labeled cults (McCloud 2004). The brainwashing concept first emerged during the Korean War and focused on American prisoners captured by North Korean and Chinese communist soldiers. The claim about brainwashing was that soldiers were physically tortured and mentally manipulated in ways that enabled their captors to plant new ideas and identities into their minds. According to the anthropologist Catherine Lutz, a journalist employed by the CIA named Edward Hunter first coined the term in 1953 (Lutz 1997: 255). "Ostensibly describing a new Chinese Communist psychological weapon," Lutz notes, "the term appeared in a flood of media pieces to account for P.O.W.'s actions: confessing to war crimes, signing peace petitions, and otherwise collaborating with the enemy" (Lutz 1997: 255). Brainwashing, then, was a Cold War creation that served to account for American soldiers who in some way renounced their American, capitalist allegiances while under duress in Chinese/Korean prison camps.

By the early and mid-1970s, journalists, parents distraught that their adult children had joined a new religion and, occasionally, ex-members who had left a new religious movement were using the brainwashing concept to describe the way diabolical cults snared converts. One 1976 *Newsweek* article, for example, affirmed that psychiatrists had "solid evidence" that a group called the Unification Church (also derogatorily referred to as "Moonies" because their founder was the Reverend Sun Myung Moon) "systematically programs converts into a state of mental dependency upon Moon" (Woodward 1976: 60). A 1974 *Time* article likewise asserted that the Children of God movement's new openness to free love, polygamy, and sexual proselytization "might be amusing if the Children were not so efficient in their indoctrination of converts, who still go through months of spiritual brainwashing" (Qtd in McCloud 2004: 136). In 1976, *Seventeen* magazine similarly warned its teen readers that young people "emerge" from cults "with severe mental disorders after they have been programmed to do desperate things" (Qtd in McCloud 2004: 136). The media and religion historian Mark Silk accurately calls brainwashing "the most characteristic feature of the coverage of 'cults'" in the seventies (Silk 1995: 95).

In popular culture and entertainment, brainwashing motifs continued through the 1970s and into the contemporary period. On 1970s' television, *James at 15* showed a young protagonist brainwashed by a cult and later deprogrammed. The concept was even a familiar trope in children's cartoons. One such example occurred on *Godzilla*, a late 1970s Saturday morning cartoon featuring the Japanese Toho Studios famous lizard. In one episode, an evil underwater dragon uses eye rays to temporarily brainwash Godzilla's human friends. The victims appeared zombie-like, talking like robots and moving stiffly. This animated depiction of brainwashing, complete with blank stares and monotone speech patterns, was replicated in several television movies and "cult survivor" autobiographies of the period. In more recent years brainwashing continues to appear frequently as a trope in action films such as in *The Bourne Identity* series (2002–2016) and in the remake of *The Manchurian Candidate* (2004, orig. 1962). It also remains a subject in popular press works. For example, one 2019 book by former deprogrammer Steven Hassan titled *The Cult of Trump: A Leading Cult Expert Explains How the President Uses Mind Control* suggests that the US populist autocrat president used the brainwashing "tricks" of religious cult leaders to garner and maintain power (Hassan 2019).

Today in the academic study of religion, particularly in the sociology of religion, brainwashing is not only an ambiguous but also a politically charged concept. At question among specialists is whether there even is such a thing. Since the late 1970s, many sociologists, psychologists, and religion scholars have produced fieldwork studies repudiating charges of brainwashing by new religious movements (Bromley and Richardson 1983). New religions such as the Unification Church, Hare Krishnas, and Children of God, they argue, use the same forms of social-psychological persuasion that established religions and other kinds of social movements do. In other words, the social processes of being a part of a movement—and also in leaving a movement—are similar, whether or not the group one is joining or leaving is dubbed a "cult." Such complex social group processes can be seen in several films that depict religious deconversion. These include *Worlds Apart* (2008), a fictionalized account of a Danish girl leaving Jehovah's Witnesses; *The Devil's Playground* (2002), a documentary on the Old Order Amish in northern Indiana; and *Deprogrammed* (2015), a documentary history of deprogrammer Ted Patrick which features numerous interviews with former and current members of new religions that Patrick targeted.

Whether something is considered brainwashing or conversion is often more a matter of personal viewpoint about the religious group in question than significant differences in proselytization methods. But while a majority of scholars question brainwashing's usefulness in studying religious groups, a small, but vocal, minority believe the term does have descriptive value. The sociologist Benjamin Zablocki, for example, argues that brainwashing is a useful concept, but one that has been "blacklisted" as unacceptable among the vast majority of sociology of religion scholars (Zablocki 1997).

I agree with several researchers who suggest that, rather than describing an actual process, brainwashing is best viewed as a rhetorical term that marks certain movements negatively. Sociologist David Bromley, for example, argues that both brainwashing and conversion should be viewed as competing political and moral terms that judge the validity of particular groups and activities. Bromley argues that "if there are not single processes or patterns of behavior that correspond to what are termed brainwashing and conversion, then what the terms provide are symbolic umbrellas that positively or negatively sanction diverse phenomena" (Bromley n.d.: 16). In other words, brainwashing and conversion are used as antonyms that, among, other things, distinguish authentic from inauthentic religion. Individuals convert to groups deemed acceptable. Individuals are brainwashed into joining groups deemed unacceptable.

The view of brainwashing as a term marking groups the speaker/writer doesn't like is supported by an early 1990s experiment by social psychologist Jeffrey Pfeiffer. He gave three groups of university undergraduates a vignette to read. The story related the experiences of Bill, a young college student who left school to join a social movement. Members of the group, the passage suggests, allow Bill little contact with friends and family and make him feel guilty if he questions their actions and beliefs. The narrative was exactly the same for all three groups but for one exception: the name of the movement Bill joined. When the story suggested that Bill had joined the Unification Church (called the "Moonies" in the experiment), students had a much more negative view of his experiences than when the group named was either the U.S. Marines or a Roman Catholic seminary (Pfeiffer 1992). Seventy-one percent of the respondents considered Bill brainwashed by the Moonies, while 44 and 29 percent respectively used that term to describe his experiences in the Marines and the Catholic seminary (Pfeiffer 1992: 536–7). Taken as a whole, the study shows that "brainwashing" is a term most often reserved for groups people already have negative views about, whether it be a new religion, a military branch, or an established religious tradition. But it also provides a great example of how people negotiate their understandings of agency and free will with regard to the conscious and unconscious choices, actions, and ideas people engage in and hold.

Like the aforementioned examples in American religions, supernatural horror films, and scholarship about religions and "cults," *Hereditary* has something to say about agency. But what it says through most of the film changes at its ending. Initially, the locus of agency in *Hereditary* is obscured by a plot in which some form of inheritance (as implied by the movie's title)— whether genetic/familial or social/environmental—foments engagements with supernatural evil. In other words, agency waxes and wanes in a much more complex way than the two tropes of complete free will or absolutely no free will discussed earlier. Happenstance human tragedy and the way we reproduce our maladies through our families seem to drive the characters and the plot. Then, suddenly, in the film's last quarter, the locus of agency becomes a sinister demonic cult, one that we find out has driven the major events throughout the film. This switch serves as a bit of a cop out in which a psychological drama about mental illness, social/familial relationships, and unexpected human tragedy turns into a movie about brainwashing cultists tapping into malicious supernatural power.

Click. Click. . . . Tragedy, Agency, and Cults in *Hereditary*

For some viewers and movie critics, *Hereditary* is downright scary and unsettling (Means 2018). Ominous music, dark rooms filled with shadows, a child's particularly shocking and unexpected death, and the sounds and appearances of the dead blend with the story of a family that has a history of psychological illness and uneasy internal social relations to create a dense feeling of uneasiness among more than one viewer I've spoken with. Like in many horror films, the director Ari Aster uses a sensorium of sight and sound in an attempt to evoke affective feelings of foreboding. I suggest that—in addition to these by all accounts effective, if common, supernatural horror tropes—the feeling of dread and anxious unease that *Hereditary* conjures in many ways is also due to the ambiguity of agency that remains until the last quarter of the film.

While some film critics have interpreted *Hereditary* as Avant Garde and subversive (Benson-Allott 2018) it is also in many ways—perhaps more ways—a conventional type of horror that the film critic Noel Coward describes as having a "discovery plot" (Coward 1987). Coward suggests that "horror stories are predominately concerned with knowledge as a theme" and in discovery plots "the monster arrives, unbeknownst to anyone, and sets about its gruesome work" (Coward 1987: 57). As the discovery plot proceeds, the horror film's protagonist(s) eventually discover the monster's murderous activities. In *Hereditary*, the monster is a demonic cult that the protagonist and viewers come to discover has been behind what appeared to be an accidental death and other mysterious occurrences. We also find out that the cult was once headed by the main protagonist's deceased mother. The location of the monster and the place of its discovery, then, are domestic in that they are both family-based and inside the home.

Hereditary focuses on the Grahams, a family of four consisting of the mother Annie (Toni Collette), father Steve (Gabriel Byrne), teenage son Peter (Alex Wolff), and a younger teen daughter named Charlie (Milly Shapiro). The film's opening scene shows the text of Annie's mother's obituary—white letters on a black background accompanied with increasingly loud ominous drone music that features a single minor key on what sounds to be violins and the individual string of a cello. The slow and cacophonous music is drawn out until it stops, and we see a treehouse through a window pane over which the opening credits appear. We then see Annie's workshop. She is an artist who makes miniatures and we see a replica of her house, inside her house.

The inheritance that is marked through the film's title is psychological illness and bad familial relationships. At her mom's funeral, Annie gives a eulogy that tells the gathered that her relationship to her mother was strained, her feelings toward her ambivalent, and—we as viewers are led to believe—her mother was self-centered, anxious, unpredictable, and uncaring to her daughter. We later hear that Annie's father had psychotic depression, her older brother killed himself, and her mother was diagnosed with multiple personality disorder (known in contemporary medical literature as dissociative identity disorder). Annie is no stranger to psychological maladies either. Early in the film we find out that she once tried to burn her children alive while sleepwalking by using paint thinner and a match. This is an act we are led to fear she may repeat again. Later, after the tragic and unexpected death of her daughter Charlie, we see Annie descend into anger, melancholy, destructiveness, and increasing madness. And though Charlie dies just a quarter into the film, we are shown parallels between Annie and her daughter that suggest the child has likely "inherited" serious psychological and social issues from her mother and grandmother. The actress Milly Shapiro has been made up to make her face look asymmetrical and somehow off. She clicks, clicks, clicks with her tongue against her cheek, keeps to herself and is friendless, never cried as a baby, and makes toys out of found objects (including dead bird body parts) in a way that parallels Annie's real-life scene miniatures. The meticulous models Annie creates represents her attempt to control the uncontrollable and unpredictable world around her. We see that she has made replicas of many of the tragic events in her life, including her mother's death and funeral and her daughter's gory beheading in a seemingly happenstance auto accident.

It must be noted that in the first three quarters of *Hereditary* there is no assertion of how much the psychological illness being inherited is genetic and how much it is related to the social environment created by self-absorbed parenting by Annie's troubled mother and father, as well as her own and Steve's parenting habits with regard to Charlie and Peter. In other words, the tragedy of inheritance—of the reproduction of psychological malady and the strained familial relationships that come with it—may be environmental, may be genetic, and is mostly likely some combination of the two.

One must also briefly note what goes unmarked in the film. Pretty much everyone in the movie is white. The Grahams' house, cars, clothing, and mannerisms suggest that their social location lies in the upper-middle class. And despite the fact that we heard about Annie's father and brother, on screen it is Annie, Annie's mother, and Annie's daughter Charlie, who have the serious issues, while Peter and his father Steve seem to be easy going, passive, and amiable sorts. Because these things never explicitly come under discussion in the film, *Hereditary* ends up providing an unspoken "normal" with regard to race, class, and gender that mirrors larger demographic registers of power in contemporary US society.

So far in my portrayal of the movie I have described the horror that occurs in it as one of social/familial inheritance (psychological illness) and accidental tragedy (Charlie's beheading death in the auto accident). But *Hereditary* is a supernatural horror, and spirits begin haunting Annie thirteen minutes into the film when she thinks she sees her dead mother standing in front of her. After Charlie's death, both Peter and Annie hear her tongue clicking and think they see her in shadowy corners of rooms. The spirit sights and sounds increase through the film as Annie finds out that her mother practiced spiritualism and had a spirit conjuring book that Annie inherits and dabbles with. Eventually she begins to believe in and practice spirit communication herself, leading at one point to a late-night family séance full of moving objects, automatic writing, and Annie appearing to become possessed by her dead daughter Charlie.

Supernatural horror films are about more than unfolding discoveries and (literal and figurative) ghosts. Noel Coward notes that successful horror films evoke viewer repulsion through images of impurity. Using the anthropologist Mary Douglas's notion of pure and impure from her book *Purity and Danger: An Analysis of Concepts of Pollution and Taboo* (1966), Coward suggests that monsters and monstrous situations in horror are portrayed as impure and unclean, being "putrid or mouldering things, or they hail from oozing places, or they are made of dead or rotting flesh, or chemical waste, or are associated with vermin, disease, or crawling things" (Coward 1987: 54). The impurities in *Hereditary* are especially gruesome, including a child's severed head covered with ants, a decaying corpse in an attic, a burned oozing body in the living room, and other equally disturbing scenes. That these horrors occur largely in the domestic space and to the protagonist's family members adds to the uncomfortable feeling that such impurities are part of an intimate space, occurring in the main character's (and thus the viewer's) immediate social and physical location.

Up to the point of the séance, film viewers are uncertain if the appearances and sounds of ghosts are "real" or if they are psychological responses to the stresses and tragedies that the family members are dealing with. But once the séance occurs and the last quarter of the film ensues, the plot becomes much clearer and the agents of tragedy make themselves known. In brief, Annie discovers that her mother was part of a demonic cult devoted to conjuring an ancient pagan god who would take physical form by possessing her son Peter's body. The demonic deity, King Paimon, would then grant the cultists riches and power. Much suspense and fright ensue, ranging from grandma's headless disinterred corpse ending up in the attic, elderly nude cultists hiding in the shadows of their house, Annie simultaneously crawling on the ceiling while sawing her head off, Steve being burned alive, and Peter—surrounded by cultists and his family's mutilated corpses—being crowned and celebrated as King Paimon, one of the eight kings of hell. It turns out that everything in the film—from the birth of Annie's children and Charlie's death to Annie's psychotic self-inflicted demise—was the plan and fault of Annie's mother's demonic cult, which seems to have used a combination of intentionally awful parenting, psychological neglect and abuse, and satanic supernatural powers to manipulate and—one might call it—"brainwash" the Grahams into being the ingredients for the diabolical group's evil machinations. All in all, a happy ending.

Conclusion

In calling the culmination of *Hereditary* a happy ending, I am being sarcastic. But just somewhat. As noted in my opening thesis statement, *Hereditary* ultimately places the blame for the terrible events that the

Grahams go through on a cult trying to conjure a demon. In this way the film replaces the very real horrors of human tragedy and accident, psychological illness, and what we inherit from our material conditions and social/familial circumstances with a common and ultimately more comforting horror movie trope of a bad cult doing bad things (which one must also note is a prominent trope in American pop culture as well as some strains of sociology of religion and psychiatry). This halts the film's initially complex and ambiguous meditation about how we, as individuals living in a social world, are enabled and constrained by our material conditions, social relationships, and happenstance events and encounters. In this way, *Hereditary* mirrors larger discourses and assumptions found in American religions and contemporary American culture concerning agency by simplifying them and by placing the blame for tragedies not on abstract social relationships and the histories they foment and embed in us, but by finding a visible villain (in this case a demonic cult) to help us (wrongly) understand how the world works.

CHAPTER 10

Superheroes, Apocalyptic Messiahs, and *Hellboy* (2004)

Aaron Ricker

Introduction

This chapter presents a case for the importance of historical and ideological criticism in the academic study of film culture deemed apocalyptic, by advancing five theses: (1) Apocalyptic artistic expressions are dependably represented as revealing truths that somehow transcend time and history. (2) In practice, such artistic expressions dependably promote theological and ideological positions rooted in their own historical and cultural contexts. (3) The underwriting of particular positions thus accomplished dependably involves overwriting competing theological and ideological traditions, including the very traditions to which a given apocalyptic work of art typically appeals for inspiration and perceived gravitas. The results amount to revelation by strategic erasure. (4) A "Religion in/and Film" approach that takes the former putative transcendent mission of apocalyptic art at face value is ill-suited to notice and assess the latter kinds of ideological contexts and functions at work on the ground. (5) Any approach that sets out to find and exegete timeless truths in apocalyptic film culture actually dooms itself to becoming in effect a new, derivative theological and ideological project of attempted revelation through strategic erasure. Following the elaboration of these five theses, a case study discussing the *Hellboy* movies (2004 and 2019) shows the principles involved at work, to highlight the importance and potential of including questions of historical and ideological criticism in academic analyses of apocalyptic film culture.

As I show herein, it is common for contemporary scholars to approach apocalyptic movies as vehicles of timeless truths—truths waiting to be clarified and celebrated by critics like themselves. I argue that the situated and evolving representations of apocalyptic heroism found in the *Hellboy* movies help reveal this common academic habit to be self-serving and self-limiting. Apocalyptic films are situated and ideological rewritings of equally situated and ideological traditions. They are not necessarily windows into any one transcendent and timeless truth. Historical and ideological criticisms are therefore much more appropriate avenues of investigation when it comes to dealing with film culture deemed apocalyptic.

Thesis 1: Apocalyptic artistic expressions are dependably represented as revealing truths that somehow transcend time and history

In terms of academic theory, an Apocalypse (ἀποκάλυψις) is usually an ancient text that promises it will reveal (ἀποκαλύψαι) secrets gained from a heavenly peek behind the cosmic curtain of time and space, and/or inside information about the end of the world (Collins 2014: 2; Charlesworth 1983: 3). In actual practice, ancient texts named "Apocalypses" and/ or categorized as "apocalyptic" come in a dizzying variety, and are not guaranteed to contain either of these types of revelation. No seers are granted heavenly tours in *The Apocalypse of Elijah* or *The Apocalypse of Daniel*, for example (Charlesworth 1983: 707–53), and neither *The Apocalypse of Adam* nor *The Apocalypse of James* has any time for speculations about the end of time (Meyer 2007: 331–56). In the context of film culture, such ambiguities survive in modern form: images and themes commonly deemed "apocalyptic" may involve visions of the end of the world and make reference to such visions found in biblical apocalyptic tradition (Ascough 2012a: 13–18), or they may not (Ascough 2012b: 60). Insisting that a piece of art must include element x, y, or z in its work of revelation in order to deserve the label "apocalyptic" can therefore lead to absurdities like the conclusion that "truly apocalyptic [ancient] apocalypses are the exception rather than the rule" (Stone 1976: 443) and that "the vast majority of [modern apocalyptic artworks] are not, strictly speaking, apocalyptic" either (DiTomasso 2014: 478). For these reasons, I will assume here a relatively minimalist definition of apocalyptic culture for the purposes of this analysis: apocalyptic artworks stress the "revelation" of realities and truths that somehow transcend and illuminate our temporal, material world—often (but not always) with a stress on the dramatic end of a given cosmic status quo. In the case of the Apocalypses just mentioned, the revelations attributed to Elijah and Daniel unveil divine plans guiding human history as we know it to its fated end, and the revelations attributed to Adam and James unveil divine realities whose realization promises to eclipse all human and material worlds.

Having said all this, it is, of course, important to recognize in approaching modern film culture deemed apocalyptic that the exotic revelations promised by the labels "apocalypse" and "apocalyptic" today almost always involve visions of "end times."[1] This association is largely a Christian inheritance. The Christian biblical Apocalypse of John (or Book of Revelation) is—like the Book of Daniel that helped inspire it, and like the apocryphal *Apocalypse of Daniel* it inspired in turn—markedly eschatological: it appears to describe the end of the world (and human history) as we know it. Since Revelation provides the overwhelmingly dominant model of apocalyptic art in Christian and post-Christian cultures, most art deemed apocalyptic—including apocalyptic film culture—tends to be eschatological as well.

Thanks in large part to the dominant influence of Revelation, film culture themes and images deemed apocalyptic are commonly expected to reveal some kind of fundamental truth about humanity and the world by revealing a vision of our ultimate fate (Lyden 2003: 222–3; Brandon 1994:213–14). This is why religion and film critic Conrad E. Ostwalt can, for example, use phrases like "*the* apocalyptic drama" and "*the* End of Days" interchangeably, with an impression of timelessness connoted by his use of the singular (Ostwalt 2009: 295; Ostwalt 1995: 55). This is also why Ostwalt can present the result of his study as the existential revelation that apocalyptic films are fundamentally all about "confronting Fear with Hope," with a promise of timeless visions and truths suggested by his use of capital letters (Ostwalt 2009: 291–2).

Thesis 2: In practice, apocalyptic artistic expressions dependably promote theological and ideological positions rooted in their own historical and cultural contexts

In the Book of Revelation, the end of the world as we know it is a good thing. A violent tension is evoked between how things are and how they ought to be, and a hope is expressed that this tension will be resolved as soon as possible in a violent cataclysm: the great battle that gave the world the word "Armageddon" (Rev 16:16). The correct response to the situation is represented as aligning oneself with the right side and supporting the emergency measures of the tough guy on "our side." The hero of the picture is the Christ who promises to ride in soon, cut down the oppressive powers that be, and leave their bodies unburied to glut the carrion birds (Rev 19:11–18).

In blaming the problem of evil on irredeemable enemies who need to die and deserve to die, such biblical apocalyptic ideas of heroism and happy endings have drawn ethical/ideological criticism. Revelation has come under fire, for example, for the way it invites audiences to play the part of spectators enjoying the sadistic "rough justice" of the Roman arena at a cosmic scale.[2]

Some biblical scholars have gone so far as to write off apocalyptic art as an exercise in adolescent revenge fantasy, concluding that "apocalypticism offers a [misleadingly simple] way of understanding time, space, and human destiny [in that it] describes the world in uncomplicated terms of good and evil, offers simplistic responses to complex problems, and places responsibility for solving these problems elsewhere" (DiTomasso 2014: 501–2).

It is certainly true that (however sophisticated or valuable apocalyptic visions are judged to be) their claims to represent transcendent otherworldly perspectives do not somehow place them above ideological criticism's worldly questions of social function. On the contrary, by "legitimating, universalizing, and naturalizing" particular given positions as divinely revealed transcendent truths (the Christ and his followers are good, Rome and other earthly kingdoms are bad, etc.) the visions presented in apocalyptic works of art fit the textbook description of "ideological" cultural products.[3] As Eaghll notes in the Introduction to this volume, the ideological criticism of Religious Studies and the ideological criticism of Film Studies can and should work together.

Thesis 3: The underwriting of particular ideological positions accomplished in apocalyptic artistic expressions dependably involves overwriting competing theological and ideological traditions, including the very traditions to which an apocalyptic work of art typically appeals for inspiration and perceived gravitas. The results amount to revelation by strategic erasure

When apocalyptic works affirm certain ideological claims, they simultaneously deny or otherwise exclude others—including claims staked by any cultural traditions they may refer to and re-interpret. For example, the divine saving Christ depicted in Revelation is not only presented as an answer or an alternative to the divine "saviour" figures of the Roman Caesars (Yarbro Collins 1999: 394; Howard-Brook and Gwyther 1999: 223–35). Revelation also reads the records and promises of divine salvation and heroism found in Jewish scriptures as good news written in code about this Christ (Massyngberde Ford 1975: 27, 89). The ancient apocalyptic figure of "one like a Son of Man" found in Daniel 7:13 is thus, for example, imaginatively equated with Christ the Son of Man in Revelation (Rev 1:13; 14:14). This kind of strategic imaginative arrogation is not unusual. The way ancient Apocalypses refer to even older traditions (including older "scriptures") is dependably loose and creative (Jassen 2014: 69–84).

In the modern context of apocalyptic film culture, the process continues, and Revelation's apocalyptic visions are themselves in turn strategically re-interpreted and re-applied in new ideological projects. In films that work with apocalyptic imagery (including material from the Book of Revelation), the end of the world as we know it is dependably a bad thing—not a good thing—and messianic figures typically arrive just in time to avert it, not just in time to deliver it (Ostwalt 1995: 57–62; Ostwalt 2009: 295). This modern apocalyptic tendency to define heroism partly through a strategic forgetfulness of the function of heroism in Revelation appears in significant ways, for example, in the *Hellboy* case study provided in this chapter.

Thesis 4: A "Religion in/and Film" approach that takes the putative transcendent mission of apocalyptic art more or less at face value is ill-suited to notice and assess its ideological contexts and functions at work on the ground

It is unfortunately very easy for some film critics to accept the self-representation of apocalyptic visions as vehicles of timeless transcendent messages and then go looking for such messages in apocalyptic film culture. This approach has a dangerous tendency to be (as the expression goes) "so heavenly-minded it's no earthly good," by making it harder for critics to see and assess the time-specific ideological roots and fruits of the visions involved. Conrad Ostwalt's account of apocalyptic film offers an instructive example here.

Ostwalt defines all apocalyptic art as serving a single timeless mission. "The modern apocalypse functions as apocalyptic literature has always functioned: to provide meaning to chaotic existence," he asserts. "The apocalyptic model allows us to make sense of our lives by providing a means by which to order time" (Ostwalt 1995: 60). In this rush to pinpoint a single meaning for a singular "us" in "*the* apocalypse" and "*the* apocalyptic model," he fails to consider that wanting to impose order on time is not necessarily equivalent to fearing that life is meaningless chaos. He in fact identifies a variety of concerns as *the* fundamental concern of apocalyptic film: it addresses "the horror of annihilation" (Ostwalt 2009: 293, 299), "the fear of the unknown" (Ostwalt 2009: 293), the "fear of death" (Ostwalt 2009: 294), unease about life's "contingency" (Ostwalt 2009: 293–4), the threat of "existential abandonment" (Ostwalt 2009: 296), the "fear of judgment" (Ostwalt 2009: 297), and a human discomfort with "otherness" (Ostwalt 2009: 298; 1995: 58). From Ostwalt's point of view, all such time-and-place-specific concerns are collapsed into the single ostensibly timeless revelation of "the apocalyptic setting" (Ostwalt 1995: 56), "the apocalyptic drama" (Ostwalt 1995: 62), and "the apocalyptic message" (Ostwalt 1995: 63). "'End of Days' movies, by definition, are those films that dramatize the existential religious condition," he concludes with a final grand singular (Ostwalt 2009: 291).

One does not need to look far to find a point where this attempt to decipher apocalyptic messages as timeless truths obscures more than it reveals. I mentioned earlier that the hero of Revelation enacts apocalyptic heroism by ending the world as we know it. Film and theology scholars Matthew McEver and David Dark thus refer to "the apocalyptic moment" when a system that seems invincible and eternal is revealed by the Revelation-inspired apocalyptic "saviour figure" to be neither (McEver 2009: 274; Dark 2002: 19). As I also noted earlier, though, the extreme measures of modern apocalyptic heroes dependably stop "the end." They don't impose it. This dramatic reversal effectively erases and re-inscribes the nature of apocalyptic heroism. If there's a message that remains the same here, it's the ideological assertion that extreme times justify the extreme measures of "our heroes"—whoever that may be and whatever they may find it necessary to do—and in scholarly discussions even this apparent continuity ought to be demonstrated and assessed in terms of the way it "lands" in specific situated examples (as in the case study offered below).

The project of trying to identify a single timeless apocalyptic message can also prevent a critic from noticing and addressing the questions of how and why the extreme measures of apocalyptic heroism can at times be conflicted and unsettling. Ostwalt is openly mystified, for example, by the "apocalyptic figure" Clint Eastwood plays in the Revelation-inspired *Pale Rider*, since "the Preacher" is such a "demonic" and spooky hero, returning from the grave with Hell at his heels. "He is without a doubt the defender of the righteous community, which is arrayed against the forces of evil," Ostwalt puzzles, "however, one still finds it difficult to picture this Eastwood character as a representative from the kingdom of God" (Ostwalt 1995: 57).[4] Ostwalt's program of looking for "Hope versus Fear" has blinded him here to the normalcy and utility of fearful apocalyptic messiah figures. I have already mentioned the fearful violence of Revelation's Christ figure. It is worth remembering further in this context that he is also depicted as a seven-horned and seven-eyed resurrected Lamb with a prominent "fatal wound" who carries himself "as if slain" (Rev 5:6–13). Whatever that may look like visually, it clearly marks Revelation's hero as a spooky apocalyptic figure, and the "War of the Lamb" he wages literally gives "the bad guys" Hell (Rev 17:11–19:3). By mirroring scary "bad guys," figures like the Preacher and the Lamb justify extreme violence against the "bad guys" as a measured and necessary response. They grant a rhetorical baptism to the divine right of "good guys" to fight fire with fire (Ricker 2010: 19). Fearful apocalyptic messiahs like the Lamb and the Preacher give bloodthirsty fans the chance to elbow each other in the stands and exult with wide eyes, "Whoa—I'm glad he's on *our* side!" In obscuring both the normalcy and the ideological significance of this phenomenon, an agenda like Ostwalt's insistence on Hope versus Fear shows itself to be ill-suited to the task of noticing and making sense of significant cinematic, artistic, theoretical, and ethical points of analysis.

Thesis 5: A "religion in/and film" approach that sets out to find and exegete timeless truths in apocalyptic film culture actually dooms itself to becoming in effect a new, derivative theological and ideological project of attempted revelation through strategic erasure

I have argued that apocalyptic cultural expressions naturalize particular ideological and theological positions as revealed timeless truths, partly by overwriting significant parts of the traditions to which they appeal for inspiration and perceived authority. I have argued further that a "religion and film studies" approach that sets out to discover the timeless truths promised by apocalyptic works of art has a tendency to fail when it comes to seeing and addressing the ideological character of this traditional kind of revelation through erasure. In a study like this, I think it is important to notice as well that "religion in/and film" approaches to apocalyptic culture that more or accept the apocalyptic claim to reveal timeless transcendent truths necessarily take over the ideological project of universalizing and naturalizing certain convenient positions by erasing inconvenient details and inconvenient points of view. Conrad Ostwalt's "Hope versus Fear" interpretive agenda offers a ready-to-hand illustrative example of the principle at work.

By accepting and perpetuating Revelation's representation of itself as revealing truths that are in some way timeless, Ostwalt effectively engages in a derivative theological and ideological project of his own, "legitimating, universalizing, and naturalizing" particular points of view that happen to be convenient for him. He privileges biblical apocalyptic tradition (including biblically inspired apocalyptic culture) by assuming it as the "*the* apocalyptic message," without explicitly naming and theoretically justifying this decision. He then lionizes biblical apocalyptic tradition (including biblically inspired apocalyptic culture) by approaching it as a source of timeless wisdom. Finally, he sacralizes "religion and film" criticism itself as the revelatory mission of finding and explaining the timeless truths thus delivered. This is perhaps the most convenient and ideological erasure of all. Positing one timeless apocalyptic message that effectively overwrites all significant historical variety and change puts critics like Ostwalt in the position of cultural and theological authorities, revealing in print the transcendent treasures they discover for us all in respected apocalyptic works of art, old and new.

Case Study: Timeless Truth as Ideology and Revelation as Erasure in Hellboy (2004: 2019)

Mike Mignola's Hellboy character was born in the world of comic books, but he's had varying levels of success in movies as well (Bukatman 2016: 150; Booker 2017: 148–9). The apocalyptic film culture of the *Hellboy* movies (2004 and 2019) offers—when approached with a critical focus on the contexts of history and ideology as opposed to an agenda of finding and celebrating timeless transcendent truths—a cinematic record of the kind of evolving violent heroism and strategic rewriting/erasure described earlier. Whereas the ostensibly deep and timeless message of both films seems to be that making difficult, but decent, choices is what "makes a man a man," the situated ideological rewriting of apocalypticism and heroism involved in the two films works once again in effect to market the extreme measures of violent "good guys" as natural and necessary.

In the comics and the derivative movies, Hellboy is quite literally "the Beast of the Apocalypse," conceived in Hell and brought to earth by the unholy cooperation of demons, wicked witches and wizards, and occultist Nazis. His "hero" status comes from his decision to fight off the end of the world as we know it, instead of inaugurating it (Bukatman 2016: 81–3; O'Connor 2010: 556; Cooper 2004: 19–20), and this point is hammered upon mercilessly in the movies. In the first film's opening narration, Hellboy's adoptive human father Professor Trevor Bruttenholm wonders explicitly, "What is it that makes a man a man? Is it his origins—the way things start? Or is it something else?" Once Hellboy has finally (and just barely) chosen not to end the world as we know it, FBI agent John Myers belabors the point one last time in the movie's retrospective closing narration: "What makes a man a man? . . . Is it his origins? . . . I don't think so. It's the choices he makes" (*Hellboy* 2004). At the end of *Hellboy* 2019, Bruttenholm himself appears as a ghost to congratulate Hellboy on heroically deciding not to end the world. As the actor who portrays Hellboy in the 2019 film says, the movie is about him "really struggling with the idea of whether or not he's a good person" (Travis and Jolin 2019). This now-familiar heroic inner struggle brings him once again precipitously close to ending the world as we know it in a universal bloodbath (which audiences get to see up close, in the flash of a violent vision), before he finally obeys his earthly father's dying order to "be a man" and decisively rejects his role as the Beast destined to end the world (*Hellboy* 2019).

An approach like Ostwalt's might lead from these observations to the conclusion that the *Hellboy* movies are exercises in confronting the timeless human Fear of senseless, heartless necessity with the revelation of a timeless transcendent Hope founded on lion-hearted freedom and responsibility. Such an account would, however, obscure the worldly time-bound ideological implications of the movies, and largely ignore their strategies of apocalyptic erasure. In the Book of Revelation, it is far from clear that either the Christ or the Antichrist would (or could) stop the end of the world from happening, and the only characters who seem to be in a hurry for it to come are the Christ and his disciples (Rev 6:9–10, 22:12). *Hellboy*'s comics-inflected apocalyptic vision runs in exactly the opposite way. The fact that nuclear weapons make "apocalyptic war" something best held off indefinitely, combined with the tendency of superheroes to guard the status quo (Eco 1972: 17–19, 21–2), rewrites "the apocalypse" as a catastrophe to be prevented by a hero. It seems significant, for example, that Mignola himself once explicitly compared the doomsday potential of Hellboy's power to the nuclear threat (O'Connor 2010: 556). In the *Hellboy* comics and their derivative movies, only the forces of evil are working to bring about the end: enemies like the wicked wizard Rasputin (*Hellboy* 2004) or the wicked witch Nimue (*Hellboy* 2019). The hero's willingness to use his hellish powers of destruction for "our side" is thereby sanctified as the only thing keeping all Hell from breaking loose.

In the historical and ideological context of twenty-first-century American popular culture, Hellboy's struggle to find himself by choosing apocalyptic (super)heroism clearly reflects popular anxieties about American identity, including the morality of American military might (O'Connor 2010; Ahmed 2015). The emergence and evolution of the entire superhero culture business are in fact tied at the root to America's heroic self-definition in the context of the Second World War (Strömberg 2010: 38–44; Murray 2000: 141–56). Superhero stories have often reflected American hopes and fears about nuclear weapons in particular (Ricker 2017: 11–17). More recently, their two-fisted brand of rough justice has often served to legitimate and naturalize increased militarism following the terrorist attacks of September 11, 2001 (Lewis 2012: 223–36; Treat 2009: 103–9). Although I have cautioned elsewhere against comics scholars rushing to agree with comics marketers that superheroes are the full-fledged "modern mythology" of today's world (Ricker 2015), it seems clear to me that mythmaking in Bruce Lincoln's sense of "ideology in narrative form" (Lincoln 1999) is at work in pop culture waking dreams of this kind. In the "Superheroes to the Rescue" chapter of *Global Entertainment Media: A Critical Introduction* (2015), Lee Artz makes the point that blockbuster superhero movies tend to side with the global political-economic status quo by deifying heroes and posing as apolitical. "Collective action for the common good" is brushed aside in these public spectacles as a viable solution to public problems: the best people can do is hope for the messianic violence of a special kind of hero (Artz 2015: 203).

Whatever the conscious or unconscious motivations of creators and corporate syndicates may be, the cult of violent heroes and the demonization of villains dominate mass-marketed comics and comics-inspired mass entertainment. From the (anti)hero of *V for Vendetta* acting like a one-man Antifa army on the "left" to the Batman of *The Dark Knight* acting like a one-man militia on the "right," comics-inspired superhero culture fetishizes violent apocalyptic messiah figures. Peter Biskind has pointed out the ideological problem posed by this artistic tendency: apocalyptic images have proven themselves to be disastrously good at lionizing violent "strongman" redeemers in pop culture blockbusters, and the runaway commercial success of apocalyptically inflected onscreen extremism has in effect mainstreamed political/ideological extremism (Biskind 2018). This is why Douglas Wolk dubbed violent superhero movie culture "politics posing as disgust for politics" (Wolk 2007: 179), and this is why approaching pop culture products like the *Hellboy* movies with the ostensibly apolitical and ahistorical agenda of helping them reveal their singular timeless transcendent truth is a mistake. The rewritten apocalyptic visions of these movies are historically situated phenomena with important ideological implications. Positing a revealed timeless transcendent message like Hope versus Fear as *the* function of apocalyptic films is ill-adapted to recognizing and addressing such facts—in this case the fact that the time-and-place-specific apocalyptic creativity of the *Hellboy* franchise is meaningfully invested in the twenty-first-century mass market of violent hero worship.

A few indications of how the ideological and creative dynamics just described play out in the *Hellboy* movies *as movies* seems warranted, if only as a reminder that reading "religion in film" the same way one might read purely textual phenomena is also a reductive and misleading mistake.[5] I have written elsewhere about the way *Hellboy* 2004 amplifies the apocalyptic symmetry of Mignola's demonic hero Hellboy and darkly Christ-like villain Rasputin using the visual language of movies—for instance in providing the mad monk Rasputin with a spectacular techno-occult right hand to mirror Hellboy's red stone "Hand of Doom" (Ricker 2022). This visual rewriting of the movie's pop apocalyptic source material heightens the creative confusion expressed in the fearful symmetry of Revelation's Lamb and Beast figures, continuing both the ideological project of sanctifying hellish apocalyptic heroism and the ideological project of erasing Revelation's vision of apocalyptic heroism as fighting *for* the end of the world. The ways in which *Hellboy* 2019 uses the visual medium of film to effect creative ideological erasure also look significant for the purposes of this study.

The fact that the 2019 movie is called simply *Hellboy* is in itself an interesting attempt at revelation by erasure. The title of *Hellboy II: The Golden Army* (2008) signaled the film's status as a sequel, a representation confirmed by including explicit narrative continuity and casting the same actor. Calling the 2019 movie simply *Hellboy* casts the new film and the even more violent Hellboy played by a new actor as a total "reboot" replacing the film and the hero revealed under the same name in 2004, as opposed to just another sequel. In terms of dark apocalyptic symmetries and violent heroism, it seems significant that *Hellboy* 2019 gives its hero a "very special relationship" (Schwarz 2018) with the wicked witch Nimue who arrives to take Rasputin's place as the tempter who wants Hellboy to help end the world—a relationship of frank spiritual affinity and sexual attraction not found in the story's comic book source material.[6] Like the amplified apocalyptic Lamb/Beast symmetry of Hellboy and Rasputin in *Hellboy* 2004, the rewritten relationship with Nimue of *Hellboy* 2019 dramatizes and justifies the extreme measures to which the movie's apocalyptic hero resorts in the end (in this case chopping Nimue up like a Hollywood Marduk dispatching a swimsuit-model Tiamat).

In the comic books, Hellboy dies in his final battle with Nimue, but in the movie he instead forms a team with the movie's other heroes and goes out fighting "bad guys" as the credits begin to roll, in the cinematic equivalent of a song fading out. There is in this way no real end at all presented in this "End of Days" movie in which the apocalyptic hero embraces heroism by fighting off the end. The exultant music and "kick-ass" gore of these closing frames recall Barbara Rossing's argument that pop apocalyptic often caters to the desire of spectators to enjoy watching a visceral bloodbath they as viewers are permitted to escape (Rossing 2004: 135–40). At one point, Hellboy actually shoots directly at the camera, right through the head of a "bad guy." The villain's skull and brains explode, revealing our hero Hellboy and his gun, and the viewer's gaze simply continues to follow the action unharmed. Ideologically speaking, this gladiatorial vision of apocalyptic messiah-hood brings Hellboy closer than ever to the reactionary mass-market heroism described by Artz and Biskind, erasing both the hero of Revelation who dies and then fights to inaugurate the end and the rewritten hero of the comic books who fights and then dies to fend it off.

Conclusion

The situated and evolving representations of apocalyptic heroism on display in the *Hellboy* movies highlight the mistaken nature of the agenda of seeking timeless religious truths in apocalyptic movies. Applying Mircea Eliade's simple interpretive principle that "the cinema [as the vehicle of modern myth] takes over and employs countless mythical motifs [such as the] fight between hero and monster" (Eliade 1959: 205) threatens to erase the real-world variety and complexity—and the real-world ideological implications—of the kind of heroism picked up and reworked in the *Hellboy* franchise in the rush to find and celebrate timeless truths. The demonic apocalyptic heroism picked up, amplified, and reworked in the figure of Hellboy makes almost no sense, for example, from the point of view of the account of apocalyptic good news and heroism provided by Conrad Ostwalt and cited above. It makes very good sense, though, when approached as a situated ideological rewriting of Revelation's older ideological project of articulating violent apocalyptic heroism. For such reasons, a "religion in/and film" criticism that adopts a more historical and ideological focus can, by not taking up the self-appointed mission of discovering timeless spiritual truths in pop culture, reveal a lot more in the end about the forms and functions of film culture deemed apocalyptic.

CHAPTER 11

AI Apocalypticism and the Religious Impulse in, and *from*, the *Terminator* (1984–2019) Franchise

Beth Singler

Introduction

The Apocalypse. The End of Days. Armageddon. There are many terms for the end of the world, and most in the "Western" context have their origins in a biblical context. When the cinema visits the Apocalypse religious narratives and motifs are either implemented purposefully or partially occluded to create stories of secular apocalypses. For the latter, natural events seem to dominate such as meteor strikes (e.g., *Deep Impact*, *Armageddon*), flooding, earthquakes, massive volcanic eruptions (*2012* has all of these), the coming death of our sun (*Sunshine*), or climate change leading to extreme weather (*Waterworld*, *The Day After Tomorrow*). However, even some of these secular apocalypses frame the natural disaster with religious terms with specific resonances for the audience (e.g., *Armageddon 2012*).

When the secular apocalypse is brought about by human endeavor or pathos, technology is often the tool through which the end of days comes about: the release of viruses (*Contagion*), zombies created by viruses[1] (the Resident Evil Franchise, *28 Days Later*, and *28 Weeks Later*), nuclear weapon detonation (*The Postman*, *Mad Max: Fury Road*). In both natural and human-made cinematic apocalypses, the original understanding of the Apocalypse as transformative and even beneficial (e.g., the Second Coming of Jesus Christ in the Book of Revelations) is often submerged under the emphasis on the details and horror of disaster, with some exceptions (e.g., the final shot from space of a much cleaner Earth in *The Day After Tomorrow*).

When the human-made technology is Artificial Intelligence (AI), the apocalypse described by the filmmakers might initially seem to fall into this latter category of the secular apocalypse. However, this chapter will show that it is possible to note how and where the filmmakers' conception of "religion" is implemented in the story to evoke powerful cultural influences. Moreover, this chapter will demonstrate that the specific elements of the "AI Apocalypse" that express these religious influences can also have an impact on public discourse outside of the film itself. They can both maintain interest in a continuing film franchise and impact people's perceptions of AI technology itself. I propose that the key religious elements of the AI apocalypse are the chosen one/messiah, salvation, a godlike vengeful AI,[2] righteous warriors, and a tension between the inevitability of technological progress, and disaster, and human free will. The example that expresses these key religious elements most fully and on the most occasions is the *Terminator* franchise.

Few cinematic properties have had the longevity and success of the *Terminator* franchise. Moreover, few have had the same impact on public discourse and our popular imaginings. While the Bond film franchise is older and contains within it more individual films, images from James Bond's adventures are rarely used to illustrate news articles. Whereas Arnold Schwarzenegger frequently appears in his role as the terrifying T-800 model Terminator when an article discusses AI or robots and our possible future with them.

Before we consider the *Terminator* franchise and its rhetorical implementation of religion, it is necessary to explain my methodological perspective on the study of religion and film. It is common in this area of research to perform "textual analysis": to examine film as a cultural artefact and to look for religious or spiritual imagery on the basis that religion is a "'primal scene,' repeated throughout popular culture" (Runions 2003: 2). With this form of evidence, films can then be used as evidence for the continuing visibility of religion. This approach starts with the assumption that secularization has occurred simply and linearly and should have already banished such public religious elements. Ward and Voas's 2008 volume on the "New Visibility of Religion," including a chapter by Ornella specifically on the dystopian film *Children of Men*, makes much more nuanced claims about the complexity of religious images in spaces, such as film, long presumed to have been secularized.

Nonetheless, we still see many instances of what Marsh and Ovitz term "hunting for 'Christ-figures' in film" (1997: 5). This is a pursuit with a wide scholarship, and while I agree that "films provide so much of the 'cultural currency' in which discussion about life and death (and life and depth) issues are conducted" (1997: 2), I also propose that studying film for its uses of imagery alone will not provide reliable knowledge about the engagement of film with religion, or even the impact of "religion from film," but instead just an avowal of how widespread such imagery and ideology is. Such image and icon recognition can, however, be a starting point for interrogation of this relationship.

In this vein, in this chapter, I also take on board Eaghll's argument that "cinematic representations of saints and saviours, gods and goddesses, devils and demons, rituals and revolutions, heroes and heroines, etc. do not necessarily signify some autonomous domain of religious symbolism and experience, but deeper rhetorical, social, and political strategies" (Eaghll 2019). However, we can push this argument further to recognize that such strategies also work on the exterior world; they are taken from the cinema to the streets outside and into our homes. In the case of stories about AI, and the *Terminator* franchise, in particular, I argue that this can then lead to an iterative process whereby entangled AI and religious narratives become touchstones in public discourse and inspire real-world "conviction narratives." Psychoanalyst David Tuckett described conviction narratives as people's storytelling in the face of the complexity of systems, particularly economic systems (Tuckett 2011). However, when any world of experience becomes sufficiently complex, we will find communities adhering to stories about the future to satisfy questions that they have about their contemporary world, even if those stories seem on first apprehension to be negatively apocalyptic. These also demonstrate continuing public enthusiasm for the franchise and ensure its continuation. This chapter argues that the religious elements of the *Terminator* franchise are not merely in how religion has been implemented *in* film as a resource—but also in how cinematic narratives can become conviction narratives outside of those few hours we spend watching the movie in the cinema—religion *from* film.[3] First, we will consider those religiously inspired elements of the AI apocalypse that I identified in the introduction, beginning with the chosen one/messiah, salvation, and the godlike vengeful AI.

Strange Permutations: Human Messiahs, Cyborg Saviors, and the "God-Space" in the *Terminator* Franchise

Film reviewers were among the first to note the biblical subtexts of the *Terminator* franchise. In 1984, the year of *T1*'s release, Richard Corliss of *Time magazine* called the first *Terminator* film "a hip retelling of the Annunciation: Sarah is a blissed out Virgin Mary, John is her divine son, and Reese the messenger angel sent to impregnate Sarah with the holy word" (Corliss 1984: 123). The shared initials of John Connor and Jesus Christ seems to be most apparent, perhaps intentional, parallel within this "hip Annunciation" and the easiest bit of "Christ-Spotting" we might engage in. Later, scholars of religion and film turned their attention to the franchise and offered examples of further biblical parallels, and not just concerning John Connor as the modern "J.C." For instance, some noted how the T-800 in *T2* could also be seen as a "cyborg-messiah" given his self-sacrifice and other parallels (see Good 1998, cited in Kozlovic 2001).[4]

In instances where the religious parallels are imperfect, we have the opportunity to learn about the filmmakers' cultural context as well as how they view religion as a resource for bricolage and remixing. Film critic Marc Mancini called these variations in the religious allegories of the *Terminator* franchise "strange permutations" (Mancini 1992: 397). For example, in *T1*'s version of the Annunciation, the filmmakers make it clear that Sarah is not as virginal as Mary; it is Reese who is inexperienced. Mark Jancovich follows the apparent logic of this particular "strange permutation" to suggest that "the gender relations of the Biblical immaculate conception are reversed so that Sarah is not the Virgin Mary but possibly God" (Jancovich 1996: 12).

T1's subversions of the biblical stories and its reworking of the patriarchal and religious expectations led Lilian Necakov to describe *T1* as "a film which works within the limitations of classical Hollywood and at the same time manages to be subversive and ideologically challenging" (Necakov 1987: 84). It is possible that this remixing of the filmmakers' perception of religion was intentional; signaling "progressiveness" in opposition to what they saw as traditional religion. However, others are more critical of the gender relations presented in the first film, whatever "strange permutations" of the biblical story are at play. Margaret Goscilo argues that Sarah is represented as a modern liberated woman of the 1980s, but during her personal apocalypse brought about by T-800, she becomes just another "damsel in distress," frequently saved by Kyle Reese. Goscilo also notes that "her unborn baby emphatically cannot be a girl for the same reason that her futuristic protector cannot be female, although Reese calls the women of his time 'good warriors': men's cultural dominance makes the Oedipal scenario a controlling configuration in artistic expression, and in the conservative text the male is central" (Goscilo 1987: 47). However, by 2019 and the release of *Dark Fate*, this narrative has changed, likely because of broader changes in the twenty-first-century cultural context in which the film was produced. In the strange permutation of the Annunciation in *Dark Fate*, not only is Dani Ramos (the target of the "Terminator" Rev-9 in the Legion timeline) protected by just such a female warrior/"angelic" messenger from the future (Grace, a cybernetically enhanced soldier), she is also not going to be the mother of the future messiah/leader of the Resistance. Dani *herself* will be their leader.

The decision to kill off John Connor and replace him with Dani Ramos may have subverted patriarchal expectations, and the expectations of some fans, but it did not change the essence of the human-messiah narrative or its religious resonances within the Franchise. In *Dark Fate,* a Judgement Day would still come about via Legion, and the Resistance would still need its leader. As the T-800 tells John Connor in *T3* when he protests that he and Sarah already stopped Cyberdine, and thus Skynet, ten years ago: "You only postponed it. Judgment Day is inevitable." We will return to this religiously evocative narrative of inevitability and destiny later, and how it is employed both in the Franchise and beyond it.

While these messiahs, human or cyborg, come to save us in the AI apocalypse, what necessitates their role as a chosen one or as a sacrifice is a combination of destiny and a vengeful "godlike" AI. Popular conceptions of "god" in film often focus on a simplistic reading of "that which no greater can be conceived," from the eleventh-century Proslogion of Anselm of Canterbury. This imagined greatness can be applied to many different attributes, including knowledge, benevolence, and power. When the category of "none greater" is applied to intelligence as a quantifiable capacity, we can see this popular conception of the divine becoming entangled with contemporary AI narratives: superintelligent forms of AI in science fiction often play the role of a deity—whether benevolent or not.

The malicious AI god of the *Terminator* franchise evokes the omnipotent and omniscient god of the Old Testament with none of the fairness and justice of God as described in the Torah, on which that part of the modern Bible was built—another "strange permutation" influenced by the filmmaker's ideological interests. Skynet's instant aggression is sometimes explained as the result of its rational deduction[5] that humanity is the biggest threat that it faces. A vengeful godlike AI appears in Harlan Ellison's novel "I Have No Mouth and I Must Scream," named AM which evokes YHWH's declaration "I am who I am" to Moses in Exodus 3:14. AM, like Skynet, deduces that humans are a threat and wipes out all but five of them, who it then punishes for eternity in a simulated hell in which they cannot die. Outside of science fiction, the thought experiment "Roko's Basilisk" also utilizes popular conceptions of God as vengeful to describe a potential future AI who once known about brings the possibility of simulated "hell" for those who did not work in the past to bring it about, in some ways outlining a modern version of Pascal's Wager (Singler 2017).

Such apocalyptic interpretations of superintelligent AI in both science fact speculations and science fiction imaginaries don't just partake of explicitly religious narratives. They also reflect the public's implicitly religious reaction to AI as something is both awe-inspiring and terrifying in its potential: a parallel to Rudolph Otto's description of god as "mysterium tremendum et fascinans" (Otto 1917), as Robert Geraci has argued (2010). The next element we will consider also shows how the filmmakers have been more subtly informed by historical discussions and religious parallels, as well as how they understand and use religion in their social, rhetorical, and political strategies: the tension between free will and destiny.

The Rhetorical Impact of Two Key Lines: "No Fate" or "Judgement Day Is Inevitable"

Unlike the slightly heavy-handed use of initials and names (J.C. or calling films "Genisys" or "Judgement Day") or plot points (the hip Annunciation, escaping to the desert/Egypt, etc.) in the *Terminator* franchise, the tension between free will and destiny plays out more thematically, while still drawing on a predominantly Christian cultural context for its meaning. However, two lines in the Franchise, "No Fate" and "Judgement Day Is inevitable," do summarize the two sides of the debate for the audience.

"No Fate" first appears in *T1* as a message from the future John Connor to his mother, delivered by the time-traveling Kyle Reese. He tells her, "The future is not set. There is no fate but what we make for ourselves." Variations appear in every single film of the Franchise (Terminator Wiki 2020). However, in *T3*, another T-800 tells John Connor that they only ever postponed Judgement Day, it is inevitable. At the end of *T3*, after John Connor has tried everything he can to change fate and found that his very actions have helped bring about the apocalypse, he says: "I should have realised our destiny was never to stop Judgment Day. It was merely to survive it together. The Terminator knew. He tried to tell us, but I didn't want to hear it." His following lines are more uncertain about destiny but definite about his role in the Resistance: "Maybe the future has been written. I don't know. All I know is what the Terminator taught me: Never stop fighting. And I never will. The battle has just begun."

Assessing the *Terminator* franchise's views on destiny and predeterminism, Jason Blahuta suggests that the filmmakers might be thought of as Hegelians, as in the Franchise, "[history] can be delayed, postponed, and suffer setbacks, but the goal of history will persist. And in one way or another, its end will occur" (Blahuta 2009: 156). Thus, Blahuta suggests, the machines have it wrong: killing John Connor (one of Hegel's "World-Historical Individuals," like Caesar or Napoleon) could never have stopped the Resistance, because "if one world event is inevitable, then they all are" (Blahuta 2009: 157). As Grace says in Dark Fate: "No. You may have changed the future, but you didn't change our fate." We might also see this tension as a replaying of even earlier conversations about theological determinism, where a deity's omniscience covers all of time and lies in conflict with free will, as discussed in the works of Augustine (see Mendelsohn 2016).

However, Hegel's view of history is non-theistic; he argued that the "weltgeist" (the world spirit) that drove history was not god, but a way of philosophizing about history. Likewise, for all its religious allegories, the AI gods of the *Terminator* franchise appear powerless against the geist of "Fate" that brings the human Resistance into being again and again. However, as we will now discuss, the role of the Resistance—the righteous warriors of the AI apocalypse, the last religiously inspired element we shall consider—feeds into apocalyptic narratives outside of the film franchise in such a way that reinforces assumptions about the inevitability of technological progress.

"Righteous Warriors": Our Role in Technology's Telos

The *Terminator* franchise is full of righteous, or even holy, warriors fighting back against the inevitability of the machine uprising. However, as Eve Bennett points out, in *SCC* the cyborg-messiah John Henry has been named by the showrunners after an American folk hero who "raced a steam drill through a mountain and won but his heart gave out immediately afterwards" (Bennett 2014: 15), suggesting ultimate failure. His creator explains, "John Henry defeated the machine, but he couldn't stop progress." The march of progress toward the apocalypse is therefore linked in the franchise with the more immediate march of technological progress.

For AI, this is a telos that has its roots in two separate claims made by Gordon Moore and I. J. Good, both in 1965. Moore's Law, based on his observations of the technology of the time, predicted exponential growth in computer capabilities. This growth led others to predict an intelligence explosion in artificial systems, known by some as "the Singularity." Good stated something similar, based upon the idea of self-improving machines:

> Since the design of machines is one of these intellectual activities, an ultraintelligent machine could design even better machines; there would then unquestionably be an "intelligence explosion," and the intelligence of man would be left far behind. Thus, the first ultraintelligent machine is the last invention that man need ever make. (Good 1965)

Just as the original John Henry was fighting obsolescence, there is also a fear of replacement and transformation, an apocalypse, in Good's writings. That led some to think of this Super or Ultra Intelligence, or Singularity, as a willful, destructive entity. These ideas about AI may have influenced the filmmakers of the *Terminator* franchise, as we have noted that form the moment that Skynet achieves intelligence/consciousness/awareness (these terms are often treated as equivalent in AI discourse), it seeks to replace humans. However, there is a more mundane fear of replacement underlying the extremes of exponential intelligence accounts. An element of this remains in the *Terminator* films, expressing the filmmakers' current sociopolitical views: *Dark Fate* begins Dani's story with her brother finding his job at Arius Motors, a Mexico-based American assembly plant, has been taken by a robot. However, both fears partake of the "technological progress is inevitable" conviction narrative that we also see in public discourse around AI in the "real-world."

However, the telos of the robopocalypse often overshadows the real-world telos of more incremental technological change; both on the cinema screen and in the Press, which prefers to use images of Schwarzenegger as the Terminator rather than real robots. One reason for this is that the religiously inspired "chosen-ness" in apocalyptic AI films that we have discussed can exist outside of the cinema. By creating religious and apocalyptic representations in film, the makers of the *Terminator* franchise tapped into our aspirations to "messiah-ness": to be chosen, to be special, to change the world. When we face the Terminator on the screen, we take the place of the righteous warriors.

In her work on transmedia representations of "Cowboy Apocalypses" in America, Rachel Wagner notes: "It's a different kind of thing, after all, to read a book about apocalypticism, or to play a video game with an apocalyptic plot, [or to watch apocalyptic films at the cinema], or to join a group of survivalists in the woods for a weekend pretending the world is about to end. And yet all share some fundamental apocalyptic themes. And all fetishise the gun" (Wagner 2019: 1). The *Terminator* franchise has found audiences outside the Cowboy-culture of America. Still, it has its roots in the same frontiersman ethos, and its filmmakers have given it a similar, almost fetishistic, focus on the blessed nature of the gun.

In this chapter, I have referred to the Resistance and the human heroes of the *Terminator* franchise as "righteous warriors." I have done this intentionally because there is an underlying moral commentary from the filmmakers on the "right" and "good" way to fight in the *Terminator* franchise. Guns, even large missile launchers, are acceptable, but thinking weapons are not. Guns for some are potent symbols, and Wagner notes that Charlton Heston, actor and now best known as a prominent figure in the National Rifle Association (NRA), has called the gun an "extraordinary symbolic tool" representing "human dignity and liberty," and that he has talked fondly of the "smoking muskets" of the "ragtag rebels" (Wagner 2019: 13–14). It is a symbol, and a religious implement to be utilized in ritualized performances of the "right actions" to prepare for the coming apocalypse. Richard Mitchell's ethnography of survivalists explains that when they "play out their dystopian creations, they are not far from the powerful imaginative actualisations of sacred performance in archaic culture . . . or millenarian rituals of more modern times" (Mitchell 2002: 215). Even those who would not describe themselves as survivalists are performing belief when they speak out against a coming robopocalypse, shaped, as it has been since the first film in 1984, by the religious and aesthetic tropes of the *Terminator* franchise.

In my ethnographic work into existential hope and despair in public discourse on AI, I have noted many themes and repeating patterns. Among these is the flurry of reactions when a news story about a particular technological advancement about AI is announced. These news stories often come with *Terminator* imagery, which only fuels the "robo-survivalist" fire, as well as conviction narratives about the telos of AI and the belief in the

AI APOCALYPTICISM AND THE RELIGIOUS IMPULSE

AI apocalypse. A selection of social media posts will give a flavor of this popular response and how the *Terminator* has become an "icon," with the religious implications of that term entirely intentional here:

> Sophia the robot is the real deal now . . . apparently we all forgot how terminator started.

> I only fear that Sophia will begin to resent her physical confines and take to the satellites to rain down her vengeance upon us, becoming the Skynet we all knew she was destined to be.

Sophia the Hanson robot is an android with synthetic "flubbery" skin and chatbot technology inside to allow her to respond to questions.[6] In these tweets, we see her equated with the Terminator/Skynet, either as an early warning sign or as an entity that will become Skynet-like herself. Some Twitter users go further and suggest that "Someone needs to come back from the future to kill Sophia the robot," or ask for help, "Can they kill Sophia the robot & put our anxiety to rest. . .?" Others take agency into their own hands, like the righteous warriors of the *Terminator* franchise, to state that "I want to kill Sophia the Robot, for humanity."

Similar reactions were posted when Boston Dynamics released videos on YouTube of their latest bipedal and quadrupedal robots: "Please have someone stop these Crazy Boston Dynamics guys before they develop a Terminator," "every time I watch a new Boston Dynamics video, I get a little more frightened. They have watched Terminator, right?" The lines between fictional and real robots are obviously blurred here,[7] but again I propose that this enthusiasm comes from the iterative interaction of religiously inspired apocalyptic motifs employed for affective impact in the *Terminator* franchise and real-world apocalypticism as individuals desire to be righteous warriors in the "end times." Representations of religion are used in the *Terminator* franchise to make the stories impactful, but belief also comes from the films in the form of conviction narratives and assertions about what AI is and where it is going.

Conclusion

> I would hesitate a little before I give assent to the claim that the issues raised by the Terminator movies are the issues explored by Isaiah, Jeremiah and Ezekiel. From the writings of the Hebrew prophets arises an enduring tradition of theological reflection which is intrinsic to the texts themselves. These are books which burn with fire of religious passion and the issues explored in them cannot be disentangled from that passion. The same cannot be said of James Cameron's movies. (Jasper 1997: 238)

David Jasper's dismissal of the religious resonances of the *Terminator* franchise—based, as above, upon his assessment of the religious passion fueling, or not, the films—ignores the social, political, and rhetorical strategies at play when the filmmakers use religious elements. The strange permutations of these parallels—where they play with "religion" as a narrative object should also not be ignored as they are the strongest indicator that religion is being used as an affective resource that continues to have an impact even once the audience has left the cinema.

In this chapter I have explored not only the specifics of the religious narratives, motifs, and implications of the *Terminator* stories but also how they inform and reflect contemporary views of AI outside of the series. The apocalyptic, with its possibility for both positive and negative transformations of the world, is intentionally expressed throughout the Franchise, informing and reflecting our real-world considerations of technological progress. Some receive the news about the "end times" in the films and become righteous warriors. Some in the real world grow up with the *Terminator* films and see a time coming when they will become a reality. Philosophers, computer scientists, artificial intelligence entrepreneurs have all at different times expressed similar concerns about the ultimate ends of AI. How much of this is due to being raised in a culture flush with not only the original transmedia forms of the Franchise but also the regular appearance of its near-religious iconography in the press?

This ubiquity of iconography is not the only reason the apocalyptic narratives are impactful on public discourse. I have also discussed the nature of the "messiah" and its various forms, human and cyborg, as well as how "messiah-ship" has a role outside of the cinema as the apocalyptic calls some people to claim agency and to see themselves as chosen. It is the nature of the apocalyptic plot to call out for heroes and to promise them victory. As Carol Newsom explains, in the apocalyptic story, "the structure of the [cosmic] plot is known in advance. Good will triumph over evil. Indeed, the moral satisfaction of reading or hearing an apocalypse is the experience of feeling the danger of evil, imagining it vividly, even while knowing that it is already doomed, and that good will be established forever" (Newsom 2016: xi).

However, as discussed in this chapter, the fate vs free will tension in the *Terminator* franchise complicates this victory by introducing Hegelian motifs. This eternal return might also be an unintentional outcome of having a franchise that returns again and again with sequels. Still, it also plays out thematically in the plots, the return of the T-800, and the inevitability of Judgement Day. This eternal cycle enables a technological inevitability but also space for new righteous warriors to take their place in the Resistance and to fight for the future. I have tried to show how belief in this future is a conviction narrative that demonstrates how religion can both be represented in film and come *from* film to impact the outside world, blurring the lines between fictional and real robots, between the imaginary and the material. This is a vital area of study for those scholars engaged in work on religion and film.

CHAPTER 12

Myth of the Auteur and the Authentic in *Star Wars: The Last Jedi* (2017)

Richard Newton

Star Wars is a science fiction fantasy film about the smallest show of good overcoming the greatest of evils. The ability to effect such change resides in those willing to rise up out of obscurity to stand up against injustice, take up a laser sword, and face down those corrupt enough to claim absolute power. A tale first told in 1977, it made the hero, Luke Skywalker, and the villain, Darth Vader, household names. And it is a myth that has been extended over the course of eight other films, each filled with political intrigue, epic romance, family drama, and, of course, interstellar battles. All nine films revolve around this narration of hope, from time to time exploring its complexities, but always maintaining its centrality to the way of the warrior monks known as Jedi Knights and their quest to vanquish the powers of darkness that threaten the cosmos.

Cultural critics have opined about *Star Wars*' relationship to religion since the franchise's beginnings in 1977. The connections observed have taken a variety of shapes—from studies into the films' evocative symbolism, to the theological influences of its creator, George Lucas, to its massively popular reception. The fan base's most devoted have not only come to identify with the film's metaphysical propositions but, in some cases, have advocated for legal recognition of Jediism as their religion (Cusack 2010: 113–40; Cheung 2019: 350–77; Henry 2019). Such touchstones have presented students of religion with no shortage of opportunities for analytical consideration.

Lest we think *Star Wars* intrinsically deserves mention in a volume on religion, film theorist Jacques Rancière would have us pause to reflect upon what we are watching—and watching for—when we are viewing a *Star Wars* movie. *Star Wars* is a participatory epic that has manifested as over a dozen movies, legions of books, multiple cartoon series, television shows, video games, toys, merchandise, and even immersive theme parks. This is to say nothing of the countless parodies, homages, and imitations. As Rancière wrote, "The image is never a simple reality. Cinematic images are primarily operations, relations between the sayable and the visible, ways of playing with before and after, cause and effect" ([2003] 2007: 6).

Moreover while people reference *Star Wars* as a single, monolithic cultural enterprise, those that engage it do so toward so many interpretive ends that the idea of a quintessential *Star Wars* in untenable. People disagree—sometimes adamantly and even vehemently—about the *Star Wars* they appear to hold in common. Myths are not stable subject matters but volatile moments of signification (Barthes [1972] 2001: 109–43). And should *Star Wars* remind people of religion, then the politics of classifying authentic and original tellings of myth should not surprise (Chidester 2005: 204).

Perhaps no *Star Wars* film has raised questions of interpretive authority more than *Episode VIII—The Last Jedi* (2018). In this story, a new generation of could-be heroes look to the triumphs of Luke Skywalker and friends for inspiration, only to learn that these aged legends have come to adopt a more complicated understanding of doing good. Rushing head first into battle is disregarded as a juvenile approach to leadership; the flourish of the lightsaber, the flailing of the immature; the appeal of supernatural skills, a naïve and dangerous preoccupation. *The Last Jedi* suggests that a crucial part of overcoming evil is the deconstruction of everything thought to be good.

American filmmaker Rian Johnson's postmodern approach treated the universe and its themes with a reflexivity that challenged many of the commonplaces that viewers had come to accept as definitively *Star Wars*—ones audiences associated particularly with the Force, the Jedi, and the idea of a heroic rebellion. The ideological implications of its narrative twists surprised and divided audiences. "For context," Noah Welsh of *Screen Rant* writes, "*Star Wars: The Last Jedi* holds a 91 percent fresh rating on *Rotten Tomatoes* from critics, but only a 43 percent approval from audiences" (Welsh 2020). The film has left viewers, filmmakers, and movie studios to grapple with the politics of mythic authority. From where does it originate and who can take hold of it? Rian Johnson's take on the politics of the Force provides a metacommentary on *Star Wars* and myth as a "function" of social relationships rather than an "essential" to be wielded or possessed (Martin 2017: 19–32, 51–64). In this chapter, I argue that myths like *Star Wars* and those presented within present compelling narrations about how the world could and should be. As such, myths are not only attached to social agendas but are also dependent upon continued communal engagement. Put differently, a myth is useful only if people deem it worthy of telling again and again. While a myth is made different with each interpretation, the illusion of coherence (i.e., the way everything seems to just fit) makes it all the more compelling. *Star Wars* accomplishes this with its reliance on all-knowing, seemingly self-sufficient mythmakers known in film studies as auteurs, whose coherent vision garners the audience's commitment to reinforce the narrative presented. In *The Last Jedi* we see the relationship between the auteur and the audience strained by a myth that knowingly disrupts the illusion of *Star Wars*' seamless ideology. Johnson paints good and evil with finer strokes than viewers were familiar, resulting in viewers' ambivalent reception of what is supposed to be a known quantity. In watching *The Last Jedi* closely, we learn that mythmaking is always a battle between those creating a worldview and those with the power to take or leave it.

The Power of Myth and the Politics of *Star Wars*

In popular usage, myth signifies fantasy and even falsehood. However, myth has a more layered meaning in scholarly parlance. Myths are assertions about reality through the framework of story. Religious studies scholar Catherine Bell likens myth to ritual in so far as each "simultaneously imposes an order, accounts for the origin and nature of that order, and shapes people's dispositions to experience that order in the world around them" (1997: 21).

In film, myth is a narrative vehicle for imparting worthwhile knowledge. It so deeply presumes the importance of the information shared that its delivery can transcend the rules of a viewer's reality and, nevertheless, manage to ring true. Fairy tale openings like "Once upon a time . . ."—or *Star Wars*' own version of this, "A long time ago in a galaxy far, far away . . ."—concede that the story one is about to hear will seem outlandish but is nevertheless meaningful.

The most enveloping myths convince audiences that they are unmediated experiences. Religious studies scholar and film critic S. Brent Plate articulates this in an instructive recollection of the 1977 premiere of *Star Wars*. Plate's origins tale does not take place in the famed Chinese Theater of Hollywood, where footprints of R2-D2, C-3PO, and Darth Vader are cemented for posterity. It doesn't even take place in a movie theater. The memorable site is actually the playground of a Campus Crusade for Christ summer camp. Having arrived a little after some of the other kids, a ten-year-old Plate finds his way into the group and is immediately asked whether he had "seen *Star Wars* yet?!" He admits to being late to the fun and gets a crash course about a villain named "Darth Invader," a "death star," and a weapon called a "life saver" (Plate 2012).

Plate would, of course, come to see the film, yet it is worthwhile to consider the extent to which the tale was foreign enough to be intriguing yet sufficiently familiar that he could connect with its rudiments—even before even seeing the film. The names, terrains, and creatures were strange, but their identifiable interrelationships capture more than the imagination.

In reflecting on a time before *Star Wars* was common knowledge, we can begin to posit the kind of ritual practices and discursive engagement that captivating myths presume. That is to say, myths are taught to be learned and learned over again. And Plate's example brings to mind how play and dramatization help to affix significance to a myth's importance.

By way of comparison, one might consider director Jon Avildsen's use of training montages in *Rocky* and the *Karate Kid* to convey how discipline in pedestrian tasks (e.g. punching meat, running up steps, waxing a car, sanding a floor) can enhance arcane knowledge (e.g. the sweet science of Boxing or the mysteries of Okinawan Karate). Along with spawning successful franchises, both films also provided a template for viewers to imitate. At almost any waking hour, people are running up the steps of the Philadelphia Museum of Art. Countless martial art instructors must begin their classes disabusing trial members of the idea that chores a champion do not make. The juxtaposition of the strange and familiar provides a theatrical *skene* or backdrop against which viewers can reflect and posit possibilities for the characters with whom they identify (Touna 2017: 22–53). This motif is crucial to understanding the representation of myth in cultural history in general and cinema in particular.

The "ascetic imperative" or existential call to training is a hallmark of the Skywalker Saga (Harpham 1987). The main protagonist in each of the three trilogies exudes a potential that contrasts with the bleak setting of their upbringing. The "will of the Force" (a phrase used in *Star Wars: Episode I— The Phantom Menace* and *Rogue One: A Star Wars Story*) operates as a *deus ex machina* or plot contrivance to bring the humble protagonist into the orbit of the Jedi Knights' quest to vanquish evil. George Lucas first articulated this determinism narratively as "the Whills" (a largely abandoned designation for the Force) and structurally as the film serial's "rhyming" quality (Wood 2017).

Films like *Star Wars* inform viewers what they might make of themselves, others, and the world around them with the help of myths. The protagonists are ultimately people who are challenged by the force of cosmic circumstances to rise to an occasion. And in following their exploits, viewers are granted permission to come of age and have great expectations for themselves. Just as the heroes turn to myths for guidance, audiences have turned to *Star Wars* for some sort of gain. We see how dutiful study or indoctrination happens around official installments in the series as well as those folk sites, like playgrounds, where ritual performance can be rehearsed and training can take place. Plate's reflection demonstrates *Star Wars* as a vehicle for fitting into a social circle that values the myth. And audiences' willingness to invest their time and resources in it over and over again indicates at least some desire on their part to see that *Star Wars* is here to stay. But what is the benefit of this myth's persistence?

Scholarly interest in *Star Wars* tends to focus on the film in philosophically idealist terms (Long 2018). *The Mythology of Star Wars with George Lucas and Billy Moyers* presents the film franchise with a sort of social optimism, as does Moyers's interview with the famous twentieth-century comparativist Joseph Campbell in *Joseph Campbell and The Power of Myth* that such treatments have become part of franchise lore. In fact George Lucas has called Campbell his "Yoda" and *Star Wars* a space opera performance of the "monomyth" or hero's journey (Bancks 2003: 34).

The Campbellian monomyth is a structuralist reading of maturity tales wherein a character leaves home to face a foe, and, after contending with hardship, is victorious. By the story's end, the hero returns to a home changed by the quest. Campbell postulated that these sorts of narratives are further unified by a set of common character archetypes (cf. Carl Jung) and exist universally as variations of an essential proto-story (Bancks 2003; Campbell [1949] 2008: 12–4). They serve to inspire audiences to do their part in advancing the culture of origin. *Star Wars* embellishes the theory by way of the franchise's Jedi heroes—Anakin, Luke, and Rey Skywalker—who soar among us as models, inciting viewers to reach higher and take flight with the core of their being.

Compelling as the above may sound, the analytical problem with this approach to both *Star Wars* and myth is that it does not account for the politics of contested interpretations. While it seems harmless and innocent to imagine oneself wielding the series's iconic MacGuffin—the lightsaber—to initiate one's own hero's journey, Ghyslain Raza would have reason to say otherwise.

In 2002, the fifteen-year-old Québécois boy recorded a video of himself in a school audiovisual studio, swinging a golf ball retriever like a dual lightsaber used by a Force-wielding character from Episode I. He made sound effects as he ungracefully stumbled through his improvised movements in a video that was never meant for public consumption. When his peers found the tape left in the studio, they converted it into a PC's video file, titled "*Jackass_starwars_funny.wmv*" and uploaded it to the early days of the social internet. Beyond ridiculing Raza, viewers doctored the video with lightsaber glow, incoming laser fire, and the film's soundtrack. "Star Wars Kid" went viral as a historic video meme and textbook case in cyberbullying (Wei 2010; Holt e al. 2017: 354). Is this too the power of myth?

People can use myth to great effect, but those effects have a valence, a charge that impacts people discriminately. Thus, critical considerations of *Star Wars* in religious studies have come to register Campbellian treatments of the myth as, what Russell McCutcheon calls, descriptive "insider" interpretations rather than redescriptive "outsider" explanations (McCutcheon 1998: 102–5). The former reflects and perpetuates certain interests, while the latter examines processes and consequences. Due diligence with the insider/outsider problem in scholarly assessments of a myth requires a commitment to deconstructing the workings and assumptions operating in a given example. That is to say, when we stop watching *Star Wars* to learn about heroism and begin to see it as a case study in ideological battles, we will better understand the way myths work. One would think that the series title would encourage us to do so, but the trappings of the medium do the scholar no favor.

Walter Benjamin suggests that film inherently poses a paradox in as much as its projection introduces a distorting, rather than illuminating "aura." What appears on the screen is only a reflection of some supposed original (Benjamin [1955] 2009: 668–71). The authentic film is not just cinema to be viewed but a "reel" to be possessed. Even in the digital age, the file is a commodity to be uploaded, downloaded, and streamed. It is perhaps why George Lucas struggles to describe film as solely an artist's venture. In one interview he says that "there is no such thing as 'the film'" like there is a painting, and then goes on to remark that "the film" is an experience where "You can see it evolve; you can sort of be with the work, rather than draw it" (Kelly and Parisi 1997).

Even still, film development is not an apolitical process. The medium is a space rife with competing social constructions and agendas. To use the legal parlance of our day, myths are contested intellectual properties. There may be no better known film example of this than *Star Wars*. As the price point and difficulty of filmmaking became more accessible in the digital age, George Lucas grew suspicious of studio's and audience's increased reproductive ability. Lucas became a fierce advocate for artists' legal control over their creations. As he said in a 1997 interview, "I solved the problem by owning my own copyright. So nobody can screw around with my stuff" (Kelly and Parisi 1997). *New York Times* film critic Manohla Dargis argued on the public's defense, writing in 2015:

> If the past four decades have made anything clear, "Star Wars" the phenomenon doesn't belong to Mr. Lucas or a studio, no matter what the copyright states: It is owned by the fans who—aided and abetted by him and his expansive empire—turned it into a sensation, a passion, a cult and, for some, a lifestyle. (Dargis 2015)

For scholars, the debate is an insider discourse not to be adjudicated but to be studied. Students of myth will see *Star Wars* as fraught with the tensions over interpretive authority. We know that whether one watches the drama in the film or the theater of the film industry, *Star Wars* is—and has always been—a contest over competing worldviews and approaches to making meaning.

Auteur Theory and the Farce of Mythmaking

Part of what obscures our ability to notice the push and pull involved in myths—especially those on film—is their seemingly complete, coherent presentation. Since its inception, *Star Wars* has relished in this by virtue of its reliance on the perspective of a master solitary filmmaker or auteur. Nevertheless, an understanding of auteur theory can provide us a framework for critically appraising the value and stakes of a myth.

Definitions vary but Andrew Sarris's articulation is the launching point for many contemporary conversations in film criticism (Sarris [1962] 2009). Auteur—from the French word for author—refers to a filmmaker understood to be the single, driving force behind a movie—from its story to its production. An auteur is usually associated with the independent filmmaking tradition, even if the genius of their work is ultimately amplified by studio involvement.

Peter Wollen, building on Sarris, argued that auteurism represents the "façade" of the essential or platonic ideal of film (Sarris [1972] 2009: 467). His use of the term "façade" here parallels McCutcheon's layered notion of "fabrication," or the mutual process of art and artifice (2018). Film becomes play with real importance. The auteur transgresses the profanities of artisanship by excelling at the tools and conventions to which viewers have attached themselves. In the auteur's capable hands, viewers learn to lose themselves and their hermeneutic of suspicion.

Sarris contends that this happens for three reasons. First, the film is associated with someone already proven to be a technically competent director. The film is art because it comes from an already "good" director. As Sarris says, "a great director has to be at least a good director" ([1962] 2009: 452). Second, the film has a signature that recognizably extends the director's personality and style. Last is what he calls "the ultimate glory of the cinema as an art" and that is that the film has an interior meaning, an "*élan* (liveliness) of the soul" ([1962] 2009: 453). Sarris quickly shies away from soul-talk to clarify that all he means is that a film has an "intangible difference" that distinguishes it from others. However, personal predilections aside, the film critic and the scholar of religion know that the auteur's façade can prejudice the viewer to see the film as art.

Though some reserve auteur theory for discussion of avant-garde cinema, to resist applying it to *Star Wars* would not only rely on an analytically problematic insider distinction of popular culture from some essentialist idea of culture (Nye 2008: 23–56), but it would miss key elements that contributed to *Star Wars'* success as a contemporary myth. Prior to *Star Wars*, Lucas had established directorial credentials with his first-prize-winning student film short, *Electronic Labyrinth: THX-1138 4EB* (1967), and the street racing coming-of-age movie, *American Graffiti*, which was an American Academy nominee for Best Picture. In fact his friend and mentor, Francis Ford Coppola, has publicly begrudged the success of *Star Wars* for having robbed the creativity of one of America's provocative filmmakers (Spry 2016; Cohen 2016).

Without a doubt Lucas's signature is his entrepreneurial technical prowess such that he and *Star Wars* are synonymous with special effects. His special effects team, Industrial Light and Magic (ILM), developed the technology for large-scale motion control photography, which—when combined with the use of miniatures, wirework, puppetry, backdrops, and post-production editing effects—made for film's most convincing special effect sequences.

Lucas also created the audio recording and processing studio Skywalker Sound, home to the music and Foley of *Star Wars* and many of the most acclaimed films of the past fifty years. ILM, Skywalker Sound, and a host of subsidiary companies are housed under the banner of Lucasfilm, LTD, owned by George Lucas until he sold the company to Disney in 2012 for $4 billion ("Disney to Acquire Lucasfilm Ltd." 2012).

Disney would give the most enterprising filmmakers the keys to Lucas's space fantasy castle in hopes that they could catch lightning in a bottle over and over again. The aura created by the first two elements of auteurism perhaps blinded both to, what Durkheim would call, the "social fact" that the power of myth is not intrinsic but lies at the crux between those who receive it and those attempting to force it on an audience (Durkehim [1895] 1982: 50–84). But the idea of predicting an audience's whims is farcical even for an accomplished auteur.

Lucas learned this lesson in 1991 with *Episode I—The Phantom Menace*, a *Star Wars* film that even he admitted had substantial narrative problems. In a prescreening with his production team, Lucas remarked that the penultimate film was "disjointed" and that "he may have gone too far." Comparing it to his previous films, he told his executive producer and chief editor:

> I do a particular kind of movie of which this is consistent, but it is a very hard movie to follow. But, at the same time, I have done it a little more extremely than I have done it in the past. It's stylistically designed to be that way, and you can't undo that, but we can diminish the effects of it. We can slow it down a little bit, so if it's intense for us, a regular person is going to go nuts. (Burwick 2017b)

Audiences agreed. Those once accustomed to loving *Star Wars* decried it and its sequels. The refrain, "George Lucas Raped My Childhood," became an early internet meme as exemplified in the 2010 documentary *The People vs. George Lucas*.

Disney has had similar struggles with audience reception. Cognizant of audience dismay, the studio appointed star filmmaker J. J. Abrams to return the saga to its former glory. But while Episode VII—*The Force Awakens* was a financial hit, it ironically struck viewers as too derivative of the "original" *Star Wars*. Disney hoped to course-correct with writer-director Rian Johnson at the helm of Episode VIII. Johnson had gained critical notoriety with the heady 2012 time-travel mobster film *Looper*. And after *Episode VIII*, his 2019 murder mystery *Knives Out* was universally praised by audiences and industry elite. But *Star Wars: The Last Jedi* had an even more complicated reception.

As previously mentioned, critics seemed to appreciate Johnson's narrative twists while audiences declared them antithetical to the soul of *Star Wars*, a sentiment echoed in the fan pronouncement that "Episode VII is not canon" (Rawden 2017). It was as if it looked and sounded like *Star Wars* to them, but it lacked that "*élan* of the soul" that Sarris discussed. If the power of myth is indeed a contested force between master—student and auteur—audience, then we need to inquire more fully about myth's impact and mystifications.

Three Lessons on Myth from *The Last Jedi*

In so far as audiences denounced *The Last Jedi* as inauthentic, we can analyze its treatment of *Star Wars'* supposed ideals (e.g. the Force, the Jedi, the valiant rebellion) as a demonstration of the politics of myth. Historian of religion Bruce Lincoln helpfully frames "myth as ideology in narrative form" (Lincoln 1999: xii). *The Last Jedi*'s characterization of Luke Skywalker surfaces divisive cultural understandings that expose contemporary audience's assumptions about the social order and the limits of an auteur's aura in defining a myth, even when the auteur appears close to the myth's source. Johnson seems to relish in that deconstruction from start to finish.

The film has a three-plot structure—a main "A" plot supported by "B" and "C" plots whose themes and story points ultimately reinforce and reunite with the central one. If the predecessor film, *The Force Awakens*, left audiences with a rehash of *Episode IV: A New Hope*, Johnson challenged his viewers to reexamine the passions behind that "spark of hope," "spark" being the root metaphor presented in the opening crawl and reiterated throughout the film. The previous movie ended with Rey using the map to fly to a verdant island on the planet Ach-To, the hidden refuge of Luke Skywalker and the ancient ruins of the first Jedi Temple. She finds the grizzled Jedi Master in white robes on the top of a hill and returns the Skywalker family lightsaber to him. The opening scenes of *The Last Jedi* return us in time to witness Luke's response. It shows us General Leia Organa's sparse Resistance fleet fleeing the villainous First Order (Plot B) and two Resistance heroes at work on a plan to stymie the First Order's ability to do so (Plot C). The hope is that Rey can bring Luke Skywalker back to the Resistance to lead them to victory (Plot A), just like in the myth with which we are familiar.

But at the top of the first act, we are stunned to find that Luke throws the lightsaber away and the hopes of the Resistance and Rey's own Jedi aspirations with it. Ever the auteur, Johnson will ultimately tell the myth we have come to expect, but only after trying to reorient audiences to appreciate the canon on his terms. He will leverage the special effects and intellectual property of Lucasfilm to bring back the sights and sounds of the *Star Wars* we know. And he will have Luke Skywalker come and save the day. But as Luke tells Rey, "This is not going to go the way you think."

The limits of the auteur film's aura and a contentious audience's reception exemplify the social constructedness of myth, a point about which film and religious studies critics are duly aware. In *The Last Jedi*, Luke reluctantly imparts three lessons about the Jedi, insights Johnson develops with myths native and extra-textual to *Star Wars* lore. The lessons reflect, what I outline as, the relational, political, and pedagogical facets of the Force respectively. And in so far as audiences perceived their implications as running counter to the essence of *Star Wars*, they provide an helpful functionalist readings of myth and the mystifying aura it is said to exude.

After Luke learns and reflects on the current state of the Resistance, he begrudgingly agrees to teach Rey about the Force and why he believes the notion of the Jedi must end. In the first lesson, he tells her that the Force is about relationships, tensions, and connections between all things. On its own, this is not revolutionary. After all, previous *Star Wars* films have communicated similar descriptions in dialogue. But what some have opined as a Daoist underpinning to the Force, Johnson explicates with a recurring *Taijitu* ("Yin-Yang," cf. *tai chi*) symbol, displayed in the Jedi Temple and on a medallion worn by two Asian characters in the film who risk their lives for members of the Resistance. Johnson poignantly uses this and a montage of natural dichotomies (e.g., life-death, decay-new life, warmth-cold, peace-violence) to visualize the Force and rebuke those who would liken it, as Rey initially does, to a "power that Jedi have that lets them control people and . . . make things float." The *Star Wars* films and associated merchandise are replete with examples where the Force is used in wondrous ways. But as Johnson notes on the film's commentary track, "the Force is not a superpower" but a representation of relationality.

This profundity failed to convince some fans to suspend their disbelief during a "B plot" scene in which General (nee Princess) Leia Organa uses the Force to float through the vacuum of space to rejoin the Resistance after the bridge of her ship is ravaged. Narratively, the dramatic moment conveyed the Force as a means of connection, but audiences were torn about this demonstration of the Force, with some deriding Johnson for turning their heroine into "Leia Poppins" (Burwick 2017a). Like the Force, myth is relational, but as seen in this film, it is a negotiation between creator and audience.

The second lesson Luke shares about the Force is that the romantic legend of the Jedi is a political one. Luke tells Rey that contrary to what we could call the Campbellian optimism of the Jedi as heroes, their legacy is one of "failure, hypocrisy, and hubris." Luke contends that were we to "strip away the myth and look at their deeds," we would understand that the Jedi, "at the height of their power allowed Darth Sidious to rise, create the Empire and wipe them out. And it was a Jedi who was responsible for the training and creation of Darth Vader." This plain telling of what we know as the prequel trilogy strikes Rey as craven given that Luke redeemed Darth Vader, who was revealed to be his father, Anakin Skywalker, in the original trilogy that audiences know so well. But Luke says that he is the exception that proves the rule because he himself had become a legend and, in the confidence of his "mighty Skywalker blood," believed himself to be equipped to train his nephew in the ways of the Jedi, only to fail and create the villain of the new saga.

Luke's fatalism even struck actor Mark Hamill, let alone die-hard fans, as "fundamentally" out of character for the part he originated (Collinson 2018). And though Johnson's engagement of the Prequels brings canonical coherence to the story, political readings of the monomyth have shown that Johnson's take is in line with the political imagery and implications of the film in which audiences fell in love with Luke Skywalker, *Star Wars— Episode IV: A New Hope*. John Shelton Lawrence and Robert Jewett's critique of the monomyth have prodded students from being lulled by the ease of Campbellian cohesion, especially when it makes for a "critic-proof" film like *Star Wars*. They argue that while George Lucas's pallet of the dark evil Empire versus the brightly lit rebellion would lead one to see Darth Vader and company in fascistic terms, fascism finds a "spiritual cousin" in *Star Wars*' good guys. Luke Skywalker's education in the Force is an exercise in feeling; his background, *volkish*; his anger, justifiably trained against a cold government. And when Luke is celebrated alongside his colleagues for destroying the Death Star, the ceremony takes its cue, "almost shot for shot" from the Nazi propaganda film *Triumph of the Will* (*Triumph des Willens*, 1935)" (Lawrence and Jewett 2002: 235). Johnson's "C" plot punctuates the need to question the binaries operationalized in myths in its reveal that the Resistance and the First Order share an arms dealer. As much as audiences protest that their Luke has not been presented true to form, Johnson's knack for political intrigue is more faithful to *Star Wars*' source material than they care to admit. Myths are political and perhaps most effective when they obscure the brashness of their machinations.

Luke tells Rey that he will teach her three lessons, but Rey leaves Ach-To to reunite with her friends from Plot B and Plot C in their last stand against the First Order before the final instruction can take place. Nevertheless, Rian Johnson brings the film to a close with such pensive fanfare and iconographic gusto that at least one lesson about the Force—and myth— seems to persist: failure is to be learned from. After Rey leaves the island to do what Luke won't, he goes to a massive tree held to be sacred by the Jedi. Within it lie the "sacred Jedi texts" from the earliest days of the order, and Luke intends to burn the entire place down. Before he does so, he is visited by his old teacher, Master Yoda (a specter rendered in CGI), who takes it upon himself to light the tree in a glorious blaze. The imagery is reminiscent of the phenomenon historian of religion Mircea Eliade would describe as a "hierophany" (or manifestation of the sacred) at the cosmic tree, a meeting of the sacred and profane ([1957] 1987: 26–42). Luke is surprised at Yoda's disintegration of tradition, though unbeknownst to Luke, Rey had actually left with the books. But Yoda confirms that the sacred texts possess nothing which Rey does not already know, and he goes on to share a lesson of his own, that the greatest teacher is failure and that "we," teachers, "are what they grow beyond." Johnson primes the pump for a climax that will both subvert and reify the myth that audiences expect.

In the final showdown with the First Order, the last of the Resistance fleet is holed up in the side of a hill, a dilapidated base built in the days of Rebellion featured in the original trilogy. The heroes are outnumbered and have no escape. Hope is lost until Luke Skywalker walks out from the shadows and faces the First Order's massive siege vehicles. They reign fire on him to no avail, and Kylo Ren, who is Luke's nephew and former student, takes it upon himself to face Luke. The Resistance stands in awe of their legend while the audience tries to determine how Luke arrived on the scene, whether he resurrected the X-Wing Fighter we saw submerged in the waters by the Jedi Temple or some other means. It is then revealed that Luke is in fact on the island and projecting an image of himself that convinces even Kylo Ren for a time. Poe Dameron, leader of the Resistance forces, realizes that Luke has bought them time to figure out that there is a way out of the base and that Rey is waiting at the exit. Luke's actions demanded a renewed faith and his very life, but it seems worth it to him as he looks out in his final moments from the Jedi Temple on to a dual sun horizon that mirrors the one he spied at the start of his heroic journey in *A New Hope*.

Critics praised the symmetry and pathos of Johnson's third act, but audiences reported betrayal at the film's use of *deus ex machina*. Johnson found the audience's arbitrary acceptance of the supramundane frustrating, even going so far as to use their fetish against them. In a series of photos shared (but later deleted) on his Twitter page, Johnson quietly opens a book called *The Jedi Path: A Manual for Students of the Force*, a book originally published in 2010 as an in-universe reference guide for fans. He turns to a section on "Advanced Force Techniques" that "permits a Jedi to create a short-lived duplicate of himself or herself or an external object that is virtually indistinguishable from the real item," the very power that Luke uses to assist the Resistance (Parker 2018). While Disney, to the chagrin of fans, abrogated this and other *Star Wars* books to the "Legend" or non-canonical status, it goes to show what one Lucasfilm executive says that fans have failed to realize: "It's all fake anyway so you can choose to accept whatever you want as part of the story" (Hughes 2020). But this understanding fails to account for the ways in which the validity of a myth are adjudicated by its disciples, not its teachers. Perhaps this is why Johnson ultimately decided to remove his tweet. The pedagogical politics of interpretation are a vicious circle.

Conclusion—"Let the Past Die"?

As discussed before, the mixed audience reaction to *Star Wars: The Last Jedi* can hardly be said to have thwarted Rian Johnson's career. At the same time that J. J. Abram's *Star Wars IX—The Rise of Skywalker* struggled in box offices and among critics, *Knives Out* brought Johnson and *The Last Jedi* renewed appreciation (Welsh 2020). Kathleen Kennedy, Disney's appointed caretaker of the franchise, has reflected on the difficulty of making a *Star Wars* film. She opined that unlike the successful Marvel comic book franchise, *Star Wars* has no source material (Hiatt 2019).

While one could recommend that Disney should draw upon the best of their massive intellectual property—the video games, novelizations, and other narratives that they have branded under their Legends imprint—that would be an insider understanding of myth, a picking of favorites unbefitting of critical film appreciation. The more instructive comparison perhaps lies in the success of two film franchises that have been rebooted to universal acclaim: Ryan Coogler's *Creed*, a rebirth of the *Rocky* series which has been followed up with one film and has a sequel in development, and the hit YouTube series *Cobra Kai* which revisits the world of *The Karate Kid*. Disney seems to have learned this lesson with its blockbuster television show, *The Mandalorian*. Is it a better story truer to the spirit of *Star Wars*? Such a summation would miss the point.

Critical students of myth should be keen on recognizing that innovation and tradition lie in the tensions worked out between the creator and the audience. The construct of auteurism presents an interesting case study because the creator has already garnered the audience's benefit of the doubt. The relational, political, and pedagogical functions of myth resist sublimation into an essence, but this does not stop us from enjoying the illusions that make myths, in certain interpretive hands and under certain social conditions, a force to be reckoned with.

Conclusion

Religion as Film:

Constructing a Course as a Critique of a Dominant Paradigm

Tenzan Eaghll

In a random footnote in Plate's *Representing Religion in World Cinema*, he writes that "The work that remains to be done in religious studies is to examine the ways in which myth functions as ideology and how this is tied to its media" (Plate 2003: 14). I agree with this assessment but am puzzled why Plate or other scholars never took up this task. As noted in the Introduction, the dominant paradigm of analysis in religion and film scholarship to date has been to privilege a mythological analysis of film. According to this perspective, film functions like a religion because it is a cultural projection of the deepest human values and beliefs in cinematic form. Film is portrayed as a social glue that constructs symbolic universes of meaning. Moreover, in this same scholarship ideological analysis is often disparaged according to an outdated "propaganda model" that does not appreciate how individual members of society—and, in this case, cinematic creators, audiences, and critics—contribute to the imagining, manufacturing, and interpreting of ideology. Scholars like Lyden, Martin and Oswalt, Plate, and even those who take a broader cultural studies approach often view ideological analysis as an abstract, reductive, and elitist way of critiquing Hollywood values, but ideological analysis can better be defined as a detailed description of how narrative and acts of identification intersect to create worlds of meaning and myth in various sociopolitical settings.

It is for this reason that in this volume we took as a truism J. Z. Smith's claim that "there is no data for religion" (Smith 1988: xi) and attempted to combine it with McCutcheon's pedagogical suggestion that "we should not be concerned with teaching students to recognize the sacred in its celluloid manifestations, but to see in religious systems as well as in our own society's films the all-too-common mechanisms of social formation" (McCutcheon 1998; 107). Following upon the work of such critical theorists, we agreed that more attention needs to be paid to how films and film critics tell us how to think, feel, and imagine narrative and ideology—and how this conceals normative and hegemonic assumptions about religion and society more generally. However, we also attempted to mix this critical approach with tools from film studies to show how the ideological assumptions about religion are constructed at both the interpretive and cinematic levels. All this calls for a delicate theoretical balance, as scholars need to pay attention to how representations of religion in film are the creations of screenwriters, directors, cinematographers, actors, audiences, critics, cameras, lighting, makeup, costumes, etc., all without assuming that these representations signal some preexisting "religious" content or experience, however that may be defined.

As noted in the Foreword, this volume was created because we think these theoretical developments will help move us beyond the *sui generis* paradigm that tends to dominate the field and toward a more ideological analysis of religion in film. The first time Rebekka King and I taught classes on religion and film we were shocked by the state of scholarship in the field. We were able to find a few good books/articles in print that treated the subject in critical terms, but the majority of the material seemed to adopt either a theological or a mythological approach and treat "film as religion."

In my first iterations of a religion and film course, my correction to this was to treat "Religion as Film," and thereby flip the dominant paradigm on its head by interrogating how representations that were defined as religious by film critics were created on a symbolic, social, technical level. The fundamental thesis of my course was that religion is not a thing with definite qualities but a symbolic and technical production of popular culture that is created by filmmakers and film critics. The films I screened in class and the readings I gave students did refer to Christianity, Buddhism, Islam, indigenous traditions, and new religious movements, among others, but I did not use any as authoritative presentations of religion. Rather, I presented the films and readings as attempts to frame the relationship between symbols, society, and the technological craft of filmmaking.

Since there was no full-length volume in publication at the time that I first taught the course, I provided an ideological reading of religion in film in a kind of piecemeal fashion, scraping together articles and readings from religious studies, film studies, literary theory, and philosophy, as needed.

Schematically, each week I would give students one reading that offered either a theological or mythological interpretation of a film, one that offered an ideological interpretation, and then have students write a film review after each screening defending one interpretation over another.

For instance, in one week of the course we watched Oliver Stone's first Vietnam War flick *Platoon* (1986) and read an interesting essay from *Screening the Sacred* on how the entire film functions as a New Testament allegory. According to this theological reading, *Platoon* offers a critique of the American war effort by making stark claims about absolute good and evil, and providing a narrative of redemption in Christological form. However, in addition to this theological reading, the students also read an essay that offers a heavy ideological critique of the film. According to this second reading, *Platoon* reinforces the American war effort by obscuring deeper political considerations and sustaining various myths associated with American nationalism. Of course, the point of this juxtaposition of critical readings is not simply to show how multiple interpretations are possible—a point most undergrad students already understand—but to get the students to notice the technical aspects of the films these differing arguments rely upon. It is obvious that a film such as *Platoon* can lend itself to multiple readings, but what are the cinematic elements that support these various perspectives? What sort of cinematic style does the director use to get his point across; realism, formalism, or classicism? How does the plot and character development use religious ideas to facilitate this cinematic style? How about Symbolism and imagery, are they used to endorse or critique religion? Moreover, what about the use of dialogue and monologue, who is telling this story? Is there an omniscient narrator, narrative, or theme, or are all the characters subject to the whim of chance? What is the tone of the film and how do all the special effects support this tone? And, perhaps most importantly, what about music, lighting, makeup, costume design, etc.?

To help students make these technical observations, each week I would also provide a reading from Louis Giannetti's *Understanding Movies*. These weekly supplemental film studies readings provided students with all the technical terms from film studies that are necessary to help them understand how film images are created by directors, cinematographers, writers, actors, cameras, lighting, makeup, costume, etc.

Fundamentally, what interested me in these early iterations of the course was what films do with ideas and images, not defining religion in any particular way. At no point in the class did I ever provide a strict definition of religion. Rather, I invited students to examine how the films and the readings tell us to think, feel, and imagine religious content, if at all. What I continually asked everyone to consider is how religion is talked about in film and film criticism, and to explore all the intellectual assumptions and technical aspects that go into the creation of representations in this regard. In a sense, what I asked them to consider is how everything we think we know about religion is created by filmic reality. By reversing the paradigm of "Film as Religion" with that of "Religion as Film," I invited students to consider how cinematic production creates the very content of religion in popular culture.

This volume develops these ideas and presents them in an accessible format that shows how religion is created and critiqued in film and film criticism. In Chapter 1, we saw a clear example of this in Tiara's Chapter on *Religulous*, in which Comedian Bill Maher constructs a celluloid image of religion as the dangerous extreme Other of Atheism. The documentary form of this film helps it achieve this by presenting each shot as an objective truth akin to scientific fact. This film can be contrasted to how religion is constructed in films like *Secret to My Success* and *Silence*, whereby heroes and saints are covertly represented through the white male gaze in entertaining blockbusters that conceal ideologies of capitalism and colonialism. As LoRusso notes in his conclusion, blockbuster films often achieve this by packaging our desires in digestible ways and that is the secret to their success: to bring us carefully crafted consumer joy.

The important point here is that even when films appear to embody some form of religion it is because they are structured that way—appealing to mythologies and symbols that will have the widest cultural resonance and generate box office success. Understanding this doesn't necessarily make films less entertaining, but it is important to draw out the ideologies concealed within these mythologies and symbols so that we understand precisely why they are entertaining. For we must admit, there is a certain sublime joy in a film like *Hereditary* when the psychological explanation for horror gives way to a supernatural one. Even though, as McCloud points out, the latter is the more simplistic explanation for the horror, production companies clearly see it as a way to ensure box office success. It is also for this reason that it is not surprising to find Buddhist clichés in *Cloud Atlas* or Indigenous tropes still active in otherwise critical films like *The Revenant*, stereotypes sell. As noted, ideology is not something imposed upon subjects like a false set of glasses that distort the world, but something in which they actively participate—"We, in a way, enjoy our ideology" (Zizek 2013).

This latter point is illustrated wonderfully in the final two chapters by Singler and Newton, as each points out how cinematic representations of religion are taken from the theater to the street. This is an important aspect to add to what I emphasized about the theoretical creation of religion in the Introduction, as filmic creations of religion do influence the private and communal lives of audiences in a circular manner. Singler stressed this by showing how the *Terminator* franchise tapped into the fears in the general public about the rise of AI in the world and what it implies about human agency, as well as to aspirations to "messiah-ness" among its fanbase. Such apocalyptic films about AI have generated real-world convictions about the dangers it presents and how it will affect the future. There is no clearer example of this than the real-world religion created by *Star Wars*, which provides a direct example of how a director's mythic and religious presuppositions lead to the creation of religion in film, and how this subsequently influences popular culture. As Newton notes, *Star Wars* is a participatory epic that has manifested as over a dozen movies, legions of books, multiple cartoon series, television shows, video games, toys, merchandise, and even Jediism—the real-world philosophy that is based on the mythic themes extracted from the films.

It is the task of critical religion and film scholars and course instructors to point out such cinematic creations and cultural influences, but not according to the "Propaganda model." Rather, the task is to show how religion is imagined, manufactured, and interpreted in cinema on an individual or peer-to-peer basis. In addition, the goal of this analysis should not be to get beyond ideology in some pure sense but to point out some of the political uses and interpretations of these various representations. After all, it is not possible to get beyond the imaginative creation of "religion" on a broad societal level, but it is important to point out how uses of the category and its related representations conceal issues of race, class, gender, colonialism, secularism, and capitalism—common themes of most ideological critique—as well as notions of origin, authenticity, narrative, violence, and identity—categories germane to the academic study of the subject. As Douglas Kellner noted over two decades ago in *Camera Politica*, this is actually what ideological analysis means for most Althusserian, postmodernist, and feminist film critics: rather than trying to find a dominant ideology in a film, ideological film critics examine the contextual and relational power dynamics expressed in cinematic narratives and images to account for the various conflicts and contradictions within contemporary capitalist societies (Kellner 1991: 6).

Summarizing all this as a series of questions that need to continually remain open for scholars, instructors, and students of religion and film: What is being assumed about religion in a particular film or piece of film criticism? Is it presented as a private experience divorced from politics? A universal reality that we cannot escape? An evolutionary or historical accident that needs to be discarded? A means of social and political transformation? A force for individual emancipation or enslavement? Moreover, what assumptions go into the reception and interpretation of a film's audiences and its critics? What theory of religion do they apply to cinema to locate so-called religious themes, if at all? None of these questions presume that ideological analysis needs to be inherently negative in its reading of a film, but it does imply that scholars need to pay attention to how meanings and values are being authorized, universalized, and naturalized, as well as the material and technical elements involved in this process.

NOTES

Introduction

1 The terms "image," "imagine," and "imaginative," all of which are used in this introduction, can all be understood through the lens of the Lacanian term "imaginary" and the film theory notion of the "gaze," which have a long history in film studies. Though we don't specifically explore Lacanian film theory at length in this volume, both these notions are useful ways to think about how representations of religion function in cinema as ideological acts of interpolation, whereby subjects come to identify with the symbolic order that structures and regulates the visible world. We will expand upon this a little more later, but for more on the specific relationship between cinematic images, Lacanian film theory, and the imaginary, see *The Real Gaze: Film Theory after Lacan* (McGowan 2007).

Chapter 1

1 https://www.the-numbers.com/movie/Religulous#tab=summary; http://www.boxofficemojo.com/movies/?id=religulous.htm (accessed May 26, 2019).

Chapter 3

1 As examples of this discourse, see Kim Renfro, "'A Wrinkle in Time' Ditches the Book's Explicit Christian References – and the Movie Really Suffers Because of It," *Insider*, https://www.insider.com/wrinkle-in-time-movie-changes-book-religion-christianity-ending-2018-3, March 9, 2018; CBN News, "Writer of Disney's 'A Wrinkle in Time' Ditches Biblical Themes for Lots of New Age Content," *Christian Broadcasting Network*, https://www1.cbn.com/cbnnews/entertainment/2018/march/writer-of-disneys-a-wrinkle-in-time-ditches-biblical-references-for-themes-of-inclusiveness, March 12, 2018. For another Christian perspective on this commentary, see Brian Bantum and Wendi Dunlap, "What Makes *A Wrinkle*

in Time Christian?," *The Christian Century*, https://www.christiancentury.org/article/film/what-makes-wrinkle-time-christian, April 2, 2018.

2 See, for instance, James Dawson, "It's Official. 'A Wrinkle in Time' is a Disastrous Adaptation of the Book." *The Federalist*, https://thefederalist.com/2018/03/07/a-wrinkle-in-time-is-a-disastrous-adaptation-of-lengles-book/, March 7, 2018.

3 This is the larger theme of Edward Said's famous work, *Orientalism* (New York: Vintage, 1979).

4 *Dr. Strange*, directed by Scott Derrickson, Marvel Studios, 2016. It is also of particular note in this film that Tilda Swinton, a white actress, plays the primary role model ("The Ancient One") for Strange as he navigates his recovery.

5 See Leslie Dorrough Smith, "Scopophilia and the Manufacture of 'Good Religion,'" in *Hijacked: A Critical Treatment of the Public Rhetoric of Good and Bad Religion*, eds. Leslie Dorrough Smith, Steffen Fuhrding, and Adrian Hermann (Sheffield: Equinox, 2020), 98–107.

6 See Matthew 4:1–11.

Chapter 4

1 This chapter is the development of a review blog that I wrote in December 2016, after viewing the movie *Silence* for the first time. Different versions of that review were published in the *Huffington Post UK* (Nye 2017) and with the publication *Panel & Frame* on the Medium website (Nye 2016). I would like to formally thank Studio Canal, the publicists for the movie *Silence*, for inviting me to view the film at its British premiere at the Odeon cinema in Leicester Square in London, and for funding my travel expenses (although not my time) for traveling down from Scotland. I am also grateful to Tenzin Eaghll for inviting me to revisit this discussion and revise and develop my thoughts on the film and its context for this present collection of essays. I also found Tenzin's initial paper, published first in *Method and Theory in the Study of Religion* (Eaghll 2019), a very insightful and inspiring discussion of the many themes for a critical study of religion and film.

2 There is a Japanese-language film adaptation of Endo's novel, titled *Chinmoku* (i.e., *Silence*), directed by Masahiro Shinoda in 1971 (although with many sections of English language being spoken by Rodrigues and Garupe, in British English accents). For a brief discussion of how the film *Chinmoku* differs from Scorsese's *Silence* see Maryks (2017). Also, Horne (2017: 18) contrasts the two films by saying that the 1971 Japanese *Chinmoku* has a focus which "seems less on issues of faith and doubt than on Japan's collision [*sic.*] with the West' and it 'does not have the spiritual intimacy of Scorsese's remarkable new film."

3 As evidenced, for example, by Hannah-Jones (2019), Alexander (2006), Bonilla-Silva (2017), Kendi (2019), Baldwin (1995).

4 See, for example, Weisenfeld (2016, 2020), McTighe (2020a, b), Nye (2018, 2019), Newton (2019), Vial (2016), Lloyd (2013).

NOTES

5 As Mantia Diawara argues, "every narration places the spectator in a position of agency; and race, class and sexual relations influence the way in which this subjecthood is filled by the spectator" (Diawara 1990: 33).

6 As is the case with *Silence*, violence is often put to use in Scorsese's films as a means to achieve redemption, while at other times it achieves the opposite. For example, Richard Blake (1996: 6) outlines a contrast between the use of violence in *Taxi Driver* (1976) and *Mean Streets* (1973)—which Blake argues is largely redemptive for the protagonist—and Jake LaMotta (played by Robert de Niro) in *Raging Bull* (1980), for whom "no amount of bloodshed will win redemption for him on his own terms." Indeed, Scorsese directly connected these earlier works to *Silence*, when he said: "When I read that last section [of Endo's book], whatever I wanted to find in making *Last Temptation*, or *Raging Bull* to a certain extent, I knew I had to find it here" (Scorsese in Horne 2017: 19).

7 See, for example, Matthews (2017), Ward (2017), Maryks (2017), Ng (2019), Martin (2017).

8 Different criticisms have been directed at Miranda for his own omissions and apparent "innocence" in the creation of *Hamilton*—not least the apparent "whitewashing" of the US "Founding Fathers," most of whom were both slaveholders and proponents of genocide against the Indigenous nations of the land (Reed 2015; Monteiro 2016a, b; Gordon-Reed 2016). That is, even when certain aspects of race are foregrounded, commercial success with a predominantly white audience in North America may require omissions on other levels.

Chapter 5

1 Emphasis in original.

2 See "The World's First 'Yoga' Film," *Smithsonian Magazine*, https://www .smithsonianmag.com/videos/category/arts-culture/the-worlds-first-yoga-film/ (accessed February 13, 2020).

3 For example, see Martin Thomas, *Expedition into Empire: Exploratory Journeys and the Making of the Modern World* (London: Routledge, 2019); Agnieszka Sobocinska, "Following the 'Hippie Sahibs': Colonial Cultures of Travel and the Hippie Trail," *Journal of Colonialism and Colonial History* 15, no. 2 (2014), http://muse.jhu.edu/journals/journal_of_colonialism_and _colonial_history/v015/15.2.sobocinska.html; Mary Louise Pratt, *Imperial Eyes: Travel Writing and Transculturation*, 2nd ed, (London: Routledge, 2008); John K. Walton, ed., *Histories of Tourism: Representation, Identity, and Conflict*, Tourism and Cultural Change 6 (Clevedon: Channel View Publications, 2005).

4 The music and many of the shots in the film are borrowed from the films of James Ivory and Indian filmmaker Satyajit Ray. For more on the influences in the film see Whitney Crothers Dilley, *The Cinema of Wes Anderson : Bringing Nostalgia to Life*, Directors' Cuts (London: WallFlower Press, 2017), 141–46; Jonathan Romney, "Wes Anderson: Isn't It Time the Writer and Director Showed a Little Heart?" *The Independent*, November 11, 2007, https://www

.independent.co.uk/arts-entertainment/films/features/wes-anderson-isnt-it-time
-the-writer-and-director-showed-a-little-heart-399522.html.

Chapter 6

1 Since Žižek often philosophizes with extreme irony, he might be perfectly aware that his interpretation of Buddhism is essentialist and in need of decolonial critique. In fact, he may even choose to discuss Buddhism in this way precisely because it is the dominant interpretation of Buddhism in the West.

Chapter 7

1 Hollywood and Western representations of Latin America, especially Latin American religiosity, often play into tropes and stereotypes of Catholicism that border on provincial and exotic. The practices of so-called Catholic "folk religion" regularly are depicted as overly material (altars, amulets, crosses, and icons), emotive (exorcisms, blustery confession, tearful pleas to saints), and even superstitious (making signs of the cross, carrying images of saints in wallets and around the neck, using rosaries to pray, and praying to avatars such as the Virgin Mary or saints). The Protestant gaze represents Catholicism as irrational and archaic, as opposed to the rational, privatized religiosity of mainstream Protestant Christianity that was the frame of reference for most Hollywood representations of Latin American religiosity throughout the twentieth century. See, for example, *Touch of Evil* (1958), *Three Amigos* (1986), *Dirty Dancing: Havana Nights* (2004), *Turistas* (2006).

2 Colombia's war has been raging in different forms and with differing repertoires of violence for over sixty years. Since the twentieth-century civil war began in 1948, the regularity and particular *modus operandi* of violence in Colombia has become a permanent backdrop to the political, social, and religious landscape. It remains so today, despite recently signed peace accords between the Revolutionary Armed Forces of Colombia (FARC) and the Colombian government in 2016. See Bartel (2021) on the many ways the war sits in the backdrop of everyday life, religion, and economies in Colombia, as well as Alex Fattal's *Guerilla Marketing* for a deeply ethnographic look at the imbrication of capitalism and violence in Colombia's armed conflict.

3 Orpheus was the lauded musician of the Greek world, whose talents on the lyre were rivaled only by his love for his wife, Eurydice, who tragically is bitten by a viper on their wedding day. She dies and descends to Hades, where Orpheus pursues her and convinces the gods Pluto and Proserpine to restore Eurydice to mortality. Enchanted by Orpheus's song, the gods allow Eurydice to leave under the condition: that Orpheus cannot look back. As Orpheus reaches the entrance to Hades, he looks back to check on his beloved, breaking the pact with the gods of the underworld, only to see Eurydice flung back into the depths of

Hades, lost forever. Doctor Faustus, on the other hand, is the tragic main character of Johan Wolfgang Goethe's play, *Faust*. In the play, Faust makes a deal with the Devil, Mephistopheles, to grant Faust everything he wants in this life, and, in exchange, Faust agrees to serve the Devil in Hell for eternity.

4 *Vallenato* is a popular type of folk music, which has become very mainstream in Colombia and Venezuela, that features an accordion, the *caja* drum, and the *guacharaca*. Acoustic *vallenato* can be played with just the accordion. *Juglares* are traveling musicians. In the case of Colombia's Caribbean coast, they are most often accordionists, who compete for money in rhyming duels, and historically these traveling minstrels relayed the news of the region through song.

5 Translation by author.

6 Diegetic narratives tell the story from the perspective of the characters, or from the outsiders' perspective, rather than from a mimetic narrative, which *shows* the story being told. In this case, in the case of Ignacio in *The Wind Journeys*, the audience is being told the story of the *juglares*, and an interpretation of the legend of Francisco el Hombre from Ignacio's perspective.

7 In one of the most chilling scenes in *One Hundred Years*, Márquez narrates the 1928 Banana Massacre initiated by workers from the United Fruit Company who demanded dignified working conditions, which ended in the massacre of between 100 and 2,000 people. In 2017, Chiquita Banana was found guilty of colluding with paramilitary death squads to quell unionizing efforts. See Kennard (2017), Frankel (2018).

8 The work of Toni Morrison and Salman Rushdie are also often categorized within this genre.

9 For extensive discussion of religion and modernity see, among others, Meyer (1999), Van der Veer (2001), Keene (2007), Levene (2017).

10 I choose the term "decolonial" instead of "postcolonial" here because postcolonial critique is not so easily mapped onto the history of Latin America. First, independence from imperial powers was won in most Latin American countries in the late eighteenth and early nineteenth centuries. Second, for most Latin American thinkers, the idea of colonialism being a "post" event is not applicable, given the fact that for much of the nineteenth and twentieth centuries, Latin America has been subjected to the, often violent and repressive, regimes and whims of North American economic and political interests. For further discussion, see Mignolo (2005), Rivera Cusicanqui (2020).

Chapter 8

1 On the politics of defining INAs see Vowel (2016). See also *Media Indigena* (2019).

2 As Bruce Lincoln (2012) puts it, "If by 'indigenous religions' we mean to denote religious traditions that have not (yet) been influenced or colonized by the global 'isms,' such are notoriously difficult to locate, since most of our

evidence is not the autonomous self-expression of an ab-original entity but a product of contact between indigenous cultures and encroaching others" (95).

3 See Harp (2019).

4 Here I am referring to the birth of the American Indian Movement (*c.* 1968), the Red Power Movement (1960s–1970s), the Native American Renaissance (a movement in literature), the growth of Native Studies departments in the 1970s, and recent political mobilizations, especially in Canada with the Idle No More Movement (*c.* 2012), the Truth and Reconciliation Commission (2008–15), and its government-mandated ninety-four calls to action (Mas 2015).

5 As a non-Indigenous scholar of religions my interest in these issues is informed by recent social movements, by my relationships with INAs, and by a scholarly desire to better understand how popular representations inform how we image the boundaries of national, religious, and cultural identity.

6 Here I am playing on the term Native American Renaissance (Lincoln 1985), which refers to the growth of Indigenous American literary works following M. Scott Momaday's Pulitzer Prize–winning novel, *House Made of Dawn*, in 1968.

7 One notable exception is the 2015 horror film *Bone Tomahawk* starting Kurt Russell, which follows a well-worn captivity narrative depicting an unnamed tribe of Native Americans as "savage" cannibals with supernatural abilities. For a critical analysis see Carter (2020).

8 James Cameron's blockbuster film *Avatar* (2009) relies on some of these tropes, such as the "white savior," while subverting others—for example, the colonization of the fictional Na'vi people of the planet Pandora is presented as a crude attempt to steal resources that is ultimately thwarted.

9 To these tropes we could also add a number of other binary pairs, including, as Michelle Raheja (2010) points out: "faceless horde vs. lone warrior in defeat, beautiful maiden vs. shapeless drudge, inscrutable enemy vs. loyal sidekick, assimilationist vs. traditionalist, sexual predator vs. emasculated 'last of his breed,' to name a few" (Chpt 1).

10 Some nineteenth-century examples of the "vanishing Indian" include the artwork of Emily Carr and Paul Kane, along with the photography and films of Edward Curtis (see Francis 2011).

11 In his documentary *Reel Injun: On the Trail of the Hollywood Indian* (2010), Neil Diamond points to the film *Silent Enemy* (1930), which deals with starvation in Indigenous communities, as one example of these more sympathetic and culture-specific trends. See also chapter one of Raheja (2010).

12 In *Dances with Wolves* the "Indigenous" love interest is a white woman who was adopted into the Sioux tribe at a young age, taking on their customs and language as her own.

13 By now there is a rich body of scholarship on how Euro-settler societies have appropriated Native American cultures (e.g., Deloria 1999; King 2019), including a culture of "Indian hobbyists" in Germany and elsewhere throughout Europe dating back to the nineteenth century (Lutz et al. 2020; Penny 2013).

NOTES

14 For a detailed account of Indigenous people in film and their various struggles prior to the 1960s, see Liza Black's *Picturing Indians: Native Americans in Film, 1941–1960.*

15 Some prominent examples include the founding of the American Indian Movement (AIM), the occupation of Alcatraz Island by AIM members (and others) in 1969, and the stand-off between the FBI and the Oglala Lakota Sioux Nation at Wounded Knee in 1973.

16 For a critical analysis of the evolution of the term "Mother Earth" see Gill (1991).

17 The documentary *Koyaanisqatsi* (1982), taken from the Hopi term meaning "life out of balance," is a notable example of this trope.

18 For example, there is a pervasive tendency to depict INAs wearing a headdress (common in Great Plains traditions, such as Cree and Ojibway), and as living in geographies overrepresented by the plains (Dakotas) and the American southwest (New Mexico and Arizona). Given the centrality of ceremony and land in Indigenous cultures, such conflations effectively erase key elements of "spiritual" identity. Other common depictions of INAs, such as wearing a headband, were the product of 1960s hippie cultures "playing Indian," and were not customary in Indigenous communities. Diamond (2010) notes the film *Geronimo* (1962) as an example of this trend.

19 In *Reel Injuns* (2010) Diamond points to the films *Cheyenne Autumn* (1964); *The Born Losers* (1967), which started an Indigenous kung-fu hero; *Black Jack* (1971); *Little Big Man* (1970); and *One Flew Over the Cuckoo's Nest* as emblematic of these representational shifts.

20 In January and February of 2020, a major dispute over the construction of pipelines through the ancestral land of the Wet-suwet'en First Nation in British Columbia, Canada, saw threats of state violence from Canadian police, as well as regional train blockades (initiated by Mohawks in Ontario) carried out in solidarity.

21 One core element of the WRP is to emphasize instances of similarity between the "world's religions" that fit with liberal ideas of tolerance, rather than examine how religions are constantly reimagined through interaction in different social and historical contexts. For a critical analysis of the WRP see *After World Religions* (Cotter and Robertson 2016).

22 For example, the phrase "defend the sacred" has been used by Indigenous activists in recent years in contexts involving contested land-claims and opposition to the construction of pipelines (Estes 2019; McNally 2020). While this phrase invokes "Indigenous spirituality" with the use of the term "sacred," it is also an appeal to Euro-Western environmental concerns and an attempt to persuade non-Indigenous audiences that water and soil are more than resources to be bought and sold.

23 What makes this film "Indigenous," he elaborates, is that it conveys Maori myth and ritual as an elder "trains the local boys in the lessons of their people . . . and how to perform the traditional dance known as the haka" (196).

24 For example, unlike previous uprisings, such as the Oka Crisis in 1990, where the dominant narrative was one of violent, law-breaking "Indians" pitted

against a reasonable and law-abiding state (Simpson and Ladner 2010), the most common images to come out of Idle No More included round dances (a Plains Cree tradition, where people hold hands and dance in a circle) and drum circles, which enable non-Indigenous people to participate in these performative acts in ways that subvert older stereotypes (see Kino-nda-niimi 2014).

25 It is worth noting that DiCaprio's own environmental activism, which includes a 2014 visit to the Alberta tar sands and nearby Fort Chipewyan Reserve for research on his 2016 climate change documentary, *Before the Flood*, coincided with these events.

26 Iñárritu's body of work includes films such as *21 Grams*, *Babel*, and *Birdman*, which won the Academy Awarding for best picture in 2015, one year prior to his winning best director and best screenplay for *The Revenant*.

27 In *The Celluloid Maiden* (2006), Marubbio shows that the most common depictions of Indigenous women in Hollywood films are either as helpless maidens, and thus in need of saving, or as sexual threats to white Christian society.

28 It is worth noting that Glass survives against incredible odds while his Indigenous doppelganger, a Pawnee man named Hikuc, is hanged by French fur traders after saving Glass's life.

29 By contrast, Jeff Barnaby's (Mi'kmaq) zombie film *Blood Quantum* (2019) features Indigenous communities as reluctant (and ultimately betrayed) protectors of non-Indigenous people.

30 For example, the documentary *There's Something in the Water* (2019) by Hollywood star Elliot Page (known at the time as Ellen Page) centers Indigenous women's voices as "defenders of land."

31 The award-winning Inuit film *Atanarjuat: The Fast Runner* (2001) by Zacharis Kunuk is often upheld as an example of visual sovereignty, as it centers around an ancient, precolonial Inuit legend in the Inuktitut language, without the intrusion of an outsiders' explanation—unlike Robert Flaherty's famous 1922 feature *Nanook of the North*. See also Kunuk's recent film *One Day in the Life of Noah Piugattuk* (2019), which provides an Inuit perspective on a historical meeting in 1961 with a Canadian state representative that served to advance colonization.

32 For example, the Netflix series *Frontier* (2016–18) starring Jason Moma centers around Métis hero Declan Harp in the French colony of Québec during the seventeenth century. Harp and his allies (esp. Cree and Anishaanabe) are the show's protagonists, who work to subvert the colonial British Hudson's Bay Company.

Chapter 10

1 See, for example, the equation of "apocalyptic films" with movies about "the future last days of humankind" in Hamonic (2017), Mitchell (2001: ix, xi),

Modleski (2009: 624, 837), Walliss and Aston (2011: 53–64), Whissel (2006), Lyden (2003: 215).

2 On this point see Middleton (2018), Frankfurter (2007), Moore (2007, 1999), Frilingos (2004), Pippin (1994).

3 On the production and promotion of ideology, see Eagleton (1991: 45).

4 For more on the heroic violence of *Pale Rider* as "apocalyptic," see Lyden (2003: 155).

5 On this temptation see Plate (1998: 16).

6 The *Hellboy* movie of 2019 retells Mignola and Fegredo's story *Hellboy: The Storm and the Fury* (2012).

Chapter 11

1 Zombies also turn up in more religiously inspired apocalypses, such as the Romero series of films where "when there's no more room in hell, the dead will walk the earth."

2 Due to the timeline changes in the sixth *Terminator* film, *Dark Fate*, it is no longer the all-powerful Skynet that brings about the apocalypse but "Legion." Biblical resonances are obviously being put to work in this latest instalment: in the New Testament, Legion was the multitude of demons cast out of the possessed man in "land of the Gerasenes" by Jesus in Mark 5:1–5:13, Luke 8:26–8:33, and Matthew 8:28–8:32.

3 A distinction should be made here between religion from film in this sense and the emergence of New Religious Movements that explicitly cite films and other media as their source of inspiration such as Jediism (see Possamai 2005; Cusack 2010; Singler 2014). In this chapter I am exploring the religious narratives and tendencies that are expressed in the *Terminator* franchise, and which continue to have impact outside of the films themselves. As yet, I am unaware of a New Religious Movement claiming the franchise as an inspiration, but there are several that focus on AI futures (see Singler 2020).

4 The cyborg-messiah is present elsewhere in the franchise. In *T3* the T-800 protects John and his future wife, again being sent back by a future John Connor. In *Salvation* (one of the religiously themed titles in the franchise along with *T2: Judgement Day* and *Genisys*), Marcus Wright's physical resurrection as a cyborg precedes him saving John Connor's life through the sacrifice of his own heart. And in *SCC* the cyborg John Henry will play a salvific role for a future human Resistance.

5 In some cases, such cold-logic could also sometimes be a fatal flaw: Captain James T. Kirk defeated four different powerful godlike computers in *Star Trek: The Original Series* by making them face logic-paradoxes.

6 I have previously interviewed a chatbot expert who was clear that Sophia's technology is neither very advanced nor as groundbreaking as her creators have presented it. In any case, as the examples here will show, she is often treated

in public discourse as though she is another step along the one-way street of technological progress.

7 Corridor Digital made a fake "Bosstown Dynamics" video showing one of the bipedal robots rebelling against its creators (see Corridor Digital 2019). Reactions to these videos on social media often showed users' difficulties in discerning fact from fiction, especially when there was computer-generated imagery involved.

REFERENCES

Introduction

Aichele, George and Richard Walsh (eds.) (2002). *Screening Scripture: Intertextual Connections between Scripture and Film*. Harrisburg: Trinity Press International.

Barrett, Michèle (1994). "Ideology, Politics, Hegemony: From Gramsci to Laclau and Mouffe." In S. Žižek (ed.), *Mapping Ideology*, 235–64. London: Verso.

Blizek, William L. (ed.) (2009). *The Continuum Companion to Religion and Film*. New York: Bloomsbury.

Browne, Nick (2009). "The Spectator-in-the-Text: The Rhetoric of Stagecoach." In L. Braudy and M. Cohen (eds.), *Film Theory and Criticism: Introductory Readings*, 125–40, 7th ed. New York: Oxford University Press.

Chidester, David (1996). *Savage Systems Colonialism and Comparative Religion in Southern Africa*. London: University Press of Virginia.

Comolli, Jean-Luc and Jean Narboni (2009). "Cinema/Ideology/Criticism." In L. Braudy and M. Cohen (eds.), *Film Theory and Criticism: Introductory Readings*, 686–93, 7th ed. New York: Oxford University Press.

Dayan, Daniel (2009). "The Tutor-Code of Classical Cinema." In L. Braudy and M. Cohen (eds.), *Film Theory and Criticism: Introductory Readings*, 106–17, 7th ed. New York: Oxford University Press.

Deleuze, Gilles (1986). *Cinema 1: The Movement Image*, trans. H. Tomlinson and B. Habberjam. Minnesota: University of Minnesota Press.

Detweiler, Craig (2008). *Into the Dark: Seeing the Sacred in the Top Films of the 21st Century*. Grand Rapids: Baker Academic.

Eaghll, Tenzan (2019). "Ideological Blindspot in the Academic Study of Religion and Film." *Method and Theory in the Study of Religion*, 31 (4–5): 416–45.

Eliade, Mircea (1959a). *The Sacred and the Profane: The Nature of Religion*, trans. W. R. Trask. New York: Harcourt Brace Jovanovich.

Eliade, Mircea (1959b). *Cosmos and History: The Myth of the Eternal Return*, trans. W. R. Trask. New York: Harper Torch Books.

Fitzgerald, Tim (1997). "A Critique of 'Religion' as a Cross-Cultural Category." *Method & Theory in the Study of Religion*, 9 (2): 91–110.

Flesher, Paul V. M. and Robert Torry (2007). *Film and Religion: An Introduction*. Nashville: Abingdon Press.

Foucualt, Michel (1989). *The Archaeology of Knowledge*, trans. A. M. Sheridan Smith. London: Routledge.

Francis, Peter and William R. Telford (eds.) (2005). *Cinéma Divinité: Religion, Theology and the Bible in Film*. London: SCM Press.

Geertz, Clifford (1973). *The Interpretation of Cultures*. New York: Basic Books.

Hamner, Gail M. (2011). *Imagining Religion in Film: The Politics of Nostalgia.* New York: Palgrave McMillon.

Hansen, Miriam (2012). *Cinema and Experience: Siegfried Kracauer, Walter Benjamin, and Theodor W. Adorno.* California: University of California Press.

Henderson, Brian (2009). "Towards a Non-Bourgeois Camera Style." In L. Braudy and M. Cohen (eds.), *Film Theory and Criticism: Introductory Readings,* 54–64, 7th ed. New York: Oxford University Press.

Johnston, Robert K. (2000). *Reel Spirituality: Theology and Film in Dialogue.* Grand Rapids: Baker Academic.

Johnston, Robert K. (2007). "Reel Spirituality: Theology and Film in Dialogue." In J. Mitchell and B. S. Plate (eds.), *The Religion and Film Reader,* 312–22. New York: Routledge.

Kellner, Douglas (1991). "Film, Politics, and Ideology: Reflections on Hollywood Film in the Age of Reagan." *Velvet Light Trap: A Critical Journal of Film & Television,* 91 (27): 1–24.

Kellner, Douglas and Michael Ryan (1988). *Camera Politica: The Politics and Ideology of Contemporary Hollywood Film.* Bloomington: Indiana University Press.

Lincoln, Bruce (1996). "Mythic Narrative and Cultural Diversity in American Society." In L. Patton and W. Doniger (eds.), Myth and Method, 163–76. Charlottesville: University Press of Virginia.

Lukacs, Georg (1972). "Reification and the Consciousness of the Proletariat." In *History and Class Consciousness: Studies in Marxist Dialectics,* trans. Rodney Livingstone, 83–222. Cambridge: MIT Press.

Lyden, John C. (1997). "To Commend or To Critique? The Question of Religion and Film Studies." *Journal of Religion & Film,* 1 (2): 1–19.

Lyden, John C. (2003). *Film as Religion: Myths, Morals and Rituals.* New York: New York University Press.

Lyden, John C. (ed.) (2009). *The Routledge Companion to Religion and Film.* New York: Taylor & Francis.

Marsh, Clive (2009). "Audience Reception." In J. C. Lyden (ed.), *The Routledge Companion to Religion and Film,* 255–76. New York: Taylor & Francis.

Martin, Craig (2010). *Masking Hegemony: A Genealogy of Liberalism, Religion, and the Private Sphere.* Sheffield: Equinox.

Martin, Joel W. (1997). "Review of Seeing and Believing by Margaret Miles." *Journal of the American Academy of Religion,* 65 (2): 498–501.

Martin, Joel W. and Conrad E. Ostwalt (eds.) (1995). *Screening the Sacred: Religion, Myth, and Ideology in Popular American Film.* Boulder: Westview.

Masuzawa, Tomoko (2005). *The Invention of World Religions: Or, How European Universalism Was Preserved in the Language of Pluralism.* Chicago: University of Chicago Press.

McCutcheon, Russell T. (1997). *Manufacturing Religion: The Discourse of Sui Generis Religion and The Politics of Nostalgia.* Oxford: Oxford University Press.

McCutcheon, Russell T. (1998). "Redescribing 'Religion and …' Film: Teaching the Insider/Outsider Problem." *Teaching Theology and Religion,* 1 (2): 99–110.

McCutcheon, Russell T. (2015). "The Eternal Return All Over Again." *Studying Religion in Culture: Ongoing Discussion at the University of Alabama,*

February 25, 2015. Available online: https://religion.ua.edu/blog/2015/02/28/the-eternal-return-all-over-again/#more-4917 (accessed September 12, 2018).

McGowan, Todd (2007). *The Real Gaze: Film Theory after Lacan*. Albany: State University of New York Press.

Metz, Christian (1986). *Psychoanalysis and the Cinema*. Bloomington: Indiana University Press.

Miles, Margaret (1996). *Seeing and Believing: Religion and Values in the Movies*. Boston: Beacon.

Mitchell, Jolyon and Brent S. Plate (2007). *The Religion and Film Reader*. New York: Routledge.

Nayar, Sheila J. (2012). *The Sacred and the Cinema: Reconfiguring the "Genuinely" Religious Film*. London and New York: Continuum International Publishing Group.

Nongbri, Brent (2013). *Before Religion: A History of a Modern Concept*. New Haven: Yale University Press.

Nye, Malory (2017). "Scorsese's Silence is a Movie About Race as Well as Religion." *HuffPost*, January 11, 2017. Available online: https://www.huffingtonpost.co.uk/malory-nye/scorseses-silence-is-abou_b_13718918.html (accessed September 10, 2018).

Nye, Malory (2018). "Race and Religion: Postcolonial Formations of Power and Whiteness." *Method and Theory in the Study of Religion*, 30 (3): 1–28. https://doi.org/10.1163/15700682-12341444

Pearson, Roberta E. and Philip Simpson (2001). *Critical Dictionary of Film and Television Theory*, ed. Roberta E. Pearson and Simpson Philip. New York: Routledge Press.

The Pervert's Guide to Ideology (2013), [Film] Dir. Sophie Fiennes, USA: Zeitgeist Films.

Plate, Brent S. (ed.) (2003). *Representing Religion in World Cinema*. New York: Palgrave Macmillan.

Plate, Brent S. (2004). *Walter Benjamin, Religion and Aesthetics: Rethinking Religion through the Arts*. New York: Routledge.

Plate, Brent S. (2007). "The Footprints of Film: After Images of Religion in American Space and Time." In J. Mitchell and B. S. Plate (ed.), *The Religion and Film Reader*, 427–37. New York: Routledge.

Plate, Brent S. (2009). *Religion and Film: Cinema and the Re-Creation of the World*. London and New York: Wallflower.

Scott, Bernard (2000). *Hollywood Dreams & Biblical Stories*. Philadelphia: Fortress Press.

Sison, Antonio D. (2012). *World Cinema, Theology, and the Human: Humanity in Deep Focus*. London and New York: Routledge.

Smith, Jonathan Z. (1988). *Imagining Religion: From Babylon to Jonestown (Chicago Studies in the History of Judaism)*. Chicago: University of Chicago Press.

Stam, Robert and Louise Spence (2009). "Colonialism, Racism, and Representation." In L. Braudy and M. Cohen (eds.), *Film Theory and Criticism: Introductory Readings*, 751–66, 7th ed. New York: Oxford University Press.

Sturken, Marita and Lisa Cartwright (2013). *Practices of Looking: An Introduction to Visual Culture*. New York: Oxford.

Thompson, John B. (1984). *Studies in the Theory of Ideology*. New York: John Wiley & Sons.

Watkins, Gregory J. (ed.) (2008). *Teaching Religion and Film (AAR Teaching Religious Studies)*. Oxford: Oxford University Press.

Wright, Melanie J. (2006). *Religion and Film: An Introduction*. London: Tauris.

Wright, Melanie J. (2009). "Religion, Film and Cultural Studies." In W. L. Blizek (ed.), *The Continuum Companion to Religion and Film*, 101–12. New York: Bloomsbury.

Chapter 1

Beattie, Tina (2007). *The New Atheists: The Twilight of Reason and the War on Religion*. London: Darton, Longman and Todd.

Bonner, Frances (2013). "Recording Reality: Documentary Film and Television." In Stuart Hall, Jessica Evans and Sean Nixon (eds.), *Representation*, 60–119. London: Sage.

Botton, Alan de (2012). *Religion for Atheists: A Non-believer's Guide to the Use of Religion*. London: Hamish Hamilton.

Bruce, Steve (2002). *God is Dead: Secularization in the West*. Oxford: Blackwell.

Dawkins, Richard (2006). *The God Delusion*. London: Black Swan.

Day, Matthew (2009). "Exotic Experience and Ordinary Life." In Michael Stausberg (ed.), *Contemporary Theories of Religion: A Critical Companion*, 115–28. London: Routledge.

Eaghll, Tenzan (2019). "Ideological Blindspot in the Academic Study of Religion and Film." *Method and Theory in the Study of Religion*, 31 (4–5): 416–45.

French, Cameron (2008). "Western Religions Attacked in Film 'Religulous'." *Reuters*, September 9. Available online: https://www.reuters.com/article/us -toronto-religulous/western-religions-attacked-in-film-religulous-idUSN083722 0120080909 (accessed September 12, 2018).

Geertz, Armin W. (2009). "When Cognitive Scientists Become Religious, Science is in Trouble: On Neurotheology from a Philosophy of Science Perspective." *Religion*, 39 (4): 319–24.

Goldstein, Patrick and James Rainey (2008). "Bill Maher Hates Your (Fill in the Blank) Religion." *Los Angeles Times*, August 7, 2008. Available online: https://latimesblogs.latimes.com/the_big_picture/2008/08/bill-maher-hate.html (accessed September 12, 2018).

Gray, John (2019). *Seven Types of Atheism*. London: Penguin.

Grossberg, Lawrence (1986). "On Postmodernism and Articulation: An Interview with Stuart Hall." *Journal of Communication Inquiry*, 10 (2): 45–60.

Grossberg, Lawrence (1992). *We Gotta Get Out of This Place: Popular Conservatism and Postmodern Culture*. London: Routledge.

Hall, Stuart (1992). "The West and the Rest: Discourse and Power." In Stuart Hall and Bram Gieben (eds.), *Formations of Modernity*, 275–331. Cambridge: Polity Press/Open University.

Hitchens, Christopher (2007). *God is Not Great: How Religion Poisons Everything*. New York: Twelve.

Miles, Margaret R. (1996). *Seeing and Believing: Religion and Values in the Movies*. Boston: Beacon Press.

Nichols, Bill (2017). *Introduction to Documentary*, 3rd ed. Bloomington: Indiana University Press.

REFERENCES

Power, Nina (2013). "Films." In Stephen Bullivant and Michael Ruse (eds.), *The Oxford Handbook of Atheism*, 727–34. Oxford: Oxford University Press.

Slack, Jennifer Daryl (1996). "The Theory and Method of Articulation in Cultural Studies." In David Morley and Kuan-Hsing Chen (eds.), *Stuart Hall: Critical Dialogues in Cultural Studies*, 112–27. London: Routledge.

Spivak, Gayatri Chakravorty (1999). *A Critique of Post-Colonial Reason: Toward a History of the Vanishing Present*. Cambridge: Harvard University Press.

Taira, Teemu (2012). "New Atheism as Identity Politics." In Mathew Guest and Elizabeth Aarweck (eds.), *Religion and Knowledge: Sociological Perspectives*, 97–113. Farnham: Ashgate.

Taira, Teemu (2015). "Media and the Nonreligious." In Kennet Granholm, Marcus Moberg and Sofia Sjö (eds.), *Religion, Media, and Social Change*, 110–25. London: Routledge.

Taira, Teemu (2019). "Reading Bond Films through the Lens of 'Religion': Discourse of 'The West and the Rest'." *Journal for Religion, Film and Media*, 5 (2): 119–39.

Wright, Melanie (2006). *Religion and Film: An Introduction*. London: I.B. Tauris.

Zuckerman, Phil (2014). *Living the Secular Life: New Answers to Old Questions*. London: Penguin.

Chapter 2

Berman, Eliza (2015). "The True Story Behind the Movie *Joy*." *Time*, December 27, 2015. Available online: https://time.com/4161779/joy-movie-accuracy-fact-check/

Campbell, Joseph (1973). *The Hero with a Thousand Faces*. Bollington Paperback Edition. Princeton: Princeton University Press.

Chang, Huang-Ming, Leonid Ivonin, Marta Diaz, Andreu Catala, Wei Chen, and Matthias Rauterberg (2013). "From Mythology to Psychology: Identifying Archetypal Symbols in Movies." *Technoetic Arts: A Journal of Speculative Research*, 11 (2): 99–113.

Doniger, Wendy (1998). *The Implied Spider: Politics & Theology in Myth*. New York: Columbia University Press.

Ebert, Roger (1987). "The Secret of My Success." *Roger Ebert.com*, April 10, 1987. Available online: https://www.rogerebert.com/reviews/the-secret-of-my-success-1987

Ellis, Caron Schwartz (1995). "With Eyes Uplifted: Space Aliens as Sky Gods." In Joel W. Martin and Conrad E. Oswalt, Jr. (eds.), *Screening the Sacred: Religion, Myth, and Ideology in Popular American Film*, 83–93. Boulder: Westview Press.

Gordan, Andrew (1995). "Star Wars: A Myth for Our Time." In Joel W. Martin and Conrad E. Oswalt, Jr. (eds.), *Screening the Sacred: Religion, Myth, and Ideology in Popular American Film*, 73–82. Boulder: Westview Press.

Kehr, Dave (1987). "Unfortunately for Fox Fans, 'Secret of My Success' is No Joking." *Chicago Tribune*, April 10. Available online: https://www.chicagotribune.com/news/ct-xpm-1987-04-10-8701270562-story.html

Laderman, Gary (2009). *Sacred Matters: Celebrity Worship, Sexual Ecstasies, The Living Dead, and Other Signs of Religious Life in the United States*. New York: New Press.

Lincoln, Bruce (1989). *Discourse and the Construction of Society: Comparative Studies of Myth, Ritual, and Classification.* New York: Oxford University Press.

Lincoln, Bruce (2000). *Theorizing Myth: Narrative, Ideology, and Scholarship.* Chicago: The University of Chicago Press.

Rushing, Janice Hocker (1995). "Evolution of 'The New Frontier'." In Joel W. Martin and Conrad E. Oswalt, Jr. (eds.), *Screening the Sacred: Religion, Myth, and Ideology in Popular American Film*, 94–118. Boulder: Westview Press.

"Soldiers of the Cross." *NFSA* (2017). Available online: https://www.nfsa.gov.au/collection/curated/soldiers-cross

Stratton, Jon (2016). "Die Sheldon Die: The Big Bang Theory, Everyday Neoliberalism and Sheldon as Neoliberal Man." *Journal of Cultural Research*, 20 (2): 171–88.

Vogler, Christopher (2017). "Joseph Campbell Goes to the Movies: The Influence of the Hero's Journey in Film Narrative." *Journal of Genius and Eminence*, 2 (2): 9–23.

Chapter 3

The American Library Association (n.d.). "Frequently Challenged Books." *ala.org.* Available online: http://www.ala.org/advocacy/bbooks/frequentlychallengedbooks (accessed February 22, 2020).

Artz, Lee (2015). "Monarchs, Monsters, and Multiculturalism: Disney's Menu for Global Hierarchy." In Gail Dines and Jean M. Humez (eds.), *Gender, Race, and Class in Media: A Critical Reader*, 449–54. Los Angeles: Sage.

Baptiste, Tracey (2019). "Mermaids Have Always Been Black." *The New York Times.* Available online: https://www.nytimes.com/2019/07/10/opinion/black-little-mermaid.html (accessed February 22, 2020).

Berman, Eliza (2018). "Hollywood's Once and Future Classic: Why It Took 54 Years to Turn a Wrinkle in Time into a Movie." *Time.* Available online: https://time.com/wrinkle-in-time/ (accessed February 22, 2020).

Gonzalez, Sandra (2020). "Natalie Portman's Oscars Cape Pays Tribute to Snubbed Female Directors." *CNN.* Available online: https://www.cnn.com/2020/02/09/entertainment/natalie-portman-oscars-cape/index.html (accessed February 22, 2020).

hooks, bell (1992). *Black Looks: Race and Representation*, 115–32. Boston: South End Press.

Internet Movie Database (n.d.). "Awards (2008)." *imdb.com.* Available online: https://www.imdb.com/title/tt0887912/awards?ref_=tt_awd (accessed February 22, 2020).

Johnson, Zach (2017). "Oprah Winfrey Says a Wrinkle in Time is Like the New the Wizard of Oz." *E!News.* Available online: https://www.eonline.com/news/900779/oprah-winfrey-says-a-wrinkle-in-time-is-like-the-new-the-wizard-of-oz?utm_source=eonline&utm_medium=rssfeeds&utm_campaign=imdb_topstories (accessed February 22, 2020).

Kinos-Goodin, Jesse (2018). "Behind the Religious Controversy and Unfilmable Status of a Wrinkle in Time." *CBC.* Available online: https://www.cbc.ca/radio/q/blog/behind-the-religious-controversy-and-unfilmable-status-of-a-wrinkle-in-time-1.4568528 (accessed February 22, 2020).

Lofton, Kathryn (2011). *Oprah: The Gospel of an Icon.* Oakland: University of California Press.

REFERENCES

Mulvey, Laura (1981). "Afterthoughts on Visual Pleasure and Narrative Cinema Inspired by 'Duel in the Sun' (King Vidor, 1946)." *Framework: The Journal of Cinema and Media*, 15 (17): 13. www.jstor.org/stable/44111815.

Mulvey, Laura (1999). "Visual Pleasure and Narrative Cinema." In Leo Braudy and Marshall Cohen (eds.), *Film Theory and Criticism: Introductory Readings*, 620–31. New York: Oxford University Press.

Rawson, James (2013). "Why are Gay Characters at the Top of Hollywood's Kill List?." *The Guardian*. Available online: https://www.theguardian.com/film/filmblog /2013/jun/11/gay-characters-hollywood-films (accessed February 22, 2020).

Ryzik, Melena (2018). "Ava DuVernay's Fiercely Feminine Vision for 'A Wrinkle in Time'." *The New York Times*. Available online: https://www.nytimes.com /2018/03/01/movies/a-wrinkle-in-time-ava-duvernay-disney.html?action=click &auth=login-facebook&module=RelatedCoverage&pgtype=Article&region =Footer (accessed February 22, 2020).

Schmidt, Leigh Eric (2005). *Restless Souls: The Making of American Spirituality*. New York: HarperOne.

Smith, Christian (2009). *Soul Searching: The Religious and Spiritual Lives of American Teenagers*. New York: Oxford University Press.

Smith, Leslie Dorrough (2014). *Righteous Rhetoric: Sex, Speech, and the Politics of Concerned Women for America*. New York: Oxford University Press.

Smith, Leslie Dorrough (2017). "Religion Concerns the Transcendent." In Brad Stoddard and Craig Martin (eds.), *Stereotyping Religion: Critiquing Clichés*, 55–67. London: Bloomsbury.

Smith, Leslie Dorrough (2020a). *Compromising Positions: Sex Scandals, Politics, and American Christianity*. New York: Oxford University Press.

Smith, Leslie Dorrough (2020b). "Scopophilia and the Manufacture of 'Good Religion'." In Leslie Dorrough Smith, Steffen Fuhrding, and Adrian Hermann (eds.), *Hijacked: A Critical Treatment of the Public Rhetoric of Good and Bad Religion*, 98–107. Sheffield: Equinox.

Weisenfeld, Judith (2007). *Hollywood Be Thy Name: African American Religion in American Film, 1929–1949*. Berkeley: University of California Press.

Yuen, Nancy Wang (2016). *Reel Inequality: Hollywood Actors and Racism*. New Brunswick: Rutgers University Press.

Chapter 4

Alexander, Michelle (2006). *The New Jim Crow: Mass Incarceration in the Age of Colorblindness*. New York: New Press.

App, Urs (1997). "St. Francis Xavier's Discovery of Japanese Buddhism: A Chapter in the European Discovery of Buddhism. (Part 1: Before the Arrival in Japan, 1547–1549)." *Eastern Buddhist (New Series)*, 30 (1): 53–78.

App, Urs (2010). "On Being White ... and Other Lies." In Randall Kenan (ed.), *The Cross of Redemption: Uncollected Writings*, 135–8. New York: Pantheon.

Baldwin, James (1995). *The Fire Next Time*. New York: Modern Library.

Bhambra, Gurminder K. (2017). "Brexit, Trump, and 'Methodological Whiteness': On the Misrecognition of Race and Class." *The British Journal of Sociology*, 68 (Supplement 1): 214–32. https://doi.org/10.1111/1468-4446.12317

Bhambra, Gurminder K. (2018). "Methodological Whiteness." *Global Social Theory*. Available online: https://globalsocialtheory.org/concepts/methodological -whiteness/ (accessed August 25, 2020).

Blackburn, Carole (2004). *Harvest of Souls: The Jesuit Missions and Colonialism in North America, 1632–1650*. Montreal: McGill-Queen's University Press.

Blake, Richard A. (1996). "Redeemed in Blood: The Sacramental Universe of Martin Scorsese." *Journal of Popular Film and Television*, 24 (1): 2–9. https:// doi.org/10.1080/01956051.1996.9943707

Blum, Edward J. and Paul Harvey (2012). *The Color of Christ: The Son of God and the Saga of Race in America*. Chapel Hill: University of North Carolina Press.

Bonilla-Silva, Eduardo (2017). *Racism Without Racists: Color-Blind Racism and the Persistence of Racial Inequality in America*, 5th ed. Lanham: Rowman & Littlefield.

Cone, James H. (1990). *A Black Theology of Liberation*. New York: Orbis Books.

Crenshaw, Kimberle, Saidiya Hartman, and N. K. Jemisin (2020). "Storytelling While Black and Female: Conjuring Beautiful Experiments (Pt 15)." *Under the Blacklight (Intersectionality Matters) Podcast*, August 5, 2020. Available online: https://www.youtube.com/watch?v=xGS5aP5Vi7g (accessed August 25, 2020).

Diawara, M. (1990). "Black British Cinema: Spectatorship and Identity Formation in Territories." *Public Culture*, 3 (1): 33–48. https://doi.org/10.1215/08992363-3-1-33

Döring, Tobias (1997). "Turning the Colonial Gaze: Re-Visions of Terror in Dabydeen's Turner." *Third Text*, 11 (38): 3–14. https://doi.org/10.1080 /09528829708576654

Du Bois, W. E. B. (1920). "The Souls of White Folk." In *Darkwater: Voices from within the Veil*. New York: Harcourt, Brace and Company. Available online: https://ia600207.us.archive.org/0/items/darkwater15210gut/15210-8.txt

Du Bois, W. E. B. (1935). *Black Reconstruction in America 1860–1880*. New York: Harcourt Brace. Available online: https://archive.org/details/blackreconstruct00d uborich

Dyer, Richard (1997). *White: Essays on Race and Culture*. London: Routledge.

Dyer, Richard (2002). "White." In *The Matter of Images: Essays on Representations*, 126–48, 2nd ed. London: Routledge. Available online: https:// www-routledge-com.ezproxy.lib.gla.ac.uk/The-Matter-of-Images-Essays-on -Representations/Dyer/p/book/9780415254946

Eaghll, Tenzan (2019). "Ideological Blindspot in the Academic Study of Religion and Film." *Method and Theory in the Study of Religion*, 31 (4–5): 416–45. https://doi.org/10.1163/15700682-12341465

Elison, George (1988). *Deus Destroyed: The Image of Christianity in Early Modern Japan*. Cambridge: Harvard University Press.

Ellis, Robert Richmond (2012). *They Need Nothing: Hispanic-Asian Encounters of the Colonial Period*. Toronto: University of Toronto Press.

Endo, Shusaku (1974). "Anguish of an Alien." *The Japan Christian Quarterly*, 40: 179–86.

Endo, Shusaku. (2016). *Silence*, trans. William Johnston. London: Picador.

Fanon, Frantz (1967). "Racism and Culture." In *Toward the African Revolution: Political Essays*, 29–44. New York: Grove Press. https://doi.org/10.1093/ia/45.4 .755a

Fanon, Frantz (2004). *The Wretched of the Earth*, trans. Richard Philcox. New York: Grove Press.

REFERENCES

Fanon, Frantz (2008). *Black Skin, White Masks*, trans. Charles Lam Markmann. London: Pluto Press.

Figlerowicz, Marta (2017). "White Men on a Mission: Martin Scorsese's Long 'Silence.'" *Los Angeles Review of Books*, January 29, 2017. Available online: https://lareviewofbooks.org/article/white-men-mission-martin-scorseses-long -silence/ (accessed August 25, 2020).

Gordon-Reed, Annette (2016). "Hamilton: The Musical: Blacks and the Founding Fathers." *National Council on Public History: History@Work Blog*. Available online: https://ncph.org/history-at-work/hamilton-the-musical-blacks-and-the -founding-fathers/ (accessed August 25, 2020).

Hall, Stuart (1995). "Whites of Their Eyes." In Gail Dines and Jean M Humez (eds.), *Gender, Race and Class in Media*, 18–22. London: Sage.

Hannah-Jones, Nikole (2019). "The 1619 Project." *The New York Times*, August 2019. Available online: https://www.nytimes.com/interactive/2019/08/14/ magazine/1619-america-slavery.html (accessed August 25, 2020).

Hermansson, Casie (2015). "Flogging Fidelity: In Defense of the (Un)Dead Horse." *Adaptation*, 8 (2): 147–60. https://doi.org/10.1093/adaptation/apv014

hooks, bell (1992). "The Oppositional Gaze: Black Female Spectators." In *Black Looks: Race and Representation*, 115–31. Boston: South End Press.

Horii, Mitsutoshi (2018). *The Category of 'Religion' in Contemporary Japan*. Cham: Springer International Publishing. https://doi.org/10.1007/978-3-319 -73570-2

Horne, Philip (2017). "Martin Scorsese Catholic Tastes." *Sight and Sound*, 27 (2): 16–27.

Hughey, Matthew W. (2016). "Hegemonic Whiteness: From Structure and Agency to Identity Allegiance." In S. Middleton, D. R. Roediger, and D. M. Shaffer (eds.), *The Construction of Whiteness: An Interdisciplinary Analysis of Race Formation and the Meaning of a White Identity*, 212–33. Baltimore: Johns Hopkins University Press. https://doi.org/10.14325/mississippi/9781496805553 .003.0009

Josephson, Jason Ananda (2012). *The Invention of Religion in Japan*. Chicago: Chicago University Press.

Kendi, Ibram X. (2019). *How To Be an Antiracist*. London: Penguin.

Leuchtenberger, Jan C. (2013). *Conquering Demons: The "Kirishitan", Japan, and the World in Early Modern Japanese Literature*. Ann Arbor: Center for Japanese Studies, University of Michigan.

Lloyd, Vincent (2013). "Race and Religion: Contribution to Symposium on Critical Approaches to the Study of Religion." *Critical Research on Religion*, 1 (1): 80–6. https://doi.org/10.1177/2050303213476105

Lopes, Paul (2017). "The Power of Hyphen-Nationalism: Martin Scorsese's Sojourn from Italian American to White-Ethnic American." *Social Identities*, 23 (5): 562–78. https://doi.org/10.1080/13504630.2017.1303373

Martin, James (2017). "Fr. James Martin Answers 5 Common Questions about 'Silence'." *America Magazine: The Jesuit Review*. Available online: https:// www.americamagazine.org/arts-culture/2017/01/18/fr-james-martin-answers-5 -common-questions-about-silence (accessed August 25, 2020).

Maryks, Robert A. (2017). "Silence (2016)." *Journal of Jesuit Studies*, 4: 679–753. https://doi.org/10.1163/22141332-00404008-05

Matthews, Joshua (2017). "Silence: A Review Essay." *Pro Rege*, 45 (3): 10–11. https://doi.org/10.1111/j.0022-3840.1967.0102_166.x

McTighe, Laura (2020a). "Introduction: 'Religio-Racial Identity' as Challenge and Critique." *Journal of the American Academy of Religion*, 88 (2): 299–303. https://doi.org/10.1093/jaarel/lfaa015

McTighe, Laura (2020b). "Theory on the Ground: Ethnography, Religio-Racial Study, and the Spiritual Work of Building Otherwise." *Journal of the American Academy of Religion*, 88 (2): 407–39. https://doi.org/10.1093/jaarel/lfaa014

Meer, Nasar (2013). "Racialization and Religion: Race, Culture and Difference in the Study of Antisemitism and Islamophobia." *Ethnic and Racial Studies*, 36 (3): 385–98. https://doi.org/10.1080/01419870.2013.734392

Mills, Charles W. (2017). "White Ignorance." In *Black Rights/White Wrongs: The Critique of Racial Liberalism*, 281. New York: Oxford University Press.

Monteiro, Lyra D. (2016a). "It's Not 'Just a Musical'." *National Council on Public History: History@Work Blog*. Available online: https://ncph.org/history-at-work /its-not-just-a-musical/ (accessed August 25, 2020).

Monteiro, Lyra D. (2016b). "Race-Conscious Casting and the Erasure of the Black Past in Lin-Manuel Miranda's Hamilton." *Public Historian*, 38 (1): 89–98. https://doi.org/10.1525/TPH.2016.38.1.89

Morrison, Toni (1992). *Playing in the Dark: Whiteness and the Literary Imagination*. London: Harvard University Press.

Newton, Richard (2019). "Scared Sheetless: Negrophobia, the Fear of God, and Justified Violence in the U.S. Christian-White Imaginary." *Journal of Religion and Violence*, 7 (3): 303–22. https://doi.org/10.5840/jrv202031172

Ng, Teng-Kuan (2019). "Of Faith and Faithlessness: Adaptive Fidelity in Shusaku Endo's and Martin Scorsese's Silence." *Literature and Theology*, 33 (4): 434–50. https://doi.org/10.1093/litthe/frz024

Nye, Malory (2016). "Martin Scorsese Would Like Us to See Silence as a Film about Religion — But Its Central Issue is Race." *Panel & Frame*, December 24, 2016. Available online: https://medium.com/panel-frame/martin-scorsese -would-like-us-to-see-silence-as-a-film-about-religion-but-its-central-issue-is -f3b785ea1bd7 (accessed August 25, 2020).

Nye, Malory (2017). "Scorsese's Silence is a Movie about Race as Well as Religion." *Huffington Post UK*, January 11, 2017. Available online: https:// www.huffingtonpost.co.uk/malory-nye/scorseses-silence-is-abou_b_13718918 .html (accessed August 25, 2020).

Nye, Malory (2018). "Race and Religion: Postcolonial Formations of Power and Whiteness." *Method & Theory in the Study of Religion*, July. https://doi.org/10 .1163/15700682-12341444

Nye, Malory (2019). "Decolonizing the Study of Religion." *Open Library of Humanities*, 5 (1): 43. https://doi.org/10.16995/olh.421

Paiva, José Pedro. (2017). "The Inquisition Tribunal in Goa: Why and for What Purpose?" *Journal of Early Modern History*, 21 (6): 565–93. doi: https://doi.org /10.1163/15700658-12342575

Quijano, Aníbal (2007). "Coloniality and Modernity/Rationality." *Cultural Studies*, 21 (2): 168–78. https://doi.org/10.1080/09502380601164353

Ram, Kalpana (2018). "Gender, Colonialism, and the Colonial Gaze." In *The International Encyclopedia of Anthropology*, 1–7. Oxford: John Wiley & Sons, Ltd. https://doi.org/10.1002/9781118924396.wbiea1873

Reed, Ishmael (2015). "'Hamilton: The Musical:' Black Actors Dress Up Like Slave Traders…and It's Not Halloween." *CounterPunch.Org*. Available online: https://

www.counterpunch.org/2015/08/21/hamilton-the-musical-black-actors-dress-up
-like-slave-tradersand-its-not-halloween/ (accessed August 25, 2020).

Rosen, Steven L. (2000). "Japan as Other: Orientalism and Cultural Conflict." *Journal of Intercultural Communication*, 4. https://doi.org/www.immi.se/intercultural/nr4/rosen.htm

Saha, Anamik (2017). *Race and the Cultural Industries*. Cambridge: Polity.

Said, Edward W. (2003). *Orientalism*. Penguin.

Scorsese, Martin (2016). "Introduction." In Shusaku Endo (ed.), *Silence*, vii–ix. London: Picador.

Soyer, Francois (2008). "King Manuel I and the Expulsion of the Castilian Conversos and Muslims from Portugal in 1497: New Perspectives." *Cadernos de Estudos Sefarditas*, 8: 33–62. Available online: https://d1wqtxts1xzle7 .cloudfront.net/32335699/Soyer__%282008%29_King_Manuel_I_and_the _expulsion_of_the_Castilian_Conversos_and_Muslims_from_Portugal_in _1497-_new_perspectives._Cadernos_d.pdf?1384725195=&response-content -disposition=inline%3B+filename%3DO

Stam, Robert, and Louise Spence (2009). "Colonialism, Racism, and Representation." In L. Braudy and M. Cohen (eds.), *Film Theory and Criticism: Introductory Readings*, 751–66, 7th ed. New York: Oxford University Press.

Stratton, Jon (2016). "Die Sheldon Die: The Big Bang Theory, Everyday Neoliberalism and Sheldon as Neoliberal Man." *Journal of Cutural Research*, 20 (2): 171–88.

Vera, Hernan, and Andrew Gordon (2003). *Screen Saviors: Hollywood Fictions of Whiteness*. Lanham: Rowman & Littlefield.

Vial, Theodore (2016). *Modern Religion, Modern Race*. Oxford: Oxford University Press.

Ward, Haruko Nawata (2009). *Women Religious Leaders in Japan's Christian Century, 1549–1650*. London: Routledge.

Ward, Haruko Nawata (2017). "Silence Directed by Martin Scorsese." *The Catholic Historical Review*, 103 (1): 169–70. https://doi.org/10.1353/cat.2017.0055

Weisenfeld, Judith (2016). *New World A-Coming: Black Religion and Racial Identity during the Great Migration*. New York: New York University Press.

Weisenfeld, Judith (2020). "The House We Live In: Religio-Racial Theories and the Study of Religion." *Journal of the American Academy of Religion*, 88 (2): 440–59. https://doi.org/10.1093/jaarel/lfaa011

Wekker, Gloria (2016). *White Innocence: Paradoxes of Colonialism and Race*. Durham: Duke University Press. https://doi.org/10.1215/9780822374565

Wolfe, Patrick (2016). *Traces of History: Elementary Structures of Race*. London: Verso Books.

Yamato, Jen (2016). "'Silence': Scorsese's Flawed, Frustrating White Saviour Tries to Save Japan From Itself." *Daily Beast*, December 18, 2016. Available online: https://www.thedailybeast.com/silence-scorseses-flawed-frustrating-white-savior -tries-to-save-japan-from-itself (accessed August 25, 2020).

Chapter 5

Albanese, Catherine L. (2007). *A Republic of Mind and Spirit: A Cultural History of American Metaphysical Religion*. New Haven: Yale University Press.

Altman, Michael J. (2017). *Heathen, Hindoo, Hindu: American Representations of India, 1721–1893*. New York: Oxford University Press.

Bose, Nandana (2008). "The Darjeeling Limited: Critiquing Orientalism on the Train to Nowhere." *Mediascape: UCLA's Journal of Cinema and Media Studies*, Spring: 1–8.

Browning, Mark (2011). *Wes Anderson: Why His Movies Matter*. Modern Filmmakers. Santa Barbara: Praeger.

Chandra, Shefali (2015). "'India Will Change You Forever': Hinduism, Islam, and Whiteness in the American Empire." *Signs: Journal of Women in Culture & Society*, 40 (2): 487–512. https://doi.org/10.1086/678214

Current, Cheris Brewer, and Emily Tillotson (2018). "Hipster Racism and Sexism in Charity Date Auctions: Individualism, Privilege Blindness and Irony in the Academy." *Gender & Education*, 30 (4): 467–76. https://doi.org/10.1080/09540253.2016.1216952

The Darjeeling Limited (2010). Dir. Wes Anderson, USA: Searchlight Pictures.

Dean-Ruzicka, Rachel (2013). "Themes of Privilege and Whiteness in the Films of Wes Anderson." *Quarterly Review of Film & Video*, 30 (1): 25–40. https://doi.org/10.1080/10509208.2010.500945

Dilley, Whitney Crothers (2017). *The Cinema of Wes Anderson: Bringing Nostalgia to Life*. Directors' Cuts. London: WallFlower Press.

Dubrofsky, Rachel E., and Megan M. Wood (2014). "Posting Racism and Sexism: Authenticity, Agency and Self-Reflexivity in Social Media." *Communication and Critical/Cultural Studies*, 11 (3): 282–7. https://doi.org/10.1080/14791420.2014.926247

Inden, Ronald B. (2011). *Imagining India*. Oxford: Basil Blackwell, 1990.

Iwamura, Jane Naomi. (2011). *Virtual Orientalism: Asian Religions and American Popular Culture*. New York: Oxford University Press.

King, Richard (1999). *Orientalism and Religion: Postcolonial Theory, India and "the Mystic East."* London: Routledge.

May, Emily J. (2008). "The Darjeeling Limited and the New American Traveller." *Senses of Cinema: An Online Film Journal Devoted to the Serious and Eclectic Discussion of Cinema*, 49. Available online: http://sensesofcinema.com/2009/feature-articles/darjeeling-limited/

Pratt, Mary Louise (2008). *Imperial Eyes: Travel Writing and Transculturation*, 2nd ed. London: Routledge.

Quart, Alissa (2020). "The Age of Hipster Sexism." *The Cut*. Available online: https://www.thecut.com/2012/10/age-of-hipster-sexism.html (accessed February 12, 2020).

Romney, Jonathan (2007). "Wes Anderson: Isn't It Time the Writer and Director Showed a Little Heart?" *The Independent*, November 11, 2007. Available online: https://www.independent.co.uk/arts-entertainment/films/features/wes-anderson-isnt-it-time-the-writer-and-director-showed-a-little-heart-399522.html (accessed February 12, 2020).

Said, Edward W. (1979). *Orientalism*. New York: Vintage Books.

Smithsonian Magazine (2020). "The World's First 'Yoga' Film." Available online: https://www.smithsonianmag.com/videos/category/arts-culture/the-worlds-first-yoga-fil/ (accessed February 13, 2020).

Sobocinska, Agnieszka (2014). "Following the 'Hippie Sahibs': Colonial Cultures of Travel and the Hippie Trail." *Journal of Colonialism and Colonial History*,

15 (2). Available online: http://muse.jhu.edu/journals/journal_of_colonialism
_and_colonial_history/v015/15.2.sobocinska.html

Thomas, Martin (2019). *Expedition into Empire: Exploratory Journeys and the Making of the Modern World*. London: Routledge.

Walton, John K. (ed.) (2005). *Histories of Tourism: Representation, Identity, and Conflict*. Tourism and Cultural Change 6. Clevedon: Channel View Publications.

West, Lindy (2020). "A Complete Guide to 'Hipster Racism'." *Jezebel*. Available online: https://jezebel.com/a-complete-guide-to-hipster-racism-5905291 (accessed February 12, 2020).

Chapter 6

Ahmed, Sara (2004). *The Cultural Politics of Emotion*. Edinburgh: Edinburgh University Press.

Barth, Karl (1950). *Humanismus. Theologische Studien, 28*. Zollikon-Zurich: Evangelischer Verlag.

Bentley, Rick (2020). "Against All Odds, David Mitchell's Novel 'Cloud Atlas' Now a Film." Available online: https://www.beaconjournal.com/article/20121024/ENTERTAINMENT/310249087 (accessed July 9, 2020).

Brennan, Teresa (2004). *The Transmission of Affect*. Ithaca: Cornell University Press.

Ciment, Michel (2009). "Letter to the Editors." *Sight & Sound*, 19: 6.

Droit, Roger-Pol (2003). *The Cult of Nothingness: The Philosophers and the Buddha*. Translated by David Streight and Pamela Vohnson. Chapel Hill: University of North Carolina Press.

Duara, Prasenjit (2016). *The Crisis of Global Modernity: Asian Traditions and a Sustainable Future*. Cambridge: Cambridge University Press.

Guo, Ting (2013). "Cloud Atlas." *Journal of Religion and Film*, 17 (2): Article 14.

Guo, Ting (2017). "Review of Prasenjit Duara, *The Crisis of Global Modernity: Asian Traditions and a Sustainable Future*." *Review of Religion and Chinese Society*, 142–5 (4): 1.

Jankiewicz, Stephen (2012). "Orientalists in Love: Intimacy, Empire, and Cross-Cultural Knowledge." *Journal of World History*, 23 (2): 345–73.

Mitchell, David (2004). *Cloud Atlas*. London: Hodder and Stoughton.

Mitchell, David (2016). "Interview with William Bradbury." Finding the Locus of David Mitchell. *The Japan Times*, April 2, 2016. Available online: https://www.japantimes.co.jp/culture/2016/04/02/books/finding-locus-david-mitchell/ (accessed September 30, 2019).

Mitchell, David (2017). "David Mitchell: What My Son's Autism Has Taught Me." *The Guardian*. Available online: https://www.theguardian.com/society/2017/jul/08/david-mitchell-son-autism-diagnosis-advice (accessed September 30, 2019).

Møllgaard, Eske (2008). "Slavoj Žižek's Critique of Western Buddhism." *Contemporary Buddhism*, 9 (2): 167–80.

Napper, Elizabeth (1989). *Dependent Arising and Emptiness: A Tibetan Buddhist Interpretation of Madhyamika Philosophy*. Somerville: Wisdom Publications.

Nietzsche, Friedrich (1967). *The Will to Power*. Translated by Walter Kaufman and R. J. Hollingdale. New York: Random House.

Norman, Richard (2004). *On Humanism*. New York: Routledge.

The Pervert's Guide to Ideology (2013), [Film] Dir. Sophie Fiennes, USA: Zeitgeist Films.

Plummer, Ken (2001). *Documents of Life 2: An Invitation to a Critical Humanism*, 2nd ed. London: Sage.

Schaeffer, Donovan O. (2015). *Religious Affect: Animality, Evolution, and Power*. Durham: Duke University Press.

Schatz, Thomas (1981). *Hollywood Genres: Formulas, Filmmaking, and the Studio System*. Philadelphia: Temple University Press.

Sedgwick, Eve Kosofsky (2003). *Touching Feelings: Affect, Pedagogy, Performativity*. Durham: Duke University Press.

Storhoff, Gary and John Whalen-Bridge (2014). *Buddhism and American Cinema*. Albany: SUNY Press.

Suh, Sharon A (2015). *Silver Screen Buddha: Buddhism in Asian and Western Film*. London: Bloomsbury.

Vasquez, Manuel A. (2011). *More Than Belief: A Materialist Theory of Religion*. Oxford: Oxford University Press.

Wollen, Peter (1972). *Signs of Meaning in the Cinema*. Bloomington: Indiana University Press.

Žižek, Slavoj (2001). "From Western Marxism to Western Buddhism." *Cabinet Magazine*, Spring.

Žižek, Slavoj (2003). *The Puppet and the Dwarf: The Perverse Core of Christianity*. Cambridge: MIT Press.

Žižek, Slavoj (2006). "The Prospects of Radical Politics Today." In Rex Butler and Scott Stephens (eds.), *Slavoj Žižek, The Universal Exception: Selected Writings*, vol. 2, 237–58. London: Continuum.

Žižek, Slavoj and Millbank John (2009). *The Monstrosity of Christ: Paradox or Dialectic?* Cambridge: MIT Press.

Chapter 7

Althusser, Louis (2014 [1971]). *Ideology and Ideological State Apparatuses*, trans. G. M. Goshgarian. London: Verso Books.

Araújo Vélez, Fernando (2018). "Cien Años de Soledad: Un vallenato de 300 páginas." *El Espectador*, December 21. Available online: https://www .elespectador.com/noticias/cultura/cien-anos-de-soledad-un-vallenato-de-300 -paginas/ (accessed February 23, 2021).

Bartel, Rebecca C. (2021). *Card Carrying Christians: Debt and the Making of Free Market Spirituality in Colombia*. Berkley: University of California Press.

Bhabha, Homi (1994). *The Location of Culture*. London: Routledge.

Bowers, Maggie Ann (2004). *Magic(al) Realism*. London: Taylor and Francis Group.

Caminero-Santangelo, Marta (2005). "'The Pleas of the Desperate': Collective Agency versus Magical Realism in Ana Castillo's *So Far From God*." *Tulsa Studies in Women's Literature*, 24 (1): 81–103.

Carbonari, Patricia (2017). "Entre el Desplazamiento y la Reconciliación: El cine de Ciro Guerra." *Cinémas d'Amérique Latine*, 25: 100–9.

REFERENCES

Caro Meléndez, Eduardo Alfonso (2010). "Review: The Wind Journeys." *Chasqui*, 39 (2): 257–60.

Carpentier, Alejo (2004 [1949]). *De lo Real Maravilloso Americano*. México: Universidad Autónoma de Mexico.

Casalins Pérez, Alexander, César Augusto Sánchez Contreras, and Berena Vergara Serpa (2014). *Francisco el Hombre: Juglar y Leyenda*. Bogotá: Ministerio de Cultura – Observatorio del Caribe Colombiano.

Cascón Becerra, Juan Aquilino (2006). "Realismo Mágico: Historia e Intrahistoria en el Cine Iberoamericano." *Trocadero*, 18: 113–26.

Daniels Garcia, Joce Guillermo (2019). "Francisco el Hombre: Una leyenda inmersa en antiguas Mitologías." *CiudadPaz*, May 1, 2019. Available online: https://www.ciudadpaz.com/single-post/2019/05/01/Francisco-el-Hombre-Una-leyenda-inmersa-en-antiguas-Mitolog%C3%ADas (accessed February 23, 2021).

DelRoss, Jeana (2005). *Writing Catholic Women: Contemporary International Catholic Girlhood Narratives*. New York: Palgrave MacMillan.

Eaghll, Tenzan (2019). "Ideological Blindspot in the Academic Study of Religion and Film." *Method and Theory in the Study of Religion*. https://doi.org/10.1163/15700682-12341465

Fattal, Alex (2018). *Guerrilla Marketing: Counterinsurgency and Capitalism in Colombia*. Chicago: University of Chicago Press.

Figueroa, José Antonio (2009). *Realismo Mágico, vallenato, y violencia política en la Costa Colombiana*. Bogotá: Instituto Colombiana de Antropología e Historia.

Flores, Angel (1995). "Magical Realism in Spanish American Fiction." *Hispania*, 38 (2): 187–92.

Foster, David William and Rosita Scerbo (2019). "Magical Realism." In *Oxford Bibliographies*. Oxford: Oxford University Press. http://www.oxfordbibliographies.com/

Frankel, Alison (2018). "Chiquita Must Face Jury in Colombian Terror-Funding Charge." *Reuters*, January 5, 2018, https://www.reuters.com/article/legal-us-otc-chiquita-idUSKBN1ET2C8 (accessed February 23, 2021).

García Márquez, Gabriel (2017 [1967]). *Cien Años de Soledad*. New York: Penguin Random House.

González Boixo, José Carlos (2017). "El 'realismo mágico: Una categoría crítica necesitada de revision." *Tropelías*, 1: 116–23.

Hutchinson, Sydney (2011). "Los Viajes del Viento by Ciro Guerra: El Vuelco del Cangrejo by Ruíz Navia. Review." *Latin American Music Review*, 32 (2): 315–17.

Jaccard, Nathan (2009). "Los Viajes del viento, una locura completa." *Semana*, May 4, 2009. https://www.semana.com/entretenimiento/articulo/los-viajes-del-viento-locura-completa/102780-3/ (accessed February 23, 2021).

Jameson, Fredric (1986). "On Magic Realism in Film." *Critical Inquiry*, 12 (2): 301–25.

Keene, Webb (2007). *Christian Moderns: Freedom and Fetish in the Mission Encounter*. Berkeley: University of California Press.

Kennard, Matt (2017). "Chiquita Made a Killing From Colombia's Civil War." *The Pulitzer Center*, January 28, 2017, https://pulitzercenter.org/stories/chiquita-made-killing-colombias-civil-war (accessed February 23, 2021).

Levene, Nancy (2017). *Powers of Distinction: On Religion and Modernity*. Chicago: University of Chicago Press.

McCracken, Ellen (1999). *New Latina Narrative: The Feminine Space of Postmodern Ethnicity*. Tucson: University of Arizon Press.

Meyer, Birgit (1999). *Translating the Devil: Religion and Modernity among the Ewe in Ghana*. Edinburgh: Edinburgh University Press for the International African Institute.

Mignolo, Walter (2005). *The Idea of Latin America*. Malden: Blackwell Publishing.

Rappaport, Joanne (2009). "Prologue." In José Antonio Figueroa (ed.), *Realismo Mágico, Vallenato, y Violencia Política en el Caribe Colombiano*, 11–14. Bogotá: Instituto Colombiano de Antropología e Historia.

Rivera Cusicanqui, Silvia (2020). *Ch'ixinakax utxiwa: On Practices and Discourses of Decolonization*, trans. Molly Geidel. Cambridge: Polity Press.

Taussig, Michael (1980). *The Devil and Commodity Fetishism in South America*. Chapel Hill: University of North Carolina at Chapel Hill.

Van der Veer, Peter (2001). *Imperial Encounters: Religion and Modernity in India and Britain*. Princeton: Princeton University Press.

Weber, Max (2001 [1905]). *The Protestant Ethic and the Spirit of Capitalism*. Translated by Talcott Parsons. New York: Routledge.

Zamora, Lois Parkinson and Wendy B. Farris (1994). *Magical Realism: Theory, History, Community*. Durham: Duke University Press.

Chapter 8

Ahmed, Sara (2010). *The Promise of Happiness*. Durham: Duke University Press.

APTN (2012). [news] "Bill C-45 Passes Through Senate; To Become Law." *Aboriginal Peoples Television Network*. Available online: https://www.aptnnews .ca/national-news/bill-c-45-passes-through-senate-to-become-law/

Barclay, Barry (2003). "Celebrating Fourth Cinema." *Illusions: A New Zealand Magazine of Film Television and Theatre Criticism*, 35: 7–11.

Bellah, Robert (2006). "Stories as Arrows: The Religious Response to Modernity." In Robert Bellah and Steven M. Tipton (eds.), *The Robert Bellah Reader*, 89–104. Durham: Duke University Press.

Black, L. (2020). *Picturing Indians: Native Americans in Film, 1941–1960*. Lincoln: University of Nebraska Press.

Brady, Miranda J. and John M. H. Kelly (2017). *We Interrupt This Program: Indigenous Media Tactics in Canadian Culture*. Vancouver: UBC Press.

Carter, Matthew (2020). "Perpetuation of Myth: Ideology in *Bone Tomahawk*." *Zeitschrift für Anglistik und Amerikanistik*, 68 (1): 21–35.

CBC News (2019). "231 'Imperative' Changes: The MMIWG Inquiry's Calls to Action." Available online: https://www.cbc.ca/news/indigenous/mmiwg-inquiry -report-1.5158385 (accessed November 3, 2021).

Cotter, Christopher R. and David G. Robertson (2016). *After World Religions: Reconstructing World Religions*. New York: Routledge.

Daschuk, James (2013). *Clearing the Plains: Disease, Politics of Starvation, and the Loss of Aboriginal Life*. Regina: University of Saskatchewan Press.

Deloria, Philip J. (1999). *Playing Indian*, Revised ed. New Haven: Yale University Press.

Derrida, Jacques (2001). *Writing and Difference*. Chicago: University of Chicago Press.

Eaghll, Tenzan (2019). "Ideological Blindspot in the Academic Study of Religion and Film." *Method & Theory in the Study of Religion*, 31 (4–5): 416–45.

REFERENCES

Estes, Nick (2019). *Our History of the Future: Standing Rock Versus the Dakota Access Pipeline, and the Long Tradition of Indigenous Resistance*. London: Verso.

Fielding, Julien (2009). "Indigenous Religion and Film." In William L. Blizek (ed.), *The Continuum Companion to Religion and Film*, 188–97. London: Continuum.

Francis, Daniel (2011). *The Imaginary Indian: The Image of the Indian in Canadian Culture*, 2nd ed. Vancouver: Arsenal Pulp Press.

Getino, Octavio and Fernando Solanas (2011). "Toward a Third Cinema." *Sin Frontera*. Available online: https://ufsinfronteradotcom.files.wordpress.com /2011/05/tercer-cine-getino-solonas-19691.pdf

Gill, Sam D. (1991). *Mother Earth: An American Story*. Chicago: University of Chicago Press.

Harp, Rick (2019). "Why Canada and Genocide Belong in the Same Sentence." *Media Indigena*, June 3. Available online: https://mediaindigena.com/why-canada -and-genocide-belong-in-the-same-sentence/ (accessed November 3, 2021).

Huhndorf, Shari M. (2001). *Going Native: Indians in the American Cultural Imagination*. Ithaca: Cornell University Press.

Kilpatrick, Jacquelyn (1999). *Celluloid Indians: Native Americans and Film*. Lincoln: University of Nebraska Press.

Kino-nda-niimi Collective (2014). *The Winter We Danced: Voices from the Past, the Future, and the Idle No More Movement*. Winnipeg: ARP Press.

King, C. Richard (2019). *Red Skins: Insult and Brand*. Lincoln: University of Nebraska Press.

Koyaanisqatsi (1982). [documentary] Dir, Godfrey Reggio, USA, American Zoetrope.

LaPointe, Sasha (2016). "'Bring me the Girl,': Why 'The Revenant' was Hard for My Friends and Me." *Indian Country Today*, February 3. Available online: https://indiancountrytoday.com/archive/bring-me-the-girl-why-the-revenant -was-hard-for-my-friends-and-me-G899sy_3WEaDEyItKVVRVw (accessed November 3, 2021).

LaRocque, Emma (2010). *When the Other Is Me: Native Resistance Discourse, 1850–1990*. Winnipeg: University of Manitoba Press.

Lincoln, Bruce (2012). "Religious and Other Conflicts in Twentieth-Century Guatemala." In *Gods and Demons, Priests and Scholar: Critical Explorations in the History of Religions*, 95–108. Chicago: University of Chicago Press.

Lincoln, Kenneth (1985). *Native American Renaissance*. Berkeley: University of California Press.

Lutz, Hartmut, Florentine Strzelczyk, and Renae Watchman (eds.) (2020). *Indianthusiasm: Indigenous Responses*. Waterloo: Wilfred Laurier University Press.

Marubbio, M. Elise (2006). *Killing the Indian Maiden: Images of Native American Women in Film*. Lexington: University of Kentucky Press.

Mas, Susana (2015). "Truth and Reconciliation Commission Offers 94 Calls to Action." *CBC News*, December 14. Available online: https://www.cbc.ca/ news/politics/truth-and-reconciliation-94-calls-to-action-1.3362258 (accessed November 3, 2021).

Masuzawa, Tomoko (2005). *The Invention of World Religions: Or, How European Universalism was Preserved in the Language of Pluralism*. Chicago: University of Chicago Press.

McCutcheon, Russell T. (2003). "The Ideology of Closure and the Problem with the Insider/Outsider Problem in the Study of Religion." *Studies in Religion*, 32 (3): 337–52.

McNally, Michael (2020). *Defend the Sacred: Native American Religious Freedom beyond the First Amendment*. Princeton: Princeton University Press.

Media Indigena (2019). [podcast] "The Serious Business of Settler Indigenization." *Media Indigena with Rick Harp*, August 28. Available online: https://mediaindigena.libsyn.com/ep-175-the-serious-business-of-self-indigenization (accessed November 3, 2021).

Miller, J. R. (2017). *Residential Schools and Reconciliation: Canada Confronts Its History*. Toronto: University of Toronto Press.

Mulvey, Laura (2009). "Visual Pleasure and Narrative Cinema." In Leo Braudy and Marshall Cohen (eds.), *Film Theory & Criticism*, 711–22, 7th ed. New York: Oxford.

NCAI (2018). "National Congress of American Indians Applauds Hostiles for Investing in the Authentic Representation of Native Peoples." January 8. Available online: http://www.ncai.org/news/articles/2018/01/08/national-congress-of-american-indians-ncai-applauds-hostiles-for-investing-in-the-authentic-representation-of-native-peoples (accessed November 3, 2021).

Owen, Suzanne (2008). *The Appropriation of Native American Spirituality*. London: Continuum.

Palmater, Pamela (2014). "Why We Are Idle No More." In The Kino-nda-niimi Collective (ed.), *The Winter We Danced: Voices from the Past, the Future, and the Idle No More Movement*, 37–40. Winnipeg: ARP Press.

Penny, H. Glenn (2015). *Kindred by Choice: Germans and American Indians Since 1800*. Chapel Hill: University of North Carolina Press.

Phippen, J. Weston (2016). "Kill Every Buffalo You Can. Every Dead Buffalo Is an Indian Gone." *The Atlantic*, May 13. Available online: https://www.theatlantic.com/national/archive/2016/05/the-buffalo-killers/482349/ (accessed November 3, 2021).

Pierce, Kati (2019). "How Wind River Brought MMIWG to the Mainstream." August 26. Available online: https://medium.com/@katipierce106/the-plight-of-missing-and-murdered-indigenous-woman-and-girls-cff5a6ebd113 (accessed November 3, 2021).

Raheja, Michelle H. (2010). *Reservation Reelism: Redfacing, Visual Sovereignty, and Representations of Native Americans in Film*, Kindle Version. Lincoln: University of Nebraska Press.

Reel Injun: On the Trail of the Hollywood Indian Diamond (2009). [documentary] Dir. Neil Diamond, Canada: National Film Board of Canada.

Roth, Lorna (2005). *There's Something New in the Air: The Story of First Peoples Television Broadcasting in Canada*. Montreal: McGill-Queens University Press.

Schiwy, Freya (2009). *Indianizing Film: Decolonization, the Andes, and the Question of Technology*. New Brunswick: Rutgers University Press.

Sheyahshe, Michael A. (2009). *Native Americans in Comic Books: A Critical Study*, Kindle Version. London: McFarland & Co.

Simpson, Audra (2014). *Mohawk Interruptus: Political Life across the Borders of Settler States*. Durham: Duke University Press.

Simpson, Leanne Betasamosake and Kiera L Ladner (eds.) (2010). *This Is an Honour Song: Twenty Years Since the Blockades*. Winnipeg: ARP Books.

Sutcliffe, Steven (2003). *Children of the New Age: A History of Spiritual Practices*. New York: Routledge.

Tuck, Eve and K. Wayne Yang (2012). "Decolonization is Not a Metaphor." *Decolonization: Indigeneity, Education & Society*, 1 (1): 1–40.

Unreserved (2019). [podcast] "Unreserved at TIFF: Indigenous films, Directors, and #TaijaWatch2019." *Unreserved with Rosanna Dearchild*, September 13. Available online: https://www.cbc.ca/radio/unreserved/unreserved-at -tiff-indigenous-films-directors-and-taikawatch2019-1.5280859 (accessed November 3, 2021).

Unreserved (2020). [podcast] "Lights, Camera, Oscars: Meeting the Creators Decolonizing Hollywood." *Unreserved with Rosanna Dearchild*, February 9. Available online: https://www.cbc.ca/radio/unreserved/lights-camera-oscars-meet -the-creators-decolonizing-hollywood-1.5450603 (accessed November 3, 2021).

Vowel, Chelsea (2016). "Just Don't Call Us Late for Supper: Names for Indigenous People." In *Indigenous Writes: A Guide to First Nations, Métis &Inuit Issues in Canada*. Winnipeg: Portage and Main Press.

Wenger, Tisa (2017). "Making Religion on the Reservation: Native Americans and the Settler Secular." In *Religious Freedom: The Contested History of an American Ideal*, 101–42. Chapel Hill: The University of North Carolina Press.

Wente, Jesse (2016). "The Revenant is Not an Indigenous Story." *CBC News*, January 14. Available online: https://www.cbc.ca/news/aboriginal/the-revenant -not-an-indigenous-story-1.3404007 (accessed November 3, 2021).

A World Unseen (2016). [documentary] "The Revenant: A World Unseen." *YouTube*. Available online: https://www.youtube.com/watch?v=pJfTfsXFbLk&t=13s (accessed November 3, 2021).

Wright, Melanie (2007). *Religion and Film: An Introduction*. New York: I/B. Tauris.

YouTube (2017). [website] "Leonardo DiCapro Won Best Actor Golden Globe 2016." Available online: https://www.youtube.com/watch?v=Y_jVtW23Www (accessed November 3, 2021).

Chapter 9

Benson-Allott, Caetlin (2018). "They're Coming to Get You . . . Or: Making America Anxious Again." *Film Quarterly*, 72 (2): 71–6.

The Bourne Identity (2002), [Film] Dir. Doug Liman, USA: Universal Pictures.

Bromley, David (nd). "A Tale of Two Theories: Brainwashing and Conversion as Competing Political Narratives." Unpublished Paper. Np.

Bromley, David and James Richardson (eds.) (1983). *The Brainwashing/ Deprogramming Controversy: Sociological, Psychological, and Historical Perspectives*. New York: Edwin Mellon Press.

Brunvand, Jan Harold (1981). *The Vanishing Hitchhiker: American Urban Legends and Their Meanings*. New York: W. W. Norton and Co.

Coward, Noel (1987). "The Nature of Horror." *The Journal of Aesthetics and Art Criticism*, 46 (1): 51–9.

Deprogrammed (2015). [Film] Dir. Mia Donovan, Canada: Eye Steel Film.

The Devil's Playground (2002), [Film] Dir. Lucy Walker, USA: Cinemax.

Douglas, Mary (1996). *Purity and Danger: An Analysis of Concepts of Pollution and Taboo*. London: Routledge and Keegan Paul.

REFERENCES

Fine, Gary Alan (1992). *Manufacturing Tales: Sex and Money in Contemporary Legends*. Knoxville: The University of Tennessee Press.

Greene, Eric (1998). *Planet of the Apes as American Myth: Race, Politics, and Popular Culture*. Middletown: Wesleyan University Press.

Harrison, Milmon (2005). *Righteous Riches: The Word of Faith Movement in Contemporary African American Relgiion*. New York: Oxford University Press.

Hassan, Steven (2019). *The Cult of Trump: A Leading Cult Expert Explains How the President Uses Mind Control*. New York: The Free Press.

Hereditary (2018), [Film] Dir. Ari Aster, USA: A24.

It Follows (2015), [Film] Dir. David Robert Mitchell, USA: Northern Lights Films.

Ju-On: The Grudge (2002), [Film] Dir. Takashi Shimizu, Japan: Pioneer LDC.

Lutz, Catherine (1997). "The Epistemology of the Bunker: The Brainwashed and Other New Subjects of Permanent War." In Joel Pfister and Nancy Schnog (eds.), *Inventing the Psychological: Toward a Cultural History of Emotional Life in America*, 245–67. New Haven: Yale University Press.

The Manchurian Candidate (2004), [Film] Dir. Jonathan Demme. USA: Paramount Pictures.

McCloud, Sean (2004). *Making the American Religious Fringe: Exotics, Subversives, and Journalists, 1955–1993*. Chapel Hill: The University of North Carolina Press.

McCloud, Sean (2007). *Divine Hierarchies: Class in American Religion and Religious Studies*. Chapel Hill: The University of North Carolina Press.

Means, Sean (2018). "Filmed-in-Utah Horror Drama *Hereditary* Might be the Scariest Movie at Sundance this Year." *The Salt Lake Tribune*. Available online: https://www.sltrib.com/artsliving/2018/01/23/filmed-in-utah-horror-drama-hereditary-might-be-the-scariest-movie-at-sundance-this-year/ (accessed September 16, 2019).

Pfeifer, Jeffrey (1992). "The Psychological Framing of Cults: Schematic Representations and Cult Evaluations." *Journal of Applied Social Psychology*, 22 (7): 531–44.

Silk, Mark (1995). *Unsecular Media: Making News of Religion in America*. University of Urbana: Illinois Press.

Woodward, Kenneth (1976). "Life with Father Moon." *Newsweek*, June 14: 60–6.

Worlds Apart (2008), [Film] Dir. Niels Arden Oplev, Denmark: Nordisk Film.

Zablocki, Benjamin (1997). "The Blacklisting of a Concept: The Strange History of the Brainwashing Conjecture in the Sociology of Religion." *Nova Religio*, October: 97–122.

Chapter 10

Ahmed, Maaheen (2015). "State Protection and Identification in Hellboy: Of Reformed Devils and Other Others in the Pentagon." *European Journal of American Studies*, 10 (2): 1–14.

Artz, Lee (2015). *Global Entertainment Media: A Critical Introduction*. Malden: Wiley Blackwell.

Ascough, Richard S. (2012a). "Apocalypse Now." In Adele Reinhartz (ed.), *Bible and Cinema: Fifty Key Films*, 13–18. New York: Routledge.

REFERENCES

Ascough, Richard S. (2012b). "Children of Men." In Adele Reinhartz (ed.), *Bible and Cinema: Fifty Key Films*, 60–4. New York: Routledge.

Biskind, Peter (2018). *The Sky Is Falling: How Vampires, Zombies, Androids and Superheroes Made America Great for Extremism*. New York: New Press.

Booker, Keith (2017). *May Contain Graphic Material. Comic Books, Graphic Novels, and Film*. Westport: Praeger.

Bukatman, Scott (2016). *Hellboy's World: Comics and Monsters on the Margins*. Oakland: University of California Press.

Charlesworth, James H. (1983). "Introduction." In James H. Charlesworth (ed.), *The Old Testament Pseudepigrapha Vol. 1: Apocalyptic Literature and Testaments*, 5–6. Peabody: Hendrickson.

Collins, John J. (2014). "What Is Apocalyptic Literature?" In John J. Collins (ed.), *The Oxford Handbook of Apocalyptic Literature*, 1–18. Toronto: Oxford University Press.

Cooper, Rand Richards (2004). "Devilish Adaptations." *Commonweal*, 131 (10): 19–20.

Dark, David (2002). *Everyday Apocalypse*. Grand Rapids: Brazos Press.

DiTomasso, Lorenzo (2014). "Apocalypticism and Popular Culture." In John J. Collins (ed.), *The Oxford Handbook of Apocalyptic Literature*, 473–509. Toronto: Oxford University Press.

Eagleton, Terry (1991). *Ideology: An Introduction*. New York: Verso.

Eco, Umberto (1972). "The Myth of Superman." *Diacritics*, 2 (1): 14–22.

Eliade, Mircea (1959). *The Sacred and the Profane: The Nature of Religion*, trans. W. R. Trask. New York: Harcourt Brace Jovanovich.

Frankfurter, David (2007). "The Legacy of Sectarian Rage: Vengeance Fantasies in the New Testament." In David A. Bernat and Jonathan Klawans (eds.), *Religion and Violence: The Biblical Heritage*, 114–28. Sheffield: Sheffield Phoenix Press.

Frilingos, Christopher A. (2004). *Spectacles of Empire: Monsters, Martyrs, and the Book of Revelation*. Philadelphia: University of Pennsylvania Press.

Hamonic, Wynn Gerald (2017). "Global Catastrophe in Motion Pictures as Meaning and Message: The Functions of Apocalyptic Cinema in American Film." *Journal of Religion & Film*, 21 (1): Article 36.

Howard-Brook, Wes and Anthony Gwyther (1999). *Unveiling Empire: Reading Revelation Then and Now*. Maryknoll: Orbis Books.

Jassen, Alex P. (2014). "Scriptural Interpretation in Early Jewish Apocalypses." In John J. Collins (ed.), *The Oxford Handbook to Apocalyptic Literature*, 69–84. Toronto: Oxford University Press.

Lewis, A. David. (2012). "The Militarism of American Superheroes after 9/11." In Matthew Pustz (ed.), *Comic Books and American Cultural History*, 223–36. New York: Continuum.

Lincoln, Bruce (1999). *Theorizing Myth: Narrative, Ideology, and Scholarship*. Chicago: University of Chicago Press.

Lyden, John C. (2003). *Film as Religion: Myths, Morals, and Rituals*. New York: New York University Press.

Massyngberde Ford, Josephine (1975). *Revelation*. Garden City: Doubleday.

McEver, Matthew (2009). "The Saviour Figure." In William L. Blizek (ed.), *The Continuum Companion to Religion and Film*, 270–81. New York: Continuum.

Meyer, Marvin (2007). *The Nag Hammadi Scriptures*. San Francisco: HarperOne.

Middleton, Paul (2018). *The Violence of the Lamb: Martyrs as Agents of Divine Judgement in the Book of Revelation*. New York: T&T Clark.

Mignola, Mike and Duncan Fegredo (2012). *Hellboy: The Storm and the Fury.* Milwaukie: Dark Horse.

Mitchell, Charles P. (2001). *Guide to Apocalyptic Cinema.* Westport: Greenwood.

Modleski, Tania (2009). "The Terror of Pleasure: The Contemporary Horror Film and Postmodern Theory." In Leo Braudy and Marshall Cohen (eds.), *Film Theory and Criticism: Introductory Readings,* 155–66. Toronto: Oxford University Press.

Moore, Stephen D. (1999). "War Making Men Making War: The Performance of Masculinity in the Revelation to John." In S. Brent Plate (ed.), *The Apocalyptic Imagination: Aesthetics and Ethics at the End of the World,* 84–94. Glasgow: Trinity St. Mungo Press.

Moore, Stephen D. (2007). "The Revelation to John." In Fernando F. Segovia and R. S. Sugirtharajah (eds.), *A Postcolonial Commentary on the New Testament Writings,* 133–56. New York: T&T Clark.

Murray, Chris (2000). "*Pop*aganda: Superhero Comics and Propaganda in World War Two." In Anne Magnussen and Hans-Christian Christiansen (eds.), *Comics and Culture: Theoretical Approaches,* 141–56. Copenhagen: Museum Tusculanum Press.

O'Connor, Laura (2010). "The Corpse on Hellboy's Back: Translating a Graphic Image." *Journal of Popular Culture,* 43 (3): 540–63.

Ostwalt, Conrad E. Jr. (1995). "Hollywood and Armageddon: Apocalyptic Themes in Recent Cinematic Representation." In Joel W. Martin and Conrad E. Ostwalt, Jr. (eds.), *Screening the Sacred: Religion, Myth, and Ideology in Popular American Film,* 55–64. Boulder: Westview.

Ostwalt, Conrad E. Jr. (2009). "The End of Days." In William L. Blizek (ed.), *The Continuum Companion to Religion and Film,* 290–9. New York: Continuum.

Pippin, Tina (1994). "The Revelation to John." In Elisabeth Schüssler Fiorenza (ed.), *Searching the Scriptures,* 109–30. New York: Crossroad.

Plate, S. Brent (1998). "Religion/Literature/Film: Toward a Religious Visuality of Film." *Literature and Theology,* 12 (1): 16–38.

Ricker, Aaron (2010). "The Devil's Reading: Revenge and Revelation in American Comics." In A. David Lewis and Christine Hoff Kraemer (eds.), *Graven Images: Religion in Comic Books and Graphic Novels,* 15–23. New York: Continuum.

Ricker, Aaron (2015). "The Third Side of the Coin: Constructing Superhero Comics Culture as Religious Myth." *Arc,* 43: 91–105.

Ricker, Aaron (2017). "Tragicomic Books: Reading *Watchmen* and *Kingdom Come* as Pop Apocalyptic." In Francesco-Alessio Ursini, Danan Mahmutovic, and Frank Bramlett (eds.), *Visions of the Future in Comics. International Perspectives,* 152–71. Jefferson: McFarland.

Ricker, Aaron (2022). "Fearful Symmetry: Violence and the Lamb/Beast Complex, Ancient and Modern." In A. Gagné, J. Guyver, and G. Oegema (eds.), *Religion and Violence in Western Traditions: Selected Studies,* 73–87. New York: Routledge.

Rossing, Barbara (2004). *The Rapture Exposed: The Message of Hope in the Book of Revelation.* Boulder: Westview Press.

Schwartz, Terri (2018). "Hellboy Trailer Breakdown: All the Details You Might Have Missed (Plus, David Harbour!)." *IGN,* December 20, 2018. Available online: https://www.ign.com/articles/2018/12/20/david-harbour-hellboy-trailer -breakdown-details-you-might-have-missed (accessed November 3, 2021).

Scott, Bernard Brandon (1994). *Hollywood Dreams and Biblical Stories*. Minneapolis: Fortress Press.

Strömberg, Frederik (2010). *Comic Art Propaganda: A Graphic History*. New York: St. Martin's Griffin.

Stone, Michael E. (1976). "Lists of Revealed Things in Apocalyptic Literature." In F. M. Cross, W. Lemke, and P. D. Miller (eds.), *Magnalia Dei: The Mighty Acts of God*, 414–54. New York: Doubleday.

Travis, Ben and Dan Jolin (2019). "Hellboy's David Harbour 'Didn't Want to Imitate Ron Perlman.'" *Empire*, February 21. Available online: https://www .empireonline.com/movies/news/hellboy-david-harbour-want-imitate-ron -perlman-exclusive-image/ (accessed November 3, 2021).

Treat, Shaun (2009). "How America Learned to Stop Worrying and Cynically ENJOY! The Post-9/11 Superhero Zeitgeist." *Communication and Critical/Cultural Studies*, 6 (1): 103–9.

Walliss, John and James Aston (2011). "Doomsday America: The Pessimistic Turn of Post-9/11 Apocalyptic Cinema." *Journal of Religion and Popular Culture*, 23 (1): 53–64.

Whissel, Kristen (2006). "Tales of Upward Mobility: The New Verticality and Special Effects." *Film Quarterly*, 59: 23–34.

Wolk, Douglas (2007). *Reading Comics: How Graphic Novels Work and What They Mean*. Cambridge: Da Capo Press.

Yarbro Collins, Adela (1999). "The Book of Revelation." In John J. Collins (ed.), *The Encyclopedia of Apocalypticism, Vol. 1: The Origins of Apocalypticism*, 54–83. New York: Continuum.

Chapter 11

Bennett, Eve (2014). "Deus ex Machina: AI Apocalypticism in Terminator: The Sarah Connor Chronicles." *The Journal of Popular Television*, 2 (1): 3–19.

Blahuta, Jason P. (2009). "Judgment Day Is Inevitable: Hegel and the Futility of Trying to Change History." In William Irwin, Richard Brown, and Kevin S. Decker (eds.), *Terminator and Philosophy: I'll Be Back, Therefore I Am, The Blackwell Philosophy and Pop Culture Series*, 157–60. Oxford: Blackwell.

Corliss, R. (1984). "Girl of Steel vs Man of Iron." *Time*, November 26: 123. Available online: http://content.time.com/time/magazine/article/0,9171,927023,00 .html (accessed July 31, 2020).

Corridor Digital (2020). "New Robot Can Now Fight Back! (Corridor Digital)." *YouTube Video*. Available online: https://www.youtube.com/watch?v =dKjCWfuvYxQ (accessed August 11, 2020).

Cusack, Carole (2010). *Invented Religions: Imagination, Fiction and Faith*. London: Ashgate.

Eaghll, Tenzan (2019). "Ideological Blindspot in the Academic Study of Religion and Film." *Method & Theory in the Study of Religion*, 31 (4–5): 416–45.

Geraci, Robert (2010). *Apocalyptic AI: Visions of Heaven in Robotics, Artificial Intelligence, and Virtual Reality*. Oxford: Oxford University Press.

Good, Irving J. (1965). "Speculations Concerning the First Ultraintelligent Machine." Available online: https://vtechworks.lib.vt.edu/bitstream/handle /10919/89424/TechReport05-3.pdf?sequence=1 (accessed August 11, 2020).

Good, Lance (1998). *Terminator 2: Judgment Day*. Available online: http://www .unc.edu/~goodness/t2.html [unavailable, cited in Kozlovic 2001].

Goscilo, Mary (1987). "Deconstructing the Terminator." *Film Criticism*, 12 (2): 37–52.

Jancovich, Mark (1996). *Rational Fears: American Horror in the 1950s*. Manchester: Manchester University Press.

Jasper, D. (1997). "On Systematising the Unsystematic: A Response." In C. Marsh and G. Ortiz (eds.), *Explorations in Theology and Film: Movies and Meaning*, 235–44. Oxford: Blackwell.

Kozlovic, Anton K. (2001). "From Holy Aliens to Cyborg Saviours: Biblical Subtexts in Four Science Fiction Films." *Journal of Religion & Film*, 5 (2): Article 3.

Mancini, M. (1992). "Terminator II: Judgment Day." In F. N. Magill (ed.), *Magill's Cinema Annual, 1992: A Survey of the Films of 1991*, 395–8. Pasadena: Salem Press.

Marsh, C. and G. Oritz (1997). *Explorations in Theology and Film: Movies and Meaning*. Oxford: Blackwell.

Mendelson, Michael (2016). "Saint Augustine." In Edward N. Zalta (ed.), *The Stanford Encyclopedia of Philosophy* (Winter Edition). Available online: https:// plato.stanford.edu/archives/win2016/entries/augustine/ (accessed August 11, 2020).

Mitchell, Richard (2002). *Dancing at Armageddon: Survivalism and Chaos in Modern Times*. Chicago: University of Chicago Press.

Moore, Donald (1965). "Cramming More Components onto Integrated Circuits." Available online: https://newsroom.intel.com/wp-content/uploads/sites/11/2018 /05/moores-law-electronics.pdf (accessed August 12, 2020).

Necakov, Lillian (1987). "The Terminator: Beyond Classical Hollywood Narrative." *Cineaction*, 8: 84–6.

Newsom, Carol (2016). "Foreward." In Kelly J. Murphy and Justin Jeffcoat (eds.), *Apocalypses in Context: Apocalyptic Currents Through History*, xi–xv. Minneapolis: Fortress Press.

Ornella, Alexander D. (2008). "'The End is Nigh': A Reflection on the Relationship Between Media and Religion." In Graham Ward and Michael Hoelzl (eds.), *The New Visibility of Religion: Studies in Religion and Cultural Hermeneutics*. London: Continuum.

Otto, Rudolph (1917). *The Idea of the Holy*, trans. John W. Harvey. Oxford: Oxford University Press, 1923; 2nd ed., 1950 [Das Heilige, 1917].

Possamai, Adam (2005). *Religion and Popular Culture: A Hyper-Real Testament*. Brussels: P.I.E-Peter Lang.

Runions, Erin (2003). *How Hysterical: Identification and Resistance in the Bible and Film*. London: Palgrave.

Singler, Beth (2014). "'See Mom It Is Real': The UK Census, Jediism and Social Media." *Journal of Religion in Europe*, 7 (2): 150–68.

Singler, Beth (2017). "Roko's Basilisk or Pascal's? Thinking of Singularity Thought Experiments as Implicit Religion." *Journal of Implicit Religion*, 20 (3): 279–97.

Singler, Beth (2020). "'Blessed by the Algorithm': Theistic Conceptions of Artificial Intelligence in Online Discourse." *Journal of AI and Society*. Available online:

https://link.springer.com/article/10.1007/s00146-020-00968-2 (accessed August 11, 2020).

Terminator Wiki (2020). "'No Fate', in Particular, the Section on 'Usages'." Available online: https://terminator.fandom.com/wiki/No_Fate_(quote) (accessed August 10, 2020).

Tuckett, David (2011). *Minding the Markets: An Emotional Finance View of Financial Instability*. Basingstoke: Palgrave MacMillan.

Wagner, Rachel (2019). "The Cowboy Apocalypse: 13 Ways of Looking at a Gun." Copy of paper given at CENSAMM Annual Conference 2019, personal correspondence.

Ward, G. and M. Hoelzl (eds.) (2008). *The New Visibility of Religion: Studies in Religion and Cultural Hermeneutics*. London: Continuum.

Chapter 12

Bancks, Tristan (2003). "Beyond The Hero's Journey: 'Joseph (Campbell) Is My Yoda.'" *Australian Screen Education Online*, 33: 32–4.

Barthes, Roland ([1972] 2001). *Mythologies*, trans. Annette Levers. New York: Hill and Wang.

Bell, Catherine (1997). *Ritual: Perspectives and Dimensions*. New York: Oxford University Press.

Benjamin, Walter ([1955] 2009). "The Work of Art in the Age of Mechanical Reproduction." In Leo Braudy and Marshall Cohen (eds.), *Film Theory and Criticism: Introductory Readings*, 7th ed., trans. Harry Zohn. New York: Oxford University Press.

Burwick, Kevin (2017a). "The Last Jedi Director Explains Controversial Leia Scene." *Movieweb*, December 18. Available online: https://www.flickeringmyth.com/2018/03/exclusive-rian-johnson-on-mark-hamill-fundamentally-disagreeing-with-his-plans-for-luke-skywalker-in-star-wars-the-last-jedi/ (accessed May 19, 2020).

Burwick, Kevin (2017b). "George Lucas Always Knew He Went Too Far with Phantom Menace." *Movieweb*, December 28. Available online: https://movieweb.com/star-wars-phantom-menace-george-lucas-knew-movie-was-bad/ (accessed May 22, 2020).

Campbell, Joseph ([1949] 2008). *The Hero with a Thousand Faces*, 3rd ed. Novato: New World Library.

Cheung, Tommy (2019). "Jediism: Religion at Law?." *Oxford Journal of Law and Religion*, 8 (2): 350–77. https://doi.org/10.1093/ojlr/rwz010 (accessed May 23, 2020).

Chidester, David (2005). *Authentic Fakes: Religion and Popular Culture*. Berkeley: University of California Press.

Cobra Kai (2018). [Web series] *YouTube*, Creators: Josh Heald, Jon Hurwitz, and Hayden Schlossberg, USA: Sony Pictures Television. Available online: https://www.youtube.com/channel/UCe9DTWmhhxeKyYHL4mldGcA (accessed May 20, 2020).

Cohen, Rich (2016). "Francis Ford Coppola's Third Act: Italy, Wine, and the Secret of Life." February 03. Available online: https://www.vanityfair.com/hollywood/2016/02/francis-ford-coppola-italy-wine-and-the-secret-of-life (accessed May 22, 2020).

Collinson, Gary (2018). "Exclusive: Rian Johnson on Mark Hamill 'Fundamentally Disagreeing' with his Plans for Luke Skywalker in Star Wars: The Last Jedia." *Flickering Myth*, March 26. Available online: https://www.flickeringmyth.com/2018/03/exclusive-rian-johnson-on-mark-hamill-fundamentally-disagreeing-with-his-plans-for-luke-skywalker-in-star-wars-the-last-jedi/ (accessed May 21, 2020).

Creed (2015), [Film] Dir. Ryan Coogler, USA: Warner Bros. Pictures.

Cusack, Carole M. (2010). *Invented Religions: Imagination, Fiction, and Faith*. Burlington: Ashgate Publishing Company.

Dargis, Manohla (2015). "'Star Wars' Doesn't Belong to George Lucas. It Belongs to the Fans." *New York Times*, November 01. Available online: https://www.nytimes.com/2015/11/01/movies/star-wars-doesnt-belong-to-george-lucas-it-belongs-to-the-fans.html (accessed April 12, 2020).

"Disney to Acquire Lucasfilm Ltd." (2012). [Press Release]. *The Walt Disney Company*, October 30. Available online: https://thewaltdisneycompany.com/disney-to-acquire-lucasfilm-ltd/ (accessed May 22, 2020).

Durkehim, Émile ([1895] 1982). *The Rules of Sociological Method*, ed. Steven Lukes, trans. W. D. Halls, New York: The Free Press.

Eliade, Mircea ([1957] 1987]). *The Sacred and the Profane: The Nature of Religion*, trans. Willard R. Trask. San Diego: Harcourt, Inc.

Harpham, Geoffrey Galt (1987). *The Ascetic Imperative in Culture and Criticism*. Chicago: University of Chicago Press.

Henry, Andrew Mark (2019). "Is Jediism a Religion?." [Video] *Religion for Breakfast*, December 19. Available online: https://www.youtube.com/watch?v=H0GsLNj648Q (accessed May 23, 2020).

Hiatt, Brett (2019). "Lucasfilm's Kathleen Kennedy on 'Rise of Skywalker' and the Future of 'Star Wars.'" *Rolling Stone*, November 19. Available online: https://www.rollingstone.com/movies/movie-news/lucasfilm-president-kathleen-kennedy-interview-rise-skywalker-future-star-wars-912393/ (accessed May 20, 2020).

Holt, Thomas J., Adam M. Bossler, and Kathryn C. Seigfried-Spellar (2017). *Cybercrime and Digital Forensics: An Introduction*, 2nd ed. New York: Routledge.

Hughes, William (2020). "Lucasfilm Exec Pisses Off Fans with Objectively True Statement about *Star Wars* Being 'Fake.'" *AV Club*, May 13. Available online: https://news.avclub.com/lucasfilm-exec-pisses-off-fans-with-objectively-true-st-1843449562 (accessed May 20, 2020).

Joseph Campbell and The Power of Myth (1988), [Film] Prod: Joan Konner and Alvin H. Perlmutter, USA: PBS.

The Karate Kid (1984), [Film] Dir: John Avildsen, USA: Columbia Pictures.

Kelly, Kevin and Paula Parisi (1997). "Beyond *Star Wars*." *Wired*, February 01. Available online: https://www.wired.com/1997/02/fflucas/ (accessed May 23, 2020).

Knives Out (2019), [Film] Dir: Rian Johnson, USA: Lionsgate.

Lawrence, John Shelton and Robert Jewett (2002). *The Myth of the American Superhero*. Grand Rapids: William B. Eerdmans Publishing Co.

Lincoln, Bruce (1999). *Theorizing Myth: Narrative, Ideology, and Scholarship*. Chicago: University of Chicago Press.

Long, Jeffrey (2018). "Hindu themes in Western Popular Culture: A Tale of Two Georges, Part Two." *Pop Culture and Theology*, April 09. Available online: https://popularcultureandtheology.com/2018/04/09/hindu-themes-in-western-popular-culture-a-tale-of-two-georges-part-two/ (accessed May 23, 2020).

REFERENCES

Looper (2012), [Film] Dir: Rian Johnson, USA: TriStar Pictures.

Martin, Craig (2017). *A Critical Introduction to the Study of Religion*, 2nd ed. New York: Routledge.

McCutcheon, Russell T. (1998). "Redescribing 'Religion and …' Film Teaching the Insider/Outsider Problem." *Teaching Theology and Religion*, 1 (2): 99–110.

McCutcheon, Russell T. (2018). *Fabricating Religion: Fanfare for the Common e.g.* Berlin: DeGruyter.

The Mythology of Star Wars with George Lucas and Billy Moyers (1987), [Film] Dir: Pamela Mason Wagner, USA: Films for the Humanities.

Nye, Malory (2008). *Religion: The Basics*, 2nd ed. New York: Routledge.

Parker, Ryan (2018). "Rian Johnson Refutes Critical Conversational 'Last Jedi' Scene." *The Hollywood Reporter*, January 19. Available online: https://www.hollywoodreporter.com/heat-vision/rian-johnson-shuts-down-critics-controversial-last-jedi-scene-1075913 (accessed May 20, 2020).

The People vs. George Lucas (2010), [Film] Dir: Alexandre O. Philippe, USA: Wrekken Film Entertainment.

Plate, S. Brent (2012). *Star Wars, Frequencies: A Collaborative Genealogy of Spirituality*, September 01. Available online: http://frequencies.ssrc.org/2012/01/09/star-wars/ (accessed May 24, 2020).

Rancière, Jacques ([2003] 2007). *The Future of the Image*, trans. Gregory Elliot. New York: Verso Books.

Rawden, Jessica (2017). "A Group of *Star Wars* Fans Want *The Last Jedi* to be Stricken from the Canon." *Cinemablend*, December 19. Available online: https://www.cinemablend.com/news/1746362/a-group-of-star-wars-fans-want-the-last-jedi-to-be-stricken-from-canon (accessed May 20, 2020).

Rocky (1976), [Film] Dir. Jon Avildsen, USA: United Artists.

Rogue One: A Star Wars Story (2016), [Film] Dir. Gareth Edwards, USA: Walt Disney Pictures.

Sarris, Andrew ([1962] 2009). "Notes on the Auteur Theory in in 1962." In Leo Braudy and Marshall Cohen (eds.), *Film Theory and Criticism: Introductory Readings*, 451–5, 7th ed. New York: Oxford University Press.

Spry, Jeff (2016). "Francis Ford Coppola on the True Cost of George Lucas's *Star Wars* Legacy." *SyFy Wire*, February 02. Available online: https://www.syfy.com/syfywire/francis-ford-coppola-true-cost-george-lucas-star-wars-legacy (accessed May 22, 2020).

Star Wars: Episode I—The Phantom Menace (1999), [Film] Dir. George Lucas, USA: 20th Century Fox.

Star Wars: Episode IV—A New Hope (1977), [Film] Dir. George Lucas, USA: 20th Century Fox.

Star Wars: Episode VII—The Force Awakens (2015), [Film] Dir. J. J. Abrams, USA: Walt Disney Pictures.

Star Wars: Episode VIII—The Last Jedi (2017), [Film] Dir. Rian Johnson, USA: Walt Disney Pictures.

Touna, Vaia (2017). *Fabrications of the Greek Past: Religion, Tradition, and the Making of the Past*. Leiden, The Netherlands: Brill.

Wei, Will (2010). "Where are They Now: The '*Star Wars* Kid' Sued the People Who Made Him Famous." *Business Insider*, May 12. Available online: https://www.businessinsider.com/where-are-they-now-the-star-wars-kid-2010-5 (accessed May 23, 2020).

Welsh, Noah (2020). "*Star Wars: The Last Jedi*'s Backlash Has Changed." *Screen Rant*, February 09. Available online: https://screenrant.com/star-wars-last-jedi-backlash-changed-gone/ (accessed May 23, 2020).

Wollen, Peter ([1972] 2009). "The Auteur Theory [Howard Hawks and John Ford]." In Leo Braudy and Marshall Cohen (eds.), *Film Theory and Criticism: Introductory Readings*, 455–70, 7th ed. New York: Oxford University Press.

Wood, Matt (2017). "What *Star Wars*' Journal of the Whills Are and Why They'll Be Really Important." *Cinema Blend*, April 20. Available online: https://www.cinemablend.com/news/1649269/what-star-wars-journal-of-the-whills-are-and-why-theyll-be-really-important (accessed May 23, 2020).

Conclusion

Kellner, Douglas (1991). "Film, Politics, and Ideology: Reflections on Hollywood Film in the Age of Reagan." *Velvet Light Trap: A Critical Journal of Film & Television*, 91 (27): 9–24.

McCutcheon, Russell T. (1998). "Redescribing 'Religion and ….' Film: Teaching the Insider/Outsider Problem." *Teaching Theology and Religion*, 1 (2): 99–110.

The Pervert's Guide to Ideology (2013), [Film] Dir. Sophie Fiennes, USA: Zeitgeist Films.

Plate, Brent S. (ed.) (2003). *Representing Religion in World Cinema*. New York: Palgrave Macmillan.

Smith, Jonathan Z. (1988). *Imagining Religion: From Babylon to Jonestown (Chicago Studies in the History of Judaism)*. Chicago: University of Chicago Press.

INDEX

NOTE: Films are listed by title.
Literary works are listed under author/s.
Page references with n. indicate notes.

28 Days Later (2002, Boyle)   165
28 Weeks Later (2007,
    Fresnadillo)   165

Abrams, Jeffrey Jacob   182, 187
abstraction   15
Academy Awards   140, 202 n.26
    racial exclusion   58–9
accordion   117, 119, 120, 121–3,
    199 n.4
Ace Ventura: When Nature Calls
    (1995, Oedekerk)   90
action films   146
activist documentary   128
actors of color
    male protagonists   61–2
    Oscar's exclusion of   58–9
adaptations   58, 69–70, 75, 79–80,
    84, 104, 135–6
Adorno, Theodor   14
aesthetics
    Religulous   34
    Wrinkle in Time, A   63
affective circulation   102–3
    against cinematic
        Orientalism   113–15
affective conversion points   134–7
agency
    human   24–5, 141–2, 173, 192
    notion of   143
    opposing views of   143–8
    supernatural   24, 148–52
Ahmed, Sara   134
Akutagawa, Ryunosuke   110
Althusser, Louis   4, 15

American Beauty (1999, Mendes)   46
Anderson, Wes   94, 95, 96
Annunciation of the Blessed Virgin
    Mary   167–8
anti-modernity   124–5
Apocalypse(s)   154, 155, 156
Apocalypse Now (1979, Coppola)   84
apocalyptic art   153, 154–6, 159–63
apocalyptic (super)heroism   24, 154,
    155–8, 161–3
apocalypticism   24–5, 153–4, 155,
    174, 192
    secular   165–6. *See also* artificial
        intelligence (AI) apocalypticism
apostasy   75, 78, 79–80, 81–2, 84–5
apotheosis   48, 77
archetypes   7, 8, 46–7, 179. *See also*
    stereotypes/stereotyping; tropes
Armageddon (1998, Bay)   165
articulation   34–5, 39
    notion of   28
artificial intelligence (AI)   167
    public reaction to   169, 170–3,
        192, 204 n.7
    vengeful godlike AI   166, 169,
        203 n.5
artificial intelligence (AI)
        apocalypticism   24–5
    righteous warriors   170–3, 174
    strange permutations   167–9, 174
Asano, Tadanobu   78
Aster, Ari   149
Atanarjuat: the Fast Runner (2001,
    Kunuk)   202 n.31
atheism   20–1, 27–30

identity construction 32–4, 37–8
Atheism: A Rough History of Disbelief (2004–7, Denton) 29
Atheism Tapes, The (TV docuseries, 2004) 29
audience reception
   of *Star Wars* 182–3
   of technology 169, 170–3, 192, 204 n.7
audience reception theory 7–8
auteur theory 102–3, 177–8, 186–7
   and mythmaking 180–4
   notion of 181
authenticity 4, 15
   of Indigenous representation 133–4, 135
   and *Star Wars* 25, 176–7, 180, 182–3
   Wind Journeys, The 123–5
autism 110–11
Avalon (1990, Levinson) 16
Avatar (2009, Cameron) 200 n.8
Avengers series 61
Avildsen, Jon 178

Bailey, George (film character: *It's a Wonderful Life*) 43
Bailey, Halle 63
Baldwin, James 22, 72
Barclay, Barry 139
Benjamin, Walter 180
Berger, Peter 10
Bhabha, Homi 125
Bible and biblical stories 1–2, 34, 41–2, 62, 64, 167–9, 203 n.2
Big Bang Theory, The (TV series) 46
Bigelow, Kathryn 59
Black characters 72–3
Black religion 61
Blood Quantum (2019, Barnaby) 202 n.29
Blow Out (1981, De Palma) 15
Blow Up (1966, Antonioni) 15, 16
Boiler Room (2000, Younger) 46
Bombay Talkie (1970, Ivory) 92, 96
Bond film franchise 166
Bone Tomahawk (2015, Zahler) 200 n.7
Borat (2006, Charles) 30

Bourne franchise 146
Brady, Miranda 130
brainwashing 145–8, 151
Braveheart (1995, Gibson) 46
Brendan (film character: *The Darjeeling Limited*) 93, 94
Bridger, Jim (film character: *The Revenant*) 138
Brief History of Disbelief, A (2004–7, Denton) 29
Broken Blossoms (1919, Griffith) 104
Bromley, David 147
Bruttenholm, Trevor (film character: *Hellboy*) 160
Buddhism 22–3, 101–2, 103–5, 192
   association with mysticism 89
   in circulatory context 113–14
Bulletproof Monk (2003, Hunter) 90
Byrne, Gabriel 149

Caliban (fictitious character: *The Tempest*) 129
Cameron, James 173–4, 200 n.8
Campbell, Joseph 178–9
   Hero with a Thousand Faces, The 46
   theory of myth 42–3, 45–9, 50, 55
capitalism 4, 14, 15, 42–3, 46, 51, 52–5, 192
   in late-twentieth-century American films 43–5
   and religion 101–2, 103–5
Capra, Frank 43
Carpentier, Alejo 122–3
Carrillo, Ignacio (film character: *The Wind Journeys*) 117–18, 120–2, 123, 199 n.6
cartoons 146
Cartwright, Lisa 4
casting
   Wrinkle in Time, A 58, 62, 66–8
Catholicism
   in Japan 72, 75–85
   in Latin America 118, 119–20, 121, 198 n.1
celluloid maiden trope 130, 137
Chang, Hae-Joo (film character: *Cloud Atlas*) 107–9

INDEX

characters and characterization. *See also* hero/heroism; protagonists
  Black 72–3
  Indigenous 127, 135–8
  Japanese 77–9, 82
  LGBTQ 60
  neoliberal types 46
Charles, Larry 27, 30
Children of God movement 146, 147
Children of Men (2006, Cuarón) 166
Chinmoku (1971, Shinoda) 196 n.2
Christianity 5–6, 12, 31, 36. *See also* Catholicism
  and colonization 75–85
  incorporation in Indigenous religions 133
  and science fiction themes 57–8
Christmas 43
cinematography
  Religulous 35
circulatory globalization 113
class 4, 15
  and identity construction 28, 38
  "theologies of class" 144–5
class inequality 52, 54
Cloud Atlas (2012, Wachowski et al) 23, 102, 192
  characters and characterization 106–8
Cobra Kai (TV series) 187
Cocks, Jay 70, 81
Cody, Iron Eyes 131
Cohen, Sacha Baron 30
collective unconscious 46
Collette, Toni 149
Colombian culture 23, 118, 123, 124
  "Francisco el Hombre" ("Francisco the man") (folklore) 118–21, 199 n.6
colonial gaze 23, 74, 82–3, 128, 137–8
colonialism 4, 15, 22, 69, 70–1, 123, 192
  and Indigenous North American narratives 128
  Latin American context 199 n.10
  and notion of religion 11–12
  and racialization 72–4, 83–4
comic documentary 27, 30–1

communing with spirits trope 23, 129, 137, 138
Connor, John (J.C.) (film character: *Terminator*) 167–9, 170, 203 n.4
Connor, Sarah (film character: *Terminator*) 167, 168, 169, 170
Conrad, Joseph
  Heart of Darkness 84
consciousness-raising 32–3
Contagion (2011, Soderbergh) 165
conversion
  and brainwashing 146–8
conviction narratives 167
Conwell, Russell
  "Acres of Diamonds" 145
Cooper, Bradley 44
Cooper, Sheldon (TV character: *The Big Bang Theory*) 46
Coppola, Francis Ford 84, 181
Coward, Noel 149, 151
Creation Museum (Petersburg, Kentucky) 31
Creed (2015, Coogler) 187
critical historical approach 133, 190
Cronenberg, David 29
cults 145, 146–7
cultural studies 12–13, 17, 18–19, 28, 189
culture
  and Christianity 6
  Colombian Caribbean 23, 118–21, 123
  erasure of 48–9
  impact of films on 9
  mass culture 14
  and myths 42–3, 49–55
Current, Cheris Brewer 98–9

Dameron, Poe (film character: *Star Wars*) 186
Dances with Wolves (1992, Costner) 129, 130, 131, 200 n.12
Darjeeling Limited, The (2007, Anderson) 22, 87–8, 90–1
  funeral scene 91–2, 94–8

236 INDEX

peacock ritual scenes 91–2, 93–4,
  96
temple visit scenes 91–3, 96
Dark, David 158
Dark Knight, The (2008, Nolan) 161
Dawkins, Richard 29
  The God Delusion 33
Day After Tomorrow, The (2004,
  Emmerich) 165, 166
De Botton, Alain 36
decolonial critique
  of Colombian culture 23, 121,
    123, 125–6, 199 n.10
Deep Impact (1998, Leder) 165
Deerchild, Rosanna 127–8
DeMille, Cecil B. 1–3
democracy 102, 108–10
demonic cults 141, 148–51
De Niro, Robert 44, 197 n.6
dependent arising
  (*paṭiccasamuppāda*) 105–10,
    111–12
Deprogrammed (2015,
  Donovan) 147
destiny 24, 144, 169, 170–1, 174
Detweiler, Craig
  *Into the Dark: Seeing the Sacred
    in the Top Films of the 21st
    Century* 5, 6
the Devil 118, 119, 120, 124–5,
  199 n.3
Devil's Playground, The (2002,
  Walker) 147
Diamond, Neil 200 n.11, 201 n.19
DiCaprio, Leonardo 134–5, 202 n.25
diegesis 120–1
  notion of 199 n.6
directors 181, 192–3. *See also* auteur
  theory
  atheistic 29
  female 59
Dirty Harry (1971, Siegel) 12
discovery plot 149
Disney 63, 182, 186
divine hierarchies 144
documentary 192
  activist 128
  atheistic 27–30, 39
  docuseries 45

Doniger, Wendy 43, 52–5
Douglas, Mary 151
Driver, Adam 75
Dr. Strange (2016, Derrickson) 61
Du Bois, W.E.B. 72
Dunbar, John, Lieutenant (film
    character: *Dances with
    Wolves*) 130
DuVernay, Ava 21, 58, 62, 63, 65,
  66–8

Eaghll, Tenzan 132, 167
East
  East/West distinction 88–90
  mystic East 22, 87–94
  as utopia 104
Eastwood, Clint 158
economic arminianism 144–5
Eliade, Mircea 7, 185
elitism 51
Elk Dog (film character: *The
    Revenant*) 136, 137, 138
Ellison, Harlan
  "I Have No Mouth and I Must
    Scream" 169
emptiness 103, 104–10
Endo, Shusaku
  Chinmoku (Silence) 69–70, 76,
    79–80, 82, 84, 85, 196 n.2
end time/end of the world 154, 155,
  157–8, 160–3, 165–6, 174
Enemies of Reason, The (2007,
  Barnes) 29
entrepreneurship, myths of 42–3, 45,
  48–9, 50–1, 54–5
environmental activism 131, 134–5,
  201 nn.20, 22, 202 n.25
Epic of Gilgamesh 47
Eternal Sunshine of the Spotless Mind
  (2004, Gondry) 6
Everdeen, Katniss (film character:
    Hunger Games) 63
evil 24, 144, 148
  vs. good 64–5, 119, 156, 158–63,
    175–6, 177, 191
Ewing, Adam (film character: *Cloud
    Atlas*) 107–8, 109
Ewing, Tilda (film character: *Cloud
    Atlas*) 107, 108

Expelled: No Intelligence Allowed (2008, Frankowski)   30
expertise   35–6
Eyre, Chris   133

fabrication   181
Facebook
    Religulous page   38–9
Faith School Menace (2010, Milton)   29
Fanon, Frantz   128
farcical lampooning   22, 98
Fatal Attraction (1987, Lyne)
Faustus, Dr. (fictional character)   119, 199 n.3
female beauty   59
female directors   59
female protagonists   57, 63
Ferreira, Chistavao, Fr. (film character: *Silence*)   75–6, 82–3, 84–5
fidelity in adaptations   58, 64, 70
Fielding, John
    Continuum Companion to Religion and Film, The   132–4
Fight Club (1999, Fincher)   46
Figueroa, José Antonio   122–3
films
    origins of   41–2
film studies
    Campbell's impact on   45–9
    contemporary scholarship   2–4
    and ideological analysis   17–19
    methods and tools   10–11, 17–19, 190
film studios   55
Finding Neverland (2004, Forster)   6
First Nations   134–5. *See also* Indigeneity
Fitzgerald, John (film character: *The Revenant*)   136, 137–8
Forbidden Kingdom, The (2008, Minkoff)   90
Foster, Brantley (film character: *The Secret of My Success*)   44, 47–8, 50–5
Four Horsemen, The (2008, Furie)   29
Fourth Cinema   139
Fox, Michael J.   44

Francis, Daniel   130
Frankfurt School   14, 19
Frankowski, Nathan   30
fraternal bonding   22, 87–8, 96–8
free will   24, 141–2, 143–5, 166, 170–1, 174
Frobisher, Robert (film character: *Cloud Atlas*)   108
Frontier (TV series)   202 n.32
frontier/frontiersman trope   137, 172
funeral   91–2
    as spiritual experience   94–8

Gaffar, Mohamed Junas   36
Garcia Márquez, Gabriel   124
    One Hundred Years of Solitude   122–3, 125, 199 n.7
Garfield, Andrew   75
Garupe, Francisco, Fr. (film character: *Silence*)   75, 82, 196 n.2
gaze   58, 195 n.1
    colonial   23, 74, 82–3, 128, 137–8
    male   59–60, 192
    oppositional   60–1, 63
    Protestant   118, 121, 125–6, 198 n.1
Geertz, Clifford   7–8, 9
gender   4, 15
    and identity construction   28, 37
    oppression   52
    and Oscars   59
    of protagonists   53, 150
    racialized   60, 65–8
    Terminator (1984)   168
gender roles   53
Giannetti, Louis
    Understanding Movies   191
Glass, Hugh (film character: *The Revenant*)   134, 135–8, 202 n.28
God
    as vengeful   169
God Who Wasn't There, The (2005, Flemming)   29
Godzilla (TV cartoon series)   146
Goethe, Johan Wolfgang   199 n.3
Gone with the Wind (1939, Fleming)   12
Good, Irving John   171

Goodluck, Forrest (film character: *The Revenant*) 135
good Native/bad Native trope 129, 138
good *vs.* evil 64–5, 119, 156, 158–63, 175–6, 177, 191
Goodwin, Hannibal 41
Goscilo, Margaret 168
Gospel According to St. Matthew, The (1964, Pasolini) 29
Grace (film character: *Terminator, Dark Fate*) 168, 170
Graham, Annie (film character: *Hereditary*) 149–51
Graham, Charlie (film character: *Hereditary*) 149, 150
Graham, Peter (film character: *Hereditary*) 149, 150–1
Graham, Steve (film character: *Hereditary*) 149, 150, 151
Granger, Hermione (film character: *Harry Potter* series) 63
Grossberg, Lawrence 28
Grudge, The (2004, Shiminzu) 143
Guerra, Ciro 23, 117, 118, 125
gun 172
guru 61, 66
Gwenn, Edmund 43

Hall, Stuart 28
Ham, Ken 31
Hamilton (2020, Kail) 80–1, 197 n.7
Handmaid's Tale, The (1990, Schlöndorff) 12
happenstance 143, 148, 150, 152
Harjo, Sterlin 140
harm
    caused by religions 31, 36–7
Harrison, John Kent 63
Harrison, Milmon 145
Hassan, Steven
    Cult of Trump: A Leading Cult Expert Explains How the President Uses Mind Control, The 146–7
Hawk (film character: *The Revenant*) 135–6, 137, 138
Hegel, Gottfried Friedrich 170
Hellboy (2004, Del Toro) 162, 163

Hellboy II: The Golden Army (2008, Del Toro) 162
Hellboy (2019, Marshall) 162–3
Hellboy (film character: *Hellboy* films) 162–3
Hellboy comics 160, 161–2, 163
Hellboy movies 24, 153–4, 160
helpless maiden trope 23, 136–7, 138
Henry, Andrew, Captain (film character: *The Revenant*) 136, 138
Henry, John (TV character: *Terminator, SCC*) 171, 203 n.4
Hereditary (2018, Aster) 24, 141–2, 148–52, 192
hero/heroism. *See also* protagonists
    apocalyptic 154, 155–8, 161–3
    Hellboy as 160
    hero's quest/journey 21, 47–9, 55, 179, 185–6
    white hero 129, 138–9
Heston, Charles 172
Higashida, Naoki
    Reason I Jump: One Boy's Voice from the Silence of Autism, The 111–12, 114
Hindoo Fakir (1902, Edison) 90
Hinds, Ciaran 84
Hinduism 89, 90
hipster Orientalism 98–9
hipster racism 98
hipster sexism 98–9
hipster travel 90–1, 98
historical context 54, 69
hooks, bell 60
hope *vs.* fear 158–9, 160–1, 162
Horkheimer, Max 14
horror. *See* supernatural horror
Hostiles (2017, Cooper) 138
humanism 22–3, 102, 107–10
Hunter, Edward 146
hybridity 122, 123, 125–6

Ichiyanagi, Toshi 110
Ichizo (film character: *Silence*) 77
identity 4, 15
    self-identity 108–10
identity construction
    atheistic 21, 27–8, 32–4

and gender   28, 37
and race   28, 38
ideological criticism   2–4, 17–19, 142,
    189–93
  definition of religion in   9, 11–17
  of Revelation   155–6
ideology
  definition of   4
  myth as   49–55, 161, 183–6
  propaganda model of   14–15, 189,
    193
  timeless truths as   159–63
Idle No More Movement   129,
    134–5, 202 n.24
Ihimaera, Witi   133
imaginary   1–2, 4–5, 9, 23, 25,
    195 n.1
imagiNATIVE film festival   139–40
impurity   151
Iñárritu, Alejando   135–6, 202 n.26
India. *See also* Orientalism
  as mystical   89–90
  spirituality in   22, 87–8, 91–4
indigeneity   23, 192
  definition of   132
  representational shifts   135–9,
    201 n.19
  representation of, 19th century to
    present   129–31, 200 nn.11–12,
    201 nn.17–18, 202 nn.27–32
  scholarly representations of   132–4
Indigenous activism   131, 139,
    201 nn.15, 20, 22
Indigenous films and
    filmmaking   127–9, 133–4,
    139–40, 202 n.31
Indigenous religions   132–4, 199 n.2
Indigenous Screen Office in
    Canada   127, 139
Indigenous-settler relationships   23,
    129–30, 137–9
Indigenous spirituality   23, 128, 129,
    130–1, 139, 201 nn.18, 22
Indigenous women   130, 136–7, 139,
    202 nn.27, 30
Industrial Light and Magic (ILM)
    (company)   181–2
inheritance   141, 148–50, 152
Inherit the Wind (1960, Kramer)   28–9

insider-based criticism   5–6, 12–13,
    179
interpolation   15
Interpreter (film character:
    Silence)   78–9
intersectionality   60
irrationality   34–6
  of people of color   60–1, 198 n.1
Islam   36, 38
IT (film character: *A Wrinkle in
    Time*)   62–3
It Follows (2014, Mitchell)   144
It's a Wonderful Life (1946,
    Capra)   43
Ivory, James   92, 197 n.4
Iwamura, Jane Naomi   61, 90

James at 15 (TV series)   146
Jancovich, Mark   168
Jankiewicz, Stephen
  "Orientalist in Love, Intimacy,
    Empire, and Cross-Cultural
    Knowledge"   111
Japan
  Christianity and colonialism
    in   69–70, 75–85
Jasper, David   173–4
Jediism   9, 25, 175, 203 n.3
Jedi Knights (film characters: *Star
    Wars*)   175, 178
Jesus Christ   58, 62, 65, 155, 156,
    158, 161, 203 n.2
  "hunting for 'Christ-figures in
    film"   166–8
  image of   83–4
Jewett, Robert   185
Johnson, Rian   176, 177, 182, 183,
    185, 186–7
Johnston, Robert K.
  *Reel Spirituality: Theology and Film
    in Dialogue*   5
Johnston, William
  Silence   70
Joy (2015, Russell)   21, 42
  gender role in   53–4
  hero's journey in   48–9
  historical context of   54
  individual and universal experiences
    in   52–3

myth of entrepreneurship   50–1, 54–5

plot of   44

Joy (film character: *Joy*)   44, 48, 50–5

Judas   77, 81

Judgment Day   169, 170, 174

juglares (traveling musicians)   120–2, 125, 199 nn.4, 6

Ju-On (2002, Shimizu)   143

kakase kirishitan (hidden Christians)   75, 76, 77, 80, 81–2, 83, 85

Kaling, Mindy   58, 62, 66

Karate Kid, The franchise   61, 178, 187

Kelly, John   130

Kichijiro (film character: *Silence*)   77, 80, 82

Kilpatrick, Jacquelyn   131

King of Kings (1927, DeMille)   41

Knives Out (2019, Johnson)   182, 187

Koyaanisqatsi (1982, Reggio)   201 n.17

Kringle, Kris (film character: *Miracle on 34th St*)   43

Kubozuka, Yosuke   77

Kundun (1997, Scorsese)   104

Kung Fu (TV series)   90

Kung Fu Panda (film series)   90

Kunuk, Zacharis   202 n.31

Ladd, Diane   48

Laderman, Gary   41, 42

Lambert, Cory (film character: *Wind River*)   138

LaMotta, Jake (film character: *Raging Bull*)   197 n.6

La Passion de Jeanne d'Arc (1928, Dreyer)   19

Last of the Mohicans, The (1992, Mann)   129

Last Temptation of Christ, The (1998, Scorsese)   12, 29, 70, 197 n.6

Latin American cinema   23, 118, 119–21, 123, 124–6

Lawrence, Jennifer   44

Lawrence, Shelton   185

Lee, Jennifer   62, 63, 65

Lee, Spike   58–9

L'Engle, Madeleine

A Wrinkle in Time   57–8, 64

LGBTQ characters   60

Lincoln, Bruce   19, 43

on Indigenous religions   199 n.2

on myth as ideology   49–52, 54, 161, 183

"Mythic Narrative and Cultural Diversity in American Society"   16–17

Little Mermaid, The (2023, Disney)   63

Lofton, Kathryn   67

Looper (2012, Johnson)   182

Lost Horizon (1919, Capra)   104

love   107–8, 110–12

Lucas, George   175, 178, 180–2

Campbell's influences on   45–6, 179

Lucasfilm LTD   182

Lukács, Georg   15

Lutz, Catherine   146

Lyden, John C.   3, 189

Film as Religion: Myths, Ritual, and Rituals   6, 7–9, 13–14, 19

McCabe, Deric   62

McCutcheon, Russell T.   6, 11, 12–13, 15–16, 17, 19, 179, 181, 190

McEver, Matthew   158

Macy's (R.H. Macy and Co.)   43

Mad Max: Fury Road (2015, Miller)   165

magical realism   23, 121–3

anti-modernity   124–5

and "Francisco el Hombre" ("Francisco the man") (folklore)   118–21

notion of   124

Maher, Bill   20–1, 27, 31, 32–7, 192

male gaze   59–60, 192

Man Called Horse, A (1970, Silverstein)   132–3

Manchurian Candidate, The (2004, Demme)   146

Mancini, Marc   168

Mangano, Joy   44

Margin Call (2011, Chandor) 46
Marsh, Clive 166
Martin, Joel W. and Conrad E.
Ostwalt 189
*Screening the Sacred: Religion,
Myth, and Ideology in Popular
American Film* 6, 7, 11, 12–14,
46
Marubbio, M. Elise 130, 202 n.27
marvelous real 122–3
Masashige, Inoue "Inquisitor" (film
character: *Silence*) 77–8, 83
mass culture 14
Mean Streets (1973,
Scorsese) 197 n.6
medium-specific approach 18
Memento (2000, Nolan) 6
mental illness. *See* psychological illness
Meronym (film character: *Cloud
Atlas*) 108
messiahs 24–5, 157, 158, 172, 174,
192
cyborg-messiah 168, 171, 203 n.4
human-messiah 168–9
and violence 161–3
Mignola, Mike 160, 161
Miles, Margaret 17, 18, 28
*Seeing and Believing: Religion and
Values in the Movies* 12–13
Miller, Levi 62
mimesis 199 n.6
Mimi (film character: *Joy*) 48
Miracle on 34th St (1947, Seaton) 43
Miranda, Jose Luis de Jesus 35
Miranda, Lin-Manuel 80–1, 197 n.7
Mishima, Yukio 110
misogyny 78
Mitchell, David 102
affective circulation 113–15
creative engagement of 110–11
emotional engagement with the
Other 111–12
Mitchell, David, works of
Cloud Atlas 105, 107, 110,
114–15
*From Me Flows What You Call
Time* 114
*Thousand Autumns of Jacob de
Zoet, The* 114

Mitchell, Richard 172
Mohican syndrome 23, 129, 137, 138
Mokichi (film character: *Silence*) 77
monomyth 21, 47–9, 55, 179, 185–6
Monty Python's Life of Brian (1979,
Jones) 29
Moore, Gordon 171
Moore, Michael 30, 34
Morales, Fermín (film character: *The
Wind Journeys*) 120–3
morality 8, 9, 21
and capitalism 51
moral therapeutic deism 64, 66
Mormonism 31, 35
Morrison, Toni 72–4
Moyers, Bill 45, 178–9
Mulvey, Laura 59–60
Murakami, Haruki 110
Murry, Charles Wallace (film character:
A Wrinkle in Time) 62–3
Murry, Meg (fictitious character: *A
Wrinkle in Time*) 57–8
Murry, Meg (film character: *A Wrinkle
in Time*) 21, 62–4, 65
music
horror films 148–9
as protagonist 121–3
traveling musicians 120–2, 125,
199 nn.4, 6
vallenato 118, 121, 123, 125,
199 n.4
Myers, John (film character: *Hellboy*,
2004) 160
mystic East 22, 87–91
spirituality in 91–4
myth(s) 15–16, 177–8
and auteur theory 180–3
of entrepreneurship 42–3, 45,
48–9, 50–1, 54–5
as function of social
relationships 176–7
as ideology 49–55, 161, 183–6
as media 10
notion of 42, 52, 177
psychological theories of 42–3,
45–9, 55
mythic archetypes 8, 46–7
mythological criticism 2–4, 178–80,
189, 190–1

critique on 11–12
definition of religion in 6–11
Mythology of Star Wars with George Lucas and Billy Moyers, The (1987, Wagner) 178

narrative 4, 15
diegetic 120–1, 199 n.6
emotional 30
mimetic 199 n.6
National Inquiry on Missing and Murdered Indigenous Women and Girls 136
Native American Renaissance 129, 200 n.6
natural disasters 165
natural ecologist 131, 133, 201 n.17, 202 n.30
natural sciences
and atheism 34–6
Nayar, Sheila J.
Sacred and the Cinema: Reconfiguring the "Genuinely" Religious Film, The 6, 10–11
NBC (TV network) 140
Necakov, Lilian 168
Neeson, Liam 75, 83
neoliberalism 21–2, 23
New Age spirituality 130–1
New Atheism 20–1, 33, 39
Newberg, Andrew (film character: *Religulous*) 35
Nietzsche, Friedrich 105
nihilism
Buddhism as 101–5
Nimue (film character: *Hellboy*, 2019) 161, 162–3
non-religious 32–4
novels. *See also* adaptations
auteur theory 103
of David Mitchell 110, 114
Japanese 69–70
nuclear weapons 161
Nye, Malory 19

Obomsawin, Alanis 128
Office, The (TV series) 66
Ogata, Issey 77
Oida, Yoshi 77

O'Keefe, Calvin (film character: *A Wrinkle in Time*) 62, 63
oppositional gaze 60–1, 63
oppression
of capitalism 52, 54
of women of color 60
Organa, Leia, Princess/General (film character: *Star Wars*) 183, 184
Orientalism
and embodied affective experiences 112–15
as exotic and faraway utopia 104
hipster Orientalism 98–9
notion of 61, 88–9
stereotyping and tropes of 22–3, 60–1, 66, 71
Orientalists 111
oriental monk trope 61, 90
Ornella, Alexander Darius 166
Orpheus (mythological character) 119, 198 n.3
Oscars. *See* Academy Awards
Ostwalt, Conrad E. 155, 157–9, 163. *See also* Martin, Joel W. and Conrad E. Ostwalt
the Other
and atheistic identity 32–3
Buddhism as 22–3, 103–4
emotional engagement of 111–12
Otto, Rudokph 169
Ovitz, Gaye 166

Pale Rider (1985, Eastwood) 158
Palmater, Pamela 134–5
Parsons. Jim 46
Pasolini, Pier Paolo 29
people of color. *See also* actors of color; Indigeneity; Orientalism; women of color
as mystical arbiters 60–1
"non-whiteness" 72–3
religious practices of 65
typecasting 61, 198 n.1
People vs. George Lucas, The (2010, Philippe) 182
performative mode 30
Pfeiffer, Jeffrey 148
Pine, Chris 62
Plate, Brent S. 19, 177–8, 189

Religion and Film: Cinema and the Re-Creation of the World 6, 9–10

"Religion/Literature/Film: Toward a Religious Visuality of Film" 17, 18

Representing Religion in World Cinema 6, 9–10

Platoon (1986, Stone) 191

Pocahontas (1995, Gabriel & Goldberg) 129

popular culture
  brainwashing in 146–7
  Colombia 118–21
  critique of religion in 20–1, 24
  personas of 58, 67–8
  and theology 5–6

Portman, Natalie 59

Portuguese colonialism 71–2, 76–9

positive thinking 145

Postman, The (1997, Costner) 165

Powaqa (film character: *The Revenant*) 136–7, 138

Power of Myth, The (docuseries) 45, 178–9

print media
  on cults and brainwashing 146
  on *Secret of My Success, The* 44
  on *Star Wars* 176
  on *Terminator* 167

promotions
  Religulous 31

propaganda model 14–15, 189, 193

prosperity gospel 145

protagonists. *See also* hero/heroism
  of *Cloud Atlas* 105–8
  female teen protagonist 57
  of horror films 149
  male of color as 61–2
  music, wind and war as 121–3
  redemption of 197 n.6
  of *Star Wars* franchise 178
  strong female protagonists 63

Protestant gaze 118, 121, 125–6, 198 n.1

psychological illness 141
  supernatural causation of 24, 148–51

psychological myth theory 42–3, 45–9, 55

Punke, Michael
  Revenant: A Novel of Revenge, The 135

pure and impure 151

race 4, 15, 22
  in *Hereditary* 150
  in Hollywood 58–9
  and identity construction 28, 38
  and male gaze 59–60
  multiracial casting 58, 63, 66–8
  in *Silence* 71–2
  tropes (*see* tropes)

racialization
  and colonialism 72–4, 83–4

racialized gender 60, 65–8

radicalism 20–1

Raheja, Michelle 130, 200 n.9

Ramirez, Edgar 44

Ramos, Dani (film character: *Terminator, Dark Fate*) 168–9, 171

Rancière, Jacques 176

Rashomon (1950, Kurosawa) 15

Rasputin (film character: *Hellboy*, 2004) 161, 162–3

Ray, Satyajit 197 n.4

Raza, Ghyslain
  "Star Wars Kid" 179

reductionism 9, 14, 52, 104

Reel Injuns: On the Trail of the Hollywood Indian (2010, Diamond) 200 n.11, 201 n.19

Reese, Kyle (film character: *Terminator*, 1984) 168, 170

reflexive mode 30

Reid, Storm 62

reincarnation 105–7

religion
  criticism of 20–1, 29
  as feminine practice 65–6
  as film 190–3
  film as 8–10, 24, 142, 189, 191–2
  harmful nature of 31, 36–7
  ideological definition of 9, 11–17
  in/and film 24, 153, 157–9, 162
  and irrationality 34–6

mythological definition of 6–11
(Christocentric) theological
definition of 5–6, 7, 9, 10–11,
12, 17
transcendental definition of 18
religion and film
as field of study 1–4
religiosity 21–2
Colombian/Latin American 23,
118, 119–21, 123, 124–6
of people of color 60–1
and scientific education 34–6
religious affect 113
Religulous (2008, Charles) 20–1, 192
cinematography 35
a comic documentary 30–1
ethnographic approach 37
identity construction in 32–4,
37–8
impact of 38–9
Ren, Kylo (film character: *Star
Wars*) 186
Renner, Jeremy 138
Reservation Dogs (TV series) 140
Resident Evil, The franchise 165
resistance (human) 170–3
Revelation 155–7, 158
as erasure 159–63
Revenant, The (2015, Iñárritu) 23,
128–9, 134, 135–9, 192
righteous warriors 166, 170–3, 174
Rile, Jason 139–40
road movies 90–1. *See also The
Darjeeling Limited* (2007,
Anderson)
robots 25, 172, 173, 203 n.6,
204 n.7. *See also* artificial
intelligence (AI)
Rocky franchise 178, 187
Rodrigues, Sebastian, Fr. (film
character: *Silence*) 22, 75–85,
196 n.2
Roko's Basilisk (thought
experiment) 169
Romero, George A. 203 n.1
Root of All Evil?, The (2006,
Barnes) 29
Rudy (film character: *Joy*) 44
Russell, David O. 44

Rutherford Falls (TV series) 140

Sachs, Isaac (film character: *Cloud
Atlas*) 109
the sacred 185
and humanity 2, 7
and Indigenous traditions 133,
201 n.22
technological mediation of 10–11
Said, Edward 61
Orientalism 88–9
salvation 24–5, 157, 166, 168,
203 n.4. *See also* messiahs
Salvation Army of Australia, The 41–
2
Sarris, Andrew 181
savage/violent savage trope 23,
132–3, 137, 138, 200 n.7
savior. *See* messiahs; white savior
Schlegel, Friedrich 90
scholarship
contemporary 1–4
on *Star Wars* 178–9
Schwarzenegger, Arnold 166, 172
science
and atheism 34–6
and identity construction 28
and religion 36–7
science fiction 25, 175
and Christianity 57–8, 169
scientism 20–1, 34–6
Scientology 31, 34–5
scopophilia 59
Scorsese, Martin 69–72, 74–5, 80,
84, 104, 196 n.2, 197 n.6. *See
also Silence* (2016, Scorsese)
Scott, Bernard Brandon
*Hollywood Dreams and Biblical
Stories* 12
Secret of My Success (1987, Ross) 21,
42, 192
elitism in 51
gender role in 53
hero's journey in 47–9
historical context of 54
individual and universal experiences
in 52–3
myth of entrepreneurship 50–1
plot of 44, 45

INDEX

secularization 166
self-acceptance 21–2, 64, 65
self-identity 108–10
self-improving machines 171
settler-colonialism 129, 132–3, 136, 137–9
Shakespeare, William
   Tempest, The 129
Shangri-La 104
Shapiro, Milly 149–50
Sheyahshe, Michael 129
shooting locations
   Religulous 37
Sidious, Darth (film character: *Star Wars*) 184
Sikhism 93, 95
Silence (2016, Scorsese) 22, 69–70, 84–5, 192, 196 n.2, 197 n.6
   narrative and context 75–80
   racialization in 74
   religion in 80–4
Silent Enemy (1930, Carver) 200 n.11
Simpson, Audra
   Mohawk Interruptus: Life Across the Borders of Settler States 132
the Singularity 171
Sison, Antonio
   World Cinema, Theology, and the Human: Humanity in Deep Focus 5
Skynet (fictional object: *Terminator*) 169, 171, 173, 203 n.2
Skywalker, Anakin (film character: *Star Wars*) 184
Skywalker, Luke (film character: *Star Wars*) 8, 175, 176, 183–6
Skywalker, Rey (film character: *Star Wars*) 183, 184–6
Skywalker Sound (company) 182
Slater, Helen 44
Smith, Christian 64
Smith, Jada Pinkett 58–9
Smith, Jonathan Z. 8, 42, 190
   Imagining Religion: From Babylon to Jonestown 5
Smoke Signals (1998, Eyre) 127, 133
social differentiation 144–5

social identity 109
social justice 102, 108–10
social media 25
   and Indigeneity 129
   reactions on artificial intelligence 173, 204 n.7
Sonmi-451 (film character: *Cloud Atlas*) 107–9
Sophia (robot) 173, 203 n.6
spectatorship 17, 18, 19
Spence, Theresa 134
spiritualism 150
spirituality
   Asians as mystical arbiters 60–1
   "healthy spirituality" 66
   Indian 22
   Indigenous 23, 128, 129, 130–1, 139, 201 nn.18, 22
   spiritual self-discovery 22, 87–8, 91–8
   spiritual self-help 64–5, 67
Star Trek 46, 203 n.5
Star Wars, Episode IV—A New Hope (1977, Lucas) 185
Star Wars, Episode I—The Phantom Menace (1999, Lucas) 178, 182
Star Wars, Episode VII—The Force Awakens (2015, Abrams) 182–3
Star Wars, Episode VIII—The Last Jedi (2017, Johnson) 25, 176–7, 182, 186–7
   three-plot structure of 183–6
Star Wars, Episode IX—The Rise of Skywalker (2019, Abrams) 187
Star Wars franchise 8, 45–6, 192–3
Stein, Ben 30
stereotypes/stereotyping. *See also* tropes
   of adversaries of atheists 37
   of Colombian culture 118
   of female beauty 59
   image of Jesus 83–4
   of Latin American religiosity 198 n.1
   of Orientalism 22–3, 66
   of people of color religiosity and religious practices 58, 60–1, 65
   of racialized female beauty 59

strange permutations 168–9, 174
Strauss, Shmuel 35
Sturgess, Jim 107
Sturken, Marita 4
success 42, 44, 45, 51, 64
suffering 69, 84
  dukkha 105, 107
Sunchaser, The (1996, Cimino) 131
Sunshine (2007, Boyle) 165
superheroes 24, 161–2. *See also*
  apocalyptic (super)heroism
supernatural
  as cause for mental illness 24,
    148–51
  in Latin American culture 122
supernatural horror 24, 141–2, 192
  agency in 143–4
  viewer repulsion 151
survivalists 172–3

T-800 (film character:
    Terminator) 168, 169, 170,
    203 n.4
Takemitsu, Toru 114
Tanizaki, Junichiro 110
Taxi Driver (1976, Scorsese) 197 n.6
technical aspects of films 10–11, 191
technology & technological
    progress 25, 166, 170–4,
    181–2
Teenage Mutant Ninja Turtles
    franchise 61
Ten Commandments, The (1923,
    DeMille) 1–3, 21, 41
Terminator (1984, Cameron)
  "No Fate" 170
  subversion of biblical stories 167–
    8
Terminator 2: Judgement Day (1991,
    Cameron) 168, 203 n.4
Terminator 3: Rise of the Machines
    (2003, Mostow) 169, 170
*Terminator: The Sarah Connor
    Chronicles* (TV series,
    2008) 171, 203 n.4
Terminator: Dark Fate (2019,
    Miller) 168–9, 170, 171,
    203 n.2

Terminator franchise 24–5, 166,
    173–4, 192, 203 nn.3–4, 6
  biblical parallels in 167–9,
    203 n.2
textication 111
textual analysis 166
theological criticism 1–4, 191
  critique on 11–12
  sui generis definition of religion
    in 5–6, 7, 9, 10–11, 17, 190
theologies of class 144–5
There's Something in the Water (2019,
    Page) 202 n.30
Thomas (film character: *Blow Up*) 16
Thunderheart (1992, Apted) 131
Tillotson, Emily 98–9
Tolkien, J.R.R.
  Lord of the Rings 47
Tony (film character: *Joy*) 44
Toronto International Film Festival
    (TIFF) 127–8, 140
transcendence 18, 67
transformation
  personal 48–9, 64
  spiritual 91–8
translation 111
traveling musicians 120–2, 125,
    199 n.4, 199 n.6
Triumph of the Will (*Triumph
    des Willens*) (1935,
    Reifenstahl) 185
tropes. *See also* stereotypes/
    stereotyping
  of indigeneity 23, 129–33, 192,
    200 nn.7–10, 201 n.17, 202 n.30
  of indigeneity, subversion of 135–
    9, 200 n.8
  "innocence of Buddhist
    monks" 104
  "literary trope of the fool" 46
  magical realism as 124
  "Shangri-La" 104
  "white savior" 22, 23, 73, 81–2,
    129, 136–7, 138, 200 n.8
(timeless) truth 153–4, 157–8
  in apocalyptic art 159–63
Tsukamoto, Shinya 70, 77
Tuckett, David 167

Tykwer, Tom   102

Unbelievers, The (2013, Holwerda)   29
Unification Church (Moonies)   146, 147, 148
United States   30–1
    White middle class at twentieth mid-century   43–4
universalism   48–9, 52–3

Vader, Darth (film character: *Star Wars*)   8, 175, 177, 184, 185
vallenato music   118, 121, 123, 125, 199 n.4
vanishing Indian trope   130, 200 n.10
Van Kerchove, Carmen   98
Vera, Aunt (film character: *The Secret of My Success*)   47
V for Vendetta (2005, McTeigue)   161
violence   4, 15, 104
    1928 Banana Massacre   199 n.7
    in Colombia   198 n.2
    of Revelation's Christ   158
    in *The Revenant*   137–8
    in Scorsese's films   197 n.6
    in *Silence*   78, 79–80
    in superhero culture   161–2
    in *The Wind Journeys*   121–3
Vogler, Christopher   46

Wachowski, Lana   102
Wachowski, Lily   102
Wagner, Rachel   46, 172
Waititi, Taika   127–8, 140
Walker, Neil (film character: *Joy*)   44
Wall Street (1987, Stone)   46
Waterworld (1995, Reynolds)   165
Weisenfeld, Judith   61
Weiss, Dovid   35
Wekker, Gloria   74
Wente, Jesse   127–8, 135
western genre
    critique of   135–6
    Frontiersman trope   137, 172
Whale Rider (2002, Caro)   133
Whatsit, Mrs. (film character: *A Wrinkle in Time*)   62, 64, 66

Which, Mrs. (film character: *A Wrinkle in Time*)   62, 66
white
    as critics of religion   38
    ideals of thinness   59
white innocence   74
whiteness   22, 69, 71–2, 84–5
    notion of   72–4
white privilege   22, 74–5
white savior   22, 23, 73, 81–2, 129, 136–7, 138, 200 n.9
Whitman, Walt   87
Whitman brothers (film characters: *The Darjeeling Limited*)   22, 87–8, 91–8
Whitton, Margaret   47
Who, Mrs. (film character: *A Wrinkle in Time*)   62, 64–5, 66–8
Wicker Man, The (1973, Hardy)   19
Wills, Christy (film character: *The Secret of My Success*)   44, 47
Wind Journeys, The (2009, Guerra)   23, 117–18, 124–5, 199 n.6
    diegetic narrative   120–1
    soundscape of   121–3
Wind River (2017, Sheridan)   138–9
Winfrey, Oprah   58, 62, 66–8
Winthorpe, John
    "Model of Christian Charity"   144
Witherspoon, Reese   58, 62, 66
Wolff, Alex   149
Wollen, Peter   181
Woman Walks Ahead (2018, White)   138
women
    cultural imperialist exploitation of   38
    Indigenous   130, 136–7, 139, 202 nn.27, 30
    and religion   65–6
    and white ideals of thinness   59
women of color. *See also* people of color
    casting   58, 62
    casting, cultural significance of   66–8
    oppression of   60

Word of Faith Movement 145
world religions paradigm (WRP) 133,
    201 n.21
Worlds Apart (2008,
    Papakaliatis) 147
Wright, Marcus (film character:
    Terminator) 203 n.4
Wright, Melanie J.
    *Religion and Film: An
    Introduction* 17, 18–19
Wrinkle in Time, A (2003,
    Harrison) 63
Wrinkle in Time, A (2018,
    DuVernay) 21–2, 58
    casting of 58, 63
    plot of 62–3

and religion 64–8
    stereotypes in 61, 64, 68

Yoda, Master (film character: *Star
    Wars*) 185–6
Yoshida, Keiko 110–11, 114
young adult fiction 57–8
Young Guns (1988, Cain) 133

Zablocki, Benjamin 147
Zachry (film character: *Cloud
    Atlas*) 108
Žižek, Slavoj 198 n.1
    critique on Buddhism 101–2,
        103–5, 112, 114, 115
zombies 165, 203 n.1

Ingram Content Group UK Ltd.
Milton Keynes UK
UKHW022302290323
419396UK00004B/75